## STACKS

How **Everything**
**Became War**
and the **Military**
Became **Everything**

Tales from the Pentagon

**Rosa Brooks**

SIMON & SCHUSTER

*New York   London   Toronto   Sydney   New Delhi*

Simon & Schuster
1230 Avenue of the Americas
New York, NY 10020

First Simon & Schuster hardcover edition August 2016

SIMON & SCHUSTER and colophon are registered trademarks of Simon & Schuster, Inc.

For information about special discounts for bulk purchases, please contact Simon & Schuster Special Sales at 1-866-506-1949 or business@ simonandschuster.com.

The Simon & Schuster Speakers Bureau can bring authors to your live event. For more information or to book an event contact the Simon & Schuster Speakers Bureau at 1-866-248-3049 or visit our website at www. simonspeakers.com.

Interior design by Paul Dippolito

Manufactured in the United States of America

10   9   8   7   6   5   4   3

Library of Congress Cataloging-in-Publication Data

Names: Brooks, Rosa, author.
Title: How everything became war and the military became everything / Rosa Brooks.
Description: New York : Simon & Schuster, [2016] | Includes bibliographical references and index.
Identifiers: LCCN 2016005348 (print) | LCCN 2016009107 (ebook) | ISBN 9781476777863 (hardcover) | ISBN 9781476777870 (pbk.) | ISBN 9781476777887 (E-Book)
Subjects: LCSH: United States—Military policy. | Strategic culture—United States. | War (International law)—Philosophy. | Armed Forces—Operations other than war. | Terrorism—Prevention—Government policy—United States. | Just war doctrine. | National security—United States. | Militarism—United States. | United States—History, Military—20th century—Anecdotes. | United States—History, Military—21st century—Anecdotes.
Classification: LCC UA23 .B7837 2016 (print) | LCC UA23 (ebook) | DDC 355/.033573—dc23
LC record available at http://lccn.loc.gov/2016005348

ISBN 978-1-4767-7786-3
ISBN 978-1-4767-7788-7 (ebook)

*For Joe, Anna, and Clara*

# Contents

# CONTENTS

# PART I

# Tremors

# A Window of Opportunity

One ordinary day in 2010, I sat in an anonymous Pentagon conference room with a dozen other people, listening as briefers from the military's Special Operations Command went over plans for an impending strike against a terrorist operative. Sending in special operations forces would be too risky, they said; we would therefore most likely strike the target using missiles fired from an unmanned aerial vehicle.

I can't tell you the region or the identity of the target. During my twenty-six months working at the Defense Department, I signed dozens of papers promising to keep the secret stuff secret, and unlike Edward Snowden, I have no desire to give out classified information—or live life as a fugitive. But I think I can say that the target was a youngish man, probably not more than thirty. I dutifully studied the small photo displayed on the briefing slides. It showed an ordinary face, the kind you might see on any street in Sana'a or Karachi—or New York or London. But this, the briefers assured us, was no ordinary young man; there was solid evidence (not detailed) of his involvement in numerous terror plots (exhaustively detailed).

For months, they explained, we had been unable to track the target, but he had finally made one of those mistakes even hardened terrorists seem apt to make, like calling his mother on his cell phone, or arranging by email to meet an old friend in a café, or allowing his picture to be included in an otherwise innocuous Facebook post. One of our intelligence agencies had noticed the slip. ("Nice!" someone murmured from the back of the room.) The target was currently occupying a house in a populated area, but as soon as a window of opportunity opened up, the briefers promised—as soon as the target moved to an isolated loca-

3

tion, reducing the danger to any innocent bystanders—we would strike.

We all nodded gravely. Of course. What was there to say? We were at war with al Qaeda and its far-flung "associated forces," and this man was an enemy combatant and a lawful target.

A day or two later, I was home eating dinner—spaghetti and meatballs, my six-year-old daughter's favorite—when I got a phone call from a colleague. "You know that thing we were discussing?" he asked. "That window? It opened up a few hours ago."

It was an open line, and he couldn't say much. But I knew what he meant. The previous day, the young man whose photo I had studied was alive; now he was dead.

"Thanks for letting me know," I said. "You can fill me in tomorrow." And I went back to dinner with the kids.

That night, I dreamed about death: someone I loved, murdered. I woke up panicky and sweating.

## War's Tentacles

I knew already that I was part of a vast, bureaucratic death-dealing enterprise. Although I pulled no triggers and signed no military orders, I, like every single man and woman working at the Pentagon, was part of a machine that sent people off each day to kill and die. Each morning, I thumbed through the latest reports of U.S. troops killed in Iraq and Afghanistan, along with intelligence reports of terrorists, insurgents, and Taliban fighters killed or presumed dead. All this sobered and saddened me, but rarely disturbed my sleep.

Somehow, though, my mind had snagged on that distant, impersonal drone strike, far from the battlegrounds of Iraq and Afghanistan.

It took me several more years to fully understand why. But even at the time, I sensed something disturbing: all our fine new technologies and fine new legal theories were blurring the boundaries of "war," causing it to spread and ooze into everyday life. That young terror suspect we killed in that 2010 strike wore no uniform and was part of no state's army; he carried no weapons, and he lived in a country with which the United States was not at war. From the outside, at least, he looked more or less like everyone else. But as he drove along an empty desert road one afternoon, someone sitting thousands of miles away entered a command into a computer, and death rained down on him from the sky.

I assumed then, and I assume now, that the intelligence information leading to that strike was developed in good faith. But what if we got it wrong? What if we got the wrong young man, or had the wrong information about the right young man?

Wars kill innocent civilians all the time. The U.S. war in Iraq killed at least sixty-six thousand Iraqi civilians, and perhaps ten times that many, while the war in Afghanistan is estimated to have killed another twenty thousand civilians.[1] For the most part, we accept some number of unintended civilian deaths as a tragic but inevitable by-product of war.

But somehow this one death seemed different. It wasn't merely that we didn't know for *sure* if the young man was a civilian or a combatant—certainty is often elusive in the fog of war—we didn't even know for sure what the word "combatant" could possibly *mean* in the context of today's shadowy conflicts. When it comes to terrorism, no one is quite sure who constitutes an "enemy," who counts as a "civilian," when isolated threats or attacks count as "war," and whether modern wars can be said to have boundaries in either time or space. If the United States could reach down from the heavens and kill this one particular man out of millions of others in Yemen or Pakistan or Somalia, what would keep any of us safe? Could war's tentacles reach into every place on earth?

•  •  •

During the time I spent at the Pentagon, I was mostly too busy to think about these uncomfortable questions. As a senior advisor to Under Secretary of Defense Michèle Flournoy, one of the Pentagon's highest-ranking civilian officials (and at the time the highest-ranking civilian woman in Pentagon history), I found myself quickly immersed in nearly every major defense policy issue.

It was an exhausting, inspiring, terrifying, and endlessly fascinating twenty-six months: I watched General David Petraeus argue about Pakistan with Ambassador Richard Holbrooke, and slid down in my seat as Holbrooke launched into one of his infamous tantrums, bellowing at two hapless young officers who had outlined a less-than-impressive strategic communication plan for Pakistan. In a windowless basement conference room, I sat behind the chairman of the Joint Chiefs of Staff as he outlined counterpiracy options for the Horn of Africa. Traveling with Flournoy in Afghanistan, I gazed out through the tiny slitlike windows of our IED-resistant vehicle at endless fields of opium poppies, and watched Afghan Special Forces commandos stage mock hostage rescue raids.

Back in Washington, I sat in on discussions of raids and strikes. I spent hours briefing congressional staff on controversial Pentagon "information operations" programs, and more hours trying to make sense of Defense Department programs intended to promote the "rule of law." I got a coveted intelligence community "blue badge," enabling me to pass freely into the sacred precincts of the CIA and other agencies—and though I wasn't nearly important enough to get face time with the president, I did manage to shake hands with Bo, the president's dog, when I encountered him one day outside the White House Situation Room. (This is the only thing I did in those two years that truly impressed my children.)

I watched nighttime flight operations from the bridge of an aircraft carrier as it pitched in post-hurricane seas, experienced the electrifying jolt of a catapult launch off the carrier's deck, and took helicopter rides from the Pentagon to a secret military bunker built beneath a mountain. (Yes, these Cold War relics still exist—and they're every bit as weird as you'd expect, complete with underwater reservoirs, nuclear power plants, and a Holiday Inn–style bedroom suite for the secretary of defense.) I flew down to Guantánamo on a military jet with several members of Congress: at the detention center, looking on through one-way glass, I watched as a notorious terrorist exercised on a StairMaster machine, climbing, climbing, climbing—and going nowhere.

Those two years were strange, almost surreal in their intensity. For me—a law professor and journalist brought up in a family of left-wing antiwar activists—working at the Pentagon was like conducting anthropological fieldwork in some exotic and unpredictable foreign tribe. The Pentagon was a world rich in mystery, full of arcane and bewildering new rituals and symbols. There was a complex code written in the ribbons and bits of metal adorning the uniforms of military personnel, for instance—and woe betide the fool who failed to understand the difference between a Navy captain and an Army captain. There was literally a new language to be learned: for several muddled months, I assumed that the constant references I heard to the "DOTMLPF Spectrum" (pronounced *dot-mil P F*) had something to do with websites or the military's Internet domain; in fact, the acronym stood for "Doctrine, Organization, Training, Matériel, Leadership & Education, Personnel, and Facilities."

Month by month, I learned to "speak DoD" as a second language. By the time I left the Pentagon, I could pontificate knowledgeably about OPSEC and MILDEC (operations security and military deception), wax eloquent about the importance of "shaping the battlespace" during "Phase Zero Operations," and explain the difference between a D-FAC (the dining facility) and an MRAP (a mine-resistant ambush-protected vehicle).

Like a total-immersion language course, my work at the Pentagon occupied every corner of my mind. For most of my first year, I dreamed about work every night. Aside from that one post-drone-strike nightmare, my dreams were tediously mundane: as I slept, my exhausted mind kept right on drafting memos and congressional testimony, designing PowerPoint slides, and trying to remember the difference between Navy and Marine Corps uniforms.

Somewhere during this exhausting period, I also met the man who would become my husband and the beloved stepfather of my two young children. Joe, an Army Special Forces officer then serving on the Pentagon's Joint Staff, had a sharp, skeptical intelligence and a well-honed sense of absurdity—both necessary attributes for career Special Forces soldiers, most of whom have been almost continuously deployed since 9/11. Joe was no exception: he had put in his time in Iraq and Afghanistan, not to mention the Philippines, North Africa, Korea, the Caucasus, and the Balkans. Initially, some of his assumptions seemed as alien to me as those of any foreign tribe. But over time, he helped me gain a much deeper understanding of the new world in which I found myself temporarily resident.

Even so, it was only after I left the Pentagon that I could truly begin to make sense of what I had seen, heard, and learned. In fall 2011, I returned to my faculty position at Georgetown University Law Center, where I taught international and constitutional law. At first, this too was disorienting: I had finally gotten used to the Pentagon and its many subtribes, and it was tough to readjust to an ivory tower world where my students called me "Professor," not "Ma'am," and no one referred to the time as "2300 Zulu" or agreed to a request with a snappy "Roger that!" At the Pentagon, an organization with an annual budget in the hundreds of billions, decisions could have life or death consequences. At Georgetown, my faculty research budget didn't even cover a new computer, and my most pressing problem was whether to give a borderline student a C or a more charitable B-minus.

But as my mind began slowly to reboot, I found myself thinking more and more about the same questions that had hovered just beneath the surface of my consciousness during my Pentagon years. In a world in which the push of a button can lead, within seconds, to the death of a specific man more than eight thousand miles away, is it possible to define "war" with any clarity? What line separates the lawful wartime targeting of an enemy combatant from the extrajudicial murder of a man suspected, but not convicted, of wrongdoing? And what is the *military* for, in a world in which future threats are as likely to come from computer hackers, terrorists, and other nonstate actors as from the armies of foreign states?

Most of all: As the boundaries around war and the military grow ever more blurry, will we all pay a price?

．　．　．

For most of recorded history, humans have sought to draw sharp lines between war and peace. Until less than a century ago, for instance, most Western societies maintained that wars should be formally "declared," take place upon clearly delineated battlefields, and be fought by elaborately uniformed soldiers operating within specialized, hierarchical military organizations.

In different societies and earlier times, humans developed other rituals to delineate war's boundaries, including complex initiation rites preceding wars, the elaborate painting and costuming of warriors, and equally elaborate rituals to mark the end of conflicts and the reintegration of warriors into ordinary life.

Old Norse literature tells of the berserkers, who changed form and personality by donning the pelts of wolves or bears before going into battle (their wild brutality after shape-shifting gave us the modern word "berserk").[2] Among the Mekeo of Papua New Guinea, men prepared for war by following a severely restricted diet and abstaining from sex for months. Only when their bodies were fully "closed" could they go to war. When they returned from battle, writes anthropologist Mark Mosko, warriors had to observe a similar period of abstinence: if a couple "did happen to open their bodies sexually while [the man] still had traces of war sorcery on his skin, it would enter both their bodies and kill them."[3]

In the American Southwest, Navajo warriors literally spoke a different dialect after setting out on raids, using what they called a "twisted language" with a special vocabulary. The Navajo also sought to carefully maintain the spatial boundaries between war and nonwar: "On the way home from a raid," noted anthropologist D. W. Murray, "a symbolic line would be drawn in the desert, the men would line up facing the enemy country, and as they sang they all turned toward home and the common language was resumed."[4]

We modern Americans are not all that different from the Old Norse or the Navajo. We think of "war" as a distinct and separate sphere, one that shouldn't intrude into the everyday world of offices, shopping malls, schools, and soccer games, and we relegate war to the military, a distinct social institution that we simultaneously lionize and ignore. For the most part, we prefer to believe that both war and the military can be kept in tidy little boxes: war, we like to think, is an easily recognizable exception to the normal state of affairs, and the military an institution that can be easily, if tautologically, defined by its specialized, war-related functions.

We're wrong on both counts.

· · ·

Two years before the September 11 terrorist attacks shattered American illusions of safety, two colonels in China's People's Liberation Army published a slender little book called *Unrestricted Warfare*. Historically, wrote Colonels Qiao Liang and Wang Xiangsui, "the three indispensable 'hardware' elements of any war" have been "soldiers, weapons and a battlefield." This, they warned, will soon cease to be true: humans are now entering an era in which even these most basic hardware elements of war will be transformed beyond recognition.

In the wars of the coming decades, predicted Qiao and Wang, the "soldiers" will increasingly be computer hackers, financiers, terrorists, drug smugglers, and agents of private corporations as well as members of organized state militaries. Their "weapons" will range from "airplanes, cannons, poison gas, bombs [and] biochemical agents" to "computer viruses, net browsers, and financial derivative tools." Warfare, they wrote, will soon "transcend all boundaries and limits. . . . The battlefield will be everywhere . . . [and] all the boundaries lying between the two worlds of war and non-war, of military and non-military, will be totally destroyed."[5]

When *Unrestricted Warfare* was first published in 1999, its dystopian predictions received little attention in the United States outside a small circle of military and intelligence officials. Seen from the vantage point of today, however, the two Chinese officers look chillingly prescient: they saw clearly a future that was unimaginable to most Americans before 9/11.

Everyone is familiar with parts of this story. Our increasing global interconnectedness has created new vulnerabilities, as has our increasing dependence on the Internet and other forms of electronic communication. North Korean hackers can now bring down major U.S. media websites; terrorist ideologues in Yemen can use the Internet to disseminate bomb-making instructions to extremists in Boston or London; Mexican drug cartels can launder money through a series of near-instantaneous electronic transactions; the self-styled Islamic State can bring videos of brutal hostage beheadings into every American living room via YouTube; and everything from pollution to bioengineered viruses can spread rapidly around the globe.

As a result, states and their traditionally organized militaries are facing more and more competition from smaller, decentralized, non-hierarchical organizations and networks. In 1941, it took a coordinated attack by 350 Japanese military airplanes to kill 2,403 Americans at Pearl Harbor.[6] Six decades later, nineteen men from four different countries—armed only with box-cutters—hijacked four civilian jets and caused the deaths of nearly three thousand Americans. Nonstate actors—even one or two individuals—can increasingly compete with states when it comes to using physical force to cause large-scale death and physical injury.

The use of physical force also has more and more competition today. War, wrote the famous nineteenth-century Prussian military strategist Carl von Clausewitz, is "an act of violence to compel our opponent to fulfill our will."[7] But our increased interconnectedness has created new means for clever actors—be they states or individuals—to achieve war's traditional ends.

Imagine a cyberattack that brought down the electrical power grid in a major population center for weeks, or a significant cyber disruption of the nation's financial infrastructure: either could rapidly cause massive economic damage and lead, albeit indirectly, to significant death and suffering. Imagine a bioengineered virus capable of killing, sickening, or weakening only individuals with specific DNA signatures. Imagine a "nonlethal weapon" capable of inducing temporary, painless paralysis or sleep—just long enough to enable an opposing force to seize control of land, money, or natural resources. Would any of these means of exercising coercion fit into the traditional Clausewitzian understanding of "war" and "acts of violence"?

Some of these technologies don't yet exist, but the September 11 attacks made it clear that the fundamental changes described and predicted by Qiao Liang and Wang Xiangsui don't lie off in some distant science-fiction future. As the nineteen al Qaeda plotters made their unimpeded way through American airport security, the era of unrestricted warfare was already well under way. We just didn't know it yet.

The U.S. response to the 9/11 attacks moved us still further into the era of unrestricted warfare. On September 10, 2001, President George W.

Bush announced during a visit to a Florida elementary school that it was "time to wage war on illiteracy,"[8] but no one expected that "war" to involve bullets or bloodshed. A few days later, with the Twin Towers in ruins and the Pentagon still smoldering, Bush announced a "war on terror." This time, no one thought he was speaking metaphorically.

Today, a decade and a half later, the United States still regards itself as being in an "armed conflict"—the legal term for what we colloquially call "war"—with "al Qaeda and its associated forces." But just as Qiao and Wang predicted, this armed conflict bears little resemblance to traditional armed conflicts. Our enemies wear no uniforms and are loyal to no state; many of those we consider "enemy combatants" don't seem to be part of any organized group at all.

In the years since 9/11, it has grown steadily more difficult to define our enemies. The United States won't define or list al Qaeda's "associated forces," and new organizations such as the Islamic State have joined our list of enemies. The "battlefield" keeps shifting too: it has ranged from Afghanistan and Iraq to Pakistan, Yemen, Somalia, and the Philippines, with forays into Mali, Nigeria, and, most recently, Syria and Libya, where U.S. air strikes and special operations troops are targeting members of the Islamic State—a perpetually changing organization that is part terrorist, part insurgency, and part de facto state. What counts as a "weapon" or an "attack" in this war is also murky: the United States has detained or killed alleged terrorist and insurgent planners, recruiters, and financiers for the purpose of disrupting everything from planned bombings to cyberattacks. But when you wage war against a nameless, stateless, formless enemy—an enemy with goals as uncertain as its methods—it's hard to see how that war can ever end.

Looking beyond the conundrums posed by terrorism and nonstate actors, the U.S. government has also made it clear that it views cyber threats primarily through the lens of "war." In 2011, the White House released an "International Strategy for Cyberspace," declaring that the United States would "respond to hostile acts in cyberspace as we would to any other threat to our country."[9] In 2012, the State Department's top lawyer announced that as a legal matter, the United States believed that "cyber activities may in certain circumstances constitute uses of force," triggering the law of armed conflict and giving rise to a right to respond with traditional physical force.[10]

War has burst out of its old boundaries.

As the lines we have drawn between "war" and "nonwar" grow indistinct, the role and mission of the U.S. military have grown similarly hazy. Today, as the military struggles to respond to novel threats from novel quarters, its once seemingly straightforward raison d'être—defending America from armed attack by foreign states—is no longer clear-cut.

For most of us, the word "war" still conjures up images of World War II, or at least Hollywood's version of World War II: we think of tank battles on open plains, or the D-Day scenes of *Saving Private Ryan*. If we can think past the 1940s, we envision long lines of green-clad soldiers snaking through the steaming jungles of Vietnam, or the miles upon miles of khaki tents pitched in the Kuwaiti desert on the eve of the first Gulf War. And just twenty-five years ago, most military personnel understood their role in a manner that would have been equally familiar to Genghis Khan or Douglas MacArthur: the military's main job, as scores of drill sergeants have bellowed at new recruits, was to "kill people and break stuff." But today's military has vastly expanded its sphere of activities.

American military personnel now operate in nearly every country on earth. In some places, they "shoot, move, and communicate" just as generations of soldiers have been taught to do in basic training. In the Iraq and Afghanistan wars, both of which were recently and ambiguously "ended" only to quietly restart, soldiers still go out on patrols, get into gun battles, call in artillery strikes, and focus on seizing and holding territory. But the vast majority of modern military personnel today spend most of their time engaged in activities that bear little resemblance to those depicted in Hollywood films.

Instead, they analyze lines of computer code in Virginia office buildings, build isolation wards in Ebola-ravaged Liberia, operate health clinics in rural Malaysian villages, launch agricultural reform programs and small business development projects in Africa, train Afghan judges and parliamentarians, develop television soap operas for Iraqi audiences, and conduct antipiracy patrols off the Somali coast. They monitor global email and telephone communications, pilot weaponized drones from simulated airplane cockpits thousands of miles away, and help develop and plan for high-tech new modes of warfare, from autonomous weapons systems operated by computers using artificial intelligence to DNA-linked bioweapons.

These and a thousand other activities now performed by the U.S. military are intended to "shape the battlespace," prevent and deter future conflict, and disrupt or destroy the capabilities of potential adversaries, whoever—and wherever—they may be. Why wait passively for the next terrorist attack—or a nuclear missile launched by a rogue state, or a cyberattack emanating from China or from a group of disaffected Estonian teens—when we could be eliminating the root causes of conflict by fostering economic development and good governance, building relationships, creating networks of agents and allies, collecting data, promoting "new narratives," or striking potential future enemies *before* they can develop the ability to harm us?

To the military, it's all about staying "left of boom." Imagine a timeline running from left to right, with potential calamity looming off to the right, somewhere in the hazy future. "Boom" might be the improvised explosive device buried under the road, a radioactive "dirty bomb," an aerosol canister filled with a bioengineered virus, or a computer worm that shuts down the New York Stock Exchange. You always, *always* want to stay left of boom—and as the varieties of "boom" expand, the military has expanded correspondingly.

## The Surface of the Moon

Even as the military's purpose and role has blurred and its activities have expanded, the U.S. military itself—as a human institution—has grown more and more sharply delineated from the broader society it is charged with protecting.

Most Americans know roughly as much about the U.S. military as they know about the surface of the moon. In post-9/11 America, troops are treated to special discounts at chain stores, airlines invite military personnel to board before other passengers, schools arrange for children to send greeting cards to "wounded warriors," and employers tout their commitment to hiring military veterans at "Hire a Hero" job fairs. But these ritualized gestures sometimes seem only to emphasize the chasm between the military and civilian society. As James Fallows noted in a 2015 *Atlantic* article titled "The Tragedy of the American Military," nearly 10 percent of the U.S. population was in uniform by the end of World War II.[11] Today, it's quite different.[12] The majority of living veterans served in wars that most Americans now consider part of our history, not part of our present.[13] Not coincidentally—and despite nearly fifteen years of war—younger Americans are far less likely than older Americans to have a member of their immediate family who served in the military.[14]

Military personnel certainly feel ignored and misunderstood by their civilian compatriots. A few years ago, the *Military Times*'s annual survey found that more than 75 percent of all active duty personnel and reservists agreed with the statement, "The military community has little in common with the rest of the country and most civilians do not understand the military." Few civilians would disagree: ask even most educated Americans to describe the basic structure of the military, estimate its size and budget, guess the locations of "forward deployed" military personnel, or describe the military's activities, and you'll get a lot of sheepish shrugs. In a 2014 YouGov survey, civilians asked to estimate the number of people currently serving in the military were, on average, off by some five million people.[15] In the same survey, majorities across all demographic groups, both military and civilian, agreed that "military culture and way of life . . . is very different from the culture and way of life of those who are not in the military," and "the military has different values than the rest of society."[16]

Speaking to West Point cadets a few years ago, Admiral Michael Mullen, former chairman of the Joint Chiefs of Staff, put it like this: "Our work is appreciated, of that I am certain. There isn't a town or a city I visit where people do not convey to me their great pride in what we do. But I fear they do not know us. I fear they do not comprehend the full weight of the burden we carry or the price we pay when we re-turn from battle."[17]

The price paid by those who go into battle has certainly been high: more than seven thousand American military personnel have given their lives in Iraq and Afghanistan, and more than fifty thousand have been wounded.[18] Deployments also bring countless nontangible costs: damaged or broken marriages, children growing up with absent parents, and the psychological strain of separation, hardship, and danger.

. . .

As a personal matter, this didn't fully come home to me until I married an Army officer.

When I first met my husband, Joe, he was a lieutenant colonel in the Army's Special Forces. Just back from a deployment in Afghanistan, he was assigned to the Joint Staff's Pakistan-Afghanistan Coordination Cell at the Pentagon. But in May 2012, he was reassigned to Fort Carson, Colorado, where he took command of an Army battalion and began to prepare for a 2013 deployment to the Middle East. A few weeks after our small backyard wedding, we began to settle in to our Army-issued house on Fort Carson—and I soon began to realize that I had entered a very different world.

My first hint came in an email from a stranger: "Good Afternoon Senior Spouses," it began briskly. "I would like to welcome you to your new assignments and cordially invite you to a private tour of Fort Carson. . . . Our hope is that the knowledge you gain from this experience will not only benefit you and your Families, but also assist you in encouraging other members of your units to take advantage of crucial Garrison services throughout their time here at Fort Carson."

When I married an Army officer, I began to understand, I did more than just acquire new in-laws—I became part of the U.S. Army. I had no enlistment papers and no commission, but I had a rank: "Senior Spouse." I apparently had "assignments" too—though I didn't have the slightest idea what they were—and was expected to encourage members of my "unit" to take advantage of "Garrison services." (This turned out, disconcertingly, to be a euphemism for getting soldiers and their wives to update their wills before the deployment began.) Ready or not, my two young daughters and I had become part of that alternately glorified and neglected entity, "the military community."

In some ways, it was like stepping into the 1950s. On Fort Carson, home of the 10th Special Forces Group and the 4th Infantry Division, being a "spouse" meant, more or less by definition, being a wife. Until quite recently, female service members were barred from both Special Forces and infantry roles, so all but a handful of young officers and soldiers at Fort Carson were male, and virtually all spouses were wives. Husbands did soldier stuff all day, often starting well before first light and coming home exhausted. Officers' wives took care of the kids, hosted "coffees" for other wives, ran the Family Readiness Groups, accepted flowers during their husbands' change of command ceremonies, and got decorously (or indecorously) plastered at Bunco Nights.

Like most other field grade officers and their wives, Joe and I were assigned a small brick ranch house with military-issue vinyl floors and industrial metal porch railings. We had a bleak backyard full of dying grass surrounded by chain link fencing, and one aged and solitary tree. Next to our driveway hung a big white sign informing the world that our house was the residence of "Commander, 2BCT Special Troops Battalion: Lonestar." Across the street, a house occupied by another battalion commander sported an identical chain link fence, an identical porch, and a nearly identical sign.

Fort Carson was an irony-free zone. Nearly every house sported multiple American flags and other patriotic symbols, as if a passerby might somehow forget she was on an American Army base and require frequent reminders. At 0630 loudspeakers around the base blared out a tinny, recorded version of Reveille, followed by the 4th Infantry Division fight song ("Our soldiers *roar* for freedom, We're *fit* for any *test!* The mighty 4th Division . . . America's *Best!*"). At 1730, the loudspeakers played Retreat; if you happened to be out and about, civilians were expected to pause respectfully with their hands over their hearts, and service members had to salute.

At 2300, the speakers played Taps. And at random intervals between bugle calls, sirens all over Fort Carson blared out stern warnings: "Attention! Attention! Severe . . . lightning . . . *warning*. . . . There is a severe . . . lightning . . . *warning*. Take . . . *shelter*. Take . . . *shelter*." When the Army isn't busy sending people into combat, it's obsessively dedicated to keeping them safe. On a hot August afternoon, the sirens would sometimes blare several times an hour, alerting everyone on post to the latest weather conditions: "Attention! High . . . *winds*. Attention! Heavy . . . *Rain*."

Fort Carson was a world unto itself. The post had everything: a military exchange (the PX) that might have been mistaken for a Walmart, a commissary that stocked multiple varieties of spicy Korean ramen noodles and English crumpets as well as the usual American brands, a Starbucks, a bowling alley, a theater, several gyms and pools, day care centers, a gas station, a post office, a liquor store, three elementary schools, and a middle school. Also, of course, there were offices, shooting ranges, barracks for single soldiers, "simulation centers" where soldiers took part in elaborate computerized war games, vast parking lots full of Humvees and tanks, and hangars for helicopters and drones.

Outside Fort Carson's heavily guarded gates was America, in which everything looked exactly the same, except messier. "America" also lacked Fort Carson's occasional grim reminders of the toll taken by a decade of bloody, inconclusive ground wars: tucked neatly between offices, parking lots, and children's playgrounds, Fort Carson—which lost more soldiers in Iraq and Afghanistan than any other Army post in the country—also had a "Fallen Heroes Family Center" and a "Wounded Warrior Transition Barracks."

On Fort Carson, everyone knew someone who had lost a family member, or seen one come home physically wounded or psychically scarred. Everyone also knew families that had been torn apart by years of deployment-related separations, and children struggling as they transferred repeatedly from one school to another with each Army reassignment. On Fort Carson, everyone knew that endless war comes with endless costs.

## Counting the Costs

Outside Fort Carson's gates, the eternally metastasizing wars of the post-9/11 era could more easily be ignored. But civilians too pay the costs of unbounded war. These costs are less tangible and thus more easily ignored, but they are nonetheless both real and steep.

The financial costs are easiest to measure. Since 9/11, budgets for most nonmilitary foreign-affairs-related government agencies and institutions (such as the State Department and USAID) have been essentially stagnant, and domestic spending on civilian social welfare programs has been slashed. But during the same time period, the defense budget skyrocketed to levels not seen since the immediate post–World War II era. Today, despite recent budget cuts, the defense budget remains at a historically high level: the Pentagon's annual base budget is still more than $500 billion. Add in funds appropriated separately for ongoing military contingency operations, the budget of the Department of Veterans Affairs, and various other pots of defense-related spending hidden in the budgets of the Department of Homeland Security, the Department of Energy, the classified intelligence budget, and so on, and the total spent on Defense-related activities is close to $1 trillion a year.[19] Even in this era of fiscal austerity, proposing significant cuts to military compensation and benefits is still considered political suicide for national politicians.

Perhaps spending money on military personnel and their families makes it easier for the rest of America not to feel guilty about the disproportionate sacrifices made by those in the military community. Before 9/11, civilian and military benefits and compensation were, on average, about the same. Today, it's different: the average member of the military is now better paid than civilian federal workers with comparable education and experience,[20] and members of the military and their families can also lay claim to some of America's most generous social programs. The military offers free health care to service members and their dependents, discount groceries, tax-free shopping, subsidized child care, tuition assistance that can be transferred to spouses and children, and a host of other services.

This creates numerous strange ironies: even as the post–New Deal welfare state continues its slow collapse, the military has become a substitute welfare state for a large swath of small-town America. In a sense, the military—despite its reputation for political conservatism—has become the last outpost of Big Government paternalism in the United States.

In a world in which fewer and fewer government institutions seem capable of performing with even minimal competence, Americans also consistently say they trust the military more than any other public institution. In a 2015 Gallup poll, for instance, 72 percent of Americans expressed "a great deal" or "quite a lot" of confidence in the military, compared to 33 percent expressing confidence in the presidency, 32 percent expressing confidence in the Supreme Court, 31 percent with confidence in the public schools, and 23 percent with confidence in the criminal justice system. Only 8 percent of Americans expressed any confidence in Congress.[21]

Little wonder, then, that Americans throw money at the military: we may not know much about it, but we view it as the only reasonably well-functioning public institution we have these days. We don't trust Congress, and the budgets of civilian foreign policy agencies have taken a beating, along with their capabilities. Faced with problems, we send in the troops—who else can we send? Unlike any other part of the government, the U.S. military can be relied on to go where it's told and do what it's asked—or die trying.

As a result, Americans increasingly treat the military as an all-purpose tool for fixing anything that happens to be broken. Terrorists and insurgents in Syria are beheading journalists and aid workers? Afghanistan's economy is a mess? The Egyptian army needs to be encouraged to respect democracy? An earthquake in Japan has endangered nuclear power plants? Call the military. We want our military busy here at home too, protecting us from cyberattack, patrolling New York's Grand Central Station, stopping illegal immigration in Arizona, and putting out summer forest fires.

But this hints at some of the less tangible costs of endless, unbounded war. We're trapped in a vicious circle: asking the military to take on more and more nontraditional tasks requires exhausting our all-volunteer military force and necessitates higher military budgets. Higher military budgets force us to look for savings elsewhere, so we freeze or cut spending on civilian diplomacy and development and domestic social programs. As budget cuts cripple civilian agencies and programs, they lose their ability to perform as they once did, so we look to the military to pick up the slack, further expanding its role in both foreign and domestic activities and further straining the volunteer force. This requires still higher military budgets, which continues the devastating cycle.

"If your only tool is a hammer, everything looks like a nail." The old adage applies here as well. If your only functioning government institution is the military, everything looks like a war—and when everything looks like war, everything looks like a military mission.

But as America grows steadily more militarized—as the whole world becomes a potential battlefield—we also risk losing something vital. After all, there's a reason human societies, from the Navajo to the Mekeo of Papua New Guinea, have consistently sought to keep war symbolically cordoned off from ordinary life. The distinction between war and nonwar may be arbitrary, but we want it to be sharp and clear, because many actions that are considered both immoral and illegal in peacetime are permissible—even praiseworthy—in wartime. Recall Shakespeare's *Henry V*:

> *In peace there's nothing so becomes a man*
> *As modest stillness and humility:*
> *But when the blast of war blows in our ears,*
> *Then imitate the action of the tiger;*
> *Stiffen the sinews, summon up the blood,*
> *Disguise fair nature with hard-favour'd rage;*
> *Then lend the eye a terrible aspect.*[22]

Peacetime moral and legal rules are radically different from wartime rules. In peacetime, killing is a criminal act; in wartime, it may get you a medal. In peacetime, the authorities can't lock people away indefinitely without charge or trial; in wartime, "enemy combatants" can be held "for the duration of the hostilities."

When war is a bounded state of affairs—a terrible but temporary departure from normality—the existence of separate and more permissive "war rules" doesn't necessarily threaten the integrity of morality or law. But when war becomes the norm, rather than the exception, both morality and law begin to lose their guiding force. As PLA colonels Qiao and Wang foresaw back in 1999, when "all the boundaries lying between the two worlds of war and non-war, of military and non-military" are destroyed, we will enter an era in which "visible national boundaries, invisible internet space, international law, national law, behavioral norms, and ethical principles [will] have absolutely no restraining effects." The two Chinese colonels just didn't expect America—a nation built on its commitment to the rule of law—to become the first major test case.

Here's the basic problem: If we can't tell whether a particular situation counts as "war," we can't figure out which rules apply. And if we don't know which rules apply, we don't know when the deliberate killing of other human beings is permitted—perhaps even required—and when killing constitutes simple murder. We don't know if drone strikes are lawful wartime acts, or murders. We don't know when it's acceptable for the U.S. government to lock someone up indefinitely, without charge or trial, and when due process is required before detention is permissible. We don't know if mass government surveillance is reasonable or unjustifiable. Ultimately, we lose our collective ability to place meaningful restraints on power and violence.

. . .

"War," wrote Clausewitz, is simply "the continuation of policy by other means."[23] Today, those "other means" have expanded beyond recognition—and at the same time, the increasing complexity of the world we live in has made American policy goals ever more difficult to define.

This book is about how we got here: how everything became war, and the military became everything. It highlights many of the more surprising aspects of the modern American way of war, and notes some of the technological, political, and legal transformations of the last half century, focusing on the often invisible impact these have had on warfare, on the military, and on the fragile web of global rules and institutions the United States helped create to constrain conflict after World War II.

*How Everything Became War and the Military Became Everything* also seeks to look into the future, asking what these changes might mean for us as individuals, for our nation, for our unstable world, and for our ability to imagine ourselves as part of a global community committed to basic human rights. When war transcends all boundaries, do the legal and moral categories we have relied upon to channel and constrain violence and coercion lose all value? Do we lose the checks and balances essential to preserving individual liberty and the rule of law? Or can we find some better, more honest way to understand and manage the paradoxes and dilemmas inherent in the era of unbounded war? Might we eventually gain something as well—a more visceral understanding of global interdependence, perhaps, or a stronger sense of shared responsibility?

While Part I of this book introduces the tensions and dilemmas that arise as war bursts out of its traditional boundaries, Part II—"The New American Way of War"—offers a brief tour through the strange world of the modern American military, from Afghan prisons, drone cockpits, and special operators to cyberwarriors, anti-malaria missions, strategic communicators, "killer robots," and the emerging science of nonlethal weapons. Part II also highlights the U.S. military's struggles to define itself in an era in which even our most basic categories—peace and war, civilian and military, national and international—are blurring almost beyond recognition.

Part III—"How We Got Here"—takes a step back, looking at the ways in which human societies have struggled throughout history to define, contain, and tame war. Part III takes us from ancient times to the rites and rituals of modern-day military boot camp, and tells the story of how the modern law of war—and institutions such as the United Nations—arose from the carnage of nineteenth- and twentieth-century conflicts. The post–World War II era saw an explosion of international lawmaking—human rights and humanitarian norms were codified into treaties and given life through global courts and other institutions.

But though these utopian new developments helped reduce interstate conflict in the post–World War II years, they were, from the start, premised on artificial categories and rife with internal contradictions— contradictions that are now beginning to tear them apart.

Part IV, "Counting the Costs," highlights the ways in which the increasingly blurred boundaries between war and "not-war" are undermining our ability to place meaningful constraints on violence and power, both domestically and globally. As "war rules" trickle down into ordinary life, they are beginning to change everything from policing and immigration policy to courtroom evidentiary rules and governmental commitments to transparency, gradually eroding the foundations of democracy and individual rights. In the international sphere, the fragile post–World War II balance between respect for sovereignty and nonintervention, on the one hand, and human rights and self-defense, on the other, has been disrupted by the legal theories put forward by the United States after 9/11, as well as by U.S. military actions such as targeted killings and the use of force in places such as Libya and Syria. The consequences may be momentous. As Part IV notes, an emboldened Russia has already begun to test the limits of legal theories put forward by the United States, and we can expect other states to follow suit. In its closing sections, Part IV also looks at the impact of war's blurriness on civilian-military relations and on the U.S. military itself.

Finally, Part V, "Managing War's Paradoxes," looks at what we can do to prevent our world from sliding toward chaos and cruelty. In an era in which threats come packaged in lines of computer code, suicide vests, and Internet propaganda as often as in tanks and missiles, we can't jam war back into its old box. But if we're courageous enough to toss away some of our old categories and assumptions, we may be able to find creative new ways to reinvent our military, to protect human dignity, and to prevent abuses of power.

* * *

This book is not a memoir. It's part journalism, part policy, part history, part anthropology, and part law, leavened with occasional stories. Only a few of the stories are my own. Still, in some ways this is a very personal book, for I'm part of this story too. Or perhaps I should say that this story is part of me: as someone who went from a childhood of antiwar demonstrations and an early career in human rights to a job at the Pentagon and life as an Army wife, I have lived many of the contradictions that brought us to our current state of unbounded war.

## My Family Values

In 1980—the year I turned ten—all the houses on our street sported American flags and yellow ribbons. I didn't really understand why; it had something to do with Iran, and hostages, and the Army, and (according to my mother) "militaristic jingoism." Only our modest suburban ranch house was bereft of both flags and ribbons. My parents instead proclaimed their politics on the bumpers of their battered old cars. "War Is Not the Answer!" "My Family Values: Peace, Not War!"

I didn't know what the term "militaristic jingoism" meant, but overall, I understood my parents' message clearly enough. War was a terrible thing. It was Not the Answer. Bad leaders sought war, but the rest of us had a duty to discourage it, though few of my neighbors seemed to know that. As for the military, its nature was just as disturbing: the military was in the business of killing, without which wars could not proceed. Like war itself, the military needed to be contained, discouraged, and ideally, it seemed to my ten-year-old self, disbanded.

On weekends throughout that year, I stood with my family and a handful of other hardy local antiwar activists in front of our neighborhood post office, protesting the newly reimposed requirement that young men register for the draft. We stood there in the summer, waving our colorful hand-painted banners as the temperature displayed on the bank thermometer across the street hit a hundred degrees, and we stood there in the winter, as the temperature display dropped to zero.

I was a dutiful child, eager to please my activist parents. As I listened to their stories of the Vietnam War, it never occurred to me to consider the draft anything other than a terrible social wrong, and the military anything more than an institution designed to exploit America's poor and inflict suffering on foreign populations. Refugees from half a dozen wars passed through our house, staying in the spare room in our basement: there were Eritreans fleeing Ethiopian military repression; a Greek Cypriot displaced by the Turkish invasion; Salvadorans and Guatemalans and Chileans fleeing U.S.-backed military juntas; Nicaraguans fleeing the U.S.-backed contras. In most of these conflicts, the U.S. military was actively assisting the same abusive actors from which our temporary guests were fleeing. I absorbed the message: sensible people stayed far away from soldiers and wars.

Well into my young adulthood, this view of the military shaped my response to politics and foreign affairs. During my senior year in college, I protested the 1991 Gulf War. We were going to war to protect U.S. access to Kuwaiti oil? It seemed like the height of cynicism. At a "candlelight vigil to support the troops," I got into a near-shouting match with an Army ROTC cadet who hastily turned off the microphone when I started to speak against the wisdom of going to war. Sure, Saddam Hussein shouldn't have invaded Kuwait, I argued in the student newspaper the next day, but "you can't stop aggression with aggression."[24]

But a few years later, footage of Rwandan corpses clogging the waters of Lake Victoria shook my previously firm opposition to military interventions. Perhaps there *were* times when aggression was the only possible counter to aggression—at least where mass atrocities were concerned. In Rwanda, couldn't the U.S. military—the strongest and best military in the world, as we were constantly told—save hundreds of thousands of innocent lives by intervening against the genocidal Hutu militias? Would such an intervention be a "war," or would it be something different?

The U.S. military did nothing in Rwanda, of course—a failure for which President Bill Clinton later apologized. But the year after the Rwandan genocide killed some 800,000 people, a U.S.-led NATO bombing campaign forced Serbian president Slobodan Milosevic and Bosnian Serb leader Radovan Karadzic to stop the ethnic slaughter in Bosnia. Watching the television news, I had decidedly mixed feelings. Dropping bombs seemed like a tragic solution, but better than doing nothing as Serbian forces brought concentration camps back to Europe and massacred thousands of unarmed civilians at Srebrenica.

After finishing law school, I worked for Human Rights Watch and saw firsthand some of the fearful consequences of unbounded war. Human Rights Watch sent me to Kenya and Northern Uganda, where I wrote a report on Joseph Kony's Lord's Resistance Army and their brutal campaign against children. In the tiny Ugandan towns of Gulu, Aboke, and Lira, I met ten-year-old boys who had been forced to hack their siblings to death with machetes, and twelve-year-old girls conscripted as "wives" for rebel commanders. Later, while teaching in the human rights clinic at Yale Law School, I worked on a lawsuit on behalf of Bosnian women who had been tortured and gang-raped in Serbian concentration camps.

Still later, during a stint at the State Department's human rights bureau, I spent time in Sierra Leone, where rebel forces in a long-running civil war were attracting global censure for their habit of mutilating civilians who wouldn't join them. Freetown, Sierra Leone's capital, was full of half-burned buildings, rotting trash, and houses pocked with bullet holes. One afternoon, Joseph Melrose, the American ambassador, brought me with him to a meeting with Ahmad Tejan Kabbah, Sierra Leone's embattled, democratically elected president. As Ambassador Melrose reiterated that the United States unfortunately would not be able to provide him with direct military assistance, President Kabbah gazed blankly past us and out the window, where a few scrawny cows grazed on the still manicured presidential lawn. Then, his head slumping over his vast, empty desk, he began, very quietly, to cry.

By 1999, when President Clinton decided to use American airpower to prevent ethnic cleansing in Kosovo, I found that I was simply relieved: in a world so chock-full of suffering, it was heartening to see the United States using military force to prevent conflict and atrocities. Visiting Kosovo for the State Department in the aftermath of the U.S.-led NATO air campaign, I saw grateful Kosovars waving "Thank You, NATO" signs—and harried but courteous U.S. troops, untrained for nation-building activities, struggling to restore order in a chaotic situation that seemed to be neither war nor peace, but something in between.

By the last years of the twentieth century, my childhood views of the military and the use of military force had come to seem simplistic and naive, or at least terribly out of date. America's military was not the dysfunctional mess it had appeared to be during the Vietnam era: this was a disciplined, all-volunteer force, in which idealistic and well-trained young men and women sought to ensure that American military force would be used to save lives, not destroy them.

My job at the State Department also brought me into direct contact with dozens of military personnel, from the midlevel officers detailed to the State Department to the young enlisted soldiers patrolling the tense streets of Pristina and Mitrovica. For the first time, "the military" was no longer an abstraction to me but an organization made up of individual human beings, many of whom I came to like and admire.

After all, I was the child of activists, brought up to believe that life had meaning only if you were committed to some cause larger than your own comfort. In my military colleagues, I recognized a similar ethos: a willingness to forgo money, comfort, and convenience for the sake of ideas and ideals. Many of my college and law school classmates had headed unabashedly off to Wall Street or large corporate law firms, with the stated intention of making as much money as possible in as short a time as possible. I found, to my own surprise, that in some ways I had more in common with my new military colleagues than with many of my old classmates.

## That's Complicated

But if my time at the State Department persuaded me that the United States and its military could be forces for good in a troubled world, the Bush administration's response to the 9/11 attacks left me reeling. Instead of a stable world in which the U.S. military kept the peace and protected the vulnerable, the 9/11 attacks ushered in a world in which unbounded war became a permanent state of affairs, and the military's role also expanded beyond recognition.

The attacks themselves were shattering. As a native New Yorker, I could hardly conceive of a skyline without the Twin Towers, and the endless television replays of falling bodies and the towers' slow collapse left me sick with horror. But I was dismayed when President Bush declared that America was now in a "global war on terror." By this time, I had left the State Department and become a member of the law faculty at the University of Virginia, where I taught and wrote about international legal issues and human rights, and I understood immediately that the war on terror was no mere metaphor—no "War on Poverty" or "War on Illiteracy." A global war on terror, I intuitively knew, was a war that could, by its nature, have no boundaries: no geographic limits, no limits on who could be targeted, captured, or killed, and no end.

All the same: if there was going to be war and struggle, I wanted somehow to be part of it. Some of my military friends were deploying to Afghanistan, and I envied them. They were going to be part of something vast and historic: they would drive out the Taliban and help restore an Afghan government that respected human rights. Even the Iraq War, however dubious its justifications and origins, seemed to promise *something* hopeful: Didn't the ouster of Saddam Hussein at least offer the Iraqi people an end to political repression?

I wanted to see for myself.

· · ·

In August 2003, I managed to pull together a trip to Iraq to research a book on military interventions and the rule of law. I organized the trip myself, tapping every network I had from the State Department and the military to the human rights community. I financed my travel with research funds from the University of Virginia, and even convinced a couple of my Virginia colleagues to come along.

My younger brother, a journalist, was working on a story in Afghanistan; in a telephone call repeatedly interrupted by static, he told me he had heard rumors that the U.S. military was torturing prisoners. I was skeptical, even offended—that wasn't the military I had come to know and respect while working for the State Department.

I asked him for his source. Someone working for Amnesty International, he said. This only increased my skepticism: I had served briefly on Amnesty's U.S. board of directors, and considered the quality of Amnesty's work uneven, and its claims sometimes unreliable.

But in the empty, looted streets of Baghdad, rumors of torture were also swirling around. One baking afternoon, exhausted and sick with a stomach bug I had managed to import to Baghdad from Charlottesville, Virginia, I was sitting outside a small restaurant, sweating and queasy—nausea had forced me away from lunch—when a pickup truck screeched to a halt in front of me. Two young Iraqi men jumped out and approached.

"Where you from, pretty lady? America?" asked one. His English was almost accent-less, his lip curled up in a sneer. "You shouldn't sit outside alone like this. Don't you know we could kidnap you and kill you? Don't you know we hate Americans? Don't you know what your soldiers are doing to our people?"

I was too nauseated to feel any fear. Instead, I just listened blearily while he ranted on, telling of torture and beatings by American soldiers, and dead Iraqi children dismissed as collateral damage. In the distance, we could hear scattered gunfire. His father, he said, had been an Iraqi consular official in the United States. He had lived in Philadelphia for much of his boyhood, enjoying the American music, the American television shows, the American freedom. But now? His siblings had all been killed in the war, he said. Now he felt nothing but hatred for America, which was destroying his family and his country.

"What do *you* think?" he finally demanded. "Is there any reason I *shouldn't* hate the Americans? Has your nation made our lives better? Is your war going well?"

No, I admitted, it appeared not.

He laughed, but it was a bitter laugh.

"At least you're honest. None of the other Americans here are honest." He shook his head violently. "You should go back inside, you know. You have nice eyes. I won't kill you, but not everyone is as soft-hearted as I am."

A few days later, my colleagues and I attended a meeting on detention policy inside the "Green Zone," where the U.S.-led multinational military coalition had set up its headquarters inside one of Saddam Hussein's former palaces. I don't remember how we wangled our way in—perhaps it was through one of my State Department contacts, or through contacts at the Army's Judge Advocate General's School, which is next door to the University of Virginia's law school. In hindsight, I'm amazed that no one thought to question the presence of three random American civilians at the meeting, but in August 2003 the Green Zone was still chaotic. Exhausted soldiers slept on cots in marble-floored ballrooms, and the palace hallways were full of anxious, rushing officers in the uniforms of half a dozen nations. No one seemed sure who was supposed to be there and who wasn't.

We sat in an echoing, high-ceilinged conference room as a discussion began about what to do with the thousands of Iraqi detainees scooped up by Coalition forces: How would they all be processed? How should officials in the U.S.-led coalition decide who should be released and who should stay in detention? What role should the largely dismantled Iraqi criminal justice system play? Were new prison facilities needed, or were existing Iraqi prisons, such as the one at Abu Ghraib, sufficient?

The meeting had been going on for ten or fifteen minutes when a dark-haired young British officer burst in. He was agitated and angry—as angry as the young Iraqi man who accosted me outside the restaurant.

The conditions in Coalition-operated prisons in Basra were appalling, he said: it was a humid 120 degrees outside, and Iraqi detainees were dying of thirst, heat, and ill treatment. "People are *dying.* We are *violating* our obligations under the Geneva Conventions," he declared, furiously slamming his palm on the table. "This *cannot* continue."

There was an uncomfortable silence. Finally, someone I never identified—an American in civilian clothes—spoke in a quiet voice. "Well, the Geneva Conventions," he murmured. "That's . . . complicated, isn't it?"

And somehow, the subject was changed.

But in August 2003, many Iraqis were still optimistic about the future. The giddy televised celebrations engendered by Saddam Hussein's fall were genuine, and it was easy enough to understand why. One day we visited a fledgling Iraqi human rights group that had "liberated" government files documenting the regime's torture and execution of thousands of political prisoners. Using a looted bulldozer, the group dumped the files into the basement of their makeshift headquarters, a large house abandoned by a fleeing Ba'athist intelligence official. Now the files lay in dozens of untidy heaps, some five or six feet high, avalanching everywhere onto the basement floor. Eager to display the evidence of Saddam's crimes to their American guests, our hosts ushered us into the basement, pulling papers out more or less at random: here, a file documenting an interrogation session; there, a photo of a young man's corpse. We walked gingerly over the photos of murdered Iraqis, but even our careful movement through the room dislodged more loose papers: records of broken lives and bodies, drifting down like falling leaves.

My colleagues and I left Baghdad by car the next week, heading for the Jordanian border. Still weak from my stomach bug, I took the back row of seats in the Chevy Suburban and tried to sleep. But somewhere on the road between Fallujah and Ramadi, I was jolted awake: our car had been forced to a stop by armed bandits.

My bandit—there were quite a few of them, but I still think of the guy who stuck a gun in my face as *my* bandit—was straight out of central casting, complete with dark stubble and a red-checkered scarf hiding his lower face. "Money money money!" he demanded in heavily accented English. His gun barrel was pointed between my eyes, and his hand shook slightly. Very carefully, I handed him my wallet. He rifled through it quickly with his free hand, pulling out the cash, then handing the wallet back to me.

"*Shukrun*," I said, producing, to my own astonishment, the Arabic word for "thank you."

My bandit looked just as surprised. "You are welcome," he said gravely, in English, before turning and running off.

We reported the incident to the bemused American soldiers at a checkpoint a few hundred miles later, but they just shrugged. It was happening, they said, to everyone: soldiers, humanitarian aid workers, journalists. We should consider ourselves lucky we hadn't been shot.

Arriving home in the States the next day, we saw on the news that a bomb had destroyed the United Nations offices at the Canal Hotel in Baghdad, killing twenty-two people (including U.N. special representative Sérgio Vieira de Mello). This shook me more than anything I had encountered while in Iraq: we had spent several hours at the Canal Hotel just a few days earlier, meeting with Vieira de Mello's aides, making use of the Internet access offered free by the U.N. to NGO workers and other visitors, and enjoying the compound's sense of safety and air-conditioned calm.

In this war, it appeared, there were no places of safety, and there could be no such thing as neutrality. This war would spare no one.

. . .

This, I was discovering, is the nature of war: It abhors a vacuum. It expands until everything and everyone is subsumed by it. It resists all efforts at categorization and containment. We keep trying to lock it into a box, but war keeps breaking out again.

Throughout the twenty-first-century's first decade, controversies swirled around the war in Iraq and U.S. detention and interrogation policies in the war on terrorism: Did the Geneva Conventions apply to the Taliban? To al Qaeda? To Iraqi detainees? Or were the Geneva Conventions—as then Attorney General Alberto Gonzales put it— "quaint" and "obsolete"? Did this "new kind of war" justify so-called enhanced interrogation techniques such as waterboarding? Could the United States lawfully capture terror suspects anywhere in the world, and detain them secretly?[25] Could the government seize a U.S. citizen inside the United States, as it did to Jose Padilla, deprive him of legal counsel, and subject him to unknown methods of interrogation?

In the years following that 2003 trip to Iraq, virtually every place we had visited was bombed. Our Baghdad hotel was bombed, as was our hotel in Amman, Jordan. The restaurant where we had lunch the day I was approached by the angry young Iraqi man was bombed. Parts of the Green Zone were mortared, along with the suburban area in which we had stepped on the files of dead political prisoners.

I wrote long academic articles about the controversies surrounding this "new kind of war." I also wrote weekly op-ed columns for the *Los Angeles Times*, many of them criticizing the Bush administration's Orwellian insistence that neither U.S. law nor human rights law nor the laws of war constrained U.S. detention and interrogation policy.

Finally, in January 2009, I watched with pride and relief as President Barack Obama, newly inaugurated, signed executive orders banning torture, closing secret CIA prisons, and initiating a working group to develop a plan to close Guantánamo. America, he promised, would abide by both the letter and spirit of international law.

"With just a few words and strokes of his pen, the president ended the war on terror," I wrote jubilantly in my weekly *L.A. Times* column.

I was wrong. Between 2001 and 2009, the entire U.S. national security bureaucracy had been revamped to fight the global war on terrorism, and truly changing course proved too much for Obama. Once set in motion, the machinery of endless war is almost impossible to stop. After all, there is no national constituency demanding an end to indefinite "law of war detention" at Guantánamo or Afghanistan's Bagram Air Force Base. There's no national movement calling for an end to the drone strikes that kill presumed terrorist masterminds.

I too was soon caught up in the unbounded war.

In April 2009, I still believed the Obama administration would turn things around, and I enthusiastically accepted a position as a political appointee at the Pentagon. Working for Under Secretary of Defense Michèle Flournoy was a dream job: Flournoy was a wonderful boss, thoughtful and empowering to her staff, and as her advisor and speechwriter, I had high-level access to almost anything I cared to learn about.

Working at the Pentagon was both glamorous and mundane, both compelling and chilling. I was walking down the hall in the Pentagon's E Ring one day with Jeh Johnson,[26] the Defense Department's general counsel, who later became secretary of homeland security. "You know, your legal scholarship has been very helpful to us," he confided. "I cited your work in a memo I just finished on counterterrorism options." He riffled through the papers he was carrying until he found the page he wanted, and handed it to me, pointing.

Yes, there were my own words: a quote from a law review article I had written a few years earlier, noting the extraordinary difficulty of fitting terrorist threats into traditional legal categories. I skimmed quickly through the memo and handed it back, unsure how to respond. Johnson was a decent, thoughtful man, and he meant to be kind, but I was thoroughly discomfited: glancing at the memo's conclusions, it seemed my words were helping to justify policies I wasn't sure I agreed with.

I wasn't sure I disagreed, either—that was the problem.

. . .

We can't turn back the clock: most of the technological and social changes that ushered in this current era of unbounded war are here to stay. But perhaps there is room for hope, as well as reason for dismay.

Crisis can lead to innovation as well as catastrophe. The wars that wracked Europe in the sixteenth and seventeenth centuries led to the emergence of the modern nation-state, a form of social organization that proved far better at promoting human welfare than the religious and feudal societies it displaced, despite its flaws. And after territorial conflicts between unconstrained, expansionist nation-states led to the twentieth century's two cataclysmic world wars, the United Nations Charter and the human rights revolution emerged from the ashes. Neither was perfect—but both were a distinct improvement on genocide and total war.

Today, we're coming again to one of history's crossroads. As the familiar distinctions between "wartime" and "peacetime," "armed conflict" and "crime," "foreign affairs" and "domestic" issues, and the "military" and "civilian" domains lose all clarity, the elaborate legal and institutional architecture designed to constrain state power and protect individual rights is growing increasingly unstable, both globally and in the United States.

There's nothing natural or inevitable about any of our familiar categories or distinctions. They are the products of human minds, conceived as a means of organizing ourselves and channeling violence and coercion at a particular moment in history. We created the categories we use, and if they're no longer serving the purpose we want them to serve, we can change them.

To do that, we'll have to first abandon the effort to draw increasingly arbitrary lines between "peacetime" and "wartime," and accept that some level of conflict will always be with us—but we don't have to let it distort our values. If we jettison the old categories and binary distinctions, perhaps we can find new ways to manage war. Perhaps we can develop institutions and norms capable of protecting human rights and the rule of law not just in peacetime, but in *all* times.

Don't imagine that our world can't collapse: there is nothing inevitable about progress or peace, and the global and national social and political order we inhabit today is no more immune from catastrophe than the pre–World War II order. And perhaps it will take another catastrophe to jolt us into designing new rules and institutions better suited to twenty-first-century challenges. But maybe—if we're honest enough to acknowledge the growing incoherence of the all-too-human rules and institutions we have created, and brave enough to imagine new ones—we can find a path that will lead us, if not toward "peace," then at least toward something kinder than perpetual war.

# PART II

# The New American Way of War

# CHAPTER ONE

# Pirates!

### Everything Was Strange

Telling people that I was going to work at the Pentagon felt like saying that I was going to work at the Death Star, or that I'd have an office inside the Sphinx. It took me weeks to shake off the slight feeling of unreality that hit me each time I entered the world's largest office building. Did *I* work *here*? How very strange.

Everything about the Pentagon was strange. My mother, visiting me for lunch, gaped at the Pentagon's food courts, banks, and shops. "The heart of American military power is a *shopping mall*?" she asked. Once you got past the shops clustered by the Metro entrance, the Pentagon's corridors were endless and echoing, lined with closed metal doors flanked by keypads and stern printed warnings: "No cell phones, cameras or other recording devices." Uniformed men and women strode about decisively, heels clicking on the shiny floors. The Pentagon had a unique scent too, some mix of cleaning fluids, wood polish, floor wax, coffee, and human stress, amplified by the canned air protecting its denizens from biological and chemical infiltration. Every time I walked in through the wide doors, the scent washed over me.

The windows in the E Ring's outward-facing offices, which house many of the most senior officials, were made of a curious green glass. I never learned the details, but I assume the thick green glass was bulletproof, or blast proof, or surveillance proof, or all those things. Regardless, from within, the green glass gave an odd chartreuse tint to the world outside the Pentagon—the endless acres of parking lots, the yacht basin, the Potomac River—and beyond, the monuments and stately buildings of official Washington. Gazing through those windows, I felt like Dorothy in the Emerald City.

There were peculiar exhibits everywhere: lurid paintings of fighter planes, elaborate dioramas illustrating the life of General Douglas MacArthur, glass-fronted displays of World War II code-breaking machines. The grand staircase leading up from the Pentagon's elegant River Entrance boasted a vast oil painting—perhaps six feet by ten—of a uniformed airman and his family kneeling at a chapel altar, rapt faces lit from above by a shaft of sunlight coming through a stained-glass window. In case the viewer was particularly obtuse, the inscription beneath the painting clarified the message: *"And the Lord God asked, 'Whom shall I send? Who will go for us?' And the reply came back: 'Here I am, send me.'"* Kitsch—but sanctified kitsch.

## Ahoy, Matey!

When I first started work at the Pentagon, it seemed that I had walked into some kind of permanent Talk Like a Pirate Week. Meetings opened with cries of "Ahoy, matey!," "Avast, me hearties!," and merry threats to make latecomers walk the plank. Occasionally, you even saw someone sporting a black eye patch or a rakish bandana.

Whatever I had expected about my new job at the heart of American military power, it wasn't this. But on April 8, 2009—less than a week before I started my new job in the Office of the Secretary of Defense—four young Somali pirates had boarded the merchant vessel *Maersk Alabama,* making it the first U.S.-flagged ship to be seized by pirates in nearly two hundred years. They demanded ransom money, but on April 12, Navy SEAL snipers shot and killed three of the pirates, rescuing Richard Phillips, the *Maersk Alabama*'s American captain, and capturing the fourth pirate.

The very next day, I started work at the Pentagon, surrounded by giddy military bureaucrats cracking pirate jokes.

And it *was* funny—sort of. Pirates! Who'da thunk it? And who could blame hardworking Pentagon action officers for uttering some celebratory cries of "Avast, me hearties"? For years, the Pentagon had struggled through the bloody and inconclusive wars in Iraq and Afghanistan. After a decade of suicide bombs and dead civilians, how nice to have an uncomplicated success story. How nice to be the good guys, rescuing American citizens and ships from the bad guys.

## He Caught a Big Fish

Admittedly, it wasn't exactly a fair fight: the four Somali pirates were scruffy, undernourished teenage boys. They were poor and untrained: the sole pirate to survive his encounter with the SEALs was Abdiwali Abdiqadir Muse, the oldest of twelve children from a Puntland family that got by on a few dollars a day. Muse grew up in a one-room home. His mother sold milk at the market; his father herded goats and camels.[1] Interviewed after their rescue, members of the *Maersk Alabama*'s crew recalled Muse's astonished delight at discovering he had unwittingly gained control of an American ship: "He kept asking, `You all come from America?' Then he claps and cheers and smiles. He caught himself a big fish."[2]

The fish was much too big for Muse, a scrawny kid of 5'2". His family told journalists that he was only sixteen, and had been duped by older criminals into trying his hand at piracy.[3] But he had no birth certificate (few Somalis do), and after a medical examination, U.S. authorities asserted that he was probably nineteen rather than sixteen. Either way, Muse and his dreams of a hefty ransom bonanza were no match for U.S. Navy SEALs.

Notwithstanding the jokes, the Navy assault on the *Maersk Alabama* pirates was in many ways a typical twenty-first-century military engagement. U.S. forces increasingly find themselves fighting nontraditional enemies: pirates, terrorists, insurgents, organized crime networks, and other actors who pose asymmetric challenges to conventional U.S. military power. Today, America's adversaries rarely engage in battles over territorial control. They'd be fools to do so, given conventional U.S. military dominance. Instead, they use kidnapping, hijacking, sabotage, theft, propaganda videos, computer hacking, suicide bombs, and IEDs to cause disruption and damage to U.S. interests.

Sometimes America's adversaries have the overt or covert backing of foreign states; sometimes they are nonstate groups acting alone. Sometimes their motives are ideological or political; sometimes purely financial. The threats they pose are real, but difficult to quantify or categorize and still more difficult to combat. You can "win" a war against Nazi Germany, but how do you win against shifting, inchoate extremist networks with little interest in controlling physical terrain, or roving bands of hungry young African pirates seeking ransom money?

No one at the Pentagon was quite sure, but Congress, galvanized by the *Maersk Alabama* incident, was demanding answers—and my boss, Michèle Flournoy, was supposed to provide them. In the absence of a designated speechwriter, she turned to me to draft her testimony.

. . .

Although I had worked at the State Department, I had no experience on Capitol Hill, and at that point I had never drafted nor given congressional testimony. But I was an international law scholar, and knew something about the intertwined history of piracy and international law. For sure, I thought, Congress would want to know about this too.

So my draft testimony began with a capsule history of piracy and law, cribbed in part from prior testimony by other DoD officials and embellished with some quick Googling:

> Mr. Chairman, piracy is a growing problem, but not a new problem. Since humans first began to travel and move valuables by ship, there have been pirates. In Roman times, Julius Caesar himself was seized by pirates in 75 B.C., and released after ransom was paid. The Vikings, too, were notorious pirates. Historically, the line between piracy and legitimate use of force on the high seas was often blurry; many states—including our own—at times issued letters of marque and reprisal, authorizing "privateers" to attack an enemy's merchant ships. The Barbary States of North

Africa were particularly entrepreneurial issuers of letters of marque, and by 1800, the young United States was paying about 20% of total federal revenues to the Barbary States, as ransom and tribute.[4]

International efforts to combat piracy also have an ancient pedigree. Since Roman times, pirates have been deemed *hostes humani generis*: the enemies of all humankind, and as a matter of customary international law, piracy was a crime of "universal jurisdiction," meaning that every state had the right and the duty to capture and prosecute piracy on the high seas, even if its own ships or nationals were not involved.

In the middle of the 19th century, the major European powers signed the Declaration of Paris, agreeing to end the practice of issuing letters of marque and reprisal. The United States, though not a signatory to the Declaration, agreed to abide by its principles. Most other states did so as well. As the anti-piracy and anti-privateering principles of the Declaration of Paris were gradually incorporated into successive treaties on the law of the sea, the long era of state-sponsored piracy came more or less to a close.

I handed this to Michèle, who read through it quickly. "This is really, ah, interesting," she finally said. "But I think we should skip the historical part. I don't think the Senate Armed Services Committee is going to want to focus on that."

I went back to the drawing board.

Getting the testimony just right proved harder than I had thought: the trick, it turned out, was to offer a little something to everyone on the committee, with enough caveats to avoid committing the Defense Department to anything that might come back to bite us. Here, we had a dual challenge: convincing any congressional skeptics that it was, in fact, entirely appropriate for the Defense Department to put resources into fighting a bunch of scruffy teen pirates (rather than solely into, say, the wars in Iraq and Afghanistan), while at the same time convincing any counterpiracy hawks that no, the entire U.S. Navy could not be sent indefinitely to patrol the Somali coastline. In the end, I came up with this:

> Mr. Chairman, we are currently seeing a dramatic upswing in reported pirate attacks, particularly off the coast of Somalia. . . .
>
> Freedom of the seas is critical to our national security and international commerce, and it is also a core principle of international law. . . . From a Department of Defense perspective, our strategic goals with regard to Somali piracy include deterrence, disruption/interdiction, and prosecution. But achieving these goals will be challenging for several reasons.
>
> First, the geographic area affected is vast. . . . When not actively engaged in piracy, pirate vessels easily blend in with ordinary shipping. . . . Second, the root causes of Somali piracy lie in the poverty and instability that continue to plague that troubled country. Third, serious gaps remain in the international community's ability to create an effective legal deterrent by prosecuting pirates for their crimes. . . . Fourth and finally, many in the merchant shipping industry continue to unrealistically assume that military forces will always be present to intervene if pirates attack. As a result, many have so far been unwilling to invest in the basic security measures that would render their ships far less vulnerable. . . .
>
> Although Somali piracy currently appears to be motivated solely by money, not ideology, and we see no meaningful links between Somali pirates and violent extremist groups, we must ensure that piracy does not evolve into a future funding source for terrorism.

Most of this draft survived. We went on to offer up a range of DoD responses to piracy: we promised that we would be "working closely with other Agencies and Departments to develop comprehensive regional counter-piracy strategies," "working directly with merchant shipping lines to undertake vulnerability assessments and disseminate best practices," working "with allies and regional states to develop their capacity to patrol the seas and protect their own shipping," and continuing "to address the root causes of most regional piracy: the ongoing poverty and instability in Somalia."

What the testimony didn't do—and couldn't do—was resolve the core underlying questions: Is the twenty-first-century U.S. military the right institution to take on ragtag bands of impoverished Africans preying on private shipping? Which U.S. institution was going to address Somalia's "ongoing poverty and instability"? At what price?—and what would constitute "success"? What rules should govern military counterpiracy operations, and how should we conceptualize them? Were they "war"? Law enforcement? Both? Something else altogether?

## Global Counterpiracy

Today, these questions remain unanswered, but the U.S. military continues to play an expansive role in global counterpiracy operations. Navy ships patrol the waters off the Horn of Africa and the Gulf of Guinea, and the number and locations of Navy patrols change in response to shifting patterns of piracy. For the most part, these patrols occur in the context of multinational counterpiracy efforts: the United States participates in Combined Task Force 151: Counter-Piracy with states ranging from Turkey and Pakistan to South Korea and Australia; and in Operation Ocean Shield with other NATO states.[5] These counterpiracy patrols play a preventive role and also have a quick response capability of the sort used in the *Maersk Alabama* rescue.

Many U.S. military counterpiracy efforts are more indirect, focusing less on military action and more on building the capacity of partner governments to effectively patrol their own coastlines. Through a maritime security exercise called Obangame Express, for instance, U.S. forces have helped train the navies and coast guards of Gulf of Guinea nations to conduct boarding operations.[6] Other U.S. military initiatives focus on providing African states with improved sensing and communications networks to enable better tracking of coastal areas. In Nigeria and Djibouti, the U.S. Navy has funded new multimillion-dollar radar systems that use "an automatic identification system and ground-based radar and sensors to enhance awareness of maritime traffic."[7] The U.S.

military donates ships to partner nations and provides training in everything from boarding techniques to "small boat maintenance." And that's not all. The military also supports counterpiracy strategic communication programs on Somali radio stations and develops training manuals to help local law enforcement officials conduct counterpiracy investigations.[8]

The effectiveness of these efforts is difficult to judge. On the one hand, piracy off the Somali Coast has dropped sharply in the last couple of years, and it seems reasonable to attribute the decline to stepped-up multinational counterpiracy programs, with the United States playing a leading role. On the other hand, piracy is up sharply on the other side of the African continent, where attacks on shipping in the Gulf of Guinea have become both more frequent and more lethal.[9] It's hard to determine causation: Is Somali piracy down because of U.S. military activity, or because of slightly improved stability and economic opportunities in Somalia? And if Somalia is more stable today, is that because of U.S. assistance, or internal factors unrelated to the United States?

Some analysts also question whether the decline in Somali piracy will be enduring,[10] noting that although there have been fewer attacks overall, those that have occurred have been more sophisticated and successful. It may be, they argue, that improved counterpiracy methods just motivate pirates to develop more sophisticated piracy methods. Brandon Prins, a professor at the University of Tennessee who has studied piracy for the Office of Naval Research, isn't optimistic about the long-term prospects: "As long as abundant targets sail in waters bordered by weak states full of jobless people, piracy will continue."[11]

That is: as long as there are hungry young men like Abdiwali Abdiqadir Muse, piracy will continue.

Adding to the difficulty is uncertainty about costs. Much of the military training and equipment the United States provides for counterpiracy purposes serves other purposes as well, and is divided under multiple budget lines. In fiscal year 2009, for instance, U.S. Central Command spent an estimated $64 million on counterpiracy, including Navy ship steaming days and air support for ships. In calendar year 2011, the Defense Department estimated that it spent $274.5 million on antipiracy programs; in 2013, that dropped to $69.4 million. It is hard to know what is included (and what is not included) in these figures, however, and in a 2014 report, the Government Accountability Office noted that "U.S. agencies have not systematically assessed the costs and benefits of their counterpiracy efforts."[12]

Needless to say, military counterpiracy efforts also carry opportunity costs: each Navy ship or plane patrolling the Gulf of Aden or the Gulf of Guinea is a ship or plane that's unavailable for other operations, and every dollar spent on counterpiracy is a dollar that can't be spent on other threats.

## "Peace Thro' the Medium of War"

In some ways, U.S. counterpiracy operations represent the new face of American warfare—and such operations wouldn't look very familiar to those steeped in World War II movies, grown accustomed to thinking of war as battles between tanks, submarines, or fighter planes.

But in other ways, military counterpiracy operations are nothing new at all. Indeed, as I suggested in the portion of Michèle Flournoy's draft testimony that she very sensibly cut, piracy is one of America's oldest military problems.

Go back in time to the days of the early American republic. The rebellious colonists had successfully cast off the British yoke—largely by doing what the weak have always done, and employing unconventional methods of asymmetric warfare against Europe's most powerful military. Flush with victory, the scrappy American rebels soon found—like so many insurgents before and after—that it's one thing to rebel, and another thing to run a nation. Before the American Revolution, British naval power had protected the thirteen colonies' shipping from predation by the state-sponsored pirates of Africa's Barbary Coast, and French assistance did the same during the Revolutionary War. After the war, the young nation found itself on its own. Without a real Navy (Congress sold off the last American warship from the Revolutionary War in 1785), America's merchant ships were easy prey for the Barbary pirates.

At first, America came to the same conclusion many shipping companies still come to today: Why fight when you can just pay the pirates to leave you alone? Fighting the pirates—a frighteningly efficient lot, backed by the leaders of Tripoli, Morocco, Tunis, and Algiers—might seem more "manly," noted John Adams, who had been appointed by Congress to negotiate with the Barbary States in 1784, but those who favored military action had "more spirit than prudence." War, Adams believed, would be far costlier than simply paying tribute to the Barbary States in exchange for safe passage for American shipping: it would not be "good economy" to spend "a million annually" on naval warfare "to save one gift of two hundred thousand pounds."[13]

But the tab grew and grew. In 1784, Moroccan corsairs captured the U.S. brigantine *Betsey*; Congress authorized the payment of $80,000 for the release of the *Betsey* and its nine-member crew. A few weeks later, Algerian pirates seized the Cádiz-bound schooner *Maria* and the Philadelphia-bound *Dauphin*.[14] More tribute was paid, though congressional unwillingness to authorize a sum beyond $40,000 meant that the twenty-one crew members of the *Maria* and *Dauphin* languished in captivity for years.

As more ships were seized, Thomas Jefferson, who had been appointed along with Adams and Ben Franklin to seek diplomatic solutions, grew impatient: ransom and tribute payments, he declared, constituted "money thrown away," for "there is no end to the demand of these powers, nor any security in their promises."[15] America should always prefer peace to war, concluded Jefferson—but when it came to the Barbary States, "it would be best to effect a peace thro' the medium of war."[16]

By 1794, Congress was beginning to agree. The Naval Act of 1794 created a standing Navy and provided funds for the construction of six ships, and in 1801, when Jefferson took office as president, he sent four of these new ships to the Barbary Coast under the command of Commodore Richard Dale. (Setting what would also become a precedent, Jefferson didn't take the trouble to request congressional authorization before sending Commodore Dale out to make war.) Dale's instructions were simple: he was to protect U.S. ships in the region through any means necessary. As for the Barbary pirates, Dale was instructed to "chastise their insolence . . . by sinking, burning, or destroying their ships and vessels wherever you shall find them."[17]

It worked, more or less. Surprised by America's new naval ferocity, several of the Barbary States quickly agreed to waive further tribute requirements. By 1805, only Tripoli still held out. When a U.S.-led land force consisting of eight U.S. Marines and several hundred mercenaries successfully occupied the city of Derna, however, the ruler of Tripoli agreed to end the war and return the remaining captured American sailors, in exchange for a onetime ransom payment.

This didn't entirely end the era of the Barbary pirates, who resumed their attacks on U.S. shipping during the War of 1812 while the Navy was once more engaged in fighting the British. In 1815, however, the United States launched another successful offensive against the Barbary States. This time, the pirates were vanquished—until piracy off the coast of Africa accelerated again in the twenty-first century.

Piracy had never fully disappeared from the world's shipping channels, of course, and the Navy has fought pirates from the Caribbean to the South China Sea over the last two centuries. The nature of piracy has changed significantly since America's first foreign military adventure, however.

Fearsome as the Barbary pirates were, they operated largely under the control of the Barbary States, making diplomacy a viable adjunct or alternative to war. State-sponsored piracy was common until the mid-nineteenth century, and the major European powers all made extensive use of privateers. The young United States embraced the practice as well: the Constitution gave Congress the power to grant "letters of marque and reprisal," and Congress did so liberally during the War of 1812. Piracy was part and parcel of state-on-state conflicts until 1856, when the major powers signed the Paris Declaration to end privateering.

Today, piracy is prohibited under international law, and state-sponsored piracy is rare. Modern piracy is engaged in largely by nonstate actors, from sophisticated international criminal networks operating off the coast of Malaysia to opportunistic teens and fishermen operating off the coast of Somalia.[18] This creates new challenges: states can use diplomacy to negotiate with other states, but it's far more difficult to negotiate with scores of individual pirates united by nothing more than a desire for money.

Technology too has proven to be a double-edged sword. Automated modern ships can operate with minimal crews—even vast oil tankers capable of holding two million barrels of oil can operate with a crew of twenty—but this makes them sitting ducks for small groups of pirates with guns and explosives. What's more, the same tracking and communications technologies governments and shipping companies use to monitor the safety of maritime traffic can be used by pirates to locate targets. For the U.S. military, the implications are clear: counterpiracy operations are probably here to stay.

As they say in the Pentagon, "Argghhh!"

# CHAPTER TWO

# Wanna Go to Gitmo?

Hey," Phil Carter asked me, "You wanna go to Gitmo?"

It was late spring 2009, and after six weeks or so at the Pentagon I was beginning to find my footing. Phil—a talented young lawyer and Iraq veteran with a gift for incisive commentary—had gone from practicing law and writing articles about detainee policy for *Slate*, the online magazine, to running detainee policy at the Pentagon. As deputy assistant secretary of defense for detainee policy, Phil was the Defense Department's point person on an Obama administration project that had not yet begun to look like a pipe dream: closing Guantánamo.

"Sure," I said.

"Great—I'm taking a congressional delegation down next week, and I think there's an extra seat on the plane."

And so I found myself at Andrews Air Force Base one morning at oh-dark-thirty, groggily shaking hands with several members of Congress. We filed onto the plane, which didn't look like any military jet I'd ever seen: this one was more like a corporate plane, with comfortable leather seats and flight attendants who served both coffee and wine. Phil and I sat across from the congressional leaders, making small talk as we flew to America's most notorious detention center.

On arrival, we were ushered into cars for transportation to a lunchtime briefing. Driving through the rolling hills, I was struck by the incongruous beauty that surrounded us: Guantánamo is gorgeous, with steep green hills and valleys unfolding down to a glittering blue-green sea. Every so often we'd pass a sign warning drivers not to run over any of the rare Cuban rock iguanas, and once or twice we caught quick glimpses of the large lizards.

If you could look beyond the barbed wire and heavily armed troops, Guantánamo might have been a nature preserve or a beach resort. Endangered sea turtles basked in the sand, and off-duty base personnel snorkeled along the coral reefs.

"We take our commitment to the natural environment very seriously here," the base commander told us over lunch. In fact, he said, conservation is one of the few issues on which Navy officials and their Cuban neighbors tend to see eye to eye. Capitalists and communists alike, everyone wants to preserve the iguanas. "They're very decent people, the Cubans we deal with," he said. "Very professional."

• • •

The Cuban government had no idea what it was getting into when it agreed to lease the land surrounding Guantánamo Bay to the United States in 1903. It wasn't precisely a voluntary transaction. After "liberating" Cuba from Spain during the Spanish-American War, the United States made the lease a condition of U.S. military withdrawal from the rest of the island. Under the terms of the Cuban-American Treaty of 1903, the newly independent state of Cuba agreed to allow the United States to lease "the lands necessary . . . for naval stations" for "the time required," giving the United States "complete jurisdiction and control over and within said areas."[1] The cost? "The annual sum of two thousand dollars," which was raised in a 1934 lease agreement to $4,085."[2] Today the United States continues to send Cuba an annual check for $4,085, but just to demonstrate how annoying they find the whole arrangement, the Cuban government refuses to cash the checks.

Throughout the twentieth century, the naval base at Guantánamo Bay remained a thorn in the side of Cuban nationalists. Until the 1990s, however, few people outside of Cuba and the U.S. Navy had heard of the base at Guantánamo. That changed in 1991, when President George H. W. Bush ordered the construction of an emergency camp at Guantánamo Bay to house hundreds of Haitian refugees.

Fleeing from the violence and political turmoil triggered by the ouster of Haitian president Bertrand Aristide, scores of thousands of Haitians took to rafts and small boats, hoping to make it to the American mainland. Many drowned, but within six months of Aristide's ouster, the Coast Guard had intercepted nearly forty thousand refugees.[3] Some were simply returned to Haiti and some were housed in temporary camps in Florida, but many of those deemed to have credible asylum claims were sent to the temporary camp at Guantánamo.

Human rights advocates around the world quickly decried the conditions there. International treaties obligate nations receiving refugees to treat them well and ensure they are not returned to a place in which they will face persecution, yet at Guantánamo the Haitian refugees were "held incommunicado behind barbed wire," wrote Yale Law School professor Harold Hongju Koh. They were given no access to lawyers who could help them with their asylum claims, and risked being returned to Haiti with little semblance of due process. Meanwhile, many lived "in squalid conditions without toilets, beds or any semblance of privacy." In March 1993, Koh recalls, the remaining detainees "went on a hunger strike that lasted more than forty days. They began to attempt suicide through hanging, throwing themselves on the barbed wire, and other devices. Nearly every day, someone would collapse from food deprivation or heat exhaustion, or attempt suicide."[4]

When I met Harold Koh in the fall of 1993, during my first year of law school, he was already something of a legend to a generation of young human rights lawyers. His passionate advocacy on behalf of the Haitian detainees at Guantánamo took him to the Supreme Court, and ultimately forced the Clinton administration to release the remaining Haitian refugees into the United States. Koh eventually became President Clinton's assistant secretary of state for democracy, human rights, and labor, and I worked for him at the State Department in 1999 and 2000. (In 2010, he was appointed legal advisor to the State Department by President Obama, and found himself defending a host of policies his younger self might well have denounced.[5] That, however, came later.)

After the Haitian refugee crisis in the early 1990s, Guantánamo faded from public view. This changed again late in 2001, when the administration of George W. Bush needed somewhere to stow detainees scooped up in the nascent U.S. war on terror.

The detainees couldn't be held just anywhere: after 9/11, the Bush administration knew the American public wouldn't warm to the notion of dangerous terrorists held inside the United States, and in any case the administration wanted to shield its detention operations from media scrutiny—and from litigious human rights advocates. Detainees held inside the United States would clearly be subject to the jurisdiction of American courts, something administration stalwarts didn't want.

In Guantánamo, they thought, they had found a perfect legal black hole: the naval base was tucked away on an island belonging to a foreign state with which the United States had no diplomatic relations. A trade and travel embargo ensured that no American tourists could stumble onto the base, and no ACLU lawyers could show up to trawl for clients among the detainees. Better still, Naval Station Guantánamo Bay was already tightly controlled by the military, and it was not, administration lawyers believed, subject to the jurisdiction of civilian courts.

This mattered, because key executive branch officials already knew that some aspects of U.S. detention policy, if discovered, would shock the world—and probably trigger a heart attack in the average federal judge.

By the beginning of 2002, the United States had begun to house detainees in a "temporary" camp at Guantánamo. The first batch of twenty detainees were flown in from Afghanistan on January 11, 2002; clad in orange jumpsuits, manacled and hooded, they were marched to the open-air metal cages in which they would be housed. Within six months, the detainee population had swelled to nearly six hundred. Ultimately, nearly eight hundred prisoners were held at Guantánamo.

From the beginning, journalists, lawyers, human rights advocates, and the International Committee of the Red Cross raised questions about the detainees and their status. U.S. officials initially refused to release information about the identities of the detainees, the circumstances of their capture, or the rules governing interrogation. What little information emerged was sketchy and often contradictory. In an article on the first detainees to arrive at Guantánamo in January 2002, the *New York Times* reported that Secretary of Defense Donald Rumsfeld "implied that there was nothing special about these prisoners— 'I don't even know their names'—and suggested that they had been sent to Cuba simply to make way for more prisoners being captured in Kandahar. 'We just have to keep the flow going, and that's what's taking place,' he said."[6]

Within weeks, administration officials had settled on a different narrative: the men sent to Guantánamo are "among the most dangerous, best trained, vicious killers on the face of the earth," said Rumsfeld. Vice President Dick Cheney agreed: "These are the worst of a very bad lot. They are very dangerous. They are devoted to killing millions of Americans, innocent Americans, if they can, and they are perfectly prepared to die in the effort."[7]

## We Need That Information

As for the law, Bush administration officials were clear: when it came to the Guantánamo detainees, there really *was* no law. At any rate, the third Geneva Convention, which governs the treatment of prisoners of war, did not apply. In a series of internal executive branch memos, the Justice Department's Office of Legal Counsel and the White House counsel came to the conclusion that Taliban and al Qaeda detainees were not POWs, and in fact not covered at all by any of the four Geneva Conventions.

The "war against terrorism is a new kind of war," asserted a now notorious January 25, 2002, memo from White House Counsel Alberto Gonzales to President Bush. "It is not the traditional clash between nations adhering to the laws of war that formed the backdrop for [the Geneva Conventions]. The nature of the new war places a high premium on other factors, such as the ability to quickly obtain information from captured terrorists. . . . In my judgment, this new paradigm renders obsolete Geneva's strict limitations on questioning of enemy prisoners and renders quaint some of its provisions."[8]

It was a neat bit of legal reasoning. Technically, the law of war is referred to using the Latin term *lex specialis*—special law. It is applicable in—and only in—special circumstances, but in those special circumstances, it supersedes ordinary law, or *lex generalis*, the "general law" that prevails in peacetime. We have one set of laws for "normal" situations, and another, more flexible set of laws for "extraordinary" situations, such as armed conflicts. As non-U.S. citizens held outside the United States, the Guantánamo detainees enjoyed no constitutional protections and had no access to attorneys or American courts. By asserting that the United States was in a "war" against terrorism, the Bush administration could make the case that neither constitutional law nor international human rights law applied to the detainees, and only the law of war was applicable.

This gave the administration the authority to hold detainees until "the cessation of hostilities" (a nebulous and possibly nonexistent point, given the nature of a "war on terror"). But being nonstate actors, al Qaeda and the Taliban were not parties to the Geneva Conventions, and therefore not entitled to any of the protections provided by the Conventions. In fact, argued Bush administration lawyers, detainees alleged to be Taliban or al Qaeda members were not even entitled to hearings in which they could challenge their status.

For most of the detainees, this created a vicious catch 22: since those believed to be al Qaeda or Taliban detainees were, according to the Bush administration, not entitled to any of the Geneva Conventions' protections—including the right to an individualized status determination—they had no ability to challenge the government's belief that they were connected to al Qaeda or the Taliban. The fact that they were believed to be "unlawful combatants" deprived them of any chance to present evidence demonstrating that this was not in fact the case.

In normal times, when ordinary criminal law and human rights law apply, the burden of proof is on the government to show evidence justifying an individual's detention. It's a core principle of English and American law, dating back to the Magna Carta: a detained person can ask that a court order the government to either produce evidence justifying imprisonment or let the detainee go. We call it the writ of habeas corpus, the Great Writ. Literally, habeas corpus translates as "you have the body"—and the principle requires the authorities controlling the body of another to justify that control.

But in wartime, different rules apply. An army can detain enemy soldiers without due process, and hold them until the end of the conflict for the sole purpose of keeping them off the battlefield. It's not about innocence or guilt, or an assessment that a particular individual poses a specific danger. It's about affiliation and status. The ninety-eight-pound weakling working in the Army chow hall can be detained right along with the Special Forces sniper.

In a traditional war, this doesn't undermine the rule of law, since military personnel wear uniforms and carry identification. There may be confusion on the margins: the occasional enemy spy may try to pass himself off as a civilian, for instance. But on the whole, the identification of enemy combatants isn't particularly tricky.

In a war on terrorism, it's a lot harder to know who counts as an enemy combatant. Almost inevitably, some people will be detained by mistake: because they were in the wrong place at the wrong time, because a rival decided to label them terrorists in order to collect a generous bounty, or because they resembled someone else or had the same name as a terror suspect. Guess how many Muslim men are named Muhammad, Ahmed, Abdullah, Ali, Omar, Hassan, Hussain, Salem, Abdul, Khalid, Rahman, or some combination or variant of those names? Given the lack of identifying papers and reliable records in places like Afghanistan, coupled with language barriers and variations in spelling and translation, it's little wonder that we sometimes nab the wrong guys.

The trouble is, the Bush administration's legal theories meant that someone nabbed by mistake was given no opportunity to explain: no hearing, no trial, no lawyer, no right to an interpreter, no right to contact friends or relatives or officials in his home nation, no information on the evidence against him—nothing. Worse, he could be detained more or less forever—and given the lack of transparency, his family might never even know what had happened to him.

Administration officials assured the world that as a matter of policy, detainees would be treated "humanely" and in a manner "consistent" with the Geneva Conventions—but only "to the extent appropriate and consistent with military necessity."[9] After all, Vice President Cheney told CNN, "These are bad people. . . . They may well have information about future terrorist attacks against the United States. We need that information. We need to be able to interrogate them and extract from them whatever information they have."[10]

These arguments helped pave the way for the biggest scandal of the post-9/11 era: the U.S. use of cruel and inhumane interrogation methods, some amounting to torture. While the worst abuses took place far from Guantánamo Bay—waterboarding mainly occurred at the secret CIA prisons that came to be known as "black sites," for instance—some interrogators at Guantánamo also demonstrated a flexible understanding of the word "humane."

A 2002 order from Defense Secretary Rumsfeld authorized the use of "stress positions," nudity, "sensory deprivation," and "the use of a detainee's individual phobias (such as fear of dogs) to induce stress."[11] A 2005 military investigation found that guards and interrogators at Guantánamo had used military working dogs to terrorize detainees and forced detainees to wear women's underwear and dog leashes,[12] and FBI agents who witnessed Guantánamo interrogations conducted by DoD personnel reported the use of sleep deprivation, bright lights, loud noises, and personal humiliation.[13] The FBI agents protested, arguing that these tactics were both illegal and ineffective, but they were ignored.

In April 2004, the Abu Ghraib scandal broke.[14] Photos of brutalized Iraqi prisoners appalled the world and contributed to a spike in violence in Iraq. In early June, reporters obtained a leaked memo,[15] authored by the Justice Department's John Yoo and Jay Bybee, arguing that interrogation techniques such as waterboarding did not constitute torture. (Under Yoo and Bybee's definition of torture, even pulling out someone's fingernails with a pair of pliers would not constitute torture.)

It's probably not a coincidence that on June 28, 2004, the Supreme Court roundly rejected the Bush administration's argument that Guantánamo was beyond the reach of U.S. courts. Instead, the justices held that U.S. courts could hear habeas corpus petitions from Guantánamo detainees.[16]

Guantánamo was no longer a law-free zone. The Supreme Court decision in *Rasul v. Bush* cleared the way for lawyers to represent Guantánamo detainees, and the worldwide scandal sparked by the Abu Ghraib revelations and the leaked government memos led to increased scrutiny of the detention facility. It soon became clear that the problems there went well beyond those related to interrogation techniques.

## The World's Jailor

While a handful of the Guantánamo detainees were unquestionably senior al Qaeda and Taliban operatives, records released in January 2005 by the Defense Department revealed that many prisoners held there and at other U.S. detention sites posed no threat to the United States, and may indeed have been detained in error.

Consider the case of Khalid El-Masri, a German citizen, who in late 2003 made the mistake of going on vacation to Macedonia, where border officials mistook him for another man by the same name who was suspected of being an al Qaeda operative. The Macedonians handed him over to CIA officials, who spirited him off to a black site in Afghanistan for brutal interrogation.

By February, several CIA interrogators began to worry that they had gotten the wrong guy. In May, El-Masri was unceremoniously released in Albania—dumped at night on an isolated stretch of road without explanation or assistance in returning home. In December 2005, Secretary of State Condoleezza Rice apologized for the error to German chancellor Angela Merkel, but El-Masri himself received neither apology nor compensation. A lawsuit filed by El-Masri in a U.S. court was dismissed in 2006 after the Bush administration argued that a trial would expose national security secrets. In 2012, however, the European Court of Human Rights ordered Macedonia to pay El-Masri 60,000 euros as compensation for his wrongful detention and subsequent torture.[17]

By 2005, the Guantánamo detainees included nationals of more than forty countries, ranging from Afghanistan and Pakistan to Sweden, Australia, and China. "It's like the United Nations around here," a guard told me cheerfully. Far from being "the most dangerous, best trained, vicious killers on the face of the earth," more than a dozen of the detainees were minors: Omar Khadr, for instance, was captured in Afghanistan at the tender age of fifteen. He grew from boyhood to manhood at Guantánamo before being transferred to Canadian custody at the age of twenty-five. Most of the detainees were captured in Afghanistan or Pakistan, but some never even came close to any active battlefields: records made public by the Defense Department in 2005 indicated that several Guantánamo detainees were captured in places as far afield as Bosnia, Gambia, Libya, and Iran.[18]

U.S. forces had captured some of the detainees, but the vast majority—86 percent, according to an analysis of Defense Department records conducted by Professor Mark Denbeaux of Seton Hall University—were captured by Pakistani agents or by Afghanistan's Northern Alliance, who later turned them over to the United States, often in exchange for large bounties. This raised obvious questions about whether the bounties motivated Afghans to turn over innocent people for cash. In fact, DoD records made it clear that quite a few of the detainees should probably never have been detained at all: as Denbeaux's analysis notes, "Fifty-five percent (55%) of the detainees are not determined to have committed any hostile acts against the United States or its coalition allies. . . . Only 8% of the detainees were characterized as al Qaeda fighters. Of the remaining detainees, 40% have no definitive connection with al Qaeda at all and 18% have no definitive affiliation with either al Qaeda or the Taliban."[19]

The Bush administration was ultimately forced by a mix of public pressure and litigation to rescind or modify many of its more outrageous legal memos and policies. In *Hamdan v. Rumsfeld*, decided in June 2006,[20] the Supreme Court declared that both al Qaeda and Taliban detainees were entitled, at a minimum, to the protections detailed in Common Article 3 of the Geneva Conventions, which the Court interpreted to prohibit both torture and "outrages upon personal dignity, in particular humiliating and degrading treatment" in conflicts between states and nonstate actors.

This effectively ended most forms of harsh interrogation at

Guantánamo—not least because under U.S. law at the time,[21] violations of Common Article 3 of the Geneva Conventions constituted war crimes, punishable by life in prison or death. The *Hamdan* decision also invalidated the military commissions in which the Bush administration had hoped to try detainees. While Congress eventually passed legislation revamping the military commissions and severely restricting detainee access to the courts, the Court decisions in *Rasul v. Bush* and *Hamdan v. Rumsfeld* were severe setbacks for the administration's Guantánamo policies.

Guantánamo had become a national embarrassment, and in 2006, President Bush implicitly acknowledged as much. "Obviously, the Guantánamo issue is a sensitive issue for people," Bush commented. "I very much would like to end Guantánamo."[22] By then, hundreds of "low-value" detainees had already been transferred into the custody of Afghan and Pakistani authorities, and many other detainees had been released to authorities in their home countries.[23]

The White House declared its intention of releasing still more of the hundreds who remained. "America does not have any intention of being the world's jailer," insisted Bush White House spokesperson Dana Perino.[24]

But closing Guantánamo turned out to be far harder than it looked. To some extent, the Bush administration fell into a trap of its own making: having told the world for years that the Guantánamo detainees were "the worst of the worst,"[25] it proved difficult to persuade other states to accept many of the remaining detainees, even though most had by then been determined to pose no threat. Other detainees presented a different problem: some, though considered too dangerous to release, could not be tried—either because the evidence against them was weak or had been obtained through torture, or because revealing the evidence even in the context of military commissions would risk exposing intelligence sources and methods. Only a handful of detainees were set to be tried.[26]

When Barack Obama took office in January 2009, he announced his intention to clean up the mess he had inherited. On January 22, he ordered a halt to the much criticized military commission trials, mandated the closure of all secret CIA prisons, required that the Red Cross have access to all U.S. detainees, and declared that interrogations of detainees—whether by the military, the CIA, or anyone else—must henceforth comply with the restrictive rules that had long been laid out in the Army Field Manual. He also ordered an immediate review of the status of the 242 remaining Guantánamo detainees, and declared, "the detention facilities at Guantánamo for individuals covered by this order shall be closed as soon as practicable, and no later than 1 year from the date of this order."[27]

Rights advocates were jubilant. I remember a photo making the rounds at the time: it depicted a man in a Navy uniform standing in front of a wall of photos emblazoned with the words "Guantánamo Bay." He was removing the official photo of George W. Bush and replacing it with one of Barack Obama.

"In his first executive orders, Obama effectively dismantled the elaborate structures that supported the Bush administration's 'war on terror,'" I wrote in my *Los Angeles Times* column that week.[28]

Once again, I spoke too soon.

## Bureaucracy Does Its Thing

The detainee review process ordered by President Obama began quickly, but soon became mired in Washington politics, bureaucracy, and interagency wrangling.

It rapidly turned into a mess: no one seemed sure who was in charge, or who was authorized to speak on behalf of the Defense Department. Phil Carter was officially the policy voice at the table. I trusted his legal and policy instincts, but he was young and relatively bureaucratically inexperienced, and it was sometimes hard for him to counter opposition from senior DoD and Joint Staff lawyers. My own role was murkier still: I attended a few of the early task force meetings with Phil, but my portfolio and authority were unclear. I was a law professor who had a policy job as senior advisor to the under secretary of defense for policy, and in that role I had both access and at least some degree of influence. But though I could try to persuade my colleagues, I had no direct authority—a fact that became more frustrating as the task force began to drift toward rec-ommending an indefinite preventive detention regime for those detain-ees viewed as dangerous but untriable.

The Obama administration was falling into the same trap as the Bush administration: having informed the world that you're holding terror-ists who have the desire and ability to kill thousands of Americans, it's difficult to pivot and say, "Actually, the risk isn't really that great, and anyway we have no valid evidence against these guys, so we've decided to let them go." Who would want to take the political heat for such a decision? If the Obama administration released someone who ended up carrying out another 9/11, the Democratic Party would be finished.

I was fully prepared to accept that some of the remaining Guantánamo detainees were very bad guys. But a core legal principle is that no one should be punished or indefinitely deprived of liberty solely because of his potential future acts. It's one thing to imprison someone who has been convicted of committing a crime after a fair trial—it's another thing altogether to imprison someone on the basis of inherent future "dangerousness," as assessed by the executive branch alone, with no judicial oversight.

I was also prepared to accept that in traditional wars there was no viable alternative to a preventive detention system. The United States detained more than 400,000 German prisoners of war in camps on U.S. territory during World War II, for instance—not to "punish" them, but simply to keep them from returning to the battlefield. These POWs re-ceived little due process, but in a war encompassing so many millions, additional due process would have been unfeasible. At the end of the war, the POWs were released and sent home; only a tiny fraction were held and prosecuted for war crimes. But in traditional wars between uniformed state militaries, there was also far less possibility for error. In the context of terrorism, it wasn't even clear that it made sense to think in terms of "war"—and even if it did, the nontraditional nature of the enemy made widespread error inevitable.

America was founded upon rule of law principles—recall the Dec-laration of Independence, with its proud commitment to "unalienable rights" and its protestations against the arbitrary exercise of power—

but the group reviewing detention policy seemed to be leaning toward jettisoning some of those core values.

It soon became clear that President Obama was leaning the same way. In a May 20 White House meeting, the president told a group of leading human rights advocates that he was considering adopting a preventive detention system.[29]

Worried that the president was being influenced by preliminary task force discussion, I emailed Michèle Flournoy with my concerns:

> The process is moving very rapidly, without much higher-level policy guidance. . . . The Task Force chairs . . . are pushing the group hard to produce draft legislation on . . . a range of even more far-reaching issues (such as potential preventive detention authority). . . . [We] asked why the timeline needs to be so accelerated. The answer . . . was that there's pressure from Congress . . . and a risk that if we don't [offer something soon], Congress could decide to move forward on its own.
>
> It's not at all clear, though, that serious thought has been given a) to whether high-level engagement with key people on the Hill could convince Congress to be a little more patient, or b) to whether rushing to push out our own possibly ill-considered legislative proposals is truly better than taking the risk that Congress acts quickly.

The next day, it became apparent that the train was already leaving the station. In a May 21, 2009, speech at the National Archives, President Obama made it clear that he was inclined to approve some sort of preventive detention framework:

> There remains the question of detainees at Guantánamo who cannot be prosecuted yet who pose a clear danger to the American people. And I have to be honest here—this is the toughest single issue that we will face. . . . I am not going to release individuals who endanger the American people.[30]

## This Guy Was My Friend

Obama's comments dismayed many who had been counting on him to reverse the Bush administration's detention policies. I was dismayed too, but tried to convince myself that the president hadn't yet fully committed to a preventive detention regime. Perhaps, I thought, there was still time to get him to rethink his remarks.

At home, I labored over a PowerPoint presentation to give to Phil Carter and Michèle Flournoy, trying to highlight the rule of law dangers inherent in adopting a permanent war framework and accepting preventive detention. If we were convinced that some detainees were dangerous, I argued, there were alternatives to holding them indefinitely: we could release them subject to ongoing electronic monitoring, for instance. In the end, I concluded, the risk of releasing potentially dangerous detainees, while not nonexistent, was outweighed by the multiple risks associated with adopting a preventive detention framework. If we adopt a preventive detention framework, I wrote, "We may alienate allies. We may create new enemies. [A] preventive detention regime may undergo 'mission creep' and undermine domestic and global legal norms. Existence of [a] preventive detention regime may incentivize capture/detention as means of thwarting threats and disincentivize [the] search for alternatives. Adversaries may claim [a] similar right to preventively detain those *they* declare to be security threats."

As with my first draft of Flournoy's testimony on piracy, I went a little overboard: my completed PowerPoint slide pack ran to twenty-eight pages. I went on about the blurring boundaries between war and not-war, and between combatant and noncombatant, and I offered several text-heavy slides about *lex specialis* versus *lex generalis*. In hindsight, I essentially created an elaborate set of slides guaranteed never to be read by anyone important enough to have a role in making final decisions. I was still new to the Pentagon, and had forgotten the lessons I had learned years before while at the State Department: most senior officials won't read anything that can't be summarized in a page or two of bullet points.

I showed my slides to Phil. He read through them and shrugged. "You know I agree," he said, "But I think this is way too academic. We can't give this to Mark Martins."

Colonel Mark Martins was the brilliant and driven Army lawyer who served as cochair of the task force reviewing detainee issues. A graduate of Harvard Law School and a protégé of General David Petraeus, Martins was viewed as a rising star: he had a reputation for cutting through red tape and getting things done. Like all top-notch lawyers, Martins could talk rings around most ordinary mortals. And as one of the task force chairs, Martins had the power of the pen: he could control the texts distributed for discussion.

"Anyway," Phil went on, "you know we're not really the DoD decision makers on this." Due to a quirk of history, the detainee portfolio, though technically part of Flournoy's domain in the Pentagon's policy office, had traditionally been handled directly by the office of the deputy secretary of defense.

Undeterred, I brought my slides to Michèle. "I think we're getting rolled in this process," I told her. "We're getting bulldozed by these Justice Department guys, who just aren't seeing the big picture here, and the deputy secretary really isn't focused on these issues yet. The president is moving toward some decisions I think he's going to regret, and I think you need to get more directly involved."

Michèle sighed. "I can convene a meeting with Mark Martins and all the other players based here at the Pentagon, and I can urge everyone to slow down and take some more time to think, but I'm not sure I can do much more."

And so we convened a meeting. Colonel Martins was charming; I made my complicated academic arguments about blurring boundaries and *lex specialis*, and everyone nodded and looked politely interested. Michèle urged everyone to slow down and take some time to consider all the issues. Everyone nodded some more and agreed that taking time to consider all the issues was an excellent idea.

But nothing changed. The president seemed unwilling or unable to negotiate to get some breathing space from Congress, and it soon became clear that he was content to leave things more or less exactly as they were: with Guantánamo still open, and indefinite detention a new de facto reality.[31]

Many of my friends and allies inside the White House were as frustrated and dismayed as I was. Samantha Power, then the National Security Staff's senior director for human rights, was characteristically blunt when I spoke to her. The detainee review process had been captured by ass-covering careerists, she told me bitterly, and the president's self-appointed gatekeepers seemed determined to keep her on the margins. "I can't even get in to see the president about this. Literally. Before the election, this guy"—Obama—"was my *friend*, but right now I can't even get ten minutes with him without going through six layers of self-important jerks." We needed to give up on this one, she concluded, and focus on the areas where we had more chance of making progress.

And so I gave up. Looking back, I wonder sometimes if I gave up too quickly. But I'm still not sure if I could have changed anything. By the time I left the Pentagon in the summer of 2011, I knew something about how to work the system: I had some hard-earned credibility, contacts throughout the executive branch, and the ability to cut through at least a little bit of the red tape that strangles most government efforts to bring about change. But in the spring of 2009, I was new, and still as green as the thick emerald glass separating those of us in the Pentagon from the world outside.

## You Must Have a Deviated Septum

By the time I went to Guantánamo with Phil Carter and his congressional delegation in mid-June, I had more or less accepted defeat. I filed away my PowerPoint slides and decided to treat the trip as a strange sort of tourism.

And it was: the sea sparkled, the endangered iguanas flicked their tongues at us, and our little group was given a warm welcome by the base commander. Lunch, which consisted of sandwiches (white bread, lunch meats, and limp lettuce) and chips, was marred by only one unfortunate incident: Congresswoman Jan Schakowsky, a longtime critic of Guantánamo, slipped on some steps and fractured her ankle.[32]

"You didn't trip her, did you?" I asked Phil.

He rolled his eyes.

Once the congresswoman's leg had been fussed over by the medics, we each received a commemorative GTMO coin before being herded together for a group photo. After that, it was time for our tour.

"Our mission here is the safe, transparent, legal, and humane treatment of detainees," the base commander told us. He seemed like a decent guy, and I didn't envy him his job. Once out of the rolling hills, the base itself was unremittingly bleak: nothing but sand, barbed wire, concrete, and prefab structures. We passed Camp Four, where a dozen or so detainees stared stonily at us through the chain link fences surrounding an exercise yard. A few shouted something. I couldn't make out the words, but it didn't sound like they were thanking us for their safe, transparent, legal, and humane treatment.

"They're on a rec strike," the base commander explained. "They refuse to leave their yard."

Overall, it was no worse than any of the other prisons I had visited over the years, and much better than some. Inside, we saw bunks and sinks and television rooms. Some of the men had copies of the Koran, though one detainee appeared to be reading an Arabic translation of *Pride and Prejudice*. Aside from the shouting prisoners in Camp Four, it was all rather quiet.

After a time, there was some discreet shuffling and murmuring, and those of us with the requisite security clearances were led off to take a peek at the section of the camp that housed "high-value" detainees who had been transferred to Gitmo from CIA custody. Despite the hush-hush atmosphere, it couldn't have been more banal: there on the Stair-Master was one of the alleged masterminds of the 9/11 attacks, idly paging through a magazine as he continued his climb to nowhere.

Twenty-nine of the detainees were on hunger strikes, the base commander told us, and most were being fed through enteral feeding tubes.

"You mean, you're force-feeding them?" asked Congresswoman Schakowsky.

The base commander didn't like that term. "We can't just let them die," he said stiffly.

Anyway, he told us, the "involuntary" nature of the feeding was overplayed by the media. Some of the detainees, he said, didn't want to participate in hunger strikes, but felt compelled to do so to avoid ostracism or abuse from other detainees. "Requiring" the enteral feeding gave them a way to avoid having to choose between starvation and ostracism. "Privately, some of them thank us." Besides, he said, enteral feeding really wasn't painful.

Maybe not. But on my next trip, one of my colleagues, a former Marine, volunteered to give enteral feeding a try. Strapped into a chair like a detainee, he waited calmly while a nurse prepared to thread the feeding tube up his nostril. Once she began, he tensed and his face flushed brick red.

The nurse frowned, murmured something apologetic, and decided to try the other nostril. This time, she managed to jam the tube in, but by then involuntary tears were streaming down his cheeks and clear liquid was running from his nose.

"I'm really sorry, sir," said the nurse, removing the tube. She looked mortified. "That really doesn't happen very often. I think you must have a deviated septum or something."

"No problem," he gasped, wiping his face. "Just remind me not to go on a hunger strike if I'm ever detained here."

# CHAPTER THREE

# Lawyers with Guns

The detainee review task force wasn't the last I saw of Colonel Mark Martins. By the autumn of 2009, he had been promoted to brigadier general, and he was assigned to serve as the deputy commander of Combined Joint Interagency Task Force 435 in Afghanistan, which was responsible for military detention operations.

But Martins's real love was programs designed to promote the rule of law. In Iraq, he had led the U.S. military effort to support the Iraqi judiciary. Afghanistan, with its less well developed legal and judicial system and a distinct dearth of lawyers, posed even steeper challenges. Without the rule of law and a well-functioning, fair, and effective criminal justice system, Afghanistan would never be stable, but Martins was convinced that rule of law promotion couldn't be left to State Department bureaucrats or Justice Department experts: given the lack of manpower and money in the civilian agencies and the pervasive security challenges of working in Afghanistan, the military would need to be closely involved with rule of law efforts.

He put his not inconsiderable persuasive powers to work, and eventually managed to talk the military powers-that-be into letting him create something unprecedented: the Rule of Law Field Force—Afghanistan. (ROLFF-A, in military acronymese.) By then, Phil had moved on from his job running the Pentagon's Detainee Policy office, and Bill Lietzau, a retired Marine Corps lawyer, had left a position working for the National Security Council and taken over Phil's old job. Meanwhile, my own amorphous advisory portfolio had evolved and clarified; with Under Secretary Flournoy's blessing, I had started a new

Office for Rule of Law & International Humanitarian Policy. The name was a mouthful, but the idea was to be a voice for human rights inside DoD without scaring away anyone likely to get the heebie-jeebies over the term "human rights."

Bill and I worked closely together: there was much overlap between his focus on detainee issues and my focus on broader rule of law issues, and our goal was ultimately to merge the two portfolios. Late in 2010, Bill proposed that we take a trip to Afghanistan with some colleagues from the Pentagon General Counsel's Office and the Joint Staff. We could check out a few of the U.S.-run detention facilities, get field briefings on the status of efforts to transfer detainees from U.S. custody to Afghan control, assess the progress of efforts to improve the Afghan judiciary and law enforcement systems, and maybe even find out what Mark Martins and his new Rule of Law Field Force were up to.

## Can Might Make Rights?

We had already heard some grumbling, mostly from NGOs and the State Department, about the Rule of Law Field Force: apparently, the notion of heavily armed lawyers didn't fill everyone's heart with delight. Why did the U.S. military think it was the right institution to promote rule of law, NGO and State Department lawyers wanted to know. Why wasn't this a civilian function? Anyway, wasn't the idea of a Rule of Law "Force" oxymoronic?

The grumbling didn't surprise me. Nineteenth-century British legal philosopher John Austin declared that law is nothing more than the commands of a sovereign, backed by the threat of force. Today, however, this version of legal positivism has fallen into disfavor; we prefer to focus on law's normative legitimacy, rather than its relationship to coercion. We thus tend to see the rule of law and the rule of force as polar opposites, and regard the idea of promoting the rule of law at gunpoint with suspicion and concern.

This was an issue I'd spent a great deal of time thinking about. I had worked on rule of law–related projects in Ghana, Kosovo, Sierra Leone, South Africa, and half a dozen other places, both for NGOs and during my time at the State Department in the late 1990s.[1] Together with two colleagues, Jane Stromseth and David Wippman, I had even written a book: *Can Might Make Rights?: Building the Rule of Law After Military Interventions.*[2] I was inclined to agree that in an ideal world, designing projects to promote the rule of law should be a civilian job, not a military job.

But we don't live in an ideal world, and particularly in the context of what the military rather politely refers to as "non-permissive environments"—meaning environments in which people are apt to get shot or blown up—it was hard to imagine civilian agencies getting much done, even if they had the resources and skills. If anything, my prior experiences and research left me with a healthy skepticism of *all* "rule of law promotion" efforts launched by cultural outsiders, regardless of whether they were undertaken by civilian government officials, military personnel, or NGOs. Over the years, governments, foundations, and international organizations have poured billions into rule of law promotion in transitional and post-conflict settings, and it's far from clear that most of these rule of law programs have led to enduring change.

One of the core projects of my new Pentagon rule of law office was to try to get a comprehensive picture of Department of Defense rule of law efforts worldwide in order to figure out if any of the DoD programs were actually helping. This wasn't an easy task. The Defense Department is vast: all told, it has nearly three million employees, including active duty military personnel, reservists, members of the National Guard, and more than 700,000 civilian workers.[3] And while only a tiny fraction of those three million people work directly on rule of law–related projects, many more work on such projects occasionally or tangentially. The Defense Institute of International Legal Studies (DIILS), based at Naval Station Newport in Rhode Island, sends mixed military and civilian teams out each year to conduct training seminars on rule of law and human rights for foreign military units all over the world;[4] the military's Southern Command provides training, technical experts, and funding to support rule of law, governance, and human rights programs in Central America; Pacific Command supports human rights and rule of law training programs for Indonesian Special Forces units.[5]

The range of military rule of law programs is vast—sufficiently vast that the Army JAG Corps has, for some years now, published a frequently updated Rule of Law Handbook for Army JAGs.[6]

Despite the plethora of rule of law–related programs, for the most part the Defense Department does not systematically track or evaluate the success of these efforts. The landscape is perpetually shifting; funding sources often draw from multiple budget lines and personnel move from assignment to assignment, making it extraordinarily difficult to get a handle on what DoD is actually doing in this area, and whether it does any good.

Mark Martins's program in Afghanistan was unusually ambitious: Martins was keenly aware of how inconsistent and unsystematic DoD rule of law work often was, and his Rule of Law Field Force was an effort to formalize and institutionalize rule of law efforts—at least in Afghanistan, at least for a while.

• • •

It was harder than you might think for a small group of Pentagon officials to set up a trip to Afghanistan. My last trip there had been with my boss, Under Secretary Flournoy, whose rank was high enough to garner her a military plane, secure communications devices, an armed security escort, and a respectful reception from four-star generals. Bill and I had to work hard just to persuade the military's Afghanistan Joint Visitors Bureau, which coordinated travel for DoD officials, to let us come.

From the perspective of the military, civilian visitors in a war zone are a great big pain in the ass. Lower-ranking civilians can be billeted with soldiers or junior officers and largely ignored, but for protocol purposes, Bill and I held civilian ranks that were equivalent to two- or three-star generals. While we were not senior enough to rate private planes or private meetings with four-star officers, we were just senior enough that protocol demanded we be treated as "distinguished visitors," with access to logistics support, decent housing, chauffeured vehicles, and in-country air transport as needed. It meant, in other words, that our visit created a whole lot of work for a whole lot of people, which gave the Joint Visitors Bureau every incentive to discourage us from showing up at all.

But we persevered, and eventually—after a series of lengthy and unpleasant coach class flights, which is all the government would spring for, followed by an overnight stopover in Dubai and a series of minor mishaps involving forgotten official passports—we made it to the Distinguished Visitor Quarters at Kabul's Camp Eggers. It was the same building I had stayed in during my previous trip with Flournoy, and it was not, in fact, very distinguished. It smelled like it had an open sewer running beneath it, and when we walked in, we surprised several enlisted soldiers engaged in surreptitious and probably unauthorized use of the Distinguished Visitor Quarters' washer and dryer. Alarmed by our arrival, they gave us surly looks, stuffed their clothes into laundry bags, and scurried away without speaking.

## It's Not Like We Point Guns at People

We spent the next few days touring prisons and courts and talking to military and civilian officials. Brigadier General Martins had rolled out the red carpet for us, setting up meetings with everyone from the vice admiral who now commanded Task Force 435 to Afghan prison guards and newly sworn-in female Afghan prosecutors.

At Sarposa Prison, the Afghan prison warden presented us with several gaudy plastic necklaces and an odd sculpture of a building, also constructed out of thousands of brightly colored plastic beads. "These items have been special handmade for you as gifts, by the prisoners," the warden said, beaming. "The prisoners, they have a love of engaging in arts and crafts." Apparently, they also had a love of hatching escape plans: just a few months after our return to the United States, almost five hundred prisoners escaped from Sarposa and rejoined the Taliban via painstakingly constructed underground tunnels.

Martins was quick to defend the Rule of Law Field Force when I mentioned the undercurrent of grumbling coming from the State Department: it wasn't, he reminded me, as if the Rule of Law Force was pointing guns at people and saying, "Respect the rule of law or die!"

Most of what the Rule of Law Force did, he explained, was provide the security and logistics support to enable the civilians to do their jobs. Rule of Law Field Force personnel worked with other military units to make sure Afghan prosecutors had safe transportation between Kabul and courts in other locations. They helped make sure the Afghan prosecutors and lawyers had safe buildings to work in and the resources and materials they needed. They made sure U.S. civilian agency staff could get to the places they needed to visit, and stay safe while there. Only when no one else was available did they take on the rule of law work themselves. "We're extremely sensitive to the concerns about militarizing rule of law," Martins told us. "We want to be in a support role." But there was a war going on, and realistically, sometimes it was the military or nothing.

From a military perspective, the rule of law matters a lot, because it's a key aspect of the giant jigsaw puzzle we call "stability." And in the context of Afghanistan, it's rarely possible to neatly separate "civilian" problems from "military" problems. Consider the detainee problem: as U.S. and other Coalition troops—or their Afghan partners—conduct military operations, they end up detaining people. Some are Taliban soldiers captured in firefights; others are scooped up during raids of suspected Taliban sites; and so on. At any given time during 2010 and 2011, the United States was holding several thousand detainees in facilities at Bagram Air Force Base, Parwan, and elsewhere.

Regardless of how we should think about the legal status of detainees held at Guantánamo, in the Afghan context there was clearly an ongoing armed conflict in 2010 and 2011, involving roughly 100,000 U.S. troops and an estimated 35,000 Taliban fighters, plus a smaller number of al Qaeda operatives. U.S. forces had the clear legal authority to detain enemy combatants in the course of these military operations, but no one was very happy about it. From the American perspective, holding thousands of detainees caused nothing but trouble, particularly in the wake of the Abu Ghraib and Guantánamo scandals. The detainees had to be provided with food, housing, and medical care, and by the end of the Bush administration everyone agreed that they had to be put through *some* sort of status determination process—although legal experts differed on precisely what process was required. None-theless, human rights groups continued to hammer the military over poor detention conditions and insufficient due process, and the Afghan government under Hamid Karzai often did the same—somewhat disin-genuously, as conditions in Afghan-run prisons were far worse than in U.S.-run detention facilities.

For the U.S. military, it was a no-win situation. Release all the de-tainees and you end up immediately fighting many of them all over again; hold them yourself and you get criticized; turn them over to the Afghan authorities and you're then morally responsible for the even worse treatment the detainees will likely encounter at the hands of their compatriots. The only way out was to improve the Afghan justice sector. If Afghanistan had better-resourced police, prison guards, pros-ecutors, and judges, humane prisons, and some credible process for deciding who should be released and who should face criminal charges, the detainees held by the United States could all be transferred to Af-ghan custody, enabling the United States to begin to transition out of Afghanistan. Seen in this light, rule of law programs could easily be seen as a military necessity—and if the U.S. military couldn't rely on U.S. or NATO civilian rule of law programs to get the Afghan system up and running, it would just have to step in itself.

If Martins's thoughts ran along these lines, it was hard to blame him. Even after nearly a decade, rule of law programs on the civilian side remained disorganized and underfunded. In Kabul, I participated in a meeting of the U.S. government rule of law community held at the embassy, listening as representatives of the State Department, USAID, DoD, the Justice Department, and others reported on their programs and ideas. It was a group of bright, dedicated, and motivated people, and they were doing their best to coordinate and work together. But they were quick to acknowledge that their programs often operated on a shoestring, and it was difficult for them to sustain their work given the lack of security and mobility and the high turnover among both Afghan and international staff.

For better or for worse, the Rule of Law Field Force was one of the few games in town.

## Hiya, Senator

Brigadier General Mark Martins wasn't the only enthusiast for military support to rule of law. One day I split off from Bill and the rest of my Pentagon colleagues to meet with rule of law experts at the U.S. Embassy in Kabul. Afterward, I was picked up by helicopter (a "rotary wing aircraft," in military parlance) to join my colleagues in Kandahar, but after a short flight we made an unexpected stop at another base. I wasn't clear why, but the pilot told me we were picking someone up; the wait would be just a few minutes. So I sat there on the tarmac, still buckled into my seat.

After a few minutes I saw a chunky figure in an Air Force uniform jogging slowly along the tarmac. He reached the helicopter, breathing hard, and hopped in across from me. "Hiya!" he said with a wink, sticking his hand out and pushing a thick lock of non-regulation-length white hair off his face. With mild alarm, I realized that I was looking at Lindsey Graham, senior senator from South Carolina, scourge of the Democratic Party and champion of Angry White Guys.[7] Graham, a lawyer by training, moonlighted as an Air Force reserve JAG colonel.

"Hiya, Senator," I said weakly. "Good to see you."

I had met a few months earlier with Senator Graham and his staff, who were strong supporters of DoD rule of law efforts—and consequently, of my new office.

"I'm jus' doin' my reserve duty here," Graham explained cheerfully as our Black Hawk rose into the Afghan sky. "Helpin' out."

Arriving, we were briefed by Martins and the admiral commanding Task Force 435. It was the only time I've ever seen a three-star Navy admiral call an Air Force reserve colonel "Sir."

"So, whaddya need, Admiral?" asked Graham.

"Sir, we need resources for detention and rule of law operations, and we need support from the Congress. The detainee review and transfer process is slow and resource intensive," responded the Admiral, "but we have to get this right if we want to transition out in 2014, as the president said we will."

Graham, who is nowhere near as dumb as he tries to appear, shook

77

his head soberly. "You know I'll do my best for you. Y'all are doing fine work. But I gotta tell ya, if you asked my colleagues in the Senate where the war in Afghanistan ranks right now in terms of their priorities, well, it probably wouldn't even make the top ten. No one cares. It's all domestic issues."

This silenced everyone for a moment. The admiral sighed, and Mark looked down. I thought of the acres and acres of dust-colored Marine Corps tents stretching out endlessly at Helmand's Camp Leatherneck, and the young Afghan boy injured by an IED I had seen being treated at a military hospital, and the female Afghan prosecutor who'd told me she'd had to lie about her job to her family, since they would never have permitted her to work in a criminal court if they'd known. I sighed too.

We went on from the briefing to sit in on a Detainee Review Board hearing, watching and listening as military lawyers questioned a young detainee about his activities. Like most legal hearings, it was terribly boring for everyone—except the poor guy whose freedom and future were at stake. He sat rigidly in his chair, his left knee twitching spasmodically as he tried to follow the proceedings. But the room was warm, and every question and answer had to be slowly and painstakingly translated.

I heard a gentle snoring noise, and glanced over at the admiral. He was sound asleep.

# CHAPTER FOUR

# The Full Spectrum

*"[It] is not a pretty thing when you look into it too much. What redeems it is the idea only. An idea at the back of it: not a sentimental pretence but an idea; and an unselfish belief in the idea—something you can set up, and bow down to, and offer a sacrifice to."*
—Joseph Conrad, *Heart of Darkness*

Rule of law programs weren't the only Defense Department activities giving heartburn to civilian experts. Across the board, the military was moving into areas more traditionally conceived of as civilian domains. It was getting into the business of health care, education, news and information, economic development, and local politics.

## A Muscle-Bound Red Cross

In 2005, Secretary of Defense Donald Rumsfeld signed DoD Directive 3000.05,[1] which declared that "stability operations" would henceforth be a core military mission with "priority comparable to combat operations." The directive defined stability operations as "Military and civilian activities conducted across the spectrum from peace to conflict to establish or maintain order in States and regions," and added that "stability operations are conducted to help establish order that advances U.S. interests and values. The immediate goal often is to provide the local populace with security, restore essential services, and meet humanitarian needs. The long-term goal is to help develop indigenous capacity for securing essential services, a viable market economy, rule of law, democratic institutions, and a robust civil society." In other words, "stability operations" is the new term for what was once derisively known as "nation building," though military jargon quickly evolved to give it a tougher-sounding moniker: "Stab Ops."

Still, Directive 3000.05 was in many ways a startling document. It's not just that President George W. Bush had, as a Republican candidate in 2000, derided anyone who "uses 'nation building' and 'the military' in the same sentence." It was also a significant turnaround for the military itself.

Not so many years ago, the military had a very different doctrinal term for such activities: they were referred to rather dismissively as "Military Operations Other Than War," or MOOTW (pronounced *moot-wah*). The implication of the term MOOTW was clear: there were the "large-scale combat operations usually associated with war," which was the military's primary mission, and then there was some other stuff the military was forced to do from time to time—stuff that was, basically, moot.[2]

In the early 1990s, fresh from triumph in the first Gulf War, many military personnel grew frustrated with the humanitarian and peacekeeping missions in which they suddenly found themselves engaged. In Somalia, a humanitarian assistance mission designed initially to provide famine relief fell to pieces after the 1993 Battle of Mogadishu, which left eighteen Americans dead and eighty-four wounded; images of dead American soldiers being dragged through the streets haunted the military for years afterward. Later, peacekeeping and humanitarian assistance missions in Bosnia, Haiti, and Kosovo forced thousands of U.S. troops into unfamiliar and uncomfortable roles: part police officers, part small-town mayors, part Red Cross.

The backlash was prompt, fueled by strategic leaks to the press. "Defense Department officials cringe at the notion of becoming a super, muscle-bound Red Cross or Salvation Army," noted a 1994 *Washington Post* article. "Such humanitarian missions are fine now and then, Pentagon officials say. But these operations sap time and attention of senior officials, cut into combat training exercises, tie up equipment and personnel and take increasingly scarce defense dollars away from other operations focused on the Pentagon's primary mission of making sure US armed forces remain strong enough to win two regional wars nearly simultaneously."[3]

Even as Clinton administration policymakers and some younger military officers began to call for more emphasis on peacekeeping and humanitarian missions in military training and education, the old guard resisted. Samuel P. Huntington, the respected Harvard political scientist whose book *The Soldier and the State* remains a classic of civil-military relations theory, was one such resister: "Such proposals are basically misconstrued," he wrote in 1993. "The mission of the Armed Forces is combat, to deter and defeat enemies of the United States. The military must be recruited, organized, trained, and equipped for that purpose alone. . . . A military force is fundamentally antihumanitarian: its purpose is to kill people in the most efficient way possible."[4]

The backlash against MOOTW—or nation building as some called it—was still manifest in the campaign debates leading up to the 2000 presidential election. Against Democratic candidate Al Gore, who as Bill Clinton's vice president was closely associated with the military interventions and subsequent nation-building efforts in Haiti and the Balkans, George W. Bush made no bones about his distaste for such military missions: "[Are we] going to have kind of a nation building corps from America? Absolutely not. Our military is meant to fight and win war. That's what it's meant to do. And when it gets overextended, morale drops."[5]

Yet a scant three years later, President George W. Bush found himself presiding over large-scale military nation-building efforts in both Afghanistan and Iraq. The 9/11 attacks had convinced policymakers of the folly of assuming that the United States could simply ignore failed states and unstable regions: after all, the 9/11 attacks were planned from deep inside the ungoverned Afghanistan-Pakistan border region. Iraq's rapid devolution into chaos after the initial U.S. military successes underscored the point: lack of stable governance gives rise to violence. Like it or not, DoD leaders concluded, the military had to get better at all those tasks once dismissed as marginal.

Defense Secretary Rumsfeld acknowledged this, albeit a few years too late to do much good in Iraq. Rumsfeld had famously ignored the many critics inside and outside the Pentagon who warned that the United States would need a plan to "win the peace" in Iraq. By 2005, he had changed his tune, recognizing that promoting stability was essential both to preventing new conflicts and resolving old ones. Under his watch, military doctrine began to evolve in significant ways.

Instead of viewing war as essentially an all-or-nothing state of affairs, military doctrine began to emphasize that conflict occurs on a continuum. The 2001 edition of the key military doctrinal publication, "JP 3-0: Doctrine for Joint Operations," emphasized only four "phases of conflict": "deter/engage," "seize the initiative," "decisive operations," and "transition." By 2008, however, joint military doctrine formally abandoned the dismissive term "military operations other than war," and instead adopted a "six phase" approach to thinking about conflict—one that reconceptualized what was once considered MOOTW as military activities that might occur at any point along the "full spectrum of conflict."

The full spectrum of conflict was defined as having six phases. In "Phase Zero"—a period without active conflict—the military's role was understood as "shaping" the character of possible future operations by building relationships, collecting information, and seeking to influence the attitudes of local actors. If conflict appeared to loom on the horizon, the military would enter Phase One, the deterrence phase: in this phase, military activities would be characterized "by preparatory actions that indicate the intent to execute subsequent phases of the operation."

If deterrence failed, Phase Two, the "seizing initiative phase," would begin, leading to Phase Three, "Dominate," in which the military would engage in "sustained combat operations." If successful, this would be followed by Phase Four, "stabilize," in which military forces would restore basic security and services. In Phase Five, the military would work with local and international actors, including NGOs, to restore civil authority. These tasks completed, the military would once again circle back to Phase Zero: the shaping phase.

Several other significant shifts occurred between 2005 and 2007: Rumsfeld signaled his newfound commitment to "stability operations" by signing DoD Directive 3000.05; the Defense Department created a new Africa Command, which was expressly designed to conduct stability operations and Phase Zero operations in Africa; and the military developed a renewed interest in counterinsurgency methods, manifested in the much-heralded 2007 Army and Marine Corps Counterinsurgency Manual, and exemplified by post-2006 operations in Iraq and Afghanistan.

## A Dying Squirrel

"A squirrel dying in front of your house may be more relevant to your interests right now than people dying in Africa," Facebook founder Mark Zuckerberg is said to have once remarked.[6] For most Americans occupying the *Now-Now-Now!* world of Facebook, this probably feels apt. And until a decade ago, Zuckerberg's statement might equally have applied to Pentagon strategists. A 1995 DoD strategy document was hardly less blunt than Zuckerberg: "Ultimately we see very little traditional strategic interest in Africa."[7]

For the military, that began to change in 1998, when U.S. embassies in Nairobi and Tanzania were bombed by al Qaeda. The 9/11 attacks accelerated the change: if terrorism thrives in failed states and ungoverned spaces, the military needed to rethink its approach to Africa, which boasts more than its fair share of basket-case states. By 2006, Africa had been bumped up to "high priority" in the U.S. National Security Strategy: "our security depends on partnering with Africans to strengthen fragile and failing states and bring ungoverned areas . . . under control."[8]

As the Pentagon struggles to adapt to a world in which security threats come from increasingly diffuse sources—and the role of the military is consequently less and less clear cut—Africa has become a key laboratory for experimentation and change.

In 2007, the United States created a new geographic combatant command to cover Africa. Africa Command—or AFRICOM—was in part an effort to rationalize a previously incoherent administrative division of labor, in which responsibility for Africa had been divided up between three geographic military commands. But it was also a bold experiment: a *new* kind of military command, designed to reflect the Pentagon's emerging understanding of a more complex security environment in which prevention would be as important as cure.

From its inception, AFRICOM was structured with stability operations—including conflict prevention—in mind. Unlike other more traditional military combatant commands, AFRICOM was also expressly designed to take a "whole of government" approach, with senior civilian officials from the State Department, USAID, and other agencies fully integrated into the command's decision-making structure.

This would, in theory, enable conflict prevention in Africa to be addressed holistically, rather than through a narrow military lens. With its integration of civilian and military power, AFRICOM would not draw sharp or arbitrary distinctions between defense, development, and diplomacy; all these would go hand in hand. And this, President Bush declared, would help "bring peace and security to the people of Africa and . . . promote our common goals of development of health, education, democracy, and economic growth."[9]

The resulting range of AFRICOM activities quickly caused heartburn for those committed to viewing military power strictly through a traditional war-fighting lens. Recent activities undertaken by or with the assistance of AFRICOM include, for instance, the construction of school classrooms in Chad; research on "the Association of Sexual Violence and Human Rights Violations with Physical and Mental Health in Territories of the Eastern Democratic Republic of the Congo"; cattle vaccination in Uganda, designed to provide healthy cattle to internally displaced civilians returning to their homes; activities to combat drug trafficking through the West Africa Cooperative Security Initiative; and the construction of closed wells with solar power pumps in Senegal.[10]

Other AFRICOM initiatives included the establishment of an East African Malaria Task Force to combat "one of the biggest killers on the continent: the mosquito";[11] the creation of a news and information website aimed toward local audiences in the Maghreb, featuring "analysis, interviews and commentary by paid Magharebia correspondents";[12] the construction of a maternal and pediatric care ward at a Ugandan hospital; collaboration with Botswana's military to "promote Botswana's national program of education, HIV screening and male circumcision surgeries"; cooperation with the Sierra Leone Maritime Wing and Fisheries Ministry, "resulting in the apprehension of an illegally operating fishing vessel";[13] and, of course, counterpiracy efforts in collaboration with host country governments through the Africa Partnership Station (APS) and Africa Maritime Law Enforcement Partnership (AMLEP).[14]

AFRICOM also conducts or facilitates a wide range of other activities, some of them more traditional, including various counterterrorism programs run through "Operation Enduring Freedom—Trans Sahara" and a range of efforts to help capture Lord's Resistance Army leaders in Central and East Africa. In 2011, AFRICOM coordinated its first large-scale military operation when President Obama approved Operation Odyssey Dawn, which aimed to enforce the U.N.-sanctioned no-fly zone in Libya and eliminate the Libyan government's ability to threaten civilians.[15]

Whether AFRICOM represents a viable model for the future of the U.S. military naturally depends on your point of view. To traditionalists within the military, the AFRICOM approach is downright dangerous: it's a slide away from the military's core competencies, and the very apotheosis of mission creep. Many civilian observers are equally skeptical, viewing AFRICOM as further evidence of the militarization of U.S. foreign policy—and of the devaluing and evisceration of civilian capacity.

"The Pentagon is muscling in everywhere," complained former State Department official Thomas Schweich in a *Washington Post* op-ed: "Why exactly do we need a military command [in Africa] running civilian reconstruction, if not to usurp the efforts led by well-respected U.S. embassies and aid officials?"[16]

AFRICOM has also been justly criticized for failing to live up to its lofty goals. A clumsy early rollout left AFRICOM struggling to allay African suspicions that the United States intended to "recolonize" Africa, and for a variety of reasons (shortage of qualified and interested personnel; inadequate career incentives; a slow-moving personnel system), many of the civilian slots within AFRICOM were never filled. Today, AFRICOM continues to struggle to coordinate its efforts with civilian agencies: as with so many other efforts, the sheer scale of military undertakings can leave underresourced civilian agencies struggling just to respond to urgent problems, with little time left over for longer-term issues.[17]

Lack of cultural awareness has also plagued programming: the distribution of used clothes in Djibouti during Ramadan offended Muslim sensibilities, for instance, and AFRICOM has also been criticized for failing to take local clan relationships into account when distributing assistance.

These problems are not unique to AFRICOM. As other military combatant commands have similarly expanded their activities into traditionally civilian domains they have struggled with similar problems and criticism.

## Information Warfare

One of my early assignments at the Pentagon was to tackle a problem no one else wanted to touch: making sense of the can of worms known as "strategic communication." "Strategic communication is important, but I feel like we're doing it really badly," Michèle Flournoy told me. My task was to fix it—if it was fixable. But first, I had to figure out what it was.

I spent much of the next few weeks on a Pentagon listening tour. I spoke to public affairs officers, had coffee with the Joint Staff's "PSYOP" and "strategic effects" teams, ate lunch with the information operations experts in the office of the under secretary for intelligence, and took careful notes as several dozen people offered several dozen conflicting accounts about what the term "strategic communication" meant, and what, if anything, DoD ought to be doing about it.

There was, it transpired, some dirty laundry left over from the Bush administration. In the corporate world, the term "strategic communication" has been used for several decades to describe the coordinated use of activities designed to make the corporate entity "look good," such as marketing, advertising, public relations, and community relations. The term carries overtones of manipulation: marketers needn't care if their product is "good" (or healthy, or durable, or safe, or whatever)—their goal is simply to make sure people buy it, regardless of its actual value.

During the early years of the Bush presidency, the term "strategic communication" was similarly used by some at the Pentagon to cover a multitude of sins. These ranged from the foolish but relatively innocuous conviction that violent extremism could be countered by simply improving U.S. "messaging" and developing "new narratives" to rather more dubious efforts, such as a 2005 initiative to pay Iraqi media outlets to run feel-good pro-U.S. "news" stories.[18]

When Flournoy took office as under secretary for policy, the Bush-era organizational chart showed a small office for "Support to Public Diplomacy" led by a deputy assistant secretary of defense. This office was identified, rather vaguely, as the office responsible for strategic communication, but Flournoy eliminated it on the reasonable grounds that none of its staff seemed able to offer a cogent explanation of its functions. I too interviewed most of the people who had worked there, but came away none the wiser; when I asked if there were office files I could look through, I was told by a nervous staffer that the files had all been shredded at the end of the Bush administration.

The Support to Public Diplomacy office turned out to be a descendant of an early Rumsfeld-era experiment called the Office of Strategic Influence, created late in 2001 to "counter extremist ideologies." After a *New York Times* story suggested it was planning to plant false news stories in foreign press outlets, the office was shuttered,[19] but most of the people and activities associated with the Office of Strategic Influence simply carried on under different organizational titles. Former Defense Secretary Rumsfeld unblushingly acknowledged the sleight of hand. Speaking to reporters in November 2002, he declared, "And then there was the Office of Strategic Influence. You may recall that. And"—he raised his voice to a mocking falsetto—"'Oh my goodness gracious, isn't that *terrible*, Henny Penny, the *sky* is going to fall!'" Returning to his normal speaking voice, he added: "I went down that next day and said 'Fine, if you want to savage this thing, fine, I'll give you the corpse. There's the name. You can have the name, but I'm gonna keep doing every single thing that needs to be done.' And I have."[20]

The opaque work of the Office of Strategic Influence was continued by various other equally opaque Pentagon entities, including the Office of Special Plans, but this office too was eventually shut down after it was accused of generating some of the misleading claims about Iraqi weapons of mass destruction used to justify the 2003 invasion of Iraq.

In the final years of the Bush administration, internal Pentagon reformers sought to jettison the more egregiously foolhardy strategic communication initiatives of the so-called Global War on Terrorism (the "GWOT"—pronounced *gee wot*). By 2009, many of DoD's remaining strategic communication activities fell under the Office of Defense Support to Public Diplomacy, until it was shut down by Flournoy on grounds of general uselessness.

By the beginning of the Obama administration, Pentagon reformers were urging a more nuanced understanding of what strategic communication might mean. Ideally, they argued, it should be less about what the Defense Department had to say than about considering how others might interpret the words and actions of U.S. defense officials. It should be a process of engaging, listening, and recognizing that *all* military activities, from speeches and meetings with local dignitaries to aircraft carrier movements and troop deployments, have "information effects." Everything communicates something.

At Flournoy's request, I became the Defense Department policy office's new point person for strategic communication issues, and built up my own small staff. I called it the "Global Strategic Engagement Team" because I disliked the term "strategic communication," and I added the term "team" to emphasize our intention of playing a coordinating and facilitating role, rather than creating a permanent new bureaucratic structure. I hoped we could finally get rid of the Bush-era programs that had caused so much trouble, and find some better ways to communicate American goals and intentions to a skeptical world.

The old hands just chuckled. A colleague who had survived the Rumsfeld era dropped by to give me an old Office of Strategic Influence lapel pin, which he dared me to wear to lunch with some reporters. I declined, but I stuck the pin on my bulletin board as a reminder of past lessons.

·   ·   ·

Sure enough, despite our best efforts, even my innocuous little team was soon drawing fire. The Defense Department's Public Affairs Office was unhappy that my staff members were brainstorming with the regional policy offices on think tank and press strategy, since they considered that their job, not ours; the State Department's Counterterrorism Office was explaining that it was actually *their* job, not ours, to develop programs to counter violent extremist ideology; staffers on the congressional armed services committees were demanding that I defend the budgets for classified information operations programs that they hated and I had never even heard of; and the CIA was insisting that DoD's classified information operations programs were interfering with *their* classified programs.

The State Department's Public Diplomacy offices —which had traditionally funded cultural exchanges, the arts, and media initiatives such as Voice of America—were annoyed that DoD was funding what they saw as classic public diplomacy projects. The military was doing everything from airdropping leaflets and posting billboards urging Iraqis to report possible IEDs to handing out soccer balls branded with anti-extremist slogans, and it didn't stop there. Under the rubric, variously, of strategic communication, psychological operations, and information operations, DoD was building and operating mobile radio stations complete with call-in chat shows, promoting new websites designed to provide alternative news and discussion forums in regions where most media had an extremist slant, and even promoting new arts and cultural events. The State Department was particularly incensed by a DoD-funded "peace concert" in Africa. I can no longer recall if the offending concert was in Mali or Mauritania, but to State Department officials, the venue didn't matter: the military needed to get out of the music business. (And the television business, the radio business, the journalism business, the film business, the education business, the sports business, and the branded product business.)

Meanwhile, Ambassador Richard Holbrooke, the president's special representative to Afghanistan and Pakistan, kept shouting that the United States—the nation of Hollywood and Madison Avenue, for God's sake!—was being out-communicated by a guy living in a cave (the late Osama bin Laden), and telling everyone that he didn't give a damn *who* was in charge of strategic communication, but could we all kindly get our heads out of other parts of our anatomy and fix the goddamned *problem*?

As with debates about whether the Defense Department should be engaged in rule of law activities, it was easy to sympathize with the civilian agencies' view that DoD was sucking up all the available oxygen. From the State Department's perspective, overt information programs intended to persuade and influence were in their domain, and it made no sense at all for the Defense Department to be funding concerts, producing television ads, sponsoring school essay contests, or giving out matchbooks advertising monetary rewards for anyone providing information about bin Laden[21]—particularly at a time when the budget for traditional State Department public diplomacy programs had been slashed.

This problem was further compounded by the existence of a number of classified DoD information operations programs of varying quality, details of which could be shared with some people within the government but not with others. Add to that the embarrassing fact that no one at the Pentagon seemed entirely sure just what programs were out there: as was the case with rule of law programs, humanitarian projects, and so much else, a combination of poor record keeping, decentralized decision making, and fragmented budgets and authorities made it difficult to feel confident that anyone had the whole picture.

But here again, it wasn't quite that simple. Congressional skepticism about the value and efficacy of DoD information programs was exceeded only by congressional skepticism about the value and efficacy of the State Department's programs. Everyone agreed that somehow the United States had to be engaged in what the Pentagon referred to as "the information domain," and only the Pentagon had the money and manpower to do so, even if some of that money was wasted and some of that manpower took a less than sophisticated approach.

My team spent the better part of a year trying to convince State Department officials to stop griping and just tell us *which* Pentagon programs they thought should be transferred to the State Department, improved through DoD–State Department collaboration, or simply canned. We got nowhere. We shared reams of budget and program information, struggling to give our State Department counterparts as full a picture as possible of what DoD was doing and why. But they kept canceling meetings with us, requesting more data, and requesting more time to review the data.

I knew it was nothing personal: Defense Department personnel outnumber State Department personnel by a ratio of about 100 to 1, and DoD personnel can sit in meetings all day, and send military information support units to dozens of embassies. The State Department's small public diplomacy staff was simply outnumbered. By virtue of its sheer size, the Pentagon frequently ends up taking on any tasks for which other agencies lack the resources or personnel. But for civilian agencies, Pentagon "help" is like being hugged by an eight-hundred-pound gorilla: it can squeeze the life right out civilian efforts.

The only thing worse than being ignored by the military, one State Department friend told me, was being embraced by the military. "If I sent a State Department political advisor to every military commander begging for one, or sent a State Department human rights or development expert to every DoD conference we're invited to, I'd have no staff left at all."

## The Coindinistas

If the Defense Department's 2005 embrace of "stability operations" marked a significant shift in how the military conceived its own role, the 2007 publication of the U.S. Army and Marine Corps' *Counterinsurgency Field Manual* was similarly significant. The relationship between stability operations and counterinsurgency operations remains somewhat murky: some see counterinsurgency as a subset of stability operations, while others see stability operations as a subset of counterinsurgency. Either way, the two are clearly close cousins: both emphasize the military's role in establishing civilian security, basic services, and governmental legitimacy, through nontraditional as well as more traditional military means.

Retired Army Lieutenant Colonel John Nagl, an early and passionate advocate of counterinsurgency methods, describes the evolution of counterinsurgency doctrine in his 2014 memoir, *Knife Fights: A Memoir of Modern War in Theory and Practice*.[22] As a young officer, Nagl served in a tank battalion during the first Gulf War, where some 400,000 American military personnel made short work of the Iraqi Army. For Nagl, however, that early sense of triumph was short-lived. A year after Desert Storm, he recalls, he found himself at the Army's National Training Center in California. Pitted against an infantry company from the Alaska National Guard in a simulated battle, Nagl's company of proud Gulf War veterans assumed they would easily prevail over the ragtag Alaskan guardsmen, many of whom didn't even speak "understandable English."[23]

Instead, something astonishing happened: the "Nanooks," as Nagl's experienced tankers dubbed the Alaskans, "crept up on us from behind, infiltrating through the mountains that protected our flanks and rear from enemy armored vehicles but not from Eskimos. Methodically, one by one, the Nanooks defeated a dug-in tank company."

Nagl was frustrated and bewildered: somehow, it turned out, "The world's most advanced ground combat systems—M1A1 tanks that only a year earlier had defeated the world's fourth largest army on its home turf with ease—were perversely vulnerable to small bands of determined human enemies whose language we could barely understand but who knew our vulnerabilities." The experience sent him back to graduate school, determined to gain a better understanding of insurgencies and irregular warfare.

Nagl's 1997 dissertation, "Learning to Eat Soup with a Knife," focused on counterinsurgency lessons from Malaya and Vietnam. At first, he couldn't find a publisher: "No one was interested in a book on how armies learn to succeed in counterinsurgency." That didn't change until the Iraq War, when, faced with a baffling and unexpected insurgency instead of the anticipated "cakewalk," many of America's top officers began to have their own version of Nagl's epiphany after his mock defeat by the Nanooks.

Suddenly, counterinsurgency—shortened to "COIN"—was all the rage. Nagl's dissertation, which had finally been published as a book called *Learning to Eat Soup with a Knife*, became an instant COIN classic, and everyone who was anyone in military circles longed to join the COINdinistas, as Nagl and other architects of the COIN revolution jokingly dubbed themselves.

The COINdinistas argued that "legitimacy is the main objective" for any military force seeking to defeat an insurgency. In a 2006 article in the *Military Review*, Nagl and three coauthors argued that in COIN, purely "military" considerations should never trump political objectives, and the military must learn to coordinate and combine its efforts with civilian and multinational actors.[24]

COIN also deemphasized offensive military action: "The cornerstone of any COIN effort is security for the populace. Without security, no permanent reforms can be implemented, and disorder will spread. To establish legitimacy, security activities must move from the realm of major combat operations into the realm of law enforcement. . . . It is best to use the minimum possible force in resolving any situation. . . . The more force you use, the less effective you are."[25]

This was a far cry from Samuel Huntington's insistence that the purpose of the military was "to kill people in the most efficient way possible." On the contrary, the COINdinistas emphasized the need for military personnel to move outside their comfort zones. As Nagl and his coauthors argued in their *Military Review* article,

> Security is important in setting the stage for other kinds of progress, but lasting victory will come from a vibrant economy, political participation, and restored hope. Dollars and ballots will have a more important effect than bombs and bullets; information is even more powerful when correctly wielded. T. E. Lawrence once observed that "the printing press is the greatest weapon in the armoury of the modern commander." This is even truer today than it was when Lawrence wrote it nearly a century ago—except that

the truly effective counterinsurgent requires not just a printing press, but radio and television programs and an Internet presence. Soldiers and Marines must be prepared to engage in a host of traditionally nonmilitary missions to support COIN operations.[26]

The language wasn't calculated to bring joy to civilian State Department officials, but these precepts soon found their way into the Army and Marine Corps' *Counterinsurgency Field Manual*, which Nagl was tapped by General David Petraeus to help draft. When it was published in 2007, the Army's COIN manual even became an improbable bestseller, garnering a fulsome review in the *New York Times* and even catapulting a uniformed Nagl onto Jon Stewart's *Daily Show*.

In the mid- and late 2000s, COIN's emphasis on "traditionally nonmilitary missions" such as population protection, basic services, and the establishment of legitimate governance fueled a surge of military interest in everything from rule of law programs to strategic communication. In Afghanistan and Iraq, commanders urged troops to get out from the safety of their bases and mingle with the people. General Petraeus, the commander in Iraq in 2007, reminded the troops that "This fight depends on securing the population, which must understand that we—not our enemies—occupy the moral high ground,"[27] and in Afghanistan, General Stanley McChrystal, who took over as commander of U.S. forces in summer 2009, immediately issued a directive reminding troops that "this is a struggle for the support of the population . . . we must respect and protect the population from coercion and violence. . . . This is different from conventional combat." Ultimately, he asserted, "working with our Afghan partners, we will overcome the enemy's influence and give the Afghan people what they deserve: a country at peace, the foundations of good governance, and economic development."[28]

In Iraq and Afghanistan, a thousand COIN-related flowers bloomed. Military engineers dug wells and fixed sewer lines; civil affairs teams refurbished schools, attended meetings of local tribal elders, and started microfinance projects for rural women; psychological operations units distributed "radio station in a box" kits and scoured the countryside for "credible voices" to put on call-in shows. Military agriculture experts encouraged Afghans to diversify their crops, and military medical teams staffed women's health clinics.

You name it, the military was doing it.

## You People

But putting COIN precepts into practice proved anything but easy. (John Nagl noted ruefully, "I thought I'd known something about COIN until I started trying to do it myself."[29]) And as with AFRICOM and stability operations, few COIN-related efforts were an unmitigated success.

Displaced civilian diplomats and development experts were often harshly critical of DoD's humanitarian, development, and governance work. Stories abounded of schools built without thought for whether they would have teachers, books, or students; bridges built three times in row in the same place, only to be repeatedly demolished by local contractors who knew the next military unit that rotated in would pay them to rebuild it yet again.

"You people, you just have no idea what you're *doing*!" a USAID development expert spluttered to me after a meeting convened by the White House on revamping development policy. "You've got these *kids*, these thirty-year-old captains who've spent their lives learning to drive tanks and shoot people, and they think they know how to end poverty in Afghanistan, in six months. They don't understand that there are people who actually *know* something about this, and it's not them— they act on whatever idea happens to pop into their heads."

Formal efforts to evaluate nontraditional military programs have offered only mixed reviews. A 2011 Government Accountability Office report on DoD humanitarian activities, for instance, found systemic management and accountability problems across the Defense Department, concluding grimly that while there have been some improvements over the years,

DOD does not have complete information on the full range of humanitarian assistance projects it conducts. . . . DOD does not know . . . when a project is going to be implemented, when it is in progress, or when and if it has been completed. . . . DOD does not know how much it has spent. . . . DOD is not consistently evaluating its projects, and therefore it cannot determine whether its humanitarian assistance efforts are meeting their intended goals, having positive effects, or represent an efficient use of resources.[30]

A later Government Accountability Office report addressing development activities in Afghanistan reached similar conclusions.[31]

Criticism of this kind also came from humanitarian assistance NGOs such as Doctors Without Borders, the Red Cross, and Save the Children. These groups worried about what they saw as the militarization of aid, and the "shrinking of humanitarian space."[32] A core tenet for most humanitarian NGOs is neutrality: aid workers don't take sides in conflicts. Food and medical aid is distributed without regard to ideology or affiliation. Neutrality is embraced by humanitarian organizations for practical reasons as well as principled ones: aid workers are far less likely to be targeted by participants in a conflict if they are viewed as above the fray. When military personnel start handing out humanitarian assistance, many NGOs argue, local actors can no longer assume that aid is neutral—instead, aid becomes an instrument of war, and aid agency personnel become targets.

It's not a misplaced fear: in the decade between 2003 and 2013, 991 humanitarian workers were killed, 236 in Afghanistan. Iraq, Pakistan, Somalia, Sudan, South Sudan, Yemen, Congo, Palestine, Uganda, and Syria have also proved particularly lethal places for aid workers in recent years.[33]

## Jagged Little Pieces

At best, the military has a mixed track record when it comes to performing such traditionally civilian functions as providing humanitarian assistance, governance support, and development aid. But though part of the problem is surely military ineptitude—clueless young officers managing tasks for which they have little instinct and less training—

it's not the military that sets national security policy, and it's not the military that sets the nation's budgetary priorities. Without strong political leadership, sensible strategic goals, and partnerships with capable, well-funded, and adaptable civilian agencies—none of which the United States has had—military initiatives can only do so much. To quote Hillary Clinton, it takes a village.

Or, more precisely: it takes a whole government to really screw up a war. A dollop of American hubris goes a long way too.

On the other hand, sometimes I think it's our best instincts that lead to our worst failures. Consider Iraq. Granted, some not-so-great instincts brought us there in 2003—but it was our best instincts that kept us there. Remember "you break it, you own it"? We took the Pottery Barn Rule seriously enough to stick around for the next eight years, trying earnestly to glue the shattered pieces back together.

The glue never stuck. We couldn't bring ourselves to believe gloomy predictions that looting might take place, and we convinced ourselves the Iraqis would be better off if we could just oust senior members of Saddam Hussein's Baathist party from the government and disband his army.[34] But instead of bringing peace and democracy, early U.S. decisions in Iraq led to chaos, revenge killings, a government that could no longer provide the most basic services, and millions of angry, unemployed—and armed—young men.

It only got worse. The continued American presence sparked an insurgency and brought al Qaeda to Iraq.[35] While the Iraq War's civilian death toll remains disputed, it was certainly stunningly high.[36] Violence began gradually to subside after 2006, for reasons that probably had more to do with the internal changes in Iraq's Sunni community known as the Sunni Awakening than with the U.S. troop surge, and in 2011 we finally slunk off, tails between our legs. Behind us, we left a squabbling, barely functional government, an economy in shambles, and a level of civil violence that remains astronomically high.

Now, we're back in Iraq, again—this time with a few thousand military "advisors" and airpower rather than scores of thousands of combat troops, and this time we're fighting ISIS, not al Qaeda or Shiite militias. But we still can't put the country back together again, and the

Iraqi troops we so expensively trained and equipped seem disinclined to fight the battles we want them to fight.

My point here is not that the Iraq War was a bad idea in the first place (though it certainly was). My point is that this cynical, foolish, arguably illegal war might still have come right in the end—if only we had tried a little less hard to fix everything that struck us as broken.

I remember Iraq in summer 2003, before the bombing of the U.N. headquarters, before suicide bombs and IEDs became near-daily occurrences. There was a brief window that spring and summer, a window in which the mood in Baghdad was cautiously celebratory. People spoke freely. NGOs and human rights groups popped up out of nowhere. Saddam was out; hope was in. We should have left then.

What would have happened if the U.S. government had been less determined to fix Iraq's broken parts? What would have happened if we'd brought our troops back home in summer 2003? What if we'd quelled our national do-gooder instincts, and left the Iraqi Army and all but a handful of top Baathist officials in place, offering the rest their lives, liberty, and some generous economic assistance in exchange for genuine cooperation on weapons inspections?

There's no way to know for sure, but I have an uneasy feeling that a more cynical U.S. government approach from the get-go—an approach that never even contemplated the restoration of democracy—might ultimately have caused less chaos and bloodshed.

Or consider Afghanistan. Since 2001, we've struggled to keep the Taliban at bay, build up a democratic government, eliminate corruption, and create an Afghan military capable of defending the population and disinclined to prey on it. All worthy aims—and to achieve them, Presidents Bush and Obama let U.S. troop levels creep up over the course of eleven years, going from fewer than ten thousand in late 2002 to more than thirty thousand in November 2008.[37] By mid-2009, Obama had doubled that number. By mid-2010, he had tripled it. But though we did substantially increase the number of U.S. civilian officials tasked to help with Afghan governance and development issues, the civilian surge never got very surgelike.[38] (In his book *Little America: The War Within the War for Afghanistan*, Rajiv Chandrasekaran quotes

Brigadier General Kenneth Dahl's sarcastic 2011 rejoinder to Karl Eikenberry, then the U.S. ambassador to Afghanistan, who informed him that the civilian surge had reached "the high-water mark." "That's great," Dahl responded. "I can feel it lapping at my ankles.")[39]

The result? Today the Afghan government remains corrupt, insecurity remains rampant, civilian deaths directly and indirectly attributable to the U.S. presence remain high, and polls suggest that ordinary Afghans are scared of American soldiers. If the Afghan population doesn't trust us much, we've come to trust them even less: green-on-blue attacks spiked in the final years of the war.[40] As in Iraq, we ended up limping ignominiously toward the exit. But in Afghanistan as in Iraq, ending the war has so far proven impossible: as I write, Taliban forces have regained control of more Afghan territory than at any time since the U.S. invasion in 2001, and ISIS now competes with the Taliban for territory and influence. U.S. troops remain engaged in hostilities inside Afghanistan, and recent White House announcements make it clear that their role and numbers are likely to continue to expand.

What if the United States had done things differently? What if we had pummeled al Qaeda's strongholds, helped the Northern Alliance oust the Taliban, and then . . . left? If we had left early in 2002, we could have continued to strike al Qaeda targets of opportunity as needed, using special operations forces and aerial attacks; we could have used diplomacy and foreign aid to urge governance and human rights reforms. Perhaps there wouldn't have been many reforms—but would things really be any worse than they are today?

Here again, my point isn't that the war in Afghanistan was a mistake, or that our efforts in Afghanistan have fallen badly short, an argument that has been made often and persuasively. Nor am I arguing that we're now "less safe" than we used to be, or insufficiently "more safe"—claims that have always struck me as hard to prove one way or the other. My point is that it has often been our best instincts, not our worst, that have led us to do harm in the world. In Afghanistan and Iraq, we spent billions of dollars and suffered thousands of American casualties. Worst of all, we caused untold suffering for the very populations we so earnestly intended to help.

The United States isn't all idealism, all the time: we're capable of plenty of cynicism, and occasional acts of plain old evil. But even our most cynical moments are accompanied by idealism. We want to help, and we want to set things right. We want everyone to share in peace, justice, and the benefits of the American way—even if it hurts.

And hurt it does. The United States and those we try to "help" are often the victims of our own idealistic commitments to democracy, human rights, and the rule of law.

This phenomenon plays out at a micro level as well a macro level. Military construction and economic development projects take far too long and cost far too much, in part because we want everything to satisfy stringent U.S. and international quality standards. Our reconstruction projects are so elaborate that only those Afghans who already have wealth and power have the capacity to serve as subcontractors.[41] By and large, the result is that power is concentrated even more in the hands of the often corrupt and violent few.[42]

Even U.S. military detention facilities in Afghanistan were built to Western specifications, complete with climate control systems and electronic security. As a result, we render them virtually useless for the Afghan officials who will inherit them—and who won't have the trained staff or the unlimited supply of electrical power to make them run. But the suggestion that the Afghans might sometimes be better off with less reeks, to us, of unacceptable double standards.

Or consider a larger and more tragic irony. By late 2009, the United States had embarked on a counterinsurgency-influenced approach to the conflict in Afghanistan: the Afghan population, we decided, was the "center of gravity."[43] Our success or failure would depend on our ability to protect the population and enable the Afghan government to provide services and thus build legitimacy. Laudable goals! But by making the Afghan population the center of gravity, we also inadvertently placed the Afghan population at the center of a big red bull's-eye. We incentivized the Taliban to combat our efforts by placing IEDs in civilian structures and targeting police, courts, governance, and economic development projects. They did so, with a vengeance.

It should be no surprise if we often fail to achieve our idealistic goals.

After all, building a culture that respects human rights, democracy, and the rule of law takes time. Our own imperfect form of democracy—rife as it still is with injustice and corruption—took us more than two centuries to build, though we stood on the shoulders of those who drafted the Magna Carta and the English Bill of Rights. So why should we imagine that durable change could come any faster in societies that start with far less—less wealth, less education, less tradition of democratic government, human rights, or peaceful change?

Simple failure to achieve our loftiest goals could be excused. But if our efforts to help only cause more harm, it's inexcusable.

Scarred by Vietnam, my parents' generation came of age with a deep distrust of American power. They suspected that American interventionism never stemmed from pure motives, and never, ever, ended well. My generation came of age at a more hopeful moment: I was a college student when the Berlin Wall came down, and the notion of non-ideological U.S. engagement with the world seemed suddenly possible again. The Rwandan genocide taught my generation that nonintervention can be as unconscionable as meddling, and Bosnia and Kosovo taught us that U.S. military power could be a force for good.

But after all the waste and bloodshed in Iraq and Afghanistan, I've lost much of my faith in our government's ability to restore peace or bring justice. I'd love to be proved wrong. But here's my fear: the more we try to fix things, the more we end up shattering them into jagged little pieces.

## An Expensive Proposition

It was virtually inevitable that post-9/11 changes in military doctrine and activities would lead to civilian-military tensions. After 9/11, resources and authorities flowed to the Pentagon. The Bush administration "always wanted military guys between themselves and whatever the problem was," recalls a retired general who served in senior positions during that period,[44] and was more than willing to pour money into DoD. "Ten to fifteen years ago, the military was much smaller and less holistic," comments retired Lieutenant General Dave Barno.

"Today, you have a more empowered military. It has expanded both in ways intended and not."[45]

Meanwhile, budgets for civilian foreign policy agencies and programs have remained largely stagnant. Former defense secretary Robert Gates touched on this theme in a landmark 2007 speech: "Consider that this year's budget for the Department of Defense—not counting operations in Iraq and Afghanistan—is nearly half a trillion dollars, [while] the total foreign affairs budget request for the State Department is $36 billion. . . . There are only about 6,600 professional Foreign Service officers—less than the manning for one aircraft carrier strike group." Gates was blunt in his analysis: the "gutting" of America's "soft power" institutions has led the Defense Department to take on "many of these burdens that might have been assumed by civilian agencies in the past."[46]

AFRICOM is a classic case. As a State Department inspector general's report commented in 2009, AFRICOM's role was "resented and challenged" by the State Department's African Affairs Bureau—but the military was essentially "stepping into a void created by a lack of resources for traditional development" and other "civilian" tasks.[47]

It's a vicious circle: as civilian capacity has declined, the military has stepped into the breach. "It's just the easiest way out of any problem," retired Major General Paul Eaton told me. "Give money to the military and let them deal with it." But the more the military's role expands, the more civilian agencies such as the State Department and USAID find themselves sidelined.

In Afghanistan, recalls Eaton, U.S. officials wanted to "help the Afghans reform their agricultural sector." Military officials asked the Department of Agriculture to develop a program, "but they couldn't spare more than a tiny number of people. So DoD pulled together an agricultural battalion made up of reservists who had agriculture expertise. Is this the best way to handle things like this? Maybe not. But it's the only mechanism we have. DoD has the only available mechanism for marshaling massive amounts of effort and talent."[48]

All the same, the ascendancy of counterinsurgency and stability operations doctrine didn't last. Whatever you want to call it—MOOTW, nation building, stability operations, COIN—it's an expensive proposition. The wars in Iraq and Afghanistan, with hundreds of thousands of troops rotating in and out of theaters, have already cost the nation more than $1.5 trillion.[49] The 2008 financial crisis made open-ended military commitments seem increasingly unaffordable, and the lack of clear success in Iraq and Afghanistan—indeed, the many failures—made such commitments more difficult for politicians to justify.

From the moment he was elected, President Obama made it clear that his top priority in Iraq was the rapid withdrawal of U.S. combat forces, not an extended counterinsurgency presence. By late 2009, it had become apparent that the war in Afghanistan could not be rapidly turned around, and Obama began to lose patience with this conflict as well: he agreed to send additional troops to Afghanistan at General Stanley McChrystal's request, but insisted publicly that most of those troops would begin to withdraw from Afghanistan eighteen months later, come what may.

In Washington, talk of counterinsurgency began to give way to talk of targeted counterterrorism drone strikes: a quick, cheap, and seemingly risk-free way for America to rid itself of its enemies.

# CHAPTER FIVE

# The Secret War

Much of what the U.S. military does is no secret: if the general public is largely unaware of the expanding scope of military activities, it's mainly due to lack of interest. If you want to know the size of the military, how much military personnel are paid, or how much it costs to provide military health care, you can do a bit of Googling and the answers will be at your fingertips. If you want details of military humanitarian assistance in Indonesia, military technical assistance to the Afghan government, or military deaths in Afghanistan, that's available too. Joint forces doctrine, Marine Corps equipment lists, the curriculum at the Army's Ranger School, a map of Fort Carson—it's all a quick Google search away.

But the military operates secret programs too—and top secret programs, and programs so terribly secret and sensitive that details are available only to those possessing the requisite "code word" clearances. "Special Access Programs" are governed by tight rules specifying how information is held and accessed. Some Special Access Programs are unacknowledged: that is, the military will not only withhold details about the program from those without the requisite clearances and "need to know," they will even deny that the program exists in the first place. "Waived Unacknowledged Special Access Programs" are even more tightly controlled: these programs aren't even reported to the full congressional oversight committees, but only to the committee chairs and ranking members of the relevant committees.

Some things have to be secret. Let's say the United States develops the capability to selectively interfere with an enemy's GPS technologies, for instance—making sure that any GPS data is just a little bit off, thus preventing the enemy from coordinating geographically or effectively targeting U.S. positions. (I made this up, by the way: I have no idea if such a capability exists.) If our ability to do this was known, enemies could compensate in other ways, or develop countermeasures; such a capability would lose much of its value if it didn't stay secret.

But some of the things the government keeps secret shouldn't be secret, or at least shouldn't be *as* secret as they are. In particular, the intentional killing of large numbers of people by the government should not be kept secret. Yet since 9/11, larger and larger swaths of national security policy have essentially vanished into the covert world—and it is in this realm of shadows that we find some of the most dangerous and lethal consequences of the hazy lines between war and not-war.

## Things Fall Out of the Sky

At Nevada's Creech Air Force Base, young Americans sit before computer terminals, dispensing remote-controlled death. Drones—or "remotely piloted vehicles," in the preferred Air Force parlance—hover over potential targets in faraway countries, and the pilots and technicians at Creech see almost everything, thanks to the sophisticated cameras mounted on the Predator and Reaper drones they control.

They see vehicles coming and going. They watch boys herding goats, and women carrying goods from the market. They see parents playing with their children, and armed men conferring in dusty compounds. Mostly, the clean-cut men and women at Creech just observe, taking eight-hour shifts as they watch endlessly unfolding images of lives lived far away. Occasionally, though, they act—and with a few computer commands and a puff of smoke viewed on a video monitor, lives end in a burst of noise and searing heat.

• • •

America's drone war began in November 2002, on an isolated stretch of road in Yemen's northwestern Marib province. One minute, a jeep containing six men drove sedately along; the next minute, the jeep was nothing but smoldering metal and blasted body parts. Qaed Salim Sinan al-Harethi, believed to be an al Qaeda leader with links to the 2000 attack on the USS *Cole*, was among those reported dead, and among the other dead was an American citizen said to have ties to al Qaeda. Local witnesses reported seeing some sort of aircraft in the vicinity around the time the jeep exploded.[1]

What happened on that Yemeni road in 2002 wasn't *exactly* a secret, but it wasn't exactly transparent, either. Unnamed "U.S. officials" suggested to the press that the jeep had been targeted in a covert CIA operation, and destroyed with Hellfire missiles fired from an unmanned Predator drone. The CIA stayed mum, and so did President Bush, though Defense Secretary Rumsfeld did comment that "it would be a very good thing if [Harethi] were out of business."[2]

Over the next few years, drones became an increasingly valuable tool for U.S. forces in Afghanistan and Iraq.[3] Because they have no human pilots in the cockpit, drones can be sent into situations deemed too dangerous for manned aircraft—and unlike human pilots, drones don't get sleepy or ask for bathroom breaks. This, along with impressive fuel efficiency, gives them "long loiter time": they can monitor targets for much longer than manned aircraft. They can be used both for surveillance purposes and to carry out missile strikes; they can even provide close air support to troops engaged in combat.

NGO and press reports suggest that it wasn't until 2004 that drone strikes were again used outside the more traditional "hot battlefields" of Iraq and Afghanistan. In June 2004, a drone strike killed Nek Mohammed, a Pakistani militant leader, along with at least six others, including two children.[4] As with the Yemeni strike in 2002, no U.S. officials would go on the record and explain exactly how Nek Mohammed ended up dead. Local residents reported hearing a drone flying nearby, and the *New York Times* later reported that Mohammed himself had "asked one of his followers about the strange, metallic bird hovering above him." Pakistani military officials dismissed reports of U.S. involvement as "absurd," however, and insisted that Pakistan had the military capabilities to carry out such strikes on its own.[5]

Over the ensuing years, the number of U.S. drone strikes outside traditional hot battlefields began to increase, slowly at first and then more rapidly. In 2005, there were 3 reported drone strikes in Pakistan, followed by 2 more in 2006 and 4 in 2007. In 2008, the last year of the Bush presidency, there were 36. In 2009, the first year of the Obama administration, there were 52. In 2010, there were 122. After that, the number of reported annual strikes began to decline again: in 2014, there were 23 strikes reported.[6] In Yemen, however, the pace of drone strikes picked up even as the number of strikes in Pakistan began to decline: there were no known strikes in Yemen between late 2002 and 2009, followed by one in 2010, 9 in 2011, and 47 in 2012, after which the number of annual strikes again began to decline. In 2015, there were reportedly about 22 strikes.[7] Today, the United States is reportedly engaging in similar targeted strikes in Libya, Syria, and elsewhere.

All the figures I have cited above are uncertain, however, for the drone war remains a largely covert war. Nongovernmental organizations and journalists have compiled information on reported strikes, basing the numbers on witness statements, evidence found at strike scenes, leaked government documents, and statements, usually off the record, by both U.S. and foreign government officials. The publicly available information suggests that U.S. strikes have killed some three to five thousand people, but no one knows for sure—just as no one outside the government knows how many of the dead were deliberately targeted, and how many were "collateral damage."

Almost everything publicly known about U.S. drone strikes comes from NGOs and the media. In 2013, for instance, a *New York Times* story by Mark Mazzetti described "a secret deal" in which the CIA agreed to kill militants the Pakistani government wanted dead, "in exchange for access to airspace it had long sought so it could use drones to hunt down its own enemies." Under the terms of the deal, "All drone flights in Pakistan would operate under the C.I.A.'s covert action authority— meaning that the United States would never acknowledge the missile strikes and that Pakistan would either take credit for the individual killings or remain silent."

The Pakistani president at the time was Pervez Musharraf, and according to Mazzetti, "he did not think that it would be difficult to keep up the ruse. As he told one C.I.A. officer: 'In Pakistan, things fall out of the sky all the time.' "[8]

The drone war is a strange sort of war. Everyone knows about it, but officially it barely exists. Until 2012, no one in the executive branch would even go on record acknowledging that the United States had engaged in drone strikes against suspected terrorists. In 2011, U.S. citizen Anwar al-Awlaki was killed in a drone strike in Yemen, but though President Obama acknowledged his death and tacitly acknowledged U.S. responsibility, he kept his comments studiously vague: "Earlier this morning, Anwar al-Awlaki—a leader of al Qaeda in the Arabian Peninsula—was killed in Yemen. . . . The death of al-Awlaki marks another significant milestone in the broader effort to defeat al Qaeda and its affiliates. Furthermore, this success is a tribute to our intelligence community, and to the efforts of Yemen and its security forces, who have worked closely with the United States over the course of several years."[9]

John Brennan, then the White House counterterrorism advisor, referred publicly to U.S. counterterrorism drone strikes for the first time in a 2012 speech: "Yes, in full accordance with the law—and in order to prevent terrorist attacks on the United States and to save American lives—the United States government conducts targeted strikes against specific al-Qaeda terrorists, sometimes using remotely piloted aircraft, often referred to publicly as drones."[10] Brennan did not, however, offer any details: he didn't give numbers, locations of strikes, or the identity of those killed.

In 2013, I was in the audience when President Obama himself referred to U.S. drone strikes in a speech at the National Defense University: "The United States has taken lethal, targeted action against al Qaeda and its associated forces, including with remotely piloted aircraft commonly referred to as drones," he said. Like Brennan, he offered almost no specifics, though he assured us that such strikes were both "effective" and "legal." Still, he admitted, "As was true in previous armed conflicts, this new technology raises profound questions."[11]

Those questions aren't likely to go away. In October 2015, an anonymous Defense Department source gave a raft of classified reports and presentations to a media source, leading to a new round of controversy.

According to the press, the leaked documents suggest that the intelligence leading to drone strikes is often far shakier than government public statements suggest, leading to a higher percentage of unidentified casualties than generally acknowledged. What's more, such secret strikes carry a cost: although captured enemies can provide the United States with valuable information, dead enemies are often literal dead ends from an intelligence-gathering perspective.[12]

## A Devilish Invention

For millennia, warriors have searched for ways to kill their enemies from a safe distance. The throwing spear had advantages over swords and clubs, and the longbow had advantages over the spear. Guns, cannons, bomber planes, and ballistic missiles each gave the militaries that first developed them a temporary edge.

Historically, virtually every significant advance in distance killing has caused anxiety. The longbow and armor-piercing crossbow were once considered immoral, or at any rate distinctly unchivalrous: in 1139, the Second Lateran Council of Pope Innocent II is said to have "prohibit[ed] under anathema that murderous art of crossbowmen and archers, which is hateful to God"—at least when used against Christians.[13] In the early 1600s, Miguel de Cervantes called artillery a "devilish invention" allowing "a base cowardly hand to take the life of the bravest gentleman," with bullets "coming nobody knows how or from whence."[14]

In our own era, the development of weaponized unmanned aerial vehicles has triggered similar controversy and discomfort. To some in the military, drones seem somehow dishonorable: "The fact our guys are sitting in safety thousands of miles away, and our targets have no opportunity to surrender—they don't even know they're targets—somehow that just bothers me," one retired general told me, shaking his head.

Others worry that drones risk creating a "PlayStation mentality," as Philip Alston, the United Nations special rapporteur on extrajudicial, summary, or arbitrary executions, and Hina Shamsi of the ACLU put it.

"Young military personnel raised on a diet of video games now kill real people remotely using joysticks. Far removed from the human consequences of their actions, how will this generation of fighters value the right to life?"[15] Others still agonize over the civilian casualties that have been caused by drone strikes.

But these concerns aren't specific to drones. You can't exactly surrender to a cruise missile, either, or to an unseen sniper hiding in the hills. And drones are surely no more "videogame-like" than other modern military technologies such as laser-guided munitions, remote sensing, satellite imaging, or cameras in the noses of missiles. Those old enough to remember the first Gulf War will recall the once shocking novelty of images taken by cameras inside Tomahawk missiles, the jolting, grainy images in the crosshairs before everything went ominously black.

There's also little evidence that drone technologies "reduce" their operators' awareness of human suffering. If anything, drone operators may have a far greater sense of the harm they help inflict than any sniper or bomber pilot, precisely because the technology enables such clear and long-term visual monitoring. Journalist Daniel Klaidman reports the words of one CIA drone operator, a former Air Force pilot, "I used to fly my own air missions. . . . I dropped bombs, hit my target load, but had no idea who I hit." With drones, it was a different story:

> I can look at their faces . . . see these guys playing with their kids and wives. . . . After the strike, I see the bodies being carried out of the house. I see the women weeping and in positions of mourning. That's not PlayStation; that's real.[16]

Increasingly, there is evidence that drone pilots, just like combat troops, can suffer from post-traumatic stress disorder. They watch a man play with his children and live his life, sometimes for extended periods of time. And then they drop ordnance on him and see his mangled body. Surely this takes a psychological toll. A recent Air Force study found that 29 percent of drone pilots suffered from "burnout," with 17 percent "clinically distressed."[17]

When it comes to civilian casualties, there is also little reason to focus on drones per se. To paraphrase the NRA, "Drones don't kill people, people kill people." At any rate, drone strikes kill civilians at no higher a rate, and almost certainly at a lower rate, than most other common means of warfare. Today's unmanned aerial vehicles (UAVs) carry highly accurate ordnance that generally produces far less widespread damage that other munitions, and their low profile and relative fuel efficiency permit them to spend more "time on target" than manned aircraft. Unlike pilots of manned aircraft, pilots of unmanned vehicles can regularly be replaced while on a mission to avoid fatigue and ensure greater accuracy.

Drones can thus engage in "persistent surveillance," spending hours, days, weeks, or even months monitoring a potential target. Equipped with imaging technologies that enable operators thousands of miles away to see details as fine as individual faces, modern drone technologies allow their operators to distinguish between civilians and combatants far more effectively than most other weapons systems.

That does not mean that civilians are not killed in drone strikes. They are. But the available evidence suggests that drone strikes cause far fewer *unintended* casualties than other types of strikes. The lack of transparency makes it impossible to say for sure, but press and NGO analyses suggest that relatively few civilians have been killed in U.S. strikes, particularly in recent years, as technologies have improved and targeting rules have tightened.

For the most part, complaints that "drones kill civilians" or "drones kill from a distance" are red herrings. We should worry about armed drone technologies, but for a different set of reasons: by lowering or disguising the costs of lethal force, their availability can blind us to the potentially dangerous longer-term consequences of our strategic choices.

Armed drones lower the perceived costs of using lethal force in at least three ways. First, drones reduce the cost of using lethal force inside foreign countries. Most drones are a bargain compared with the available alternatives. Manned aircraft, for instance, are quite expensive: Lockheed Martin's F-22 fighter jets cost about $190 million each, and F-35s are roughly $100 million. But the 2015 price of an MQ-9 Reaper drone was $13.7 million, while Predator drones cost only about $5 million to make. (Hellfire missiles are a steal at less than $100,000 each; you could buy one with a home equity loan.)[18]

Second, relying on drone attacks reduces the domestic political costs of using lethal force. Sending special operations forces after a suspected terrorist places the lives of U.S. personnel at risk, and full-scale invasions and occupations endanger even more American lives. In contrast, using armed drones eliminates all short-term risks to the lives of the personnel involved in the operations. And because drone attacks don't involve "sustained fighting . . . active exchanges of fire . . . [or] U.S. ground troops," any need for congressional notification and approval under the War Powers Act can conveniently be avoided.[19]

Third, by reducing accidental civilian casualties, precision drone technologies reduce the perceived moral and reputational costs of using lethal force.[20] Contrary to assumptions in some quarters, most officials care greatly about avoiding civilian casualties. Even those willing to discount the moral cost of civilian deaths understand the reputational costs: dead civilians upset local populations and host country governments, alienate the international community, and sometimes even disturb the sleep of American voters.

I don't believe that humans can be reduced to *Homo economicus*, but as a group, government officials are remarkably sensitive to financial, political, and reputational costs. Thus, when new technologies appear to reduce the costs of using lethal force, their threshold for deciding to use lethal force correspondingly drops.

If killing a suspected terrorist based in Yemen or Somalia or Libya will endanger expensive manned aircraft, the lives of U.S. troops, and/or the lives of many innocent civilians, officials will reserve such killings for situations of extreme urgency and gravity (stopping another 9/11, finally getting Osama bin Laden). But if all that appears to be at risk is an easily replaceable drone, officials will be tempted to use lethal force more and more casually.

And this, of course, is exactly what has been happening over the last few years. Increasingly, the publicly available information suggests that drone strikes appear to have targeted militants who are lower and lower down the terrorist food chain, rather than terrorist masterminds.[21] Strikes also seem increasingly to target individuals who pose speculative, distant future threats, rather than only those posing urgent or catastrophic threats.[22] And drone strikes have spread ever farther from hot battlefields, migrating from Pakistan to Yemen to Somalia and, according to press reports, to several other states as well.[23]

## Shot with a Machine Gun

Although President Obama has himself acknowledged that U.S. drone strikes raise "profound questions," it's strangely difficult to articulate just what it is that's troubling about them. Our instinct that they may lower the threshold for using armed force is part of it, but perhaps it's also the apparent individualization of warfare that bothers us.

We're accustomed to thinking of war as simultaneously awful and purely impersonal. On the rare occasions we pause to think of the war dead—on Memorial Day, perhaps—we picture them in their countless, serried ranks: the neat, symmetrical lines of white headstones at Arlington Cemetery, or images conjured up from half-remembered poems. "In Flanders fields the poppies blow/ Between the crosses, row on row . . ."

For most of the last few centuries, the wartime dead have been equally anonymous to their enemies. In my office, I have an old black and white family photo of eight smiling young Canadian soldiers posing together in August 1914, on the eve of the First World War. One of those soldiers—jaunty and confident in his high-necked tunic with its gleaming buttons down the front—was a relative of mine: a great-great-uncle, or maybe a cousin, named Robert George MacFarlane. On the back of the photo, the names and fates of those grinning young men are listed in my great-grandmother's careful script:

*L. B. Reynolds*
*B. T. O'Grady*
*G. H. Revell, Killed*

*A. Davies*
*Tom Brown Jr.*
*A. J. Evans, Killed*
*L. B. North*
*R. G. MacFarlane, Shot with a machine gun*

Thanks to Internet archives and a few old family stories, I know a fair amount about Robert George MacFarlane. At the time of his death he was a second lieutenant attached to the British Army's Royal Engineers. He was born in Huntingdon, Quebec, on January 28, 1889; he had a brother named James and a sister named Elsie. He was a Presbyterian, like his Scottish emigrant forebears, and he attended McGill University, graduating in 1910 and finding work as a mining engineer in Nelson, British Columbia. According to Canadian military records, he stood just 5'6" inches tall at the time of his enlistment in 1914, and he had a 38" chest. In July 1915, he was badly injured. He recovered, but only to be shot and killed on March 6, 1916, in the Battle of Railway Wood, near Ypres.[24]

I know all this, and my great-grandmother, who loved him, knew much more, but the German soldier who killed him knew none of this. The German who pulled the machine gun trigger hadn't been stalking Robert MacFarlane for days or weeks, watching his every move, waiting for the perfect moment to end his life. No one in the German military knew anything at all about MacFarlane, and presumably they didn't much care: a German soldier shot him not because he was Robert Mac-Farlane, height 5'6", brother of Elsie and James, but because he was an enemy soldier in a brutal war that killed millions of soldiers. He just happened to be one of them, in the wrong trench at the wrong time.

To the friends and families of the dead, war will always seem personal: the dead are beloved brothers, cousins, husbands, sons, daughters, sisters, and wives, each one unique and precious. But to those on the other side, the enemy dead have generally only been numbers: so many rotting corpses in the muddy trenches of Ypres; so many Viet Cong bodies in the jungles of Vietnam; so many dead Iraqi soldiers on Highway 80 north of Al Jahra, their burned flesh merging with the melted metal of their smoldering tanks.

Drone strikes are the polar opposite: they're "targeted killings," usually aimed at specific, known individuals.[25] Most of the time, U.S. officials know quite a lot about those they target: their names end up on "kill lists" precisely because military and intelligence analysts have built up a painstaking dossier on them, sometimes over many years. Between human informants and high-tech surveillance, we often know where our targets were born, where they went to school and college, the names of their siblings and children, their favorite pastimes, and much more.

Even those individuals whose names are not known often have detailed dossiers based on their observed behaviors over weeks or months. Their faces and details appear on the "baseball cards" studied by administration officials and discussed at "Terror Tuesday" meetings, where individuals are added to (or, more rarely, removed from) the list of approved targets. My former professor, Harold Hongju Koh—the former dean of Yale Law School and former State Department legal advisor—recalls the jarring intimacy of the targeting reviews: "As the Dean of Yale Law School I spent many, many hours looking at the résumés of young twenty-year olds, students . . . trying to figure out who should be admitted. I now spend a comparable amount of time studying the résumés of terrorists, same age. Often I know their background as intimately as I knew my students."[26]

In a 2013 *GQ* profile, the late journalist Matthew Power wrote of the "voyeuristic intimacy" between a drone pilot and his targets: a drone pilot could watch the targets "drink tea with friends, play with their children, have sex with their wives on rooftops, writhing under blankets. There were soccer matches, and weddings too." Pilots watched their targets die in agony too:

> The smoke clears, and there's pieces of the two guys around the crater. And there's this guy over here, and he's missing his right leg above his knee. He's holding it, and he's rolling around, and the blood is squirting out of his leg, and it's hitting the ground, and it's hot. His blood is hot. But when it hits the ground, it starts to cool off; the pool cools fast. It took him a long time to die.

I just watched him. I watched him become the same color as the ground he was lying on.[27]

Targeted killings are surely better than indiscriminate killings—after all, parties to a conflict have a legal and moral obligation to try to distinguish between combatants and noncombatants. But it's precisely the personalization of killing that makes drone strikes seem uncomfortably similar to assassinations or simple murders.

During my time at the Pentagon, I had no direct involvement in planning or approving targeted strikes, though I was one of scores of officials whose work occasionally brought me into contact with the world of "deciders" and operators, usually to discuss the "information effects" of a particular drone strike or to debate the long-term legal and political implications of the strikes. But even from my perch on the periphery, I couldn't shake a queasy sense of dismay. How had it come to pass that I, who was skeptical about military approaches to countering terrorism to begin with, could end up sitting calmly in quiet conference rooms, flipping through photos and biographies of young men who would be dead within days?

There's something undeniably chilling about a "kill list" reviewed each week by a hundred or so administration officials meeting via videoconference. Press reports suggest that President Obama is personally involved in most decisions about who should go on the kill list. The *New York Times* described the process:

> This was the enemy, served up in the latest chart from the intelligence agencies: 15 Qaeda suspects in Yemen with Western ties. The mug shots and brief biographies resembled a high school yearbook layout. Several were Americans. Two were teenagers, including a girl who looked even younger than her 17 years.
>
> President Obama, overseeing the regular Tuesday counterterrorism meeting of two dozen security officials in the White House Situation Room, took a moment to study the faces.[28]

After successful strikes, a military officer serving in the Joint Staff's special operations office told me, civilian administration officials often ask to see video of the killings. "It's totally fucked up," he said. "We call it Kill TV. Those guys always want to come over to the Pentagon and watch the video."

.  .  .

It's the secrecy surrounding drone strikes that's most troubling.

Wars—the organized use of violence to achieve political ends, to use Clausewitz's formulation—are quintessential public acts. Yes, every war has its secrets—every war has its codes and spies and covert operations—but the wars themselves are no secret. In World War II, the Allies tried hard to keep the Germans from figuring out where and when they would invade France, using classic tools of military deception—but the fact that the United States and Britain were at war with Germany and hoped to push the Germans out of occupied France was no secret, and after the D-Day invasion the Allies didn't pretend their forces hadn't landed at Normandy.

The wars in Iraq and Afghanistan also hold secrets, but the American public—and indeed, the world—can easily ascertain the basic details. The approximate number of troops deployed at any given time is no mystery, and neither is the budget. Specific operations are generally disclosed after the fact, at least in broad outline. Deaths and injuries of U.S. troops are promptly made public, and journalists willing to take the risks inherent in war reporting can move freely around to report on Iraqi and Afghan casualties. Although there have been some notable exceptions, particularly in the early days of each war, allegations of significant numbers of civilian casualties are also generally acknowledged and investigated by the military.

Contrast this to the government's continued silence about the drone war. It took a full decade for the existence of drone strikes against terrorists to be acknowledged even in the abstract, and as of this writing the United States has specifically acknowledged its role in the deaths of a handful of individuals (most of them American citizens).

We don't know the targeting criteria, or whether the rules for CIA and military drone strikes differ; we don't know the details of the internal process through which targets are vetted; we don't know the chain of command, or the details of congressional oversight. The United States does not release the names of those killed, or the locations or number of strikes, making it impossible to know whether those killed were legitimately viewed as combatants or not. We also don't know the cost of the secret war: How much money has been spent on drone strikes? What's the budget for the related targeting and intelligence infrastructures? How is the government assessing the costs and benefits of counterterrorism drone strikes?

That's a lot of secrecy for a targeted killing program that has reportedly caused the deaths of several thousand people.

## Spooks and Special Operators

If armed drones are the weapon of choice in America's expanding secret war, intelligence agency operatives and military special operations forces have provided most of the secret war's manpower. Indeed, if the post-9/11 era has been marked by the expansion of the military into traditionally civilian domains, America's secret war epitomizes yet another kind of blurriness: the increasing erosion of any distinctions between the military and the intelligence community.

When it comes to counterterrorism strikes, the overt has gone semi-covert, and the covert has gone semi-overt. The CIA has moved increasingly into paramilitary activities, while the military has moved increasingly into what look like covert intelligence activities. These trends are the result of natural and to some extent praiseworthy efforts by the Pentagon and the intelligence community to respond to changing threats with creativity and agility, but the end result is confusion and lack of accountability.

Start with the intelligence community. After the CIA debacles of the 1960s and 1970s (remember the Bay of Pigs, and the exploding cigar?),[29] the intelligence community shifted away from lethal covert action. A presidential executive order prohibited assassinations,[30] and Congress tightened covert action notification requirements.[31] Espionage remained a dangerous game, operating in a sort of legal twilight,[32] but in the 1980s and 1990s the intelligence community focused mainly on collection and analysis rather than on the covert use of force. The 9/11 Commission report concluded that prior to 9/11, many in the intelligence community in fact believed that using covert lethal force was prohibited.[33]

After 9/11, this changed fast. CIA personnel were the first American government agents to enter Afghanistan, paving the way for Army Special Forces; in some cases, CIA personnel fought (and died) alongside Afghan Northern Alliance soldiers.[34] CIA personnel also participated actively in the Battle of Tora Bora and Operation Anaconda, and in the years that followed the CIA has substantially beefed up its paramilitary side, recruiting heavily within the military special operations community.[35] Today, the CIA is widely reported to engage in raids against high-value terrorist targets, and is reportedly responsible for scores—possibly hundreds—of drone strikes.[36]

Officially, none of this is happening. Or, rather, although U.S. officials are happy enough to take credit for turning live terrorists into dead terrorists, the U.S. government officially insists, "Whether or not the CIA has the authority to be, or is in fact, directly involved in targeted lethal operations remains classified." What's more, asserts a 2012 Justice Department legal brief, "Notwithstanding widespread reports that drone strikes occur, the CIA has never confirmed or denied whether it has any involvement or intelligence interest in any of those drone strikes."[37]

In response to Freedom of Information Act requests for records relating to drone strikes, the CIA itself has been unambiguously ambiguous. Writing to the ACLU, for instance, the CIA's Information and Privacy Coordinator offered only a stock response: "The CIA can neither confirm nor deny the existence or nonexistence of records responsive to your request. The fact of the existence or nonexistence of requested records is currently and properly classified."[38]

So is the CIA conducting lethal drone strikes, or not? The investigative journalism group Pro Publica has compiled a list of press reports in which "anonymous senior" officials have discussed those reported CIA drone strikes, together with seemingly confirmatory quotes from several people who ought to know, including former secretary of defense and former CIA director Leon Panetta and President Obama.

In 2009, for instance, then CIA director Panetta responded to a reporter's question about CIA drone strikes by saying, "These operations have been very effective. . . . I can assure you that in terms of that particular area, it is very precise, and it is very limited in terms of collateral damage, and, very frankly, it's the only game in town in terms of confronting and trying to disrupt the al-Qaeda leadership."[39]

Two years later, after taking over the helm at DoD, Panetta cheerfully told a military audience, "Having moved from the CIA to the Pentagon, obviously I have a hell of a lot more weapons available to me in this job than I had at the CIA, although the Predators weren't bad."[40]

What happens when activities that are officially covert become so extensive and sustained that they effectively move into the overt world? We know *someone* is using drones to go after Pakistani militants, and the U.S. military insists that it's not them. After a decade of drone strikes and dead bodies, it gets harder and harder to insist that what the CIA is doing is covert. As former director of national intelligence Dennis Blair put it in December 2011, "Covert action that goes on for years doesn't generally stay covert. . . . If something has been going for a long period of time, somebody else ought to do it, not intelligence agencies."[41]

But even as covert CIA lethal activities appear to have become more and more overt, more and more military activities appear to be moving into the covert realm. In particular, the role of special operations forces—Navy SEALs, Army Green Berets, Air Force Special Tactics, and the like—has dramatically expanded in recent years,[42] and special operations forces are increasingly engaging in activities designed to remain unattributable and unacknowledged.[43]

After 9/11, the expansion of special operations forces activities was virtually inevitable. America's conventional general-purpose forces are fantastically good with tanks and artillery and moving large numbers of people and machines from one place to another, and as the 1991 Gulf War demonstrated, they can roll over enemy armies with ease. But as we know, terrorist organizations don't fight like conventional armies. They eschew uniforms and traditional military command structures and rely instead on stealth, subterfuge, and asymmetrical attack. They blend easily into local civilian populations. As a result, they often confound American conventional forces.

Special operations forces, in contrast, were designed to handle unconventional threats. Various organizations within the SOF community emphasize different skills. SEALs take pride in their ability to conduct lightning raids on high-value targets. The raid on Osama bin Laden's compound is a classic example. Army Special Forces emphasize their ability to keep a low profile and work closely with foreign armed forces, something that takes sophisticated linguistic and cultural skills as well as all-around military expertise. Other organizations within the SOF community bring their own unique skills to the table—including, not coincidentally, skills related to the operation of armed drones.

Put all these skills together, and you have a group of military personnel with precisely the skills needed for the long war. No surprise, then, that both the Bush and Obama administrations have come to rely heavily on special operations forces. Army Special Forces worked closely with CIA officers to help Afghanistan's Northern Alliance defeat the Taliban in the fall of 2001, and SEALs—again in close coordination with the CIA—played a crucial role during Operation Anaconda.

Since those early post-9/11 days, special operations forces have played an ever-larger role in an expanding number of countries. SOF personnel embedded in over a dozen U.S. embassies conduct counterterrorism-related information operations, and SOF personnel embedded with foreign militaries continue to serve as trainers and advisors. Special Operators can offer quiet assistance to foreign governments interested in capturing or killing terrorists in their territory, and, if necessary, they can take direct action themselves. As a result, they have increasingly been relied upon to capture or kill suspected terrorists outside of hot battlefields, both through quick cross-border raids and through the use of drone strikes.

Much of the time, their precise role is—of necessity—kept secret. Foreign governments may want U.S. military help, but only if they can deny any American role. And when military operations raise difficult questions about sovereignty, keeping them secret is often less diplomatically embarrassing for all concerned. Still other military activities rely on secrecy even more directly. For instance, some foreign information operations may be ineffective if everyone knows that a particular radio show or television program is U.S.-funded.

Of course, engaging in covert activities has traditionally been an intelligence community job, not a military job. The CIA and other intelligence agencies must report to the House and Senate select committees on intelligence, but the military reports to the armed services committees, and both the Pentagon and the armed services committees have a strong aversion to letting the intelligence committees horn in on their territory.

Regardless of who's doing what, all activity designated as "covert" requires a presidential finding and subsequent notification of the intelligence committee, even if just the so-called Gang of Eight: the Senate and House majority and minority leaders, and the chairs and ranking members of the House and Senate intelligence committees. This gives the Pentagon a strong incentive to insist that whatever it is that special operations forces are doing, they're *not* engaging in covert activities. Conveniently, the Intelligence Authorization Act, which lays out most of the rules for covert activities, exempts "traditional military activities" from its definition of covert action—though the definition and scope of "traditional military activities" remains hotly contested.[44]

In practice, military and CIA personnel generally work together quite closely when planning and engaging in drone strikes or raids. CIA and other intelligence agency personnel play a vital role in providing targeting information to military teams planning strikes, and military personnel are often detailed to assist with intelligence agency activities.

But the increasing fuzziness of the line between the intelligence community and the military creates confusion and uncertainty: Who decides which agency should take the lead, and on what basis? How are activities coordinated? What's the chain of command? What law governs each entity's activities? Does the CIA use the same targeting rules as the military? Does covert military activity risk depriving the military personnel involved of protection under the Geneva Conventions?

No one's saying.

The blurred lines also create a risk of "forum shopping," tempting the executive branch to place a given targeted strike under the direction and control of whichever entity is deemed to have the most accommodating congressional overseers. Give the CIA the formal lead on a particular operation and it need only be reported to the intelligence committees; give DoD the formal lead and, depending on the type of operation, it may be reported to the armed services committees, or not reported to anyone in Congress at all.[45]

All this also creates a strange irony. As the United States continues to expand its use of lethal force overseas, the CIA is fighting to insist that its alleged drone strikes are and must remain covert. At the same time, the Pentagon is fighting to insist that its secret special operations missions should *not* be categorized as covert action. In both cases, the intent—or at least the result—is to shield the activities at issue from scrutiny. The CIA wants to keep journalists and the ACLU off its back; the military mostly just wants the intelligence committees to leave it alone. The end result is the same: when the covert goes semi-overt, and the overt goes semi-covert, the public is left in the dark.

Just to add to the blurriness and complexity, many of the participants in America's secret war are neither military personnel nor CIA paramilitary officers but private contractors[46]—and the presence of contractors in the mix makes it even harder to decide if what we're looking at is war, or something else, and makes it difficult to know how to apply the law of armed conflict. Is a contractor who provides intelligence analysis that supports targeting decisions a combatant? A civilian participating in hostilities? Can he or she be lawfully targeted by U.S. adversaries? What rights and duties do contractors have?

The U.S. government's increasing reliance on private military and security contractors has been well documented, but it remains extremely difficult to get precise and detailed information about the number of contractors, the cost of contracted services, the specific functions contractors perform, and their fates. During the first Gulf War, fewer than ten thousand civilian contractors accompanied some 500,000 military personnel.[47] During the height of the Iraq and Afghanistan wars, contractors outnumbered U.S. troops. And they paid heavily: some estimates suggest that more contractors than troops were killed in those wars.[48]

## That's Classified

*Why* are most of the details about U.S.-targeted counterterrorism strikes—whether they involve military service members, paramilitary intelligence personnel, or paramilitary private contractors acting at the behest of the government—kept in the secret world?

I'll return to this subject later, but for now it's worth noting that the U.S. government has a long history of overclassifying information that shouldn't be classified at all—and keeping information classified until long after any justification for classifying it has disappeared.

My first government job was at the State Department, during the waning days of Bill Clinton's second administration. During that period, I recall reading top secret memo after top secret memo, all signed by the same senior colleague, all dealing with a particular issue.

I'd tell you what the issue was, but then, as we say, I'd have to kill you. Believe me, that's not because revealing it would do the slightest damage to national security. I'm keeping mum for one reason only: long ago, I signed a large number of terrifying forms swearing to donate my firstborn child to the Justice Department if ever I should reveal the contents of a classified document.

Aside from that, there's no reason for secrecy. Suffice it to say that those memos I remember from my time at the State Department contained absolutely no information worthy of a top secret designation. But I was young and inexperienced, so at the time I assumed I must be missing something. I finally worked up the courage to ask my senior colleague directly: "Why," I wondered tentatively, "are all these memos classified top secret? Is this issue more sensitive than meets the eye?"

His response was brisk and unapologetic. "No, not really, but if I don't put 'top secret' on my memos, people will think they're not important, and no one will bother to read them."

Since then, I've seen the same phenomenon over and over. To mix metaphors, classified information is the currency of the realm inside the national security sausage-making machine. It's the only way to be special.

You don't have a security clearance? You're no one. You only have a secret level clearance? I'm sorry, a top secret clearance is required for you to be part of this meeting. You have a top secret clearance? Regrettably, this document is part of a compartmented code word special access program and you're not read-in. In fact, it's part of a waived, unacknowledged special access program that only I and four other people can know about! Sorry 'bout that.

As the national security bureaucracy has expanded and more and more classified documents are produced, more and more people need security clearances in order to do their jobs. But as more and more people receive security clearances, the iron law of supply and demand kicks in, and the value of clearances goes down.

According to an excellent 2010 *Washington Post* series on "Top Secret America," an estimated 854,000 people hold top secret clearances.[49] That's not a very exclusive club: any secret that can be accessed by 854,000 people isn't much of a secret. Throw in the people with lower-level clearances and we get up to more than four million, or nearly 2 percent of the adult population of the United States.[50] Who let all those people into the club?

As a result, the government keeps finding new ways to distinguish between levels and types of access, and more and more documents and programs are reflexively given a high classification, even when there's really no secret to keep. The government's Information Security Oversight Office reported that 92 million decisions to classify information were made in 2011 alone, representing a 20 percent increase in classification decisions from 2010 and a 40 percent increase from 2009.[51]

And as I said, this problem isn't new. A 2011 report by the Brennan Center for Justice offers some choice glimpses into history. By 1956, only a decade and a half after an executive order signed by Franklin Roosevelt launched the modern classification system, a DoD panel was already warning that "overclassification has reached serious proportions." In 1970, a Defense Science Board task force reported that "the volume of scientific and technical information that is classified could profitably be decreased by perhaps as much as 90 percent." In 1985, yet another DoD committee concluded that "too much information appears to be classified." In 1994, a joint CIA-DoD commission found that "the classification system . . . has grown out of control."[52]

Fast-forward to the 9/11 Commission's report, which was every bit as damning: "Current security requirements nurture overclassification and excessive compartmentation of information among agencies."[53] Even more recently, the congressionally established Public Interest Declassification Board (PIDB) concluded, in a November 2012 report, "The system is compromised by over-classification and, not coincidentally, by increasing instances of unauthorized disclosures."[54]

Documents overclassified by government employees range from the embarrassing and illegal to the merely goofy. According to the Brennan Center report, FBI efforts to "completely discredit" Martin Luther King Jr. "as the leader of the Negro people" were classified, as were government radiation experiments involving human subjects. Ditto, oddly, a 1940s Navy study on sharks attacking human beings.

A 2003 report by the National Security Archive notes that during a 1999 declassification review, a CIA employee even redacted a portion of a tongue-in-cheek 1974 memo dealing with a fictitious effort by an "organization of uncertain makeup, under the name of 'Group of the Martyr Ebenezer Scrooge' . . . to sabotage the annual courier flight of the government of the North Pole. Prime Minister and Chief Courier S. Claus has been notified."[55]

Closely linked to the problem of overclassification is the failure of government officials to declassify documents when the need for secrecy is over. In theory, most classified documents are classified for ten years or less, after which they are "automatically" declassified. Under a Clinton-era executive order those exceptional documents classified for longer periods must be "automatically" declassified after twenty-five years.[56]

But as report after report has demonstrated, "automatic" declassification is usually anything but. Agencies can review documents subject to "automatic" declassification to ensure that they don't fall into any exceptions to declassification, and agencies lack the authority to declassify information initially classified by other agencies. As a result, the "automatic" declassification process can take years. In the era of electronic information, documents of all kinds have proliferated, worsening the backload still more.[57]

. . .

Ironically, our government's tendency to overclassify information—and the sheer complexity of the rules for dealing with classified information—ends up increasing the number of cases involving the mishandling or unauthorized disclosure of classified information. Those with security clearances are obligated to abide by a confusing, arbitrary, and ridiculously cumbersome set of rules to safeguard classified material, but the rules are so incoherent that even the most conscientious employees tend to fall afoul of them at one time or another.

Find someone you know who has a security clearance, and ask him or her the following questions:

Can you swear that you never discussed classified information outside of a Sensitive Compartmented Information Facility, or never, ever wandered out of a meeting held at a classified level with some notes you really shouldn't have taken jotted down on your totally unclassified legal pad? Can you swear that you never sat down at home to draft an outline of a memo on classified issues because you were struck by an important insight at 10 p.m. and feared you might forget it, but didn't want to go all the way back to the office to write it down? That you never discussed an interesting issue with a colleague who had a clearance but probably no real "need to know"? Or that you never scribbled your randomly generated eighteen-character computer password on a Post-it because you just could not seem to commit it to memory, no matter how hard you tried?

If they're being honest, most people with security clearances will start looking a little red in the face.

I remember a particularly surreal period during my stint at the Defense Department. When the first WikiLeaks cables became public, every media outlet in the world began quoting from the leaked documents. At the Pentagon, however, we were all warned not to even read any of those stories quoting leaked documents, because classified documents remain classified even if they're splashed all over the front page of the *New York Times.*[58] Thus, anyone who read media quotes from any leaked classified documents above his or her clearance level was accessing unauthorized information.

Even those who had clearances higher than those needed to see any secret cables (most of which were, at the time, easily accessible on classified networks to anyone with a secret-level clearance) were forbidden from reading the media reports online, because if the news reports did contain any classified information, looking at them would constitute the unauthorized downloading of classified material onto unclassified government or private computers.

This was a head-scratcher, particularly for anyone charged with dealing in any way with the media or the public. It forced the frequent use of bizarre circumlocutions to avoid accidentally messing up: "If it is the case that classified information is contained in a *Washington Post* article, a fact I can neither confirm nor deny, that would be a security breach, and we certainly wish people would not read or discuss any such material that might or might not be genuine and might or might not be classified."

As I noted earlier, some classified material obviously *should* be kept secret. Even the most ardent WikiLeaks supporter might accept that launch codes for U.S. nuclear weapons don't belong in the public domain, and the claim that we need to protect "intelligence sources and methods" isn't a frivolous one. Some of the intelligence the United States collects comes from individuals who pass information at great personal risk. Even when the information itself has little value to the United States, revealing that we have it can lead foreign organizations to identify our source—sometimes with lethal consequences.

The problem, of course, is that from the outside there's no way for a reporter or a citizen to know for sure: Is access restricted because it contains information that, if revealed, could truly harm the nation? Or is access restricted to cover up crime, fraud, or stupidity, or to make an uninteresting issue seem more important, or help a midlevel bureaucrat gain status?

# CHAPTER SIX

# Future Warfare

The murkiness surrounding war and the military isn't likely to dissipate. If anything, many just-around-the corner technologies and trends are likely to increase the perceived military benefits of secrecy and further erode the lines between the world of war and the world of peace. It would take many books to describe all these trends, but consider just a few: our increasing global reliance on the Internet, advances in robotics, and the emergence of autonomous weapons systems; and the conjunction of precision weapons, bioengineering, and mass data collection (along with easily accessible tools for analyzing all that data, such as facial recognition programs). Consider also what the evolution of what the military calls "nonlethal" weapons: technologies designed to incapacitate or control without killing.

## War in Cyberspace

In suburban Maryland, hundreds of young men and women sit at computer terminals. They're "cyberwarriors," assigned to the military's newest combatant command, Cyber Command (or CYBERCOM, which is conveniently located in the same compound as the National Security Agency). CYBERCOM's task: protect America's Internet infrastructure from all enemies, whether they be teenage hackers in Romania, Chinese government spies, or Islamic terrorists. If necessary, America's cyberwarriors can go on the offensive, monitoring, disrupting, or destroying the cyber capabilities of others.

Most of these young American cyberwarriors have never heard

a gun fired in anger; many have never left the United States. They're trained in information technology, not in hand-to-hand combat. Yet the lines of code they produce have the potential to disable Russian websites, sow confusion within ISIS and al Qaeda, or even, according to press reports, damage centrifuges in Iran.

It goes beyond computer code. One summer day a few years back, I visited a small, unmarked office building in an anonymous Maryland strip mall. Inside, the rooms were always kept dimly lit: for security reasons, the shades were always kept down, and the windows were made of special glass, designed to foil electronic eavesdropping. The men and women who worked in these dim rooms were pleased to have a visitor from "mission control," as someone jokingly called the Pentagon—they were glad to show off their clever technological tricks.

I can't tell you what any of those tricks are: they're the most secret kind of secret, since if any bad guys came to know about them, they wouldn't work anymore. But just imagine. Imagine the things you think you already *know* the NSA can do, thanks to Edward Snowden and press reports, and multiply that. Imagine we had the ability to take technologies our adversaries trust and turn them to our own uses.

That's the sort of thing CYBERCOM and a handful of other small Defense Department and intelligence organizations exist to do. It's not just about protecting email and financial software, or monitoring websites used by U.S. adversaries. Some of it's even more sophisticated and surprising. But in a world in which more and more things—from our alarm clocks and our cars to our home security systems and cell phones—are (or can be) connected to the Internet—more and more things can also be manipulated and controlled from afar. You can bet American adversaries are developing similar technologies to use against us too.

We assume that "war" involves physical violence. For this reason, military recruitment and training still emphasize physical strength and fitness. But today's military is also preparing for a possible future in which "battles" take place mainly in cyberspace, and "winning" or "losing" may have little or nothing to do with threats to life, limb, or property. Cyber battles will most likely be about information and control: Who will have access to sensitive health, personal, and financial information about individuals—individuals who may, in some cases, make key individuals vulnerable to blackmail? Who will be able to control the machinery of daily life: the servers relied upon by the Pentagon and the New York Stock Exchange, the computers that keep our cars' brakes from activating at the wrong time, the software that runs our household computers?

We might have decided to view cybersecurity as a purely civilian issue, and conceptualized both current and future cyber "attacks" as criminal matters. But as with humanitarian assistance, rule of law programs, strategic communication, and so much else, the military has jumped in to fill the vacuum created by squabbling and under-resourced civilian agencies. CYBER Command and the National Security Agency, both of which are under the command of the same four-star military officer, have become America's primary cyber offense and defense agencies. Technically, the Department of Homeland Security is the lead agency for defending U.S. cyber infrastructure, but budget figures tell a different story: the 2016 budget request for DoD's cybersecurity activities—not including those carried out by the NSA, which has a separate, classified budget—was over $5 billion, while Homeland Security's 2016 cyber budget request was just $1.4 billion.[1]

The emerging era of cyberwar also creates new legal puzzles. If cyberattacks can be a form of "warfare," what law should apply? International law on this question remains unsettled, but the government has already staked out a position: cyber operations are subject to the law of armed conflict, and any cyberattacks that cause injury, death, or "significant destruction" could be considered "armed attacks" for legal purposes, triggering, among other things, a legal right to retaliate using conventional armed force. But this still leaves numerous unanswered questions. In the "real" world, distinguishing between civilians and combatants and civilian versus military infrastructure is hard enough. In the cyber world, it can be nearly impossible.

## The Individualization of Warfare

If we have traditionally conceived of war as violent, we have also traditionally tended to think of it as impersonal. As we have seen, however, improved surveillance technologies and precision targeting technologies have already begun to "individualize" warfare, primarily through targeted drone strikes. In the future, this trend will continue: more and more, we will see highly individualized "attacks" on specific individuals, in addition to—or in place of—impersonal assaults on "enemy forces." This too will further blur the boundaries around "war."

Consider the world of big data and the world of bioscience.

On the Internet, more and more data is available about more and more people. Governments keep census data online; banks keep financial data; hospitals keep health data; Amazon.com keeps purchasing date; social media sites keep our photos, videos, and personal musings. Data from cell phone cameras and security cameras is stored in the cloud. Add in rapidly improving facial and voice recognition software and rapidly advancing data analysis technologies, and it will soon be possible (and probably quite cheap) to build up detailed dossiers on half the people on earth. As former Air Force deputy judge advocate general Charles Dunlap notes in a recent article on what he calls "the hyper-personalization of war," these capabilities are rapidly being militarized: "In the not-too distant future, the U.S. military—and likely other militaries—will be able to launch swarms of drones equipped with facial recognition software to roam battlefields looking for very specific members of an enemy's force."[2]

In the bioscience world, breakthroughs in our understanding of genetics are opening up the possibility of personalized medicine: cancer treatments tailored to a specific person's genetic code, for instance. But the same discoveries that may soon allow doctors to tailor life-saving treatments to the needs of specific individuals may also allow the development of DNA-linked bioweapons: a virus designed to disable or kill only a specific individual.

In some ways, the individualization of warfare may be a good thing. Targeted killings may be troublingly intimate, but they are surely better than indiscriminate killings. The law of war obligates parties to a conflict to avoid the intentional targeting of civilians and take all reasonable measures to avoid causing incidental civilian deaths, and the technologies that enable the individualization of warfare represent significant leaps forward in our ability to ensure that wars kill as few people as possible. Compared to the firebombing of Dresden or the dropping of the atom bomb on Hiroshima, weapons capable of killing only specific individuals seem like a moral advance. Wouldn't it be nice if we could spare frightened young conscripts and kill only their bloodthirsty leaders, or target only terrorist masterminds and the architects of genocidal campaigns, sparing those with lesser culpability and influence?

Indeed, the individualization of warfare raises the possibility that warfare itself will be utterly transformed, becoming, as Harvard Law School's Gabriella Blum suggests, more like policing, with its focus on individual harms, individual victims, and individual culpability.[3] When individual malefactors can be reliably taken off the field, there's no reason to send hundreds of thousands of soldiers off to fight their counterparts in foreign lands. As warfare becomes more individualized, it may also become possible to add to warfare some of the due process protections common in law enforcement.

We take it for granted that soldiers can't be expected to prove probable cause or obtain warrants from a judge before taking prisoners on a battlefield, much less provide evidence that proves a suspected combatant's enemy status "beyond a reasonable doubt" before using lethal force. In the context of, say, the invasion of Normandy, it makes perfect sense to accept a "shoot first, ask questions later" standard. But why couldn't we have a different standard for different types of "battlefields"? In the context of targeted drone strikes, for instance, those we target have often been on kill lists for weeks or even years before the opportunity to kill them arises. In such a context, a modified judicial or quasi-judicial enquiry couldn't get in the way. On the contrary: greater due process could offer needed legitimacy. The individualization of warfare thus has the potential to bring war more in line with core human rights norms.

Today, individualized killing technologies are still the prerogative of only the wealthiest and most technologically advanced states. But this will change. Al Qaeda, ISIS, and other malignant nonstate actors are already attuned to the emerging possibilities of personalized warfare. In 2007, for instance, terrorist sympathizers hacked into the email and telephone records of Danish soldiers serving in Afghanistan, and used the information to harass and intimidate service members' families.[4]

More recently, an Islamic State website posted the names and home addresses of selected U.S. military personnel and their families in March 2015, urging "our brothers in America" to "take the final step" of killing them.[5] Drone technologies and facial recognition technologies are commercially available already, and will become steadily more sophisticated; bioscience information, techniques, and materials also will become increasingly available to individuals and small groups. Even if we believe our own government will use these technologies responsibly—not a foregone conclusion—there's little reason to imagine others will do so.

The individualization of warfare also raises some dismaying Orwellian possibilities. Andrew Hessel, Marc Goodman, and Steven Kotler noted in a 2012 *Atlantic* article that DNA-linked bioweapons may usher in a future in which "politicians, celebrities, leaders of industry—just about anyone, really—could be vulnerable to attack-by-disease." Some attacks might be geared toward sowing disruption: imagine a targeted bioweapon that could dramatically degrade cognitive functioning. "Even if fatal," Hessel, Goodman, and Kotler argue, "many such attacks could go undetected, mistaken for death by natural causes; many others would be difficult to pin on a suspect, especially given the passage of time between exposure and the appearance of symptoms."[6]

Writing in the seventeenth century, Thomas Hobbes famously asserted that humanity's original "state of nature" must have been a "warre of all against all." The growing individualization of warfare suggests that this may be our all too real future, as well as our imagined past.

## Killer Robots

Or perhaps future wars won't involve humans at all. Perhaps we will leave war to the robots.

Today, the overwhelming majority of even our most advanced weapons technologies still require humans in the loop. There are a few relatively minor exceptions: some missile defense systems are programmed to fire immediately if an incoming missile fits certain preset parameters, for instance, since once an incoming missile is detected it may impact in seconds, with too little time for a human to decide how to respond. But these situations are exceptional. For the most part, humans still make the important calls. Predator drones can't decide for themselves whom to kill: it takes a human being—often dozens of human beings in a complex multiagency command chain—to decide that it's both legal and wise to launch missiles at a given target.

In the not so distant future, this could change. Imagine robots programmed not only to detect and disarm roadside bombs but to track and fire upon individuals concealing or emplacing IEDs. Or imagine an unmanned vehicle that can fire missiles when a computer determines that a given individual is behaving like a combatant, based on a preprogrammed set of criteria. Or imagine tiny insect-sized nano-drones that operate in "combat clouds" or swarms, remaining in constant real-time communication with one another and instantly modifying their flight paths and making decisions about targeting based not on human intervention, but on software instructions. Advances in artificial intelligence make this a real possibility—and the fact that other states, including some U.S. adversaries, are pursuing research into such weapons systems means that the United States may have to do the same, for purely defensive purposes: human reaction time won't be able to keep pace with machine reaction time.

A growing number of ethicists and rights advocates are troubled by this. Indeed, some are calling for a global ban on the development, production, and use of fully autonomous weapons systems, which are, according to Human Rights Watch, "also"—and rather conveniently— "known as killer robots."[7]

The term does tend to have a chilling effect even upon those harboring a soft spot for R2-D2 and WALL·E. I'm less concerned, however: not because I'm fond of killer robots, but because I'm inclined to think ethicists and rights advocates are far too generous in their assumptions about human beings.

Their core concern relates to military research into weapons systems that are "fully autonomous," meaning that they can "select and engage targets without human intervention." According to the Campaign to Stop Killer Robots, this is troubling because, first, such killer robots might not have the ability to abide by the legal obligation to distinguish between combatants and civilians, and second, "Allowing life or death decisions to be made by machines crosses a fundamental moral line" and jeopardizes fundamental principles of "human dignity."[8]

Neither of these arguments persuades me. Granted, the thought of a robot firing indiscriminately into a crowd is dismaying, as is the thought of a rogue robot, sparks flying from every rusting joint, going berserk and turning its futuristic super-weapons upon its own "side." But setting science fiction aside, real-life computers have an excellent track record. When was the last time Siri staged a rebellion and began to systematically delete all your favorite videos, just to mess with you? When was the last time a passenger plane's autopilot system got depressed and decided to plow into a mountain, notwithstanding human entreaties to remain airborne?

Computers may be far *better* than human beings at complying with international humanitarian law. After all, we humans are fragile and panicky creatures, easily flustered by the fog of war. Our eyes face only one direction; our ears register only certain frequencies; our brains can process only so much information at a time. Loud noises make us jump, and fear floods our bodies with powerful chemicals that can temporarily distort our perceptions and judgment.

As a result, we make mistakes in war, and we make them all the time. We misjudge distances; we forget instructions, we misconstrue gestures. We mistake cameras for weapons, shepherds for soldiers, friends for enemies, schools for barracks, and wedding parties for terrorist convoys.

In fact, we humans have historically been quite bad at distinguishing between combatants and civilians, even in traditional conflicts between the militaries of opposing states. Even when we manage to correctly distinguish between civilians and combatants, we often make risk-averse calculations about necessity and proportionality, preferring dead civilians to dead comrades. If the U.S. conflicts in Iraq and Afghanistan produced a surfeit of dead and mangled civilians, it's not because of killer robots, it's because of fallible human decision making.

Computers, in contrast, are excellent in crisis and combat situations. They don't get mad, they don't get scared, and they don't act out of sentimentality. They're exceptionally good at processing vast amounts of information in a short time and rapidly applying appropriate decision rules. Missile approaching, with impact projected in nineteen seconds? For humans, that's not much time, but nineteen seconds is an eon for a computer. Computers aren't perfect, but they're a good deal less flawed than those of us cursed with organic circuitry.

We assure ourselves that we humans have special qualities no machine can replicate: we have "judgment" and "intuition," for instance. Maybe, but computers often seem to have *better* judgment. This has already been demonstrated in dozens of different domains, from aviation to anesthesiology. Computers turn out to be better than humans at distinguishing between genuine and faked expressions of pain; Google's driverless cars fare better at avoiding accidents than cars controlled by humans.[9] Given a choice between relying on a human to comply with international humanitarian law and relying on a well-designed, well-programmed robot, I'd take my chances with the killer robot any day.

Opponents of autonomous weapons ask whether there's a legal and ethical obligation to refrain from letting machines make decisions about who should live and who should die. If it turns out, as it may, that machines are better than people at applying the principles of international humanitarian law, we may end up having to ask an entirely different question: Might there be a legal and ethical *obligation* to use "killer robots" in lieu of "killer humans"?

Confronted with arguments about the technological superiority of computers over human brains, those opposed to the development of autonomous weapons systems argue that such consequentialist reasoning is insufficient. Ultimately, as a 2014 joint report by Human Rights Watch and Harvard's International Human Rights Clinic argues, it would simply be "morally wrong" to give machines the power to "decide" who lives and who dies: "As inanimate machines, fully autonomous weapons could truly comprehend neither the value of individual life nor the significance of its loss. Allowing them to make determinations to take life away would thus conflict with the principle of [human] dignity."[10]

I suppose the idea is that any self-respecting person would naturally prefer death at the hands of a fellow member of the human species—someone capable of feeling "compassion" and "mercy"—to death inflicted by a cold, unfeeling machine.

But death is death, and I don't imagine it gives the dying any consolation to know their human killer is capable of feeling bad about the whole affair.

We shouldn't romanticize our own species. We humans are capable of mercy and compassion, but we also have a remarkable propensity for violence and cruelty. We're a species that kills for pleasure: every year, more than half a million people around the globe die as a result of intentional violence, and many more are injured, starved, or deliberately deprived of shelter, medicine, or other essentials. In the United States alone, more than fourteen thousand people are murdered each year, and many more are the victims of other violent crimes.[11] Humans, not robots, came up with such ingenious ideas as torture and death by crucifixion. Humans, not robots, came up with the idea of firebombing Dresden and Tokyo; humans, not robots, planned the Holocaust and the Rwandan genocide.

Plug in the right lines of code, and robots will dutifully abide by the laws of armed conflict to the best of their technological ability. In this sense, "killer robots" may be capable of behaving far more humanely than we might assume. But the flip side is also true: humans can behave far more like machines than we generally assume.

In the 1960s, experiments by Yale psychologist Stanley Milgram demonstrated the fearful ease with which ordinary humans could be persuaded to inflict pain on complete strangers; since then, other psychologists have refined and extended his work.[12] If you want to "program" an ordinary human being to participate in genocide, both history and social psychology suggest that it's not much more difficult than creating a new iPhone app.

Admittedly, I'm assuming we'll have robots that obey the instructions we humans give them. Many of the alarmist scenarios involving autonomous weapons systems make the opposite assumption, however, envisioning intelligent, autonomous robots that decide to override the code that created them, and turn upon us all.

But when the robots go rogue—when lust for blood, money, or power begins to guide their actions—they'll have ceased to be robots in any meaningful sense. They'll finally be able to pass the Turing Test. For all intents and purposes, they will have become humans—and it's humans we've had reason to fear, all along.

## Nonlethal Weapons

If we fought a war with weapons that did no permanent physical harm to our enemies, would they still be weapons, and would it still be a war? The advent of cyberwar forces us to ask this question, but similar questions also arise when we consider advances in "nonlethal weapons."

The military is already experimenting with a number of technologies that can incapacitate or control enemies without causing injury or death. For instance, there's the "active denial technology," which can shoot a focused beam of radio frequency millimeter waves at a frequency of 95 gigahertz toward a specific area. "Traveling at the speed of light, the millimeter wave directed energy engages the subject, penetrating the skin to a depth of only about 1/64th of an inch, or the equivalent of three sheets of paper," asserts a Defense Department fact sheet.[13] Three painful sheets of paper: anyone caught in the beam will feel a sudden, searing heat all over his or her body, making further forward movement impossible; one's natural instinct will be to move out of range. Once out of the beam, the sensation of unbearable heat immediately ceases, with no permanent ill effects—not even a bruise or burn.

The value of such technology to the military is obvious. As the DoD fact sheet explains:

Active Denial technology can be used for both force application and force protection missions. Applications include crowd control, patrol and convoy protection, perimeter security and other defensive and offensive operations from both fixed-site or mobile platforms. Non-lethal directed energy weapons using Active Denial Technology have the potential to provide a non-lethal effects at distances up to and beyond small arms range, providing U.S. military forces with additional time and space to assess the intent of potential adversaries.

Imagine, for instance, U.S. troops on patrol in an area that has seen multiple insurgent ambushes. Suddenly, a figure bursts out of an alleyway and races toward the patrol vehicles. Troops have only a split second to decide how to react: is the figure a local teen running from an angry parent, or a suicide bomber who will detonate his vest as soon as he's close enough? Soldiers armed only with lethal weapons will tend to shoot first and ask questions later, but soldiers equipped with non-lethal directed energy weapons can stop the figure before he gets close enough to cause harm, and let him go if he poses no threat.

Similarly, improved "flash-bang" grenades can temporarily disorient adversaries, using light and sound to create transient blindness and deafness. The new flash-bang grenades can be thrown by hand, and another variant can be fired through existing mortar tubes from a distance of up to a kilometer. In the future, these nonlethal mortar rounds may also "paint" those caught near detonations with infrared or ultraviolent ink, invisible to the naked eye, but easily detected by U.S. troops trying to track enemies escaping through crowded city streets.[14] Other emerging technologies fire lasers that cause temporary blindness, or high-powered radio waves that can cause vehicle engines to stall.[15]

As with technologies that enable the individualization of warfare, these nonlethal weapons have the potential to make warfare less bloody. Enemies can be incapacitated, disarmed, and detained instead of killed, and the failure to distinguish accurately between civilians and combatants will do no permanent harm.

But here too, the evolution and expansion of warfare raises distinctly Orwellian possibilities. Imagine the development of nonlethal DNA-linked bioweapons that cause hallucinations or crippling schizophrenia symptoms, aimed at political, economic, or military leaders, for instance. Or imagine linking nonlethal weapons to individualization technologies and distance warfare technologies in other ways. A world in which swarms of miniaturized drones with facial recognition software can seek out and incapacitate specific individuals in a crowd will be a world in which suicide bombers can be stopped in their tracks—but also a world in which repressive governments can exercise near-total control over dissenters. It will be a world in which lines between the worlds of war and peace will no longer exist.

It will be a brave new world, for sure.

# CHAPTER SEVEN

# What's an Army For?

It's raining in the Kuwaiti desert.

It's not supposed to rain in the desert, and the downpour is snarling traffic, flooding barracks, and leaving military vehicles sodden and afloat at Camp Arifjan, the forward headquarters of U.S. Army Central and Kuwait's largest American base. "I guess no one thought it was important to have good drainage in the middle of the desert," Colonel William Eubank tells me glumly. Eubank, the commander of Kuwait's Area Support Group, is the man in charge of keeping everything up and running at Arifjan and nearby Camp Buehring, which together housed some twelve thousand soldiers when I visited in 2014—the largest concentration of deployed Army personnel outside of Afghanistan, Germany, and South Korea. It's no easy task, particularly when many of those soldiers seem to have no clear idea what they're doing in Kuwait.

"So what are you guys doing here?" I ask the young private behind me in line at Camp Arifjan's spacious Starbucks. "I mean, in Kuwait. What's your mission here?"

He offers a sheepish shrug. "Got me, ma'am. That's above my pay grade. I'm just trying to stay dry."

"Ours not to wonder why, ours but to try and stay dry," quips the lieutenant in front of him, carefully maneuvering a lid onto his overflowing cup of caramel latte.

• • •

In an age in which even the lowest-ranking soldiers are expected to be able to understand and articulate U.S. strategic goals, "Got me!" is of course the wrong answer to journalistic queries. It has the distinct virtue of honesty, however: as the boundaries of war grow ever blurrier and the tasks we assign to the military grow ever more varied, the U.S. military is increasingly struggling to understand and articulate its own role. For the Army—America's largest service and the historical center of America's military—the problem is particularly acute. The Iraq War is over, the war in Afghanistan is winding down, and Washington's budget cutters are sharpening their knives. In a world of cyber operations, pirates, humanitarian missions, and high-tech unmanned aerial vehicles, the Army is struggling to define—and defend—its role and mission.

Why *should* the United States Army keep roughly twelve thousand soldiers stationed in peacetime Kuwait? And, more broadly, why does a nation so seemingly determined to avoid another land war need a large standing Army, with troops deployed all over the world? Won't the conflicts of the future be better suited to the Navy and Air Force, with their drones and computers and other technologically advanced toys, than to the Army's 540,000 grunts, with their tanks, rucksacks, and muddy boots?

Former Army chief of staff General Raymond Odierno thought he could answer those questions—and whether they knew it or not, the twelve thousand soldiers stationed in Kuwait were part of his ambitious effort to reimagine the Army of the future.

Odierno, who served as Army chief of staff from 2011 until his retirement in 2015, believed that the Army's future lies in regionally aligned forces: Army units—from whole divisions down to the small-unit level—that will have long-term relationships with particular geographic combatant commands and perhaps even with particular subregions and countries, such as the Gulf States or Kuwait. These regionally aligned forces—or RAF, since the Army instinctively acronymizes everything from meals to weapons—will receive significant region-specific linguistic and cultural training, making them more effective across the entire "spectrum of conflict"—and better able to stay well to the left of boom.

More culturally attuned soldiers will be better equipped to identify brewing conflicts *before* they get out of hand, enabling more timely and effective "shaping" and deterrence activities. "Shaping" means activities designed to make conditions favorable for U.S. military success, and can include efforts to influence local populations, establish friendly relations with host populations and local leaders, strengthen military-to-military cooperation, and the like. If conflict breaks out, soldiers with a deeper understanding of local cultural dynamics will have both a better understanding of the enemy and a greater ability to work effectively with the host population, making tactical, operational, and strategic success more likely.

"Before the most recent set of conflicts," wrote Odierno in March 2012, "it was generally believed that cultural awareness was only required in select Army units, such as Special Forces."[1] Most units in the general purpose force were deployed without regard to building up regional expertise. Thus, a brigade could find itself in Korea one year, Iraq two years after that, Germany a few years later, and then in Afghanistan. Implicit in this force management system was the assumption that "military skills" exist in a realm outside of culture, and local populations are mostly just background noise.

Like many others in his generation of senior officers, Odierno—who spent four years commanding troops in Iraq—learned the hard way that military skills don't exist in a cultural vacuum. "We went in there with a complete misunderstanding—regionally and inside Iraq—of what was going on," he told me, shaking his head at the memory. "I don't ever want that to happen again."[2] The U.S.-led military coalition easily defeated Saddam Hussein's conventional forces, but lack of cultural, linguistic, and political understanding consistently hampered efforts to restore stability and comprehend the insurgency's roots, structure, and asymmetrical tactics. Meanwhile, many American successes in Iraq hinged on painstaking efforts to build up cultural knowledge: mapping clan and family relationships turned out to be key to identifying Saddam Hussein's hiding place, for instance.[3]

The regionally aligned forces concept represents the Army's effort to lock in the lessons of Iraq and Afghanistan, on a global scale. We don't know which threats will prove most serious in the future, and we don't know which part of the world will give rise to the most serious threats—so to leaders like Odierno and his successors, the best way to hedge against risk is for the Army to align forces to *every* geographic region. No one can be an expert on every region, speak every language, or develop strong personal ties with people in every country—but aligning Army units with each geographic Combatant Command increases the odds that the United States will have at least *some* knowledgeable forces able to predict, prevent, and respond effectively to future crises.

The concept of regionally aligned forces represents an ambitious effort to rethink the Army's role and mission in the uncertain, globalized post-post-9/11 world. It's an effort to take a large, clumsy, industrial behemoth and turn it into an agile, regionally engaged, globally responsive, and culturally sophisticated force—one that's more Mao than Bismarck, and more T. E. Lawrence than George Patton.

It's also smart marketing for the Army at a moment when budget cutters in the executive branch and on the Hill are sharpening their knives. "There are many people that believe that through technology advancement, we can solve all of the issues of warfare," Odierno commented. "I absolutely reject that concept. . . . Human interaction in a complex environment is key to our success in the future." The United States needs a force that is "skilled in understanding the physical, cognitive, the information, cultural and social environments we have to operate in the future."

There's a not so subtle subtext here: the Navy and Air Force can brag all they want about their technologically sophisticated systems, but you can't build human relationships from the deck of an aircraft carrier or the simulated cockpit of a Predator drone. Building relationships on a global scale requires putting human beings on the ground in regions all over the world—and only the Army has the manpower to do this.

Nevertheless, formidable obstacles stand in the way of the Army's vision for regionally aligned forces. Some of those obstacles are external: to succeed with their plans for regional alignment, Army leaders will need buy-in from the other services, the State Department, the White House, and the Hill, and getting that is far from a foregone conclusion. But many of the obstacles are internal: the Army may not resemble an aircraft carrier in most ways, but it shares an aircraft carrier's inability to make rapid turns. Any effort to rethink long-standing practices generates anxiety, confusion, and bureaucratic resistance.

It's like the old joke:

"How many psychiatrists does it take to change a light bulb?"

"Only one, but the light bulb has to *want* to change."

Senior Army leaders know that if the Army wants to remain relevant and useful, it *needs* to change.

But does it want to change?

## We're Not in Kansas Anymore

Before the regionally aligned forces concept was developed, recalls Odierno, geographic combatant commanders would complain about the unpredictability and inefficiency of the military's byzantine global force management system: combatant commanders never knew precisely what forces would be made available to them, and couldn't count on being able to access the capabilities they considered most useful in their region. The problem was particularly acute for AFRICOM, the neglected stepchild of the geographic combatant commands: with no assigned forces, the command often found itself last in line when troops were allocated.

But with the advent of regionally aligned forces, declared the *Army Times* in June 2013, "Everything you know about deployments is about to change." For smaller geographic combatant commands such as AFRICOM, RAF would create a reliable source of Army troops that could be drawn upon at will by the combatant commander. For individual soldiers, promised the *Army Times*, "The immersion in language, regional expertise and culture training will be the big difference. Indeed, units assigned to the new deployment model will quickly find themselves on the cutting edge of the 'human dimension' doctrine."[4]

The Army's efforts to operationalize the RAF concept started small, and in the middle of Kansas. At Fort Riley, the 1st Infantry Division's 2nd Brigade Combat Team (BCT)– the "Dagger Brigade"—was designated the Army's first regionally aligned brigade in spring 2012. The brigade and its several thousand soldiers "aligned" with Africa Command, the smallest and youngest of the military's geographic combatant commands (COCOMs).

In Kansas, Fort Riley's Dagger Brigade struggled to figure out what it meant to be "regionally aligned" to AFRICOM. With no template for how to increase their sociocultural knowledge, brigade leaders got creative, scrounging up African students and faculty experts on Africa at nearby Kansas State University. With their help, the brigade developed a training course for troops preparing to deploy.[5]

The training course was short—just a week long—but the brigade's regional deployments were also short: the brigade as a whole remained at Fort Riley, sending small units off for days or weeks at a time to train or conduct exercises with African partner forces. Two dozen soldiers from Fort Riley helped train Mali-bound U.N. peacekeeping troops in Niger; several hundred Dagger Brigade soldiers conducted exercises in South Africa; two Fort Riley snipers conducted a short-term mission in Burundi, and so on.

It wasn't "immersion," but the Army deemed this initial regional alignment experiment a success, and stepped up efforts to align forces to other geographic combatant commands. The 7th Infantry Division's 3-2 Stryker Brigade Combat Team has been aligned to the Pacific Command,[6] for instance, while the 1st Armored Division has been aligned to Central Command.[7] And this, Army officials say, is just the beginning.

## The Question of What Wars and Where Can Be Worked Out at Their Leisure

Outside Army circles, the regionally aligned forces concept generated little interest beyond a few media mentions.

Most were respectful, if slightly bemused. ("U.S. Army Hones Antiterror Strategy for Africa, in Kansas," the *New York Times* reported.)[8] On the left, however, RAF has been viewed as further evidence of the United States' sinister, hegemonic ambitions.

An article by Nick Turse in the *Nation* charged that "AFRICOM releases information about only a fraction of its activities . . . preferring to keep most information about what it's doing—and when and where—

secret." But, Turse continued, "previously undisclosed US Army Africa records reveal" that, in 2013, Fort Riley's Dagger Brigade took part in "128 separate 'activities' in twenty-eight African countries" as part of the Army's regionally aligned forces effort. "So much else . . . remains in the shadows," Turse wrote, including, he suggests, US training of coup plotters and war criminals. "It remains to be seen just what else we don't know about US Africa Command's exponentially expanding operations."[9]

On Antiwar.com,[10] a post by news editor Jason Ditz warned that "Gen. Raymond Odierno's 'Regionally Aligned Forces' plan [gives] the US the ability to quickly deploy troops anywhere on the planet. . . . With enough troops and enough countries involved, the question of what wars and where can be worked out at their leisure."

Lieutenant General James Terry, the commander of U.S. Army Central (ARCENT), shakes his head at the notion that anyone could view RAF as a sign of growing U.S. bellicosity. "After twelve years of war," he tells me, "I don't wish another protracted conflict on my grandkids. If we get regionally aligned forces right, if we get the shaping right, we can hopefully help prevent another conflict."[11]

Odierno agrees: RAF, he says, is premised on the "need to *prevent* conflicts." He has better reason than most to understand that war isn't an impersonal game of chess; among the thousands of soldiers killed or grievously injured during the Iraq War was his son Tony, who lost his left arm in 2004 when his vehicle was hit by a rocket-propelled grenade.

Still, it's not hard to understand why some might feel a flicker of unease when contemplating RAF. Even if it doesn't reflect hegemonic ambitions, the RAF concept—taken to its logical extreme—does suggest that senior Army officials view the entire globe as a potential battlefield.

Most Americans think of "peace" as a time in which the military is more or less irrelevant. But military doctrine takes a different view: recall that to the military, what most would call "peace" is merely "Phase Zero," the first phase on the six-phase "spectrum of conflict." In Phase Zero—a period without active conflict—the military's role is understood as "shaping" the character of possible future operations by building relationships, collecting information, and seeking to influence attitudes of local actors.

"It's always five o'clock somewhere," says the dedicated drinker. The RAF concept suggests that to General Odierno and other senior Army leaders, it's always Phase Zero somewhere. In fact, at any given time, it's Phase Zero almost everywhere—so why not have regionally aligned Army forces everywhere?

.  .  .

In late 2013, Army officials launched a full-court press to publicize the regionally aligned forces concept. At the 2013 annual meeting of the Association of the United States Army, a nonprofit advocacy and research organization, senior Army officials offered multiple presentations on RAF, from a speech by General Odierno to panel discussions featuring numerous senior Army officials. "Regionally aligned forces will ensure that the Army's 'Prevent—Shape—Win' Strategy is operationalized," proclaimed a handout distributed at the meeting by FORSCOM, the Army's manpower command. "In the Human Domain, people-to-people relationships matter!"

Several years after Odierno first unveiled his vision for regionally aligned forces, however, it remains remarkably difficult to penetrate the cloud of jargon-laden rhetoric and pin down Army officials on what any of this *really* means.

Oddly, the Army's day-to-day point person for the initial development of the regionally aligned forces construct wasn't a U.S. Army officer at all, but a British Army officer. After a stint at the U.S. Army War College, Colonel James Learmont found himself assigned to U.S. Army headquarters at the Pentagon as a British exchange officer, where he was handed the unenviable task of figuring out how to turn General Odierno's ambitious concept into a reality for the U.S. Army.

In some ways, Learmont was the perfect man for the job. Every British Army officer has a bit of T. E. Lawrence in his DNA (and the British know a little something about both the seductions and perils of empire). Learmont's own military career brought him to Germany, Norway, Iraq, Australia, Bosnia, and Afghanistan, often working in close coordination with U.S. and other NATO forces. As a friendly outsider, he's seen the U.S. Army up close, in all its glory and with all its warts—and he's seen the distinct benefits of a U.S. Army that's better trained, more professional, and more culturally aware.

What Learmont couldn't bring to the table, however, is an insider's understanding of the culture and bureaucracy of the U.S. Army itself. Yet if anything sabotages General Odierno's vision of RAF, it's most likely to be the tendency of any large bureaucracy to water down transformational concepts until they cease to have much real meaning.

Sitting in Learmont's windowless Pentagon office one afternoon after my Kuwait trip, I explain that even after weeks of research and interviews, I'm still having trouble getting a handle on what RAF is—and what it isn't. Everyone I speak to seems to have a different understanding of RAF, I tell Learmont. Some see it as an overdue transformation of the whole Army; some see it as a tool of imperialist intervention, and others see it, in the words of one former Pentagon official, as "another giant Army nothing-burger." Also, I tell Learmont, no one seems able to offer clarity on which Army units are regionally aligned, which are not, and which are slated to be regionally aligned in the future.

Learmont obviously gets these questions a lot. He sighs. "One of the biggest problems we have is the straightforward education piece," he tells me. "For one thing, he says, RAF isn't just for combat troops. RAF, he insists, encompasses "the Army total force," including the active duty force, the Army reserve, and the National Guard—and it includes headquarters elements and "enablers" such as engineers, transportation and logistics units, and even organizations like the Army's Training and Doctrine Command (TRADOC)—the whole kit and caboodle. "Everything the Army's got," says Learmont, "is in some way regionally aligned." With its emphasis on giving the Army a "better understanding" of each region, he says, RAF will constitute "a fundamental shift in how the Army is doing business."

## A New Hood Ornament

At Kuwait's Camp Arifjan, the persistent rain seems to carry with it a general sense of malaise and confusion. People slog grimly through the mud, heads down.

The Kuwaiti desert is bleak to begin with, and the scenery isn't much improved by the mud or the drab architecture of military barracks and office buildings. Soldiers stationed in Kuwait still get combat pay (though this is scheduled to end in June), and Arifjan *looks* like a base in a combat zone, surrounded by multiple layers of barbed wire, concrete barriers, and guard posts operated by heavily armed soldiers and contractors. Kuwaiti military and government officials rarely visit Camp Arifjan, I'm told—there's nothing worth seeing, and in any case, the elaborate security measures don't create a welcoming atmosphere for our host country partners, who refer to Arifjan and Buehring as "the American prisons."

Perhaps because he's only visiting, Colonel Tom Weikert is a pleasant exception to Arifjan's gloom. Weikert is based out of Camp Shaw, North Carolina, where he serves in the chief of staff's office for ARCENT, the Army component supporting CENTCOM. He's also cheerleader in chief for ARCENT's efforts to turn the regionally aligned force concept into reality: back in October, Weikert gave his own presentation at the annual AUSA conference, touting ARCENT's plans for hundreds of exercises and partnership activities to take place next year in some nineteen different nations. "ARCENT Says Future Hinges on Regional Alignments," trumpeted the headline of the Army News Service report on Weikert's remarks.[12]

Weikert greets me with an enthusiastic handshake, and blushes when I tell him I've been reading about him in the news. "A lot of folks are wondering if this RAF stuff is just a new hood ornament," he tells me. "But the answer is, it's not! It's real. We've been building partnerships in this region for years—I like to say, 'we were doing RAF *before* it was cool.' But we're going to be doing even more, and we're going to be doing it better."

RAF's goal, says Weikert, is "building partner capacity." That's DoD-speak for giving partner militaries the ability to fight alongside us—or, better still, the ability to fight the fights America would prefer to avoid. The more the United States can strengthen the militaries of our allies and partners, the more we can step back ourselves, letting our partners manage their own regional security.

Weikert's not alone in assuming that this is the primary purpose of RAF—many in the Army's Africa Command seem to take the same view. "Our goal is to help Africans solve African problems, without having a big American presence," declared Dagger Brigade battalion commander Robert Magee in October 2013.[13] Similarly, a February 2014 article produced by AFRICOM's public affairs office quotes Major Albert Conley of U.S. Army Africa (USARAF) on the virtues of RAF: "By helping Africans help themselves, it means that we don't have to get involved ourselves."[14]

This version of RAF is quite different from the left's conspiracy theory vision of unbridled hegemonic U.S. aggression: far from suggesting a United States determined to become ever more interventionist in an ever-expanding list of countries, it suggests, on the contrary, an exhausted empire struggling to hand over its global cop responsibilities to others, as rapidly as possible.

But it also bears little resemblance to the version of RAF that seems to lie at the heart of General Odierno's initial conception. I ask Weikert how RAF will be carried out by ARCENT: Will it closely resemble RAF, AFRICOM style? Not really, he says: tiny AFRICOM can offer a "boutique" version of RAF, while RAF in the CENTCOM region will have to be "large-scale and industrial strength." But even in the CENTCOM region, he assures me, culture and language training will enable ARCENT forces to step up their efforts to "build trust-based relationships," which will, in turn, "improve inter-operability, reduce unpredictability, and give U.S. senior leaders a better understanding of the region than they would otherwise have."[15]

Pressed on what the improved ARCENT cultural training will entail, Weikert looks a little uneasy: "Well, we create the training requirements, but we don't do the training here. We're asking FORSCOM to set that up. But," he adds, brightening, "We'll have an ARCENT Internet portal, which will offer video training. Everyone is going to have a computer avatar, and the avatar will take each soldier immersively through the culture. That training will be required for all soldiers."

Can I look at a sample training module, I ask?

Unfortunately, no, says Weikert. "The modules have not been developed yet."

## I Don't Like Cultural Food

What's the appropriate cultural training for life in Kuwait, a nation that often feels more like a transit lounge than a country? Kuwaiti citizens make up less than a third of Kuwait's resident population. Everyone else is from somewhere else, and plans to go somewhere else.

Arriving in Kuwait City, I find that the airport taxi dispatcher is Egyptian, and the taxi driver is Indian. At my hotel, the bellboy is Bangladeshi, the maids are Filipina, and the desk clerk is a cheery Tunisian.

At the hotel restaurant on day two, I finally stumble upon a genuine Kuwaiti at the breakfast buffet. I express my astonishment, and he laughs. "Kuwait? It is a place to make money," he informs me. "You come, you make money, you go. That is all. What brings *you* here?"

Oversimplifying, I explain that I'm researching an article on U.S. Army efforts to develop deeper relationships with Kuwaitis. He's intrigued. "Excellent! I was concerned that the American soldiers had all returned to America when the war in Iraq ended," he says. "I did not know that there are still many thousands of American soldiers in Kuwait!"

RAF or no RAF, most of the American soldiers I met seemed equally unaware that there are still many thousands of Kuwaitis in Kuwait. The average American soldier has virtually no direct contact with Kuwait's population, and less contact still with Kuwaiti citizens.

If entering Camp Arifjan is a formidable endeavor, requiring multiple document and vehicle inspections, exiting Arifjan is harder still. On several occasions, I wasn't sure I'd be allowed to leave: explaining that I was a visiting journalist rather than a member of the military cut no ice with the private contractors who serve as Arifjan's gate guards, who only agreed to let me out when my ARCENT public affairs escort produced signed memos authorizing me to move around freely.

"We try very hard to encourage people to get to know Kuwait," Area Support Group Commander Colonel Eubank tells me. "We offer an hour-long cultural briefing every Friday. It's mandatory for anyone leaving the base." So, unfortunately, is an "06 Departure Approval Memo": everyone below the rank of 06 needs a colonel's signed authorization to be allowed to leave the base.

Even the officer who runs Arifjan's public affairs office seems surprised (and more than a little disconcerted) when I insist that yes, I really do want to leave Arifjan and interview some Kuwaitis.

"In your own work, do you partner with the Kuwaitis?" I ask.

She frowns. "I tried to partner with the Kuwaitis for the first time just this week, but they haven't gotten back to me."

Perhaps it's just as well. The next evening, we attend a banquet hosted by Kuwait's former deputy prime minister, Sheikh Mohammad Sabah Al-Salem Al-Sabah, a member of Kuwait's ruling family and a former ambassador to the United States. There's an elaborate buffet, with dozens of traditional Kuwaiti dishes. My ARCENT public affairs escort pokes suspiciously at some shrimp.

"We should have stopped at McDonald's," she mutters. "I don't like cultural food."

Overhearing this, Sheik Mohammed's son Sabah Mohammad Al-Sabah—a young West Point graduate who now serves as a Kuwaiti army intelligence officer—comes up to us. "Do you get off the base much?" he enquires.

"Not much," she admits.

"Ah," says Captain Sabah. "I can tell."

My public affairs escort was hardly unique, however: except at the senior-most level, few of the Army personnel I met seemed to have much direct contact with either the Kuwaiti people or even with their Kuwaiti military counterparts.

As one senior U.S. embassy official tactfully put it: "U.S. troops keep a very low profile here, which is very wise. Across the political spectrum in Kuwait, there's agreement that a U.S. military presence is desirable and good. This may partly be because the U.S. military is virtually invisible."[16]

. . .

Predictably, civilian U.S. government agencies responded skeptically to this latest Army innovation. Asked his opinion of the shift to regionally aligned forces, former ambassador to Kuwait Matthew Tueller purses his lips. "Well. Within the United States, we have *so many* centers for ideas to come through. . . . I applaud the Army for developing this new concept. That said," he adds delicately, "the regionally aligned forces idea will, ah, bump up against other ideas coming from parts of the State Department."

In other words, the State Department may not share the Army leadership's enthusiasm for an Army that is "globally responsive and regionally engaged." Many at the State Department think it's their job, not the Army's, to develop cultural and regional expertise and relationships. In such quarters, the RAF concept looks less like an innovative approach to global risk management than yet another military effort to replace diplomats with soldiers.

"Their concern is always the militarization of foreign policy," admits Odierno. But, he says, the Army is planning more outreach to senior-level State Department officials. "What we're trying to tell them is, we are not conducting foreign policy—we are an instrument available to you . . . and we can do a lot of humanitarian assistance, disaster relief, we can do medical support, engineering support that builds things. So it's not just combat capabilities, it's a broader array of things that we can bring."

Odierno concludes optimistically: "I think once we lay it out for them they'll understand. They just want to make sure we are not driving the diplomatic process. And that's not our intent at all."

Back at the Pentagon, Colonel Learmont winces slightly when I tell him how much difficulty I had finding anyone able to offer a clear account of the RAF concept or how individual units fit into it. RAF, he reminds me, is still a work in progress.

At times, RAF seems to reflect a rather modest strategic vision: an assumption that the United States needs to retrench and look inward, coupled with a conviction that for a weary and financially strapped global cop, the only viable route to retirement involves an intense but time-limited investment in building the military capacity of allies and partners. As ARCENT's Brigadier General John Roberts put in an interview, "We've learned that it's really expensive to be in Phase Three and Four. Most Americans get that we need to invest in preventative maintenance for our equipment, or in insurance on our cars and houses—so why don't we do that globally, by investing in building partner nation capacity? It's the way to save on costs way down the road."

But Odierno and his successors often seem to lean toward the opposite vision: an assumption that the whole world's a potential battlefield, and a conviction that the United States should double down on its role as global cop. "Looking into the future," Odierno told the House Appropriations Subcommittee on Defense in 2013, "we are reposturing our force to be globally responsive and regionally engaged. . . . In this uncertain world we need an Army that conducts many missions at many speeds, in many sizes, under many conditions."[17] The 2015 "Army Vision," the Army's top-level strategic planning document, adopts the same view, declaring the importance of

> Enhanced country access and theater presence . . . to support the Army's expeditionary capability. . . . We must maintain a rotational presence with pre-positioned military equipment to expedite readiness in the event of crisis abroad. . . . We must capitalize on our success with Regionally Aligned Forces to further augment this capability . . . [and] expand [our] ability to rapidly place U.S. land forces anywhere in the world.[18]

We need an Army, in other words, that can do everything, everywhere—in a world where war may be everywhere, and forever.

# CHAPTER EIGHT

# What We've Made It

The U.S. military also fights wars the old-fashioned way, with things that go boom and results inscribed in flesh and bone. In addition to two major ground wars in Afghanistan and Iraq, since 9/11 the United States had also used military force in Libya and Syria. American airpower destroyed Muammar Gaddafi's Libyan forces, and as I write, missiles and bombs from American planes and ships continue to pound targets inside Iraq and Syria. That's on top of episodic special operations raids in half a dozen other regions.

While these conflicts have posed many novel challenges for the military, they also have features that would be familiar to any soldier who fought in World War II, Korea, or Vietnam—and they have exacted a high price in both dollars and blood. Some estimates suggest that the total price tag for the wars in Afghanistan and Iraq will eventually reach $4 trillion, once the deferred costs of medical care, disability payments to veterans, and the like have been factored in.[1] Thousands of American and coalition military personnel lost their lives, and although no one knows exactly how many Iraqis and Afghans have been killed and wounded, the number almost certainly runs into the hundreds of thousands, taking into account both military and civilian casualties.

If I have not spent much time discussing these more traditional ways of making war, it is not because I consider them unimportant. Far from it: their human, financial, and geopolitical costs will reverberate for decades to come. But the story of these wars is a story most Americans already know something about. Hollywood doesn't make movies about soldiers providing technical assistance to the Iraqi parliament, or sailors operating mobile health clinics in coastal Africa. Violence and danger—preferably lots of it—is what sells movies and books. The news too is dominated by stories of firefights, missile strikes, and IEDs, not stories of the countless military personnel whose jobs have little to do with traditional forms of combat. To the extent that the media focuses on noncombat stories relating to the military, the focus is generally on combat's aftermath: grieving families, injured veterans, or soldiers struggling with PTSD.

We think of war—of violence, blood, and mortal combat—as central to the mission of any military. And it's no accident that the military's uniformed leadership is populated disproportionately by those coming from combat arms backgrounds: military logisticians, lawyers, nurses, and communications experts may be important, but the Army still draws most of its senior leadership from the infantrymen, armor officers, and artillery officers, just as most Navy leaders are former fighter pilots or surface warfare commanders. Indeed, most would say that violence and killing are what define wars and the military. Recall Clausewitz: "War is nothing but a duel on an extensive scale . . . an act of violence intended to compel our opponent to fulfill our will."[2] As for the military, it is the institution that fights in wars: the armed forces.

I'm not sure Clausewitz would say the same today.

## Their Job Is to Kill People

One weekend day, I walked through the Pentagon with my father and stepmother, who were visiting from their home in Connecticut. The building was mostly empty on a Saturday morning, and my children raced through the long corridors of the Pentagon's E Ring, giggling and trying to wrap themselves up in the flags that stood outside the secretary of defense's office. Occasionally, someone in uniform unlucky enough to be working the weekend shift would wander by and stop to chat.

After one of those brief exchanges, my father shook his head. "This is just so strange, being in the Pentagon, surrounded by photos of tanks and fighter planes, with uniformed soldiers walking by and talking to us."

I laughed. It had taken me several months to get over that feeling myself.

"They're just people."

My father nodded. "Sure. It's just hard to get past the fact that they're people whose job is to kill *other* people."

But this isn't quite accurate. Certainly, some people in the military kill other people on behalf of the United States. But not all of them do, and not all of them think of themselves that way. Speak to a Marine infantryman, and he'll probably tell you that killing—or at least being prepared to kill—is central to his role. But many military personnel don't see killing as central to their jobs any more than the average police officer sees it as central to his. Notwithstanding recent scandals about police shootings, most police officers think of themselves as people who try to keep their communities safe, not people who try to use violence. Similarly, many in the military see their goal as preventing conflict, not engaging in it. Some don't even go that far: ask an Air Force supply clerk or a Navy cable installation technician if his job is to kill other people and he'll look at you like you've gone crazy.

Contrary to popular assumptions, only a small minority of military personnel have combat-related jobs. In 2015, even after two lengthy wars, the percentage of military personnel in combat specialties was only 14 percent overall—with substantial differences between the services: for instance, 28 percent of enlisted Army personnel serve in jobs that are classified as combat positions compared to just 3 percent of Navy enlisted personnel.[3]

To be sure, many military personnel in noncombat positions end up in combat anyway: a truck filled with supply clerks can be ambushed or hit by an IED as easily as a truck full of infantrymen. But even when deployed in combat zones, most members of the military never end up fighting; instead, they maintain vehicles, enter data into computers, write articles for the base newsletter, monitor satellite imagery, make sure the right number of MREs have been ordered, and so on.

And though deployment rates have varied substantially by branch of service, a solid third of military personnel never deployed at all to the Iraq or Afghanistan theaters. As of 2011, the most recent year for which there are reliable statistics available, 41 percent of active duty Air Force personnel, 39 percent of Marines, 34 percent of Navy personnel, and 27 percent of Army soldiers had never deployed to either of these conflicts.[4] Army personnel were far more likely than personnel in any other service to have endured multiple deployments to combat theaters: 25 percent of Army personnel in 2011 had been deployed to Iraq or Afghanistan for three or more years, compared to fewer than 7 percent of sailors, airmen, or Marines. The Army has also taken the lion's share of the casualties from these wars: of the roughly 0.6 percent of military personnel deployed to Afghanistan and Iraq who were killed in action in the decade after 9/11, more than two thirds were Army soldiers, and most of the rest were Marines.[5]

To the average civilian, a soldier's a soldier, and the differences between the various military services may seem arcane and unimportant. But it's not just a matter of football rivalries: the services get different training, have different traditions and protocols, have different demographic profiles, specialize in different capabilities, and experience the nation's wars in quite different ways.

These differences can have a substantial impact on national debates about defense strategy and foreign policy. In the mid-2000s, with large numbers of American troops engaged in sustained ground combat, the Army and Marines were ascendant. Decades of preparation for a Soviet invasion of Europe quickly proved irrelevant, and military journals were soon full of articles proposing radically different ways of approaching conflict and ground combat. Counterinsurgency doctrine became influential, and shaped not only military debates but broader foreign policy debates.

But as the war in Iraq petered out and U.S. efforts in Afghanistan produced only ambiguous gains, the pendulum swung away from the land forces and back in the direction of the Air Force and Navy. Largely sidelined in the Iraq and Afghanistan wars, the two more tech-heavy services were quick to declare counterinsurgency dead. COIN was too labor intensive and too complex—and surely the United States would retire from the nation building business once and for all. Failing states and nonstate actors could be addressed through smaller scale strikes or training and advisory missions led by special operations forces. The United States should refocus on the "real" future threat: possible conflicts with other states.

In particular, argued Air Force and Navy leaders, the United States needed to step up its ability to counter new technologies being developed by peer and "near-peer" competitors such as China and—well, China. Specifically, the concern related to emerging Chinese "anti-access and area denial" methods: technologies designed to render U.S. ships and planes impotent by scrambling their communications, hijacking their control systems, countering their stealth capabilities, targeting them with sophisticated antiship and antiaircraft missiles, and so on. The U.S. military can move more ships, planes, and ordnance more quickly than any other nation—but the strength, speed, and firepower we possess will be irrelevant if our adversaries can keep us from getting ships, planes, or missiles close enough to pose a threat.

Air Force and Navy officials argued that their services were the best positioned to take on such challenges. Thus the concept of "Air-Sea Battle" was born—integrated naval and aviation operations to counter high-tech new anti-access and area denial capabilities possessed by adversaries. It's a concept that, not coincidentally, would require substantial investment in Navy and Air Force platforms.[6]

Cultural differences *within* the services can be as significant as cultural differences between the services, or between the military and the civilian population. Consider the cultural differences between Army Special Forces (the Green Berets) and the conventional Army—what the Special Forces community calls "Big Army." Special Forces enlisted personnel tend to be older and better educated than their Big Army counterparts, and the Special Forces community is less hierarchical. Special Forces soldiers operate in very small groups, and much of their focus is on working in an advisory capacity within foreign militaries. As with the differences between the services, cultural differences within the services can lead to deeply divergent views on strategy and policy: Special Forces soldiers tend to place a high value on linguistic and cultural knowledge, for instance, and to favor small-footprint efforts that leverage the energy and skills of foreign militaries over the large-scale, U.S.-heavy operations the Big Army prefers.

To military personnel, the different services and different occupational specialties might as well be different tribes—and an old hand can tell from a quick glance at another service member's unit insignia and patches as much as most civilians could glean from reading a résumé. To those in the know, there's nothing uniform about a uniform: it displays fine gradations of rank, experience, and institutional prestige. For the Army, the presence or absence of Ranger tabs and combat patches are instant indicia of credibility, and the crossed arrows of Special Forces personnel or the crossed muskets of the infantry send a far different message than the Transportation Corps' gold ship's wheel or the red, white, and blue shield of the Adjutant General's Corps.

## What We've Made It

So who are these men and women who fight in our wars, program computers in anonymous cubicles for CYBERCOM, weld together damaged Humvee parts at Fort Bliss, or oversee well-digging projects in Botswana?

The Defense Department is the nation's largest employer. At the end of fiscal year 2013, there were roughly 1.4 million active duty military personnel, along with 843,000 reservists. More than 14 percent of active duty personnel were women, and 30 percent were members of minority populations. The average age of active duty personnel was about twenty-nine, and more than a quarter of officers were over forty. More than half of active duty personnel were married, and 36 percent were married with children.[7]

Today's military is distinctly middle-class in origin,[8] and military personnel are more likely than comparable age groups in the civilian population to have graduated from high school. More than 80 percent of military officers have bachelor's degrees, compared to just 30 percent of the overall population over the age of twenty-five.[9] After leaving the military, most veterans do well economically, relative to their civilian counterparts: they have higher median incomes than nonveterans, are less likely to be unemployed, and are less likely than nonveterans to live below the poverty line.[10]

Popular stereotypes hold that military personnel tend to be politically conservative. Studies suggest a more complicated reality, however. In a recent study of Army personnel, for instance, Jason Dempsey, an Army lieutenant colonel and veteran of West Point's social science faculty, found that "on the whole, military opinions tend to parallel civilian opinions." Older officers tended to be more conservative than younger officers and enlisted personnel, but political labels turned out to be poor predictors of views on particular issues. Overall, Dempsey concluded, "the idea that service members have a distinctly different worldview... [that is] conservative and dramatically out of step with the rest of society—is a myth that must be constantly debunked."[11]

Geographically, the South, Southwest, and the mountain states are overrepresented within the military, while Northeastern states are underrepresented, relative to their overall populations.[12] But while this is often assumed to be a product of regional ideology—with "red" states being more "pro-military" than "blue" states—here too the reality is more complex. The geography of military recruitment and accessions is less a product of ideology than of two somewhat related phenomena: population density and the location of large military installations, which create, in effect, self-replicating military clusters.

Military personnel are disproportionately likely to come from nonurban areas,[13] and states with high population densities have, on average, lower per capita military recruitment than states with low population densities.[14] To some degree, this is a story of economic and cultural opportunity: An eighteen-year-old from a sparsely populated rural area doesn't have as many options for employment or seeing the world as an eighteen-year-old from New York or Chicago. But new military recruits are also likely to come from areas that *already* have large military populations. Thus, decisions about where to locate large military installations are a major driver of military demographics.

For complex historical reasons—including the post–Civil War occupation of the American South by federal troops, the Mexican and

Indian Wars of the nineteenth century, and the military's need for large tracts of cheap land—the South and Southwest have long hosted a disproportionate share of America's major military bases. This pattern has been exacerbated by base closure and realignment policies, which in recent decades have consolidated military bases into a relatively small number of states. Of the roughly 1.2 million active duty service members stationed in the United States, 49 percent are currently stationed in only five states: California, Texas, Virginia, North Carolina, and Georgia.[15]

Base location decisions create self-fulfilling prophesies: young people's career choices are profoundly influenced by the career choices of the adults around them, so it's not surprising that those who grow up in communities with substantial military populations end up joining the military in higher numbers than those who grow up far from large military bases, just as the children of military personnel are themselves more likely to join the military. Look at the list of the one hundred counties that produce the highest number of military recruits each year; to a great extent, it's a list of the counties that house the largest military installations. High recruit-producing counties include, for instance, Cumberland County, North Carolina, home to Fort Bragg; El Paso County, Texas, home to Fort Bliss; San Diego County, California, home to Naval Base Coronado and Naval Base San Diego; Montgomery County, Ohio, home to Wright-Patterson Air Force Base; Bell County, Texas, home to Fort Hood; El Paso County, Colorado, home to Fort Carson; Muscogee County, Georgia, home to Fort Benning; and so on.[16]

If Americans wanted a more geographically diverse military (and one that might become more ideologically and culturally diverse as a result), there's a simple solution: redistribute military installations with an eye to equalizing recruitment across the nation's major geographic regions. If we wanted more liberals in the military, for instance, we'd want bases in the nation's major urban areas, which, regardless of state, tend to be more liberal than rural areas. This would be expensive, of course: try finding thousands of square miles of unoccupied land to train in in the Boston or New York metro areas.

But it's a useful thought experiment to imagine what the military would look like with bases located in quite different places. It's common to hear people insist that only a draft would give America a truly representative military, but that's probably not so; both base locations and military recruitment priorities have a profound effect on military demographics. The military pours money into ensuring a steady stream of high-caliber minority recruits, for a simple reason: as a society, we've decided it's important to have a military that's as ethnically and racially diverse as the overall population. If we decide we're worried about urban-rural divides or cultural and ideological divides in the military, tinkering with base location decisions is an obvious way to make the military more geographically and ideologically representative of American society. Yes, it would cost money, just like many other important but difficult things—but if Congress made it a priority, it could be done.

Most fundamentally, the U.S. military is—and will continue to be—a product of our culture and our collective decisions. Whatever it is, it's what we have made it.

# PART III

# How We Got Here

# CHAPTER NINE

# Putting War into a Box

War, in one form or another, appeared with the first man," declared President Barack Obama in his 2009 Nobel Peace Prize acceptance speech.

Whether or not this is true is hotly contested. Some anthropologists and historians view organized warfare as a relatively recent human invention, a product of culture rather than nature. Others are convinced that warfare is as old as humanity itself, hardwired into the human psyche.[1] To Thomas Hobbes, the "state of nature" was characterized by "warre of all against all"; writing a century later, French theorist Jean-Jacques Rousseau was equally convinced that warfare was a disease of civilization, unknown in the golden age of primitive man.

In virtually every major civilization, ancient literature and art memorialize war and warfare. The Narmer Palette, from about 3100 BC, memorializes the battle victories of the first king of unified Egypt.[2] Similarly, the story of Gilgamesh, from around 2100 BC, depicts an ancient Sumerian society in which warfare was elaborate, organized, and deeply entwined with notions of honor and masculinity. Even Gilgamesh's death is described using the metaphors of war:

> *He who was perfect in combat is lying down, never to rise*
> *  again,*
> *The warrior girt with a shoulder-belt is lying down, never to*
> *  rise again. . . .*
> *The battle that cannot be fled has caught up with you,*

*The combat that cannot be matched has caught up with you,*
*The fight that shows no pity has caught up with you!*[3]

In Bronze Age China, Shang Dynasty rulers built elaborate fortified cities and engaged in war to replenish their supply of slaves. In Europe, *The Iliad*, which is thought to date from around 700 BC, describes the ten-year siege of Troy, recounting scenes of battle in gory detail. The first verse of India's Bhagavad Gita, written sometime between the fifth and second centuries BC, opens on a battlefield. The Bible too is full of war stories, from small-scale skirmishes to all-out wars between massed armies, waged with little mercy.

But if war is as old as humanity itself, so too is the human effort to define and control it, differentiating warfare from other forms of violence and conflict and establishing rules to govern and constrain it.

In our own era, clear definitions of war have generally proven elusive: efforts to define war tend to degenerate quickly into versions of Supreme Court Justice Potter Stewart's famous quip about the meaning of the term "obscene": "I shall not today attempt further to define the kinds of material I understand to be embraced within that shorthand description . . . and perhaps I could never succeed in intelligibly doing so. But *I know it when I see it.*"[4]

The *Stanford Encyclopedia of Philosophy*'s entry on "war" informs us that:

> War should be understood as an *actual, intentional* and *widespread* armed conflict between political communities. . . . War is a phenomenon which occurs *only* between political communities, defined as those entities which either are states or intend to become states (in order to allow for civil war). . . . *All warfare is precisely, and ultimately, about governance.* . . . The mere *threat* of war, and the presence of mutual disdain between political communities, do not suffice as indicators of war. The conflict of arms must be *actual*, and not merely latent, for it to count as war. Further, the actual armed conflict must be both *intentional* and *widespread*. . . . The onset of war requires a conscious commitment,

and a significant mobilization, on the part of the belligerents in question. There's no real war, so to speak, until the fighters *intend* to go to war and until they do so with a heavy *quantum* of force.[5]

This is in line with the views of the great German military strategist Carl von Clausewitz, who saw war as "nothing but a duel on an extensive scale . . . an act of violence intended to compel our opponent to fulfill our will." To this, he famously added, " 'War is nothing more than the continuation of politics by other means. . . . For political aims are the end and war is the means, and the means can never be conceived without the end." War, to Clausewitz, "is only a branch of political activity . . . it is in no sense autonomous."[6] But the element of violence remains critical: as historian Michael Howard notes, political or economic conflicts such as "trade wars and tariff wars may involve conflicting interests, but unless there is an element of organized, sanctioned and purposeful violence, these are not war."[7]

Most of us intuitively follow these definitions when we try to understand war. Thus, we don't tend to view a game of chess as war: it is a rule-bound, organized competition, but it does not involve force or coercion, and lacks a political purpose. Similarly, although a spontaneous barroom brawl is violent, it is not a war: it is not rule-bound and organized, nor extensive nor engaged in for political purposes. For similar reasons, isolated and sporadic homicides are not war.

Rugby competitions are also not war: although they are violent, organized, rule-bound, and often extensive, they too lack a political purpose. Urban gang fighting, drug interdiction raids, and organized crime are similarly not viewed by most of us as war. Economic sanctions are organized, coercive, and have political goals, but we don't view them as war either, even though they may lead directly and predictably to suffering and even death.

·  ·  ·

Oddly, even the modern law of war—more formally known as the international law of armed conflict (LOAC, to aficionados)—does not offer a precise definition of armed conflict. The Geneva Conventions apply on their terms to "all cases of declared war or of any other armed conflict," but how much violence equals an armed conflict, for legal purposes? No one is entirely sure. As two respected European legal scholars noted in a 2009 article in the *International Review of the Red Cross*, this is "one of the glaring gaps" in the law of armed conflict, a gap that "concerns its very foundation—namely the question of the definition of war, or rather 'armed conflict.'"[8] Several international court decisions have sought to clarify the meaning of armed conflict. Thus, the International Criminal Tribunal for the Former Yugoslavia declared in a 1997 ruling, "an armed conflict exists whenever there is a resort to armed force between States or protracted armed violence between governmental authorities and organized armed groups or between such groups within a State." This definition "focuses on two aspects of a conflict: the *intensity* of the conflict and the *organization* of the parties to the conflict. In an armed conflict of an internal or mixed character, these closely related criteria are used solely for the purpose, as a minimum, of distinguishing an armed conflict from banditry, unorganized and short-lived insurrections, or terrorist activities, which are not subject to international humanitarian law."[9]

There is, however, no consensus about how to define the key terms: what "level of intensity" is enough? How "organized" does a force have to be to be a "party" to a conflict?

## Containing War

But even if we can't define war with precision, we know it's a dangerous thing. Leaving definitional efforts to one side, nearly every human society has sought ways to mark the distinction between war and not-war— between acceptable and socially sanctioned violence and unacceptable forms of violence. Societies have made use of a very wide range of rules and rituals to draw spatial and temporal lines between war and not-war, and between those who participate in wars and those who do not.

Earlier, I mentioned Norse berserkers, and the Navajo's "twisted language" and lines drawn in the desert sand. To these examples, we can add many more.

When the Blackfoot Indians prepared for raids, writes anthropologist John C. Ewers, "the evening before departure the prospective raiders walked around camp drumming on a piece of buffalo rawhide and singing their wolf (war) songs." On raids, when the enemy camp had been sighted, the warriors "set up a pile of sticks," which their leader would then kick over, "and all the men scrambled for them. Each stick was considered a prophecy of a horse he would take from the enemy." The raiders would then don war paint and war medicine, and move toward the enemy, singing war songs.[10]

Many Native American groups, including the Cheyenne, the Choctaw, Shawnee, the Iroquois, and the Tetons, divided authority between "peace chiefs" and "war chiefs." Among the Cheyenne, for instance, peace chiefs "led the nation's ten or so bands, supervised their trade, and adjudicated disputes. When war threatened, they gave control of the nation to war chiefs, who planned strategy and tactics and led the attacks."[11] When the war ended, war chiefs handed control back to the peace chiefs. The locus of authority—and whether power was hereditary, in the case of many tribes' peace chiefs, or meritocratically earned, as was often the case for war chiefs—thus depended entirely on the ability of a tribe to distinguish readily between peacetime and wartime.

In nineteenth-century Liberia, warriors wore special masks during raids, and war was prohibited while "bush school" was in session for boys and girls.[12] Among the Zulu in southern Africa, conflict prior to the early-nineteenth-century military innovations of Shaka Zulu was similarly ritualized. Disputes between tribes were settled through combat: on a mutually agreed upon day and time, each tribe's warriors would draw up "in lines at a distance of about 100 yards apart," writes anthropologist Keith Otterbein, an expert on early warfare. "Behind the lines stood the remaining members of each tribe. . . . Chosen warriors would advance to within 50 yards of each other and shout insults" before opening the battle "by hurling their spears."[13]

The Jíbaro Indians of Ecuador and Peru engaged in elaborate ritual dances prior to battle, using stylized language and movements of their lances as pairs of warriors faced one another:

*Let us speak loudly! . . .*
*Let us quickly assemble!*
*Let us avenge the blood guilt!*
*Tomorrow we will sleep far away.*
*Let us quickly take our enemy. . . .*
*Let us go, to return quickly, youths!*
*Quickly, quickly!*
*We have been fighting!*
*We have killed!*
*We have revenged the blood!*
*Let us cut off the head (of the enemy)!*
*Let us carry it with us!*

This elaborate dance, wrote Finnish anthropologist Rafael Karsten, was "a magical ceremony by which the Jíbaros believe themselves to be able to conjure forth victory," and was followed by additional ritual acts as the warriors traveled to meet their enemies. "During the whole journey to the scene of a war, a journey that takes several days, sometimes even weeks," the warriors were prohibited from speaking except when absolutely essential, and then only in a whisper. "Only the chief has the right to speak in a loud voice." Before the attack, warriors removed their usual head ornaments and donned special caps made of monkey skins, along with necklaces made of jaguar teeth, then painted their bodies black. "The Indians say that by blackening themselves in this way they become like the demons (*iguanchi*)," explains Karsten, "which means that they also get their ferocity and strength."[14]

Among the Avotip in Melanesia,

When men went to war they quite literally took on a different face. Each man wore around his neck a chest ornament, called a kwa'ahsapi, which has the form of a stylized face. It was the focal embodiment of his Spirit, and when he went into battle he held it in his teeth by a tag at the back, so that it covered up his face except for the eyes. A man's spirit in this way 'went before the man. . . .' Men can therefore imply that it is not entirely they themselves who killed in war, but those spirits that killed through them.[15]

Even the masks are insufficient, however: immediately before battle, Avotip men placed an herb called akar on their tongues; "this could only be administered after the men were well away from Avotip, because, once bespelled" by this most powerful war magic, "they became capable of killing anyone . . . even their own wives and children. . . .They call this state, 'bristling skin,'" and "claim not even to have perceived the enemy corpses until the magic was removed 'and our eyes became clear again, and we saw all the fine men and women we had killed.'"[16]

The Mekeo of Papua New Guinea similarly saw war as toxic to ordinary life and relationships. "To reach a state of war readiness," writes anthropologist Mark Mosko, Mekeo men had to fast and refrain from sexual relations for at least six months. The goal of such abstinence was to "close or tighten the body" so that "enemies' aggressive war sorcery" would remain outside. Once "closed" and ready for war, a man could "devote himself completely to war." During that time, however, he could not touch his wife sexually: if a couple "did happen to open their bodies sexually while [the man] still had traces of war sorcery on his skin, it would enter both their bodies and kill them."[17]

The idea of war as toxic to ordinary civil life is common. If going to war generally required a variety of rituals designed to mark a man's transition from ordinary life to warrior, prepared to kill and die, many societies viewed the return from war as requiring additional rituals to facilitate that transition back to safety, community, and normality.

The Old Testament speaks frequently of the need for warriors to cleanse themselves before returning to their communities: Numbers 31:19 instructs the Israelites returning from battle with Midian to "abide without the camp seven days: whosoever hath killed any person, and whosoever hath touched any slain, purify *both* yourselves and your captives on the third day, and on the seventh day."[18] In medieval Europe, warriors returning from fighting in the Crusades nonetheless were often required to take part in public ceremonies of repentance, even though they had killed in "just" wars; these penances included fasting, acts of charity, avoidance of Communion for a period of time, and so on.[19]

Native American tribes made similar use of purification rituals:[20] "those who became warriors must of necessity assume a changed psychological state in order to kill," write psychologists Steven Silver and John Wilson, but "after battle," warriors must undertake rituals to "purge, purify and heal the physical and psychological wounds of warrior." The Navajo "Enemy Way Ceremony, for instance," purifies and heals those who have killed in battle, transforming them from their warrior identities back into their normal identities.[21]

Many societies still use such rituals today. In 1990s Mozambique, for instance, soldiers returning from participating in the country's bloody civil war would undergo public cleansing rituals. Under the direction of a traditional healer, they would participate in "kuguiya," a public simulated battle: "The patient must imitate, with a pestle pole instead of a weapon, the fights and killings he performed during the war." This is followed by cleansing with incense, taking a type of herbal sauna, and a ritual in which the healer removes any spirits afflicting the body of the returned fighter. If the spirits belong to those the fighter has killed, the fighter may have to perform various acts of expiation, in addition to providing compensation to the families of those he killed.[22] In post-genocide Rwanda, the court system couldn't cope with the hundreds of thousands of people accused of participating in the slaughter: many were instead sent into the Gacaca system, which mixed together aspects of modern criminal trials and traditional cleansing and reconciliation rituals.[23]

## We Had to Become Clean

Even newly emerged modern groups often rapidly develop rituals of initiation and purification for fighters. In the mid-1990s, a colleague and I traveled to Northern Uganda for Human Rights Watch and interviewed children who had been captured by the Lord's Resistance Army, a notoriously brutal group that maintains its strength by abducting children and teens to serve as soldiers and servants.[24]

It was my first real experience of war, though initially I didn't realize it. In the mid-1990s, few people outside Uganda had heard of the LRA, which arose in the late 1980s out of the ashes of Alice Lakwena's Holy Spirit Movement, a rebel movement that fought in opposition to Uganda's central government. Between the late 1980s and the mid-1990s, LRA raids killed thousands of villagers in Northern Uganda. Hundreds of thousands of people were displaced, and an estimated ten thousand children were forcibly abducted by the LRA and brutally coerced into becoming killers, sex slaves, or both. By the late 1990s, CNN's Christiane Amanpour was covering the LRA and Hillary Clinton was writing op-eds about the group's atrocities. In 2012, the viral YouTube video "Kony 2012" even made the Lord's Resistance Army a household name for a few brief weeks.

But in the spring of 1997, the LRA had yet to make CNN, and even at Human Rights Watch, an organization institutionally committed to championing the forgotten, most people knew nothing about the conflict. It was a low-intensity, low-tech war of filth and grief and blood, and it was all happening in a distant and obscure corner of a distant and strategically insignificant country. It didn't map onto anything familiar. So when a Human Rights Watch colleague and I arrived in the Northern Ugandan town of Gulu, we had only the vaguest understanding of what we were getting into. We had heard that "Christian fundamentalist" rebels were abducting children, but we had no notion of what this meant. We had received no special training on operating in a conflict zone, and no special training on working with severely traumatized children. We were as unprepared as it is possible to be.

Nevertheless, I found myself in May 1997 dropped off in a grass airfield in what turned out to be a war zone. The tiny, rattling plane that had delivered us promptly flew away with its remaining cargo: one motorcycle, a nun, and several chickens. A solitary cow, grazing at the airfield's edge, didn't even look up as the plane wheezed off overhead.

The town of Gulu was little more than a dusty, sprawling mess of thatch-roofed huts and crumbling cinder block, huddled near Uganda's northernmost tip. Everything in Gulu spoke of catastrophe: half the huts we saw had their roofs burned off, and our dingy hotel had been burned half to the ground a few days earlier. Our questions about how the fire had started (rebels? arson? a kitchen mishap?) met with apathetic or frightened shrugs from the remaining staff. There was no electricity or hot water, and small bugs swam through the beans and rice offered up by the hotel kitchen.

Just outside the courtyard where we ate, a ragged woman nursed a baby with a distended belly. When she spotted us, she came toward us slowly, holding the infant up in silent display. I offered her some money, but she ignored it. Instead, she continued to silently hold out her sick baby to me, her eyes pleading, tears on her cheeks. I didn't know what to do, so I gently patted the baby's stomach, and shook my head helplessly. Finally, she pulled the baby back into her chest, took the bills I was still holding out, and walked dejectedly away.

We spent the next week talking to people about the war, and it was bad—worse than I can really say. Almost everyone we met cried at some point: the aid workers cried; the journalists cried; doctors at the hospital cried; local officials cried; children cried. Even the American ambassador in her spacious embassy office cried when we told her what we had learned.

Interviewing children who had escaped from the Lord's Resistance Army (or, in some cases, been captured in battle by the Ugandan army), we soon learned that the LRA had developed its own odd mix of traditional Acholi tribal religion, Islam, and Christianity. Children captured by the LRA were compelled to undertake a variety of rituals designed to transform them into soldiers—and these rituals were no less elaborate for being largely invented by illiterate teens, borrowing from half-remembered tribal stories.[25]

"After we were first abducted, before they gave us food, they said we must become clean," one boy told us.

We had to spread shea butter oil on our chests and our backs, because we were unclean, and had to become clean enough to eat with them. This is because we Acholi are a very bad people, and we must all become better before we can rule in our land. This is what the Holy Spirit has ordered. This also is why some people must be killed: we must become pure, and many Acholi do not follow the orders of the Holy Spirit anymore. Many of them are working with *jok* [spirits]. So they must be killed. This is what the rebels told me.

"Everything they did was because of the *malaikas* [angels]," explained a girl:

For an example: there was a malaika from Sudan that sent a message at one time that they should not sleep with their wives before fighting. And there were very many rules: before they crossed water they must pour water over their head. Also, you must not throw or step on certain stones. If a girl was during her period, she must not touch anything that a man will touch, and she must sit very far away from the fire. Also, you must not greet anyone who is not a rebel with your hands.

LRA captives were often forced to participate in the slaughter of other captives to reinforce their new identities. "On the third day, a little girl tried to escape," recalled another girl:

They made us kill her. They went to collect some big pieces of firewood. Then they kicked her and jumped on her, and they made us each beat her at least once with the big pieces of wood. They said, "You must beat and beat and beat her." She was bleeding from the mouth. Then she died.

In battle too, the children explained, rituals are required:

When you go to fight you make the sign of the cross first. If you fail to do this, you will be killed. You must also take oil and draw a cross on your chest, your forehead, and each shoulder, and you must make a cross in oil on your gun. Also you take a small stone, you sew it on a cloth and wear it around your wrist like a watch. That is to prevent the bullet that might come, because in battle it is acting as a mountain. So those people on the other side will look at you, but they will see only a mountain, and the bullets will hit the mountain and not hurt you.

You also have water: they call it "clean water," and they pour it into a small bottle. If you go to the front, you also have a small stick, and you dip it in the bottle and fling the water out. This is a river and it drowns the bullet that might come to you. Finally you wear a cross on a chain. But in the fighting you wrap it around your wrist and hold it in your hand. Should you make a mistake and not wear it on your hand, you will be killed.

These rituals were central to the LRA rebels' sense of self, and constituted a vital aspect of maintaining some sense of personal purity and virtue even as they engaged in the most horrific acts. A schoolgirl kidnapped by the LRA from her boarding school dormitory related this exchange with one of the rebel leaders:

They said they wanted Uganda to become a paradise. . . .

One day, I asked our commander, "Why are you killing mostly your own people, people from the North?"

He said, "We do not kill them because they are from the North, but because they are misbehaving."

I said, "Why do you kill those who try to escape?"

And he said, "Jesus did not ask his disciples to come with him, he just told them, 'Follow me.' But today Ugandans do not follow the Holy Spirit, so they must be forced."

I said, "People of Northern Uganda would not refuse to follow you if what you did was truly right."

He said, "Stella, you are joking with the Holy Spirit. You don't know what we are doing. We are pretending we are bad, but we will be the first to enter God's Kingdom. One day you will believe in us and you will see we are God's people."

Most of the children we interviewed had escaped or been rescued from the LRA, and though these children had been under extreme duress throughout their time with the LRA, several spoke of the need to return to their home villages so they could undertake purification rituals. As one teenage girl recalled:

> One boy tried to escape, but he was caught. . . . His hands were tied, and then they made us, the other new captives, kill him with a stick. I felt sick. I knew this boy from before. We were from the same village. I refused to kill him and they told me they would shoot me. They pointed a gun at me, so I had to do it. The boy was asking me, "Why are you doing this?" I said I had no choice. After we killed him, they made us smear his blood on our arms. . . . They said we had to do this so we would not fear death and so we would not try to escape.
>
> I feel so bad about the things that I did. . . . When I go home I must do some traditional rites because I have killed. I must perform these rites and cleanse myself. I still dream about the boy from my village who I killed. I see him in my dreams, and he is talking to me and saying I killed him for nothing, and I am crying.

. . .

Don't imagine that only ancient or exotic societies engage in peculiar rituals designed to mark the boundaries between war and peace, warrior and ordinary human. We modern Americans have such rituals too: we're simply so accustomed to our own rituals that we rarely recognize them as such.

Think of military boot camp, or the first week for new cadets at West Point. New recruits and cadets are separated from their families; their civilian clothing is packed away and replaced with uniforms. Their hair is shorn in a kind of ritual disfigurement. Literally stripped of their old identities, they go through a series of initiation rites remarkably similar to those used by a thousand different societies through history. They are deliberately disoriented: they are yelled at and subjected to ritualized insults; their sleep patterns are disrupted; they miss meals; they are forced to exercise to the point of exhaustion; they submit to detailed and often arbitrary new rules; they learn a new language. (You wear a cover, not a hat, and do PT, not exercise; you eat in the DFAC or the chow hall, not the cafeteria.) Special items of clothing gain near talismanic properties; the recruit must learn to walk differently and hold himself differently. At West Point, new cadets—"plebes"—must memorize and be prepared to recite bits of arcane lore, little of which serves any purpose beyond emphasizing group membership and the plebe's subordinate status: to the question "How many lights in Cullum Hall," the cadet must answer, "340"; to the query "How is the cow," the cadet must respond, "She walks, she talks, she's full of chalk, the lacteal fluid extracted from the female of the bovine species is highly prolific to the nth degree!"[26]

Once initiated, the new soldier progresses through various further challenges; successive steps are marked with ceremonies, brightly colored ribbons to be displayed on the chest, and bits of metal forged into the shape of totem animals or weapons. Just as Native Americans wore war paint and Melanesians and Liberians wore masks into battle, modern American soldiers don helmets and mirrored sunglasses and display images of fierce warriors, weapons, and animals on their unit patches: the Army's 2nd Infantry Division patch shows a Native American warrior with a feathered headdress; the 101st Airborne patch depicts a screaming eagle. Panthers, skulls, Tasmanian devils, wolves, and dragons all make appearances on other military patches.

Weapons and vehicles are similarly named after fearsome figures and predatory animals: hornets, predators, reapers, black hawks, cobras, and so on. Often, military personnel paint their vehicles to resemble predators: I remember a particularly colorful A-10 Thunderbolt, its nose painted to resemble a shark's eyes and teeth. Other military planes have tigers, hawks, eagles, and skulls painted on the side. Just as donning the skins of bears and wolves to go into battle helped Norse berserkers take on the borrowed ferocity of the predatory animals whose skins they wore, American troops today hope that they too will become as fierce and courageous as the animals for whom they name their weapons and units.

Perhaps, like the berserkers, they also hope for absolution: that any ruthless or inhuman acts will belong not to them, but to the animals and spirits whose attributes they have temporarily taken on.

# CHAPTER TEN

# Taming War

War's appeal has always been counterbalanced by its horror.

For millennia, war has been a proving ground for manliness, the field of honor; it has been a means of dispute resolution, wealth accumulation, and territorial expansion. But its violence appalls us so much that we have found a thousand ways to symbolically separate ourselves from war's brutality and keep war's poison leaking into ordinary human society and destroying it: we wear masks, engage in initiation and cleansing rituals, and change our very language to fight. We are constantly trying to keep war in a tidy box, separate from ordinary life.

Humans have also long sought to tame war, imposing rules on its chaos and violence and seeking to temper its brutality. The ancient Indian Laws of Manu, dated to somewhere between 1000 BC and AD 200, offer a list of prohibitions:

> When he fights with his foes in battle, let him not strike with weapons concealed (in wood), nor with (such as are) barbed, poisoned, or the points of which are blazing with fire.
>
> Let him not strike one . . . who joins the palms of his hands (in supplication), nor one who (flees) with flying hair, nor one who sits down, nor one who says "I am thine."
>
> Nor one who sleeps, nor one who has lost his coat of mail, nor one who is naked, nor one who is disarmed. . . .
>
> Nor one whose weapons are broken, nor one afflicted (with sorrow), nor one who has been grievously wounded, nor one who

is in fear, nor one who has turned to flight; (but in all these cases let him) remember the duty (of honourable warriors).[1]

In ancient China during the Warring States period, the seven feuding states agreed on rules concerning declarations of war and the treatment of prisoners, and prohibited the use of ruses, severely injuring, and capture of the elderly.[2] While Ancient Greek law permitted the massacre of civilians and disabled enemy soldiers, it required parties to conflicts to respect the inviolability of heralds, ambassadors, sacred places, and religious festivals, and required the "respectful treatment and return of enemy dead."[3]

In ancient Rome, Cicero wrote in 44 BC that

The only excuse . . . for going to war is that we may live in peace unharmed; and when the victory is won, we should spare those who have not been blood-thirsty and barbarous in their warfare. . . . Not only must we show consideration for those whom we have conquered by force of arms but we must also ensure protection to those who lay down their arms and throw themselves upon the mercy of our generals.[4]

In the fifth century, following Cicero, St. Augustine drew a distinction between just and unjust wars, noting that "They who have waged war in obedience to the divine command, or in conformity with His laws, have represented in their persons the public justice or the wisdom of government, and in this capacity have put to death wicked men; such persons have by no means violated the commandment, 'Thou shalt not kill.'"[5]

The Koran tells believers to "fight in God's cause against those who fight you, but do not overstep the limits; God does not love those who overstep the limits." Abu Bakr, the father-in-law of the Prophet Muhammad and the first caliph, is said to have told his men, "Do not act treacherously, do not act disloyally, do not act neglectfully. Do not mutilate. Do not kill little children or old men or women. Do not cut off the heads of palm trees or burn them. Do not cut down fruit trees. Do not slaughter livestock except for food."[6]

tance who had risen to a senior position in the Union Army. The meeting proved fateful: Halleck was able to help him locate Hamilton, who had lost an arm, and in the months that followed, Halleck and Lieber struck up a correspondence on issues ranging from politics to military tactics. Ultimately, Halleck—by then a Union general—invited Lieber to propose a new legal and ethical code for the Union Army.[16]

The draft code that Lieber produced in February 1863 remains famous even today. "Military necessity admits of all direct destruction of life or limb of armed enemies, and of other persons whose destruction is incidentally unavoidable in the armed contests of the war," wrote Lieber. As a result, the violence of war must be carefully circumscribed: "Peace is [the] normal condition; war is the exception." What's more, he insisted, even in wartime there must be clear rules and limits, for "Men who take up arms against one another in public war do not cease on this account to be moral beings, responsible to one another and to God." His code thus laid out detailed rules for the treatment of civilians, prisoners, and the wounded during war and occupation. Torture and "the infliction of suffering for the sake of suffering" must be considered always impermissible, for instance, and "the private citizen" must "be spared in person, property and honor."[17]

Lieber's draft met with prompt approval from General Halleck and other Union Army officials, and in April 1863 it was signed by President Abraham Lincoln and distributed to Union troops as "General Order 100: Instructions for the Government of Armies of the United States in the Field." Today, it is better known as the Lieber Code.

•  •  •

Lieber was not the only man focused on moving constraints on war out of the realm of morality and into the realm of law. In 1859, Swiss businessman Henry Dunant traveled to the small Italian city of Solferino. He hoped to meet there with Napoleon III, the emperor of France, and solicit his favorable intercession in a matter involving land and water rights in the French colony of Algeria, where Dunant had started a company. Instead, much to his own surprise, Dunant became a witness to a bloody battle between French and Austrian troops. "I was a mere tourist with no part whatever in this great conflict," he wrote the next year, "but it was my rare privilege, through an unusual train of circumstances, to witness the moving scenes that I have resolved to describe."[18] The Battle of Solferino involved some 300,000 men, and lasted more than fifteen hours, and Dunant was stunned by the suffering and bloodshed:

> Austrians and Allies trampling each other under foot, killing one another on piles of bleeding corpses, felling their enemies with their rifle butts, crushing skulls, ripping bellies open with sabre and bayonet. No quarter is given; it is a sheer butchery; a struggle between savage beasts, maddened with blood and fury. . . .
>
> Here come the artillery, following the cavalry, and going at full gallop. The guns crash over the dead and wounded, strewn pell-mell on the ground. Brains spurt under the wheels, limbs are broken and torn, bodies mutilated past recognition—the soil is literally puddled with blood, and the plain littered with human remains.[19]

The aftermath of the battle was equally horrific:

> Some, who had gaping wounds already beginning to show infection, were almost crazed with suffering. They begged to be put out of their misery, and writhed with faces distorted in the grip of the death-struggle. . . . Anyone crossing the vast theatre of the previous day's fighting could see at every step, in the midst of chaotic disorder, despair unspeakable and misery of every kind.[20]

Dunant began to organize relief parties to aid the wounded, raising money for food and medical supplies, and mobilizing the local civilian population to assist. He left Solferino convinced of the need for institutions and rules that could help reduce the suffering occasioned by war. In 1862, he published a short book describing the battle and its aftermath. "There is need," he concluded, "for voluntary orderlies and volunteer nurses, zealous, trained and experienced, whose position would be recognized by the commanders or armies in the field, and their mission facilitated and supported." Could not, asked Dunant, military leaders and diplomats meet

> to formulate some international principle, sanctioned by a Convention inviolate in character, which, once agreed upon and ratified, might constitute the basis for societies for the relief of the wounded in the different European countries? . . . Is it not a matter of urgency, since unhappily we cannot always avoid wars, to press forward in a human and truly civilized spirit the attempt to prevent, or at least to alleviate, the horrors of war?[21]

In 1863, just as Francis Lieber's new code was being developed, Dunant got his wish, and the International Committee of the Red Cross was founded. The following year, in 1864, ten European states ratified the Geneva Convention for the Amelioration of the Condition of the Wounded in Armies in the Field (First Geneva Convention).

Efforts to constrain armed conflict continued; in 1899 and 1907, international peace conferences at The Hague led to the drafting and later the entry into force of the various Hague Conventions on the laws and customs of war,[22] and in the interwar period, the Kellogg-Briand Pact between the United States and fourteen other nations made it illegal to have "recourse to war for the solution of international controversies."[23] Morality and philosophy were being transformed into international law, binding on all states.

## To Save Succeeding Generations

At the beginning, these heroic efforts to overpower war with law were largely unsuccessful. The Kellogg-Briand Pact failed to prevent the Second World War, and the Geneva and Hague Conventions did little to restrain its savagery. The Second World War remains the most destructive conflict humanity has yet seen. An estimated 50–60 million people were killed in the space of half a decade, and at least 20 million of those deaths were among the civilian population. Nazi Germany slaughtered some six million civilians, most of them Jews, during the Holocaust, and Japanese atrocities against civilians were legion. The Allies, meanwhile, killed hundreds of thousands of civilians through aerial bombing, culminating in the use of the atomic bomb in Japan.

It was against this backdrop of carnage and devastation that modern international law and institutions emerged: the United Nations Charter and its rules on the use of force, the codification of international human rights law, and the further codification and elaboration of the laws of armed conflicts.[24]

When I teach international law, my students are apt to view the United Nations as a dull and largely irrelevant institution. It's always a struggle to convey to them the sense of grief, horror, and urgency that led to the U.N.'s founding: today, when fifteen years of war have left fewer than ten thousand Americans dead, they have trouble wrapping their minds around the concept of a six-year war that literally decimated much of Europe, flattening great cities and killing some 15 percent of Central Europe's population.

As the realities of that terrible war recede further and further into the past, they have increasingly lost their power to shock. For those reaching adulthood today, World War II is as distant as the Franco-Prussian War or the American Civil War was to those who reached adulthood in the 1930s and 1940s.

For the diplomats who gathered to draft the United Nations Charter in San Francisco in April 1945, however, the war was no fading historical memory, but an ongoing reality. The Nazi concentration camps at Auschwitz-Birkenau had been liberated by Allied forces just months before the San Francisco conference began. On the Pacific front, the March 9 firebombing of Tokyo had left an estimated 100,000 dead—most of them civilians—in a single aerial raid.[25] And new horrors were revealed each day, even as the conference delegates in San Francisco busied themselves with the making of formal speeches and the endless, legalistic revision of carefully worded drafts. Dachau was liberated two days after the San Francisco conference began. Adolf Hitler's suicide came a few days later, and Germany's surrender a week after that.

And this did not yet mark the end of the Second World War's

slaughter. In the months following that first conference in San Francisco, a devastated Europe struggled to assess the carnage and begin the painful task of rebuilding. Meanwhile, the war in the Pacific raged on. In August, the United States dropped atomic bombs on the Japanese cities of Hiroshima and Nagasaki, killing another 135,000 people, mostly civilians. Japan signed formal documents of surrender on September 2, 1945, and on October 24, less than two months after the war's end, the United Nations Charter entered into force.

Today—some seven decades on from that increasingly unimaginable time—legal commentators and international relations experts still refer frequently to Chapter I of the United Nations Charter, which rather dryly declares that the U.N.'s purpose is "to maintain international peace and security." But we refer less often to the charter's preamble, with its poignant opening lines: "We the peoples of the United Nations" are determined "to save succeeding generations from the scourge of war, which twice in our lifetime has brought untold sorrow to mankind."

We are today apt to view this as mere rhetoric, hortatory language without legal effect or words that can be safely ignored by procedurally focused technocrats. It would be a mistake not to take these words seriously, however. Most of the men and women who drafted the U.N. Charter had experienced the "untold sorrows" of war firsthand, as had the leaders and populations of the states that employed them.

Historically, war had been viewed as a prerogative of states: an acceptable mode of territorial expansion, revenue production, or political dispute resolution. Clausewitz saw war as the continuation of politics by other means, and just war theory was simply that: theory. But the U.N. Charter sought to cement into law the Kellogg-Briand Pact's earlier prohibition on waging aggressive war—this time, with considerably more success.

Under the charter, U.N. member states pledged "to establish conditions under which justice and respect for the obligations arising from treaties and other sources of international law can be maintained, and . . . to practice tolerance and live together in peace with one another as good neighbors, and to unite our strength to maintain international peace and security, and to ensure, by the acceptance of principles and the institution of methods, that armed force shall not be used, save in the common interest." To that end, the charter declared that "all Members shall settle their international disputes by peaceful means . . . [and] refrain in their international relations from the threat or use of force against the territorial integrity or political independence of any state."[26]

For U.N. member states, this was a significant commitment—and the prohibition on the use of force proved surprisingly effective. While the U.N. Charter's collective security system certainly did not end all wars, it did succeed in greatly reducing the number of conflicts between states, and overall, deaths due to armed conflicts have declined.[27]

It was also significant that the charter's preamble is offered not in the name of nations, states, governments, or leaders, but as a commitment by and to the "peoples" of the United Nations. Like all institutions created by human beings, the United Nations was compromised by the cold realities of politics from its earliest moments. But though it has never fully lived up to the hopes once attached to it, it is nevertheless worth recalling its founding vision: a vision of a world that valued *human beings* above all, and a world in which those artificial political constructs we refer to as "states" and "governments" were at the service of the people who populated them, rather than the other way around.

The charter marked the symbolic beginning of the age of human rights. Prior to it, "human rights" lay largely in the realm of morality, theology, and ethics, not in the realm of international law. International law was viewed as governing the relations between states; insofar as individual human beings were concerned, international law regarded violations of their rights as violations of the rights of their parent states: a state that violated the rights of a foreign national might owe apologies and reparations to the foreign nation's government, but not to the injured individual himself.

After World War II, this changed.[28] After the Holocaust—after the U.N. Charter and the Universal Declaration of Human Rights; after the Nuremberg and Tokyo tribunals, which tried German and Japanese officials charged with war crimes and crimes against humanity— the language of human rights began to spread around the globe.

New treaties sprang up to protect human rights: one treaty prohibited genocide, another prohibited torture, and others laid out basic civil and political rights. Today, although human rights treaties are still only inconsistently enforced, we take it for granted that states shouldn't lock up dissidents, torture prisoners, or prohibit dissent. But in the 1940s and '50s, the notion that individual humans were entitled to be treated by their states with respect and concern—that they held "rights" not at the pleasure of their governments but simply by virtue of their humanity—was a revolutionary idea.

But it was also an idea that was, from the beginning, fundamentally in tension with the U.N. Charter's embrace of the principles of "sovereign equality" and sovereign "nonintervention." The charter prohibits member states from using force against each other, and Article 2.7 also declares that "Nothing contained in the present Charter shall authorize the United Nations to intervene in matters which are essentially within the domestic jurisdiction of any state." But if individuals hold rights by virtue of their humanity, and all states have a legal obligation to protect and defend the human rights of individuals, this, by definition, appears to place some limits on state sovereignty.

The evolution of the law of war in many ways complemented and paralleled the evolution of international human rights law. Although most scholars view human rights law and the law of armed conflict as conceptually distinct, both bodies of law share a concern with establishing an irreducible sphere of human dignity that nothing, not even war, can justify breaching. The trials of German and Japanese leaders by the Nuremberg and Tokyo tribunals helped establish that even during wartime, certain acts were legally prohibited, and the four Geneva Conventions of 1949 added additional clarity.[29]

Common Article 3 of the Geneva Conventions famously lays out minimum standards of conduct for all parties to conflicts, including nonstate actors:

Persons taking no active part in the hostilities, including members of armed forces who have laid down their arms and those placed "hors de combat" by sickness, wounds, detention, or any other cause, shall in all circumstances be treated humanely, without any adverse distinction founded on race, colour, religion or faith, sex, birth or wealth, or any other similar criteria.

To this end, the following acts are and shall remain prohibited at any time and in any place whatsoever with respect to the above-mentioned persons:

(a) violence to life and person, in particular murder of all kinds, mutilation, cruel treatment and torture;

(b) taking of hostages;

(c) outrages upon personal dignity, in particular humiliating and degrading treatment;

(d) the passing of sentences and the carrying out of executions without previous judgment pronounced by a regularly constituted court, affording all the judicial guarantees which are recognized as indispensable by civilized peoples.

(2) The wounded and sick shall be collected and cared for.

The process of seeking to constrain and "humanize" armed conflict has continued into the present time, and though the enforcement of human rights and humanitarian law remains uneven, both national and transnational courts at times have held states and individuals liable for violations of these core norms. Several of the leaders who ordered genocide and ethnic cleansing in Rwanda and Bosnia are now behind bars, for instance, convicted of war crimes or crimes against humanity by international tribunals. The law still does not speak with a loud voice in time of war, but it is no longer wholly silent.

The U.N. Charter also sought to lay out clear rules about the limited circumstances in which states could use military force. While the charter expressly prohibited "the threat or use of force against the territorial integrity or political independence of any state" and obligated states to settle disputes by "peaceful means," it also laid out certain exceptions to the general prohibition on armed force. First, the charter empowers the U.N. Security Council to identify "any threat to the peace, breach of the peace, or act of aggression." In such cases, the Security Council may "take such action by air, sea, or land forces as may be necessary to maintain or restore international peace and security." For practical purposes (since the United Nations never got the standing army envisioned by its founders), this means the Security Council can pass a resolution authorizing member states to use force to carry out its mandates (this occurred in the first Gulf War, for instance, and in the 2011 air campaign in Libya).

A second exception to the prohibition on the use of force relates to self-defense. In Article 51, the charter says, "Nothing in the present Charter shall impair the inherent right of individual or collective self-defense if an armed attack occurs against a Member of the United Nations, until the Security Council has taken the measures necessary to maintain international peace and security." Aside from Security Council authorization and self-defense, there is one other implied exception to the prohibition on using force inside a sovereign state. By definition, it is not a violation of sovereignty if one state consents to another state's use of force inside its borders.

Today, states generally accept that decisions about when and how to use force must comply with core legal principles—and though some aspects of the law of armed conflict can seem numbingly trivial (prisoners of war must be permitted to wear badges and declarations, for instance, but are obligated to salute military officials of the detaining power), most of the law's important principles are familiar even to laypersons.

To begin with, the law of armed conflict accepts that certain behaviors that are illegal and abhorrent in time of peace are both permissible and desirable in time of war. Most obviously, the deliberate killing of other humans is considered morally abhorrent in peacetime, but in time of war soldiers are not only permitted but *required* to try to incapacitate members of enemy forces, if necessary by killing them.

In peacetime, the willful killing of another human would normally lead to prosecution, trial, and possibly conviction for the crime of murder. During and after wars, however, soldiers have what the law calls "combatant immunity": they cannot be prosecuted for killing enemy combatants, destroying enemy property, and so on. Similarly, combatants can be captured and detained by opposing forces, but they can't be punished for their legitimate wartime acts, and they must be released when hostilities end.

But the law of armed conflict offers benefits only to those who play by its rules. The law draws a clear distinction, for instance, between violence that is justified by "military necessity"—the need to weaken opposing forces—and violence motivated by simple callousness or cruelty. The law of armed conflict also draws a sharp line between violence directed against enemy combatants, which is permissible, and violence against "protected persons" (civilians, prisoners, etc.), which is not.

To put this in legal terms, military violence, to be lawful, must seek to avoid "unnecessary" suffering and must be in accordance with the principles of "proportionality" and "distinction." The principle of proportionality requires that "loss of life and damage to property incidental to attacks must not be excessive in relation to the concrete and direct military advantage expected to be gained." That sounds technical, but is essentially just a restatement of common sense morality: don't use nuclear bombs when conventional artillery will do the trick; don't flatten an entire village if a targeted raid on a single house will accomplish the same objective.

The principle of distinction is similar: it requires that military violence must "distinguish between combatants and noncombatants; military objectives and protected people/protected places." Translated into common sense terms, this is perhaps the most familiar rule of all: it's fine to shoot at enemy soldiers, but not at children or other civilians; it's fine to drop bombs on the enemy's military positions, but not okay to bomb schools or hospitals. Targeting and killing enemy combatants is a lawful and accepted part of war, but the deliberate slaughter of civilians or helpless prisoners is a war crime.

Of course, these simple principles aren't always so simple to apply. Take the principle of proportionality. The principle of proportionality would clearly prohibit carpet bombing an entire city in order to eliminate the threat posed by a single sniper—but how much incidental loss of life is too much, and how can one measure the "concrete and direct military advantage expected to be gained"? Would bombing an entire apartment building full of civilians be acceptable if the purpose of the attack was to eliminate a sniper known to be somewhere in the building? (Almost certainly not.) Bombing a whole house? (Maybe.) If the sniper is firing a shoulder-mounted antiaircraft missile capable of bringing down troop transport planes or passenger jets, how many incidental civilian deaths would be permissible as part of an effort to get the sniper?

Even the principle of distinction, so clear in theory, gets murky in practice. When the enemy is a terrorist group rather than an organized state military, it's not obvious who should count as a "civilian." What's more, even civilians can be deliberately targeted and killed if they take "direct part in hostilities." No one would dispute that a civilian who picks up a weapon and starts firing at opposing forces becomes a lawful target—but was Osama bin Laden's driver an enemy combatant or a civilian? If he was a civilian, did he take a "direct part" in "hostilities"? All the time? Only while driving? Only while driving with explosives in the trunk? Only while driving bin Laden to an attack, or to a planning session for an imminent attack? Only while carrying a weapon? Only while firing a weapon?

## I Have No Respect for Those Guys

To laypersons, this may seem like so much legal hair-splitting. But a great deal hinges on such questions, and by and large U.S. military lawyers take them exceptionally seriously.

Most military lawyers are Boy Scouts: hardworking, sincere, and absolutely dedicated to applying the law of war, as they understand it, in an ethical and responsible manner.

Indeed, U.S. military as a whole takes the laws of war very seriously. All military personnel receive training on the law of war, and Defense Department directives mandate that "members of the DoD Components [must] comply with the law of war during all armed conflicts, however such conflicts are characterized, and in all other military operations."[30] The Uniform Code of Military Justice incorporates international law of armed conflict principles into U.S. law, and service members who flagrantly violate the law of armed conflict tend to wind up in prison.

The relative size of the Judge Advocate General's corps has increased over the last fifty years, and military lawyers have been increasingly integrated into operational decision making.[31] During the Vietnam War, there were about 1,800 active duty Army JAG lawyers in an army of nearly 1.5 million soldiers.[32] Today, there are some 1,600 active duty JAG lawyers in an army less than a third that size: relative to the size of the total force, the size of the JAG corps has increased threefold. [33]

Military lawyers undertake a wide variety of tasks, including training local judges and lawyers in conflict and post-conflict environments. They also teach law of war classes for U.S. and foreign soldiers, help commanders determine rules of engagement, conduct investigations in cases involving civilian casualties, and participate in real-time decision making about targeting. As Geoffrey Corn, a retired Army JAG lawyer now teaching at the South Texas College of Law, puts it, "It is no exaggeration to state that at no time in history have legal advisors been more integrated into [the targeting] process than today."[34]

Not everyone appreciates this, of course. Search military blogs or the right-wing media, and you'll find plenty of complaints that all those lawyers are just getting in the way. "When Capt. Zinni spotted the four men planting the booby trap on the afternoon of Feb. 17, the first thing he did was call his lawyer," notes a 2010 *Wall Street Journal* article. "'Judge!' he yelled. . . . Capt. Matthew Andrew, judge advocate for 1st Battalion, 6th Marine Regiment, advises the battalion about when it is legal to order the airstrikes. He examined the . . . video feed closely. 'I think you got it,' Capt. Andrew said, giving the OK for the strike."[35] Stories like this send some into conniptions: "Pull the trigger . . . and leave the lawyers out of it!" fulminates a blog post on HotAir.com.[36]

Ironically, as the *Wall Street Journal* article makes clear, it was the lawyer who was willing to err on the side of striking, and the nonlawyer—in this case, Captain Anthony Zinni, son of the general of the same name—who decided not to order airstrikes in the end. As he studied the video feed more closely, he saw something he had missed earlier: "Children. Maybe 50 feet from the men planting the booby trap. 'It's not a good shot,' Capt. Zinni said, ordering the Predator drone to delay the strike. 'It's not a good shot.'"

In 2005, the University of Virginia's *Journal of International Law* hosted a conference called "The Politics of the Geneva Conventions." I spoke at the conference, as did a number of lawyers from the Army's Judge Advocate General's School, which is physically located right next door to UVA's law school. Also speaking at the conference were several former Bush administration lawyers, including John Yoo, the Justice Department lawyer many blame for giving the legal green light to the torture of detainees, and Jack Goldsmith, who served both in the Bush Justice Department and in the Defense Department general counsel's office (and who promptly rescinded Yoo's memoranda on torture during his own stint at the Justice Department).

After the conference, the speakers gathered for dinner at a Charlottesville restaurant. The JAG lawyers had said their goodbyes, and only a small group remained, including myself, Goldsmith, and Yoo. Somehow, the conversation turned to the role of JAG lawyers, and Yoo complained that JAG lawyers tend to be very literal-minded about the law. Goldsmith agreed, but added, "I have a lot of respect for JAG lawyers."

John Yoo didn't share the sentiment.

"I have *no* respect for those guys!" he burst out. "None! They just don't get it! They don't understand that the laws they love so much just can't be applied anymore. They just can't seem to change with the times!"

Everyone courteously ignored this outburst, because polite law professors don't accuse each other of being torturers over dinner. But we all knew what Yoo was talking about.

Recall White House counsel Alberto Gonzales's January 2002 memo arguing that "the war against terrorism is a new kind of war. . . . It is not the traditional clash between nations adhering to the laws of war that formed the backdrop for [the Geneva Conventions]. The nature of the new war places a high premium on other factors, such as the ability to quickly obtain information from captured terrorists. . . . In my judgment, this new paradigm renders obsolete Geneva's strict limitations on questioning of enemy prisoners and renders quaint some of its provisions."[37]

Yoo—then a young lawyer at the Justice Department's Office of Legal Counsel—shared the sentiment, and took it a few steps further, authoring a series of memos giving the green light for a range of harsh interrogation techniques, including hooding, sleep deprivation, use of dogs, sensory deprivation, nudity, the placement of prisoners in painful positions for extended periods, and waterboarding.

He and his Justice Department colleagues also elaborated on a theory of executive power that effectively makes the president above the law: since the Constitution makes the president the chief executive of the United States and the commander in chief of the armed forces, any congressional effort to pass laws limiting or criminalizing certain forms of interrogation would restrict the president's inherent powers, and thus be unconstitutional; as a result, the president need not obey any laws that, in his view, infringe on his inherent powers.[38]

In 2004, when photos of egregious abuses at Abu Ghraib prison in Iraq brought U.S. interrogation practices under increasing scrutiny, many commentators linked the Abu Ghraib abuses to the Bush administration's insistence that the "war against terrorism" was a "new kind of war" and that neither Congress nor international law could limit presidential discretion.

But Alberto Gonzales wasn't wholly wrong when he noted that traditional law of war concepts couldn't easily be applied to a war against terrorism—he and his cronies were simply wrong to conclude that the blurriness of *some* legal categories should permit the deliberate flouting of any rules they happened to find inconvenient. However much genuine uncertainty there is in efforts to apply the law of armed conflict to new kinds of conflicts and threats, the rules prohibiting torture are entirely clear and unambiguous.

Regardless of which set of rules one chooses to invoke (criminal law, the law of armed conflict, human rights law, and so on), and regardless of how one categorizes detainees (as prisoners of war, unlawful combatants, criminals, or civilians participating in hostilities), the minimum standards concerning humane treatment are essentially the same. Common Article 3 of the four Geneva Conventions prohibits "cruel treatment and torture," as well as "outrages upon personal dignity, in particular, humiliating and degrading treatment." Torture is prohibited under federal criminal law and under military regulations, as well as by international law—and as noted above, the Convention Against Torture makes it clear that torture is justified by "no exceptional circumstances whatsoever."

When Bush administration lawyers such as John Yoo argued that waterboarding and the like didn't legally constitute torture, they were not simply mistaken about the conclusions warranted by statute, treaty, and case law—they were engaging in illegitimate and unethical forms of legal argumentation, ignoring and selectively misreading various relevant texts in order to reach a predetermined conclusion.

Think of law—the enterprise of legal interpretation—as a game, like basketball or football or tennis. The "game" of legal interpretation has rules, some written, some customary, some bright-line, some ambiguous. But although it is difficult to say just what elements make tennis *tennis*, we all know that there is a difference between playing tennis in a way that pushes the envelope between the permissible and the impermissible, "cheating," and leaving the game altogether.

Thus: Calling a ball "in" when it just touches the outside of the baseline is skirting the edge of the permissible, but it is clearly within the rule. Calling a ball "in" when you know it landed outside the baseline is cheating, but it's still "playing tennis": it's just *cheating* at tennis. Pausing to beat up your opponent when he complains that you're cheating is no longer tennis, however; the resort to force destroys the game entirely.

Map this onto three of the different kinds of Bush administration legal arguments I mentioned above. The claim that war on terror detainees were not entitled to any of the protections of the Geneva Conventions was surely wrongheaded in a strategic and moral sense, but if we think of law as a game, the Bush administration's lawyers were still playing by the rules here, though perhaps pushing the boundaries a bit.

Yoo and his colleagues' claims about torture are different: the conclusion that waterboarding and such don't constitute torture relies on cheating, insofar as it depends on selective and misleading citations and odd logical leaps. Nonetheless, cheating, however reprehensible, is still a way to play the game; by definition, if you are cheating at a game, you are still accepting most aspects of the game itself.

But the Bush administration's claims about "inherent executive powers" is of a different order. Though couched in legal terms, such claims constitute a game-ending move, the rough equivalent of a threat: "Play by my rules or I'll crush you."

Of course, though law is "game-like," it's not truly a game. Law differs from tennis because the "rules" of law and legal interpretation are not there for the entertainment of the players: they're not merely self-referential. Law is supposed to bear some relation to facts on the ground, and law enables coercive action to be taken in ways that can permanently alter the facts on the ground. If we create a legal system in which cheating is widespread—or, worse, if we overlook game-ending moves by those with power and treat them as legitimate modifications of the game—then it isn't merely the rules that get bent, but the rule of law itself.

•   •   •

Unlike their civilian counterparts at the White House, the Justice Department, and the CIA, most military lawyers had no trouble understanding that however much a war on terrorism might present a "new paradigm" and "render obsolete" aspects of the law, nothing about this "new kind of war" justified the kinds of "enhanced" interrogations that John Yoo was inclined to permit.

A series of 2003 memos from the nation's top military lawyers made this clear. Major General Jack Rives, then deputy judge advocate general of the Air Force, warned the general counsel's office at the Pentagon that "several of the more extreme interrogation techniques [described], on their face, amount to violations of domestic criminal law and the [Uniform Code of Military Justice]." His Navy JAG colleague, Rear Admiral Michael Lohr, wrote that at least one of the interrogation techniques suggested by the Justice Department "constitutes torture under both domestic and international law."

The Army's judge advocate general, Major General Thomas Romig, added that John Yoo's analysis could damage military "interests worldwide . . . putting our service personnel at far greater risk and vitiating many of the POW/detainee safeguards the United States has worked hard to establish over the past five decades." Similarly, Marine Corps JAG Brigadier General Kevin Sandkuhler cautioned that the interrogation techniques green-lighted by the Justice Department would "adversely impact . . . public support and respect of U.S. armed forces [and] pride, discipline, and self-respect within the U.S. armed forces."

It was the Navy's Rear Admiral Lohr who made the point most poignantly. If questionable and harsh interrogation techniques are used, he asked, "will the American people find we have missed the forest for the trees by condoning practices that, [even if] technically legal, are inconsistent with our most fundamental values?"[39]

# CHAPTER ELEVEN

# An Optimistic Enterprise

## Law in the Heart of Darkness

Law is an optimistic enterprise. It is premised on the conviction that even the almost unimaginable extremes of human emotion and behavior can be made subject to the law's rationalizing power—the conviction that law can reach into the very heart of darkness, and make us better than we have so far proven to be. Francis Lieber and Henry Dunant believed that law could bring both honor and compassion to the horrors of the battlefield; more recently, top military lawyers sought to use law and assertions about the fundamental values behind the law to counter the Bush administration's utilitarian arguments for "enhanced interrogation."

While it is a truism to observe that if humans were angels, law would be unnecessary, we could equally turn the truism around, and note that if humans were devils, law would be pointless. In this sense, the law-making project always presupposes the improvability, if not the perfectibility, of humankind. Whether our view of human nature tends toward Hobbesian grimness or Rousseauian equanimity, we tend to think of law as critical to reducing brutality and violence.

But what actually happens when law is operating at the extreme edge of human behavior and emotion? Can law truly tame war, or is that just a dream? Does the law of war have anything particularly satisfying to offer those people who find themselves caught in the dark places of the earth—or any lessons for those of us who have not so far been tested?

. . .

Here is a story about law and war, and an ordinary man who found one day that the moral terrain around him had changed beyond recognition.[1]

This story comes out of the first judgment handed down by the International Criminal Tribunal for the Former Yugoslavia, better known as the Hague Tribunal. The case, *Prosecutor v. Erdemovic*, was decided in 1997,[2] but for years it received only minimal attention. This is probably because, to many observers of the tribunal, it seemed like an unimportant and even disappointing case: it involved the wrongs of an obscure young Croatian soldier, not those of a general or a president, and its outcome, to many critics, was hardly a resounding victory over the forces of evil.

But it's a fascinating case. It can be seen as a parable about the limits of law and its inherent inability to completely tame war's savagery—but it might equally be seen as a parable about law's vital role in marking the boundaries between good and evil, even when its practical impact seems most attenuated.

Drazen Erdemovic was an ethnic Croat who lived in the Yugoslav republic of Bosnia-Herzegovina. In 1990, Erdemovic, aged eighteen, began his mandatory military service in the Yugoslav National Army, which was at that time still more or less multiethnic in composition. In 1992, voters in Bosnia-Herzegovina opted for independence from the Federal Republic of Yugoslavia in a referendum in which most of the region's Bosnians and Croats participated, but most of the Serbs boycotted. The Republic of Bosnia and Herzegovina declared its independence from Yugoslavia shortly thereafter, and Erdemovic, who had just finished his service with the Yugoslav National Army, was briefly mobilized into the new republic's army as civil war engulfed the region. In November 1992, however, Erdemovic left the Bosnian army to serve with the Croatian Defense Council's police force. His tenure there was equally short.

By all accounts, Erdemovic was an accidental and unwilling soldier. He came from a pacifist, cosmopolitan background, and opposed the war; when he left the Croatian Defense Force, he sought work as a locksmith. He eventually married a Serbian woman he had known since childhood, and the young couple drifted around Serbia for a time, trying to find work and a place where a multiethnic family could live unmolested. Finally, with his wife pregnant and his savings almost gone, Erdemovic turned to one of the few remaining sources of steady employment in the region, and in 1994 he enlisted once more, this time in the Bosnian Serb army of Radovan Karadzic's self-proclaimed "Republika Srpska," the Serb enclave within Bosnia.

Although whispers of concentration camps, torture, and other atrocities had already reached well beyond the region, most of these rumored atrocities were attributed to vicious Serb paramilitaries and police, not to regular soldiers. When he joined the Bosnian Serb army, Erdemovic asked to serve in the 10th Sabotage Detachment because its members included Croats as well as Serbs, and because it was not a combat unit. For a time, all went well; Erdemovic's wife bore a son, money came in, and Erdemovic's military duties were not too onerous.

On July 16, 1995, however, the 10th Sabotage Detachment was ordered to the Branjevo collective farm in Pilica, not far from the city of Srebrenica, for a mission that was not disclosed to the soldiers until five buses pulled up and several hundred Muslim men and boys were let off, hands tied together. The Muslims—all in civilian clothes—were lined up with their backs to the soldiers, and Erdemovic and his comrades were told that upon their commander's word, they were to shoot the civilians.

## Are You Normal?

Drazen Erdemovic was incredulous. It didn't take a law of war expert to understand that this was an illegal order: shooting the civilians would clearly constitute a war crime. As Erdemovic later told the judges of the Hague Tribunal's trial chamber, "I said immediately that I did not want to take part in that and I said, 'Are you normal? Do you know what you are doing?'" But his commander told him bluntly that he had a choice: he could participate in the executions of the Muslim civilians, or, if he felt "sorry for them," he could "stand up, line up with them and we will kill you too."

Faced with such a choice, Erdemovic reluctantly agreed to obey the order. He made one more effort to be merciful when he spotted an elderly man whom he recognized among the civilians. He told his commander that the man had helped save the lives of Serbs on an earlier occasion, and suggested that at least his life might be spared. But his commander said that it was not possible to spare any of the civilians: none of them could be left alive as witnesses.

At this, Erdemovic gave up his efforts to resist, and participated, however unwillingly, in the slaughter. He later told journalists that he tried to kill as few people as possible, and he made an effort not to shoot at the youngest victims. But the buses kept leaving and returning with more victims, and by the day's end, Erdemovic estimated that his bullets might have killed as many as seventy or eighty people. Soldiers of the 10th Sabotage Unit killed some 1,200 civilians that day, a good fraction of the estimated seven to eight thousand Srebrenica civilians slaughtered that week by the Bosnian Serb army.

Four months later, the Dayton Accords brought an ambiguous end to the war in Bosnia, and Drazen Erdemovic, now twenty-five years old, again found himself demobilized. But his personal war was not quite over. Erdemovic poured out his story to a journalist from the French newspaper *Le Figaro*, and informed her that he wanted to go to The Hague and tell his story there as well.

He did not have to wait long. The story in *Le Figaro* caused a sensation; it was the first acknowledgment by any of the perpetrators that Europe's worst massacre since the Holocaust had definitely occurred. In the wake of the Dayton Accords, Yugoslav premier Slobodan Milosevic was eager to throw a few bones to the international community. Handing over a general or a president like Ratko Mladic or Radovan Karadzic would have been costly for Milosevic, but picking up a Croat foot soldier who seemed desperate to incriminate himself in any event was an easy way to keep everyone happy. Shortly after the *Le Figaro* article was published, Erdemovic was arrested by Yugoslav authorities and transferred to The Hague.[3]

## They Would Have Killed Me

At this point, the story of Drazen Erdemovic also becomes a story about the age-old human dream of taming war with law.

At The Hague, Erdemovic repeated and amplified the confession he had made to *Le Figaro*. His own confession was the only incriminating evidence against him, and prosecutors were at first reluctant to charge him; the Hague Tribunal had been established in 1992 with much fanfare and with pledges to bring to justice the most high-ranking perpetrators, and a conscience-stricken twenty-five-year-old Croatian foot soldier was no one's idea of a good start. In May 1996, however, Erdemovic was charged with one count of crimes against humanity and one count of war crimes.

In November 1996 (after delays due partly to Erdemovic's shaky mental and emotional state), he pled guilty to the first charge. But as he entered his plea, he reiterated to the trial court that he had participated in the massacre only to save his own life: "Your Honour, I had to do this. If I had refused, I would have been killed together with the victims. . . . I could not refuse because then they would have killed me."

After his guilty plea, Erdemovic was sentenced by the trial court to ten years in prison. On appeal, however, a new attorney assigned to his case argued that Erdemovic's guilty plea had been uninformed and equivocal, and that since he had told the judge he participated in the massacre only to avoid certain death, his statements should properly have been understood as a plea of "not guilty" due to duress.

This raised a novel question for the tribunal: Can duress be a complete defense to charges of crimes against humanity or war crimes, when the crimes at issue involve the killing of innocent people? The trial court had assumed that duress might serve as a mitigating factor in sentencing, but could not fully exonerate a defendant. The Appeals Chamber, however, acknowledged that the precise scope of the defense of duress was uncertain, and undertook to determine the appropriate international law rule relating to the scope of the duress defense.

There was no issue of fact at stake. The prosecution stipulated that they accepted the truth of Erdemovic's version of events, and acknowledged that he probably would have been shot by his commander had he refused to take part in the slaughter. Thus, the only question for the Appeals Chamber was whether duress should exonerate Erdemovic, leading to a verdict of "not guilty," or merely reduce his sentence following a guilty verdict.

The judges of the Appeals Chamber agreed, after a survey of possible sources of international law on the issue, that there was no unambiguous international legal standard on the scope of the duress defense. As far as national legal systems were concerned, there was also no consensus: virtually all civil law jurisdictions permitted duress as a complete defense to all crimes, while virtually all common law jurisdictions precluded the defense of duress to charges of murdering innocent people.

By a vote of 3–2, the Appeals Chamber ultimately decided to adopt the general common law rule. The plurality opinion, authored by Justices Gabrielle Kirk McDonald and Lal Chand Vohrah, declared that while duress might be a *mitigating* factor that would affect sentencing, duress was *not* a complete defense to charges of crimes against humanity.[4] Drazen Erdemovic had properly entered a guilty plea, for no amount of duress could exonerate him altogether.

In some ways this seems like an astonishing conclusion. Erdemovic had had no desire to kill innocent civilians, and he did so only when threatened with his own imminent death. Given the context, his death would probably have served no purpose: the Muslim civilians would surely have been killed with or without his participation, and refusal to participate in the massacre would merely have added Erdemovic to the list of victims.

By establishing this standard, the majority of the Appeals Chamber essentially declared that Erdemovic's legal guilt was foreordained when he was ordered to Srebrenica. Erdemovic could have preserved his legal innocence only by sacrificing his life. At Srebrenica, the only way to be innocent was to be dead.

## A Heroic Example

There is, of course, a possibility that his commander would have spared him and allowed him to sit out the massacre, but the possibility must have seemed to Erdemovic to be vanishingly small. Even if Erdemovic had heroically declared, "Go ahead, shoot me, but I won't kill these civilians," the civilians would almost surely have been slaughtered anyway by the other soldiers in his unit. There is also a faint possibility that Erdemovic's refusal to participate might have sparked a broader resistance among the other soldiers, but again, the possibility was vanishingly small; Serbian war crimes in Bosnia were numerous and systematic, and it is overwhelmingly likely that with or without Erdemovic, and even with or without his comrades in the 10th Sabotage Detachment, the Muslims of Srebrenica would have been slaughtered sometime that week.

So, Erdemovic was effectively faced with a choice: He could violate one of the most fundamental tenets of the laws of war by participating in the massacre, and the civilians would die, but he would stay alive. Alternatively, he could obey the law by refusing to participate in the massacre, in which case he would die right alongside the civilian victims. Expecting Erdemovic to have acted other than as he did seems thoroughly unreasonable.

Recall his anguished question to his commander and comrades when faced with an order he knew to be both illegal and unconscionable: "I said, 'Are you normal? Do you know what you are doing?'"

Sadly, Erdemovic's colleagues were "normal" indeed: they were average humans who followed orders and didn't stick their necks out to save people they did not know. It was only Erdemovic who was atypical enough to lodge a protest, however ineffectual.

From this perspective, Erdemovic appears to have made a defensible choice. Writing for the two-judge dissent in the Erdemovic case, Judge Antonio Cassese took this view. Had Erdemovic "compl[ied] with his legal duty not to shoot innocent persons," wrote Cassese, "he would [have] forfeit[ed] his life for no benefit to anyone and to no effect whatsoever apart from setting a heroic example for mankind (which the law cannot demand him to set)."[5]

This, argued Cassese, was hardly fair. "Law is based on what society can reasonably expect of its members. It should not set intractable standards of behaviour which require mankind to perform acts of martyrdom, and brand as criminal any behavior falling below those standards." To do so, he argued, would be the purest hypocrisy.

. . .

The Appeals Chamber plurality was ready enough to acknowledge the harshness of its rule, but viewed this harshness as no more than was necessary:

> Surely it is at the moment when the temptation to crime is strongest that the law should speak most clearly and emphatically to the contrary. . . . The law should not be the product or slave of logic or intellectual hair-splitting, but must serve broader normative purposes in light of its social, political and economic role.

The plurality decision went on to cite a number of policy reasons for their decision, insisting that "It would be naive to believe that international law operates and develops wholly divorced from considerations of social and economic policy. . . . There is no avoiding the essential relationship between law and politics."

In the end, the plurality did not rest its decision upon a utilitarian calculus. "The approach we take does not involve a balancing of harms for and against killing . . . our rejection of duress as a defence to the killing of innocent human beings does not depend upon what the reasonable person is expected to do. We would assert an absolute moral postulate which is clear and unmistakable for the implementation of international humanitarian law." Citing the eminent British jurist Sir William Blackstone, they concluded that "a man . . . ought rather to die himself, than escape by the murder of an innocent."

Implicitly, we have here a statement about the acceptable moral contours of a human life, a statement about what it is that makes us human beings, without which we might as well be dead.

We also have a statement about the purpose of law. To the plurality, law cannot be predicated wholly on expedience or on what the average man can reasonably be expected to do. Law should instead be seen as having "broader normative purposes": it is part of politics, not an edifice that stands apart from the ongoing collective project of building a better future. By providing moral guidance and assigning moral meaning to our acts and our choices, the creation and interpretation of legal rules helps shape the world to come.

## Because of Everything

Erdemovic himself seemed to have agreed with the plurality's view of the issue. During his sentencing hearing in November 1996, he wept as he explained to the judges why he had decided to plead guilty, despite his conviction that he had acted under duress. At Srebrenica, he said,

> [My commander] said, "If you do not want to [participate in the executions], stand with them . . . so that we can kill you too. . . ."
>
> I was not afraid for myself at that point, not that much . . . but what would happen to my child and to my wife? So there was this enormous burden falling on my shoulders. . . . I knew that I would be killing people, that I could not hide this, that this would be burning at my conscience. . . .
>
> [My attorney] told me, "Drazen, can you change your mind, your decision [to plead guilty]? . . . I do not know what will happen. . . ."
>
> [But] I told him because of those victims, because of my consciousness, because of my life, because of my child and my wife, I cannot change what I said . . . because of the peace of my mind, my soul, my honesty, because of the victims and war and because of everything. Although I knew that my family, my parents, my brother, my sister would have problems because of that, I did not want to change it. Because of everything that happened I feel terribly sorry, but I could not do anything. . . .
>
> Thank you. I have nothing else to say.[6]

Perhaps for Erdemovic, pleading guilty and accepting his sentence was part of restoring his sense of himself as a moral person. Perhaps, from his point of view, serving his prison sentence was his own small contribution to building a better future.

. . .

The story of Drazen Erdemovic's life and trial is full of painful ambiguities. This may lead some to dismiss its significance, either on the "hard facts make bad law" theory, or on the theory that the situation Erdemovic faced was so extreme and complex that it offers no useful lessons. But it is the very ambiguities in this story that should give us pause.

How should we feel about this instance when the law seems to demand something unreasonable—this moment when the law seems to require heroism and martyrdom? Where we come out on this has a great deal to do with our conceptions of the appropriate temporal framework for understanding the events at issue. Do we see wartime as standing almost outside of ordinary time, in binary opposition to ordinary peacetime life? Or do we see war—and that farm outside Srebrenica on July 16, 1995—as just another point along the continuum between peace and war, with one moment blurring almost indistinguishably into another, until, suddenly, we look around and everything seems different?

On the spot, it seems unfair to punish someone as a criminal just because he could not quite bring himself to die for the sake of a legal and moral principle. But if we go back far enough—before the choices became so stark and unforgiving, before the threat of violence became so palpable and imminent—perhaps it is fair after all. Here, taking a different temporal view, the focus shifts to how the actor ended up in such a bad situation in the first place, and to what each moment had in common with the long line of moments preceding it.

Put another way: when we evaluate Drazen Erdemovic's behavior on the farm outside Srebrenica, a lot depends on whether we see his story as a narrative about inevitability and determinism, or a narrative about choice. To Antonio Cassese, writing for the Appeals Chamber's minority, Erdemovic's story is a tale about inevitability, and the very worst sort of moral luck. Erdemovic was caught up in events beyond his control, and he had no more freedom than a pawn on a chessboard: he was an ordinary man who one day simply found himself in an untenable situation. *Someone* was guilty of a terrible crime at Srebrenica, no question—but it was not Drazen Erdemovic, young and frightened and anxious about the fate of his wife and child.

To the majority on the Appeals Chamber, however, Erdemovic's story is fundamentally a narrative about choice. The majority treats Erdemovic as a moral agent whose failure was consummated at Srebrenica, but begun, perhaps, much earlier. Erdemovic's crime, on this view, goes back some years: Erdemovic drifted from army to army, committed to nothing but unable to bring himself to resist wholly. He was complicit, little by little, in allowing Bosnia to become one of the earth's dark places. By the time he tried, finally, to take a stand, it was much too late.

We prefer to imagine brutal wars and atrocities as events that "just happen" every now and then, much like tornadoes or lightning strikes; this metaphor suggests that we can't generalize from them, since they are radically discontinuous with ordinary life. But wars and atrocities do not "just happen": societies and individuals slide into them, little by little, one tiny decision or omission at a time.

Keeping this in mind, perhaps we can make more sense of the common-law rule permitting duress as a complete defense to all crimes except murder. The rule is puzzling if we think that "ordinary life" always remains ordinary, for if it does, why not just be consistent, and allow the duress defense across the board? But if we realize that the ordinary can become the extreme in the blink of an eye, the Appeals Chamber's refusal to permit duress as a defense to murder seems less an anomaly than a stern warning of how easily events can slide out of control.

Perhaps the rule is meant to say to us, "If you find yourself having to choose between killing an innocent person and preserving your own life, you have already chosen wrong." Perhaps the rule is meant to warn us that the contours of darkness and war are often indistinct—and by the time we see that war has swallowed us whole, it's usually too late.

Of course, the Srebrenica massacre could not have occurred without countless political and moral failures of the first order, made by people and institutions with far more power than Drazen Erdemovic.

Recall that in 1995, unable to summon the political will to take sides in the Bosnian conflict or impose a peace, but dogged by media reports of atrocities against civilians, the United Nations Security Council came up with the idea of declaring certain areas within Bosnia U.N. "safe areas," to which civilians could go and be protected by U.N. peacekeeping troops. Srebrenica was one such "safe area," and in the summer of 1995 thousands of Bosnian Muslim civilians poured into Srebrenica to seek protection from the incursions of the Bosnian Serb army and paramilitaries. As the plurality opinion in the Erdemovic case dryly notes, however, the Dutch U.N. troops protecting the "safe area" of Srebrenica (the judges had enough sense of shame to keep the term in quotation marks) surrendered their weapons to the Serbs and withdrew rather than risk a fight. It was their abandoned civilian charges who were brought by the busload for Erdemovic and his fellow soldiers to slaughter.

Naturally, none of the Dutch U.N. peacekeepers were ever brought up on criminal charges for their failure to protect the civilians they were pledged to protect, and no high-ranking U.N. officials were charged as accomplices in the murder of the thousands who died, and none of the Security Council powers who gave the U.N. leaders their marching orders will ever be called to account in a court of law.[7]

When the Hague Tribunal was established by the United Nations Security Council in 1993, it represented the first major international judicial effort to punish and deter atrocities since the Nuremberg and Tokyo tribunals nearly fifty years earlier. Its formation was linked in the minds of many of its creators with the long-term goal of creating a permanent international criminal court, one that could truly act as the conscience of humankind and ensure the end of impunity for war criminals and those committing genocide or crimes against humanity. But the tribunal was a creature of the U.N. bureaucracy. It was accountable to no one in particular, unrooted in any legal or political culture, and unable to connect in any meaningful way to the people whose lives it claimed to affect. Since it depended upon the military muscle and intelligence reports of its Security Council sponsors, the tribunal was, by itself, nearly toothless: it couldn't get the NATO powers to arrest any of its most wanted but still politically useful criminals.

Despite its lack of coercive powers, the tribunal could, and did, lock up former Private Drazen Erdemovic. There had to be a sacrificial lamb: given the failure of the international community to prevent the Srebrenica massacre, and the embarrassing inability of the tribunal to get its hands on any high-ranking suspects, how could the tribunal let the very first defendant brought before it—a man who *admitted* killing scores of innocent people—walk free?

Perhaps, then, Erdemovic's conviction was an act of expiation, one that allowed the majority on the Appeals Chamber to use law as a mechanism for bearing witness to the moral failures of our collective institutions—including the law itself.

Or perhaps the ultimate message is this: law cannot fully tame war, despite the dreams of Francis Lieber and Henry Dunant. But it can still serve as a signpost pointing us toward one future rather than another, and reminding us that we always have choices to make.

# CHAPTER TWELVE

# Making War

*War made the state, and the state made war.*

—Charles Tilly[1]

Return for a moment to the question of whether we can define war. I noted that international law does not offer a precise definition of armed conflict, and different societies have sought to delineate the boundaries of war in different ways. But causation runs in both directions: just as different societies define war in different ways, different ways of understanding and defining war can end up shaping quite different societies.[2]

Political sociologist Charles Tilly famously argued that the history of the Western state is inextricably bound up with the history of European warfare. To oversimplify Tilly's nuanced and complex arguments, the story goes something like this: As power holders (originally, bandits and local strongmen) sought to expand their power, they needed capital to pay for weapons, soldiers, and supplies. The need for capital and new recruits drove the creation of taxation systems and census mechanisms, and the need for more effective systems of taxation and recruitment necessitated better roads, better communications, and better record keeping. This in turn enabled the creation of larger and more technologically sophisticated armies.

The complexity and expense of maintaining more professionalized standing armies made it increasingly difficult for nonstate groups to compete with states, giving centralized states a war-making advantage and enabling them to increasingly monopolize the means of large-scale violence. But the need to recruit, train, and sustain ever-larger and more sophisticated armies also put pressure on these states to provide basic services, improving nutrition, education, and so on. Ultimately, we arrive at the late-twentieth-century European welfare state, with its particular tradeoffs between the state and its subjects.[3]

By now, Tilly's claim that "war made the state, and the state made war" is so widely accepted among scholars that it has become almost a truism, at least with regard to European history[4]—so much so that we're apt to forget that the process of war making and state transformation remains ongoing, and isn't merely a matter for the history books. Though there is nothing deterministic or teleological about it, the cycle described by Tilly still continues: today as in the past, the state makes war—and the manner in which the state makes war drives further changes in the shape of the state itself and in the relationship between individuals and the state.

"The state makes war" in several different senses.

Most obviously, it is the state that *wages* war: the state chooses which wars to fight, and how to fight them. In 2001, for instance, the United States decided to go to war in Afghanistan, first relying largely on airpower in conjunction with small numbers of Army Special Forces troops and CIA paramilitary personnel, then expanding the military effort until, by 2010, the force in Afghanistan consisted of roughly 100,000 troops.[5] Similarly, in 2003 the United States chose to invade Iraq, launching an eight-year war; by 2007, troop levels in Iraq peaked at nearly 170,000.[6] These "traditional" forms of state war making have budgetary implications and opportunity costs, and fit into Tilly's paradigm in obvious ways.

But the state "makes" war in other senses as well.

Scholars and lawyers can argue until they're blue in the face about the proper theoretical definition of war, but for all practical purposes, war is whatever powerful states say it is. From an institutional perspective, it is the state, through the apparatus of government, that decides which tasks to assign to civilian entities and which tasks to assign to the military. And from a legal perspective, it is the state that *defines* what will be considered a war and what will not.

The United States' initial response to 9/11 is a case in point. The attacks might have been defined as egregious acts of criminality—mass murders, or massive crimes against humanity, for instance. The United States instead chose to define the 9/11 attacks and the U.S. response as an "armed conflict"—with consequences more far-reaching than almost anyone could then have imagined.[7]

In the days and weeks immediately after September 11, 2011, the 9/11 terrorist attacks became, for many, the legal equivalent of a Rorschach test. While most commentators insisted that there was a manifestly correct and a manifestly incorrect way to understand which legal framework should be applied to the attacks, there was little agreement on just what that legal framework should be. Depending on the observer, the 9/11 attacks were variously construed as criminal acts, acts of war, or something in between.

In liberal and libertarian-leaning circles, for instance, many scholars took the view that since the 9/11 attacks were carried out by nonstate actors, using nothing that resembled traditional weapons, they were best understood as criminal acts. Though they were crimes of a frightening magnitude and complexity, the attacks were considered by such scholars to be appropriately addressed through an ordinary law enforcement paradigm. Such commentators roundly dismissed the notion that the attacks could trigger a "war" between the United States and al Qaeda. As Antonio Cassese, the first president of the International Criminal Tribunal for the Former Yugoslavia, wrote in 2001, "It is obvious that in this case 'war' is a misnomer. War is an armed conflict between two or more states."[8]

James Cole, a prominent government and private attorney who was later appointed Deputy Attorney General by President Obama, similarly insisted in a 2002 article that "for all the rhetoric about war, the Sept. 11 attacks were criminal acts of terrorism against a civilian population, much like the terrorist acts of Timothy McVeigh."[9] September 11 was a "devastating crime," Cole continued, but one for which ordinary criminal law offered the most appropriate framework.[10] Amnesty International took the same view.[11]

But others insisted with equal certainty on the correctness of the opposite proposition: insofar as the 9/11 attacks stemmed from overseas and caused death and destruction on a scale more commonly associated with armed conflict than with crime, they should be conceptualized as acts of war, triggering the law of armed conflict.

On the evening of September 11, with smoke still swirling above the ruins of the World Trade Center and estimates of the dead ranging as high as ten thousand, President Bush promised that America would "win the war against terrorism."[12] Two days later, he told reporters that on 9/11 "an act of war was declared on the United States of America." Although his phrasing was murky, his meaning was not: the war on terrorism, said Bush, would be "the first war of the 21st century."[13]

Bush administration lawyers elaborated on the president's words. As Justice Department lawyers John Yoo and James C. Ho put it,

> The attacks were coordinated from abroad, by a foreign entity, with the primary aim of inflicting massive civilian casualties and loss. . . . The head of al Qaeda, Osama bin Laden, declared war on the United States as early as 1996. Finally, the scope and the intensity of the destruction is one that in the past could only have been carried out by a nation-state, and should qualify the attacks as an act of war.[14]

Although the Obama administration has moved away from the "global war on terror" language favored by the Bush administration, its legal analysis has been strikingly similar.[15] As former White House counterterrorism advisor John Brennan, now the CIA director, put it a few years ago, "We are at war with al-Qa'ida. In an indisputable act of aggression, al-Qa'ida attacked our nation and killed nearly 3,000 innocent people."[16] President Obama has repeated the same sentiment on numerous occasions, leaving little room for doubt: "Under domestic law, and international law, the United States is at war with al Qaeda, the Taliban, and their associated forces."[17]

## Duck-Rabbits

So who was "right"? Were the 9/11 attacks "crime," or "war," or something in between: Isolated attacks triggering a temporary U.S. right to use force in self-defense, but not a full-fledged armed conflict?

Despite the vociferousness with which they were defended, none of the positions outlined above can be said to be clearly right or clearly wrong from a legal perspective. To a significant extent, the legal status of 9/11 is effectively indeterminate.[18]

If we think of law as being game-like, you could say that these positions posed entirely novel questions that the rules of the game simply didn't address.

Until about forty years ago, tennis rackets were made of wood and generally all strung the same way. When a professional tennis player in the mid-1970s began to play with double-stringed rackets, some players gained an immediate advantage—one that many critics viewed as unfair. But the rules of tennis didn't specify whether any particular racket stringing techniques were prohibited. Only in 1978 did the International Tennis Federation clarify the rules. Since then, new racket technologies have raised similar issues: wooden rackets were replaced by steel, then aluminum, then graphite and composites containing titanium and tungsten. Each new racket was lighter and stronger, permitting more powerful strokes with less effort. And each new technological leap raised similar questions: When is a tennis racket no longer a tennis racket? At what point does a new technology change things so fundamentally that the players aren't even playing tennis anymore, but a new game that will require new rules?

In the "real world" of law and war, new actors and new technologies present similar challenges: sometimes the rules just don't offer a right and wrong answer.

Or take a different metaphor. At the end of Georgetown Law's 2015 spring semester, a student in my Law and War seminar knocked on my office door. "Hey, Professor Brooks," he said cheerfully, reaching into his backpack. "We got a present for you." Grinning, he pulled out a six-pack of beer.

"Beer?" I asked. "Was there something about my teaching style that made you think I need to drink more beer?"

"No, no," he said. "You have to look more closely at this."

He held it out to me, and I started to laugh. "You found Duck-Rabbit Beer! I can't believe it!"

The six-pack was emblazoned with an image of Ludwig Wittgenstein's famous duck-rabbit, which could equally be viewed as a representation of a rabbit or a representation of a duck:

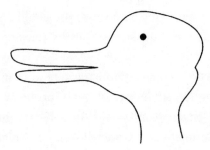

Over the course of the semester, my students became convinced that I was obsessed with the duck-rabbit, which Wittgenstein used to illustrate his theory of language games. The duck-rabbit, I informed anyone who would listen, offered a full explanation of legal indeterminacy in applying the law of armed conflict to modern realities.

No, really. Stay with me here.

To Wittgenstein, it was erroneous to imagine that words were straightforward representations of some fixed external reality. Rather, he insisted, language itself is inseparable from context: "the speaking of language is part of an activity, or a form of life."[19]

He noted, "The picture [of the duck-rabbit] might have been shewn me, and I never have seen anything but a rabbit in it. . . . [But imagine now] I see two pictures, with the duck-rabbit surrounded by rabbits in one, by ducks in the other."

When the duck-rabbit is surrounded by images that are unambiguously rabbits, engaged in typically rabbitlike activities, one would never think to see the duck-rabbit as anything but a quickly sketched rabbit. But when the duck-rabbit is surrounded by images that are unambiguously of ducks, engaged in ducklike activities, one would be equally unlikely to see the duck-rabbit as anything other than a duck.

"I do not notice that [the original duck-rabbit image is] the same," in each of these two pictures, wrote Wittgenstein. "Does it follow from this that I see something *different* in the two cases?"[20]

Like Wittgenstein's duck-rabbit, the 9/11 attacks can be viewed as crime, as war, or as isolated armed attack—and just as the duck-rabbit may strike the viewer differently when surrounded by a backdrop of rabbits versus a backdrop of ducks, a great deal depends on whether one views 9/11 against a backdrop of crimes or a backdrop of military attacks.

Considered alongside the Oklahoma City bombing, the murderous activities of Mexican drug cartels, or the Rwandan genocide, the 9/11 attacks look like crimes: crimes on a massive scale, even crimes against humanity, but crimes all the same. Considered alongside the 1976 hijacking of an Air France jet or the 1998 bombings of U.S. embassies in Kenya and Tanzania, the 9/11 attacks might look like isolated violent incidents that could nonetheless trigger a temporary right to respond with armed force in self-defense. Considered alongside the 1993 World Trade Center bombing, the 1998 embassy bombings, and the 2000 attack on the USS *Cole*, the 9/11 attacks look like another stage in an ongoing armed conflict.

Ultimately, as with Wittgenstein's duck-rabbit, it would be quite mistaken to insist that one description of the attacks is somehow ontologically "truer" than any other, and equally mistaken to insist that there is a "right" and "wrong" legal paradigm through which to make sense of the 9/11 attacks.

To say that there is neither a right nor wrong legal framework is not the same as saying that one might as well pick one as another, for the choice of legal frameworks is far from inconsequential. Indeed, if it comes to that, the choice of duck versus rabbit is also far from inconsequential, if one is a hunter—or, for that matter, if one is a rabbit or a duck. If it's duck-hunting season but not rabbit-hunting season, ducks are fair game but rabbits are immune from violence; if it's rabbit-hunting season but not duck-hunting season, the opposite is true. The lawfulness of the hunter's shot depends on whether we view the duck-rabbit as duck or as rabbit. For the duck-rabbit, survival itself is at stake.

So it is with the post-9/11 choice of legal frameworks. If the 9/11 attacks were a crime, they trigger law enforcement rules that place substantial constraints on the state's ability to monitor, search, detain, and use lethal force against individuals. If the 9/11 attacks were part of an armed conflict or initiated an armed conflict, they trigger the law of war, which places far fewer constraints on the state's use of coercion and lethal force.

Ontologically, there may be no right answer—but power has a way of reshaping reality. In the world we inhabit, the United States is the only superpower still standing, and though its relative global power may be in decline, it still has an outsized ability to impose its vision of the facts and the law on the rest of the world.

What is more, when a state "makes" war in this manner—redefining what counts as war—the shape of the state itself may begin to change, along with relationships between individuals and the state.

Trust me: this makes even more sense once you've enjoyed a few bottles of Duck-Rabbit beer.

# CHAPTER THIRTEEN

# Making the State

The state makes war—and war, plus a good dollop of Western imperialism, made the modern state. Today, the state continues to "make war," both in the traditional sense and by moving a range of new and nontraditional activities—from counterterrorism to cyber operations—into the legal and policy box labeled war. This too is eroding the customary boundaries between the world of war and the world of peace. New kinds of war and state war making are, in turn, re-making—and in some ways *un-making*—the state itself, and are also transforming the international order and relationships between individuals and states.

To trace these changes, it's worth thinking briefly about where states come from, and what they do.[1] And just as we sometimes end up trying to make sense of war by emphasizing those things that are *not* war—chess, rugby, homicide, riots, economic competition, trade sanctions—perhaps the best way to understand states is to start by thinking about what we call "failed states."[2]

In the years since the end of the Cold War, the international community—and the community of international lawyers—has become increasingly preoccupied with "failed states."[3] Successful states control defined territories and populations, conduct diplomatic relations with other states, monopolize legitimate violence within their territories, and succeed in providing adequate social goods to their populations. Failed states, their dark mirror image, lose control over the means of violence, and cannot create peace or stability for their populations or control their territories.[4]

Recent examples of failed states are familiar to us all, from the total collapse of state institutions in Somalia and the disintegration of the former Yugoslavia to the varied crises in Syria, Iraq, Libya, Afghanistan, Sudan, Rwanda, Haiti, Congo, and Sierra Leone. One notch up the food chain from failed states are the numerous "weak" or "failing" states, which together constitute much of sub-Saharan Africa (consider Côte d'Ivoire, Zimbabwe, Mali, Burundi, Mozambique, Liberia, and Angola, to name but a few of the most notorious), significant chunks of Central Asia, and parts of Latin America and South Asia.

Failed states make it even harder to keep war in a box. They can become breeding grounds for extremism and insurgencies, or staging points for organized terrorist groups. Failed states cannot enter into or abide by treaties; they cannot participate in the increasingly dense network of international trade or environmental or human rights agreements and institutions; they cannot enforce contracts between their citizens and foreigners or protect settled property interests. Even weak states pose this problem. How do we determine whether Pakistan has "consented" to U.S. drone strikes, for instance, when the locus of legitimate government authority within Pakistan is itself contested?

So far, the international community has not proven particularly adept either at staving off state failure or at reconstituting failed states. From Bosnia and Sierra Leone to Afghanistan and Iraq (where the collapse of a government institutions was, of course, externally induced), efforts to turn failed states back into successful states have produced tenuous stability at best.

There are many reasons for this. Most are complex, but for now, focus on one: the "international community" is itself a fiction, at least insofar as the term implies a cohesive community of states with the capacity to act in a reliably coordinated and effective fashion.

The international community is a hodgepodge of actors and institutions, with divergent interests, natures, and capacities. There are states, to begin with; some of these are powerful (the United States; China; Russia; Germany; the United Kingdom) and some are weak (Ukraine; Afghanistan, Georgia; Bosnia); some are (relatively) outward-looking (Canada) while others are (relatively) inward-looking (China), and many are in between. States differ in territory, population, ideology, culture, and wealth, though as a matter of international law they are united by the shared myth of sovereign equality.

And states are far from the only actors on the world stage. Their influence is simultaneously challenged and extended by an ever-widening range of nonstate actors. Some of these are more or less benevolent (Save the Children, Human Rights Watch), while others are fundamentally disruptive (the self-styled Islamic State, al Qaeda, Hezbollah, the Lord's Resistance Army). Of these, some are extraordinarily rich and powerful: the Islamic State, for instance, has an estimated $500 billion kitty;[5] others operate on a shoestring.

Still other nonstate entities are more ambivalent in nature: consider for-profit corporate entities, for instance, which may be exceptionally powerful (Walmart's and ExxonMobil's annual revenues exceed those of all but the world's richest states).[6] And these are only some of the publicly declared world actors. Illicit regional and global networks— such as drug cartels, weapons smugglers, and human traffickers—also abound.[7] What's more, many of these nonstate actors, whether licit or illicit, also have complex and sometimes hidden links to states.

Little wonder, then, that "the international community" struggles to respond effectively to the challenges posed by "failed" states. From the perspective of an alien observer from another planet, the "international community" of the planet earth would surely appear like a failed state writ large; it has proven consistently unable to control the violence of powerful actors (whether states or nonstate entities such as terrorist organizations), control environmental catastrophes such as climate change; remedy astronomically large economic inequities between individuals and societies, constrain the devastating scramble to exploit the earth's dwindling natural resources, or address crises such as global epidemics.

Just as Syria, Afghanistan, and Iraq are fractured into numerous competing ethnic and religious groups dominated by warlords and other regional power brokers, the international order still better resembles a Hobbesian struggle for survival than a coherent system of governance. If there is some sense in which all the world's people constitute a society (and why not insist on that, in this era of globalization and human rights?), it is hard not to conclude that the international community is simply a failed state on a global scale.

## But That's Silly

The obvious rejoinder to this claim is that it makes no sense at all to think of the international order as a failed state, since the international order has never been—and has never truly sought to be—a successful state. If we see chaos, poverty, disease, environmental depredation, and enormous unchecked violence around the globe today, this can be attributed to many causes (from original sin to collective action problems: take your pick). But it can hardly be attributed to some sort of state failure—to the collapse of once functioning global governance institutions—since such institutions never existed. By definition, the international order cannot be considered a failed state on a global scale, because there never existed a global state that could fall apart.

But is it so silly to analogize the international order to a failed state? True, there never was a global state that existed, so it seems odd to speak of the international community as a failed state. But much the same could be said of many failed states on the national level. That is: most so-called failed states were never really states in the first place, at least not in anything more than a strictly technical sense.

Afghanistan was never a fully functioning modern state; neither was Congo, or Sierra Leone, or Syria, or Iraq, or Somalia, or most of the dozens of states that have been characterized in the past decades as failed or failing. With their boundaries often drawn by colonial and imperial powers, these faux states made for tidy maps and had seats at the United Nations and an international juridical personality, but they rarely possessed the attributes of robust states in other than a purely formal legal sense.[8]

From their inception, such states rarely exercised anything approaching a monopoly on violence within their territories; to a significant extent, their borders were unmanageably porous, and the reach of government authority either barely extended beyond their capital cities and a handful of other urban centers or extended only in predatory form. Whether through incapacity, lack of resources, massive corruption, repression, or all four, most provided basic services only sporadically and poorly, and left their populations to fend more or less for themselves. At best, these "states" were, for a time, fragile facsimiles of the nation-states that appeared to thrive in Western Europe and parts of the Americas.

During the Cold War, they were propped up by the competing superpowers; with the end of the Cold War, many were revealed as the faux states they had been all along. If the "descent" into failed state status requires some prior period as a functioning state, places such as Syria, Sierra Leone, and Afghanistan can hardly be considered failed states. They never really were states to begin with.

## Born in Blood

We can go further: maybe the apparent permanence and ubiquity of the nation-state is just a mirage. We take it for granted that states are (and ought to be, and must be) the building blocks of world order, viewed historically, the nation-state is a transient and contingent form of social organization.[9] In fact, the history of the modern state is short—and not particularly happy. Since prehistory, groups of human beings have found a very wide range of ways to organize themselves into societies. The world has seen tribes, sects, feudal kingdoms, city-states, and religious empires, among other modes of social organization. The idea of the territorial nation-state as the locus of authority, within a system of formally equivalent similar states, is of quite recent vintage.

It was not until 1648, when the Peace of Westphalia ended the Thirty Years War, that the modern international system of sovereign states began to develop. Even after this symbolic starting point, it took centuries of conquest and many more wars before anything truly resembling today's state system took shape.

In Europe, state consolidation was rarely peaceful: consider the three wars of the German unification, or the bloody excesses of the Italian unification. (It was the carnage of the Battle of Solferino that inspired Henry Dunant to form the International Committee of the Red Cross, and led indirectly to the emergence of the modern law of armed conflict.) Or think of France: during the "reign of terror" that followed the French Revolution, France's revolutionary government publicly beheaded an estimated thirty to forty thousand people—all in the name of *liberté, égalité,* and *fraternité*. In the early 1790s, at least 150,000 other unfortunate French *citoyens* were shot, burned to death, hacked to pieces, or deliberately drowned in France's Vendée region.[10] "I crushed the children under the feet of the horses," French general François Joseph Westermann is said to have written after one particularly brutal campaign. "I massacred the women who, at least for these, will not give birth to any more brigands. . . . I have exterminated all. The roads are sown with corpses."[11]

National identity for the peoples of Europe didn't come about naturally: it had to be created, in a process that only accelerated in the nineteenth century. Monuments were built and national anthems composed; regional dialects and various particularisms stamped out by central authorities, often ruthlessly.[12] In the brutality of its state-building efforts, the so-called Islamic State is less historically atypical than we might prefer to imagine.[13]

One can see the ferocious militarism that has characterized Europe until the post–World War II period as a direct result of state expansion and nationalism—or, alternatively, in line with Charles Tilly's argument, one can see state formation and nationalism as incidental by-products of militarism, as warlords required ever more elaborate infrastructure support to fund and sustain their armies.[14] Either way, few scholars would dispute that the history of the state as the dominant form of social organization is a history dripping with blood.[15]

This has been as true in the rest of the world as in Europe. Although empires and kingdoms have long existed around the globe, the modern state largely spread outward from Europe through imperialism and colonial expansion. In the Americas, indigenous populations were small and lacked sophisticated military technologies, and European colonists soon killed or marginalized them; then, drawing on their own political traditions, the colonists quickly replicated the state structures of Europe. Soon enough, the colonists insisted on independence from their parent states, and new states were born, often through violent rebellion.

Meanwhile, in Africa, Asia, and South Asia, where they found indigenous populations more formidable, the European powers (often loosely represented by commercial enterprises acting under state charters, such as the British East India Company) first established nominally independent puppet-states, which they often molded out of far more varied local forms of social organization such as tribe and city. Quickly enough, however, most abandoned the charade of local rule in favor of straightforward colonial regimes. Ultimately, Africa's and Asia's most portable natural resources were depleted, and two world wars made maintaining colonies an expensive luxury.

At the same time, and not coincidentally, emerging global norms of self-determination, nondiscrimination, and human rights made colonial regimes more difficult to justify. As indigenous elites began to demand independence, often through violence, still more states were formed. Their governance structures generally mirrored the internal governance structures bequeathed them by Europe's colonial powers, and their borders notoriously reflected happenstance and inter-European conflicts and compromises rather than any precolonial political or social units.

## The State as Failure

The state as we know it today is thus of recent origin, and there is little that is natural or inevitable about this system. States are the product of both a unique history and of multiple conscious human choices, and there is no reason to view the state as a particularly successful or benign mode of social organization. Even in Europe, the birthplace of the modern state, the history of the state has been a history of repression and war. As states expanded they consumed or trampled on other, weaker social systems; as they vied for dominance they sent millions to be slaughtered on battlefield after battlefield, and as they sought to create unified national cultures they frequently cannibalized their own citizens, a process that reached its terrible apotheosis in the Nazi state's genocidal policies.

This is a story familiar to international lawyers, and a happy ending is usually proffered: the United Nations Charter and the emergence of human rights law. But these new norms and institutions have hardly ended state predation. Even in Europe, ethnic cleansing in the former Yugoslavia is only the most recent chapter in that story. The best that can be said of the state in Europe and the Americas may be that it proved a form of social organization well suited to the era of industrialization,[16] and that its excesses have to some extent been tamed by the U.N. Charter system on the outside and by relatively robust internal checks and balances on the inside.

Outside of Europe, the state has hardly been kinder or gentler, and it has certainly been less successful as state success is traditionally evaluated. In most places—much of Africa, much of Central and South Asia, parts of the Americas—the state was never more than a semi-fictional overlay of institutions that masked more protean forms of social organization such as tribal systems or patronage networks. When the Cold War ended, some of these states simply reverted, more or less messily and painfully and visibly, into whatever it was that they had always been; in other societies, new and often even more lethal modes of social organization emerged.

In Afghanistan, for instance, the secular Russian-influenced state that had displaced the traditional tribal system was itself displaced, first by violent and corrupt warlords and then by the Taliban, which forced its extremist version of Islam and Sharia law onto all populations under its control. In parts of Africa, tribal networks weakened by foreign rule and urbanization were superseded, after decolonization, by brutal and anarchic rebel groups intent only on seizing resoures, regardless of the mayhem left in their wake.

To a significant extent, the state in the developing world has offered its citizens all the violence that accompanied European state formation, and few of the corresponding benefits. Weak, failing, and failed states are not the exception in many parts of the world. They are the norm, and have been since their inception.

Despite the many weak and failing states and the increasing number of nonstate entities that compete with them, the modern international order still relies on the fiction of sovereignty. States make international law, and they create, finance, and staff the international organizations designed to enforce international law, from the United Nations itself to the International Criminal Court. Without states—without their votes at the U.N., their militaries, their treasuries and their bureaucracies, however weak and dysfunctional—the world currently has no mechanism for solving global problems.

But from the inception of the post–World War II international system, human rights have run smack into sovereignty—a contradiction at the heart of the U.N. Charter itself. Principles of sovereignty tell us that if Saudi Arabia prefers to prohibit voting by women or the Serbian government wants to slaughter its own citizens, that's sad, but it's no one else's business—just as it's no one else's business if Afghanistan is run by corrupt warlords or the government of Thailand is ousted in a military coup. Principles of human rights tell us the opposite: people are people, whether they were born in Riyadh, Beijing, Srebrenica, or Damascus. And when a government oppresses or slaughters its own people, stopping the abuses is *everyone's* business.

For Americans, this is a familiar concept: our own nation is premised on the "self-evident" idea that there are "unalienable rights" that predate and trump the rights of government. Recall the Declaration of Independence: it is "to secure these rights" that "governments are instituted . . . deriving their just powers from the consent of the governed. [But] whenever any Form of Government becomes destructive of these ends, it is the right of the people to alter or abolish it."

Such a philosophy, which is also implicit in the concept of international human rights, has inescapable implications for sovereignty and international law: If the rights and needs of individuals trump those of the artificial constructs we call "states," why *should* international law prohibit intervention into the affairs of sovereign states? If a state can't or won't protect the human beings who live within its borders, why should the international system protect that state? Why should those of us living in other states hesitate to intervene to help our fellow human beings if necessary?

States created an international architecture built upon a joint commitment to sovereignty and human rights—but today, that very same joint commitment is also contributing to the unraveling of the state itself.

# CHAPTER FOURTEEN

# Un-Making Sovereignty

The United Nations Charter system that arose out of the devastation of the Second World War was far from perfect, but most scholars nonetheless credit it with dramatically reducing the number of wars between states. When the Cold War ended, many believed the world was poised for an era of genuine peace: the threat of nuclear war between the Soviet Union and the United States was finally over, and the threat of proxy conflicts between puppet states aligned with one or the other superpower also appeared to be over.[1]

But even as the threat of interstate conflict receded, the post–Cold War world began to experience what looked like a resurgence of messy internal conflicts within states, exemplified by the ethnic conflicts that wracked Rwanda and the former Yugoslavia in the early 1990s.

During the 1994 Rwandan genocide, the international community stood by as the bodies piled up: nearly a million people were slaughtered in a matter of a few short months. In the former Yugoslavia, the situation was not *quite* as shameful for the international community, which did ultimately act—with Security Council approval—to end the savage and bloody conflicts in Bosnia and Croatia, but most critics felt that the international community did too little, too late.

The glaring inadequacy of the international community's response to the crises in Rwanda and Bosnia led to a good deal of hand-wringing, and an understandable and appropriate sense of guilt: being "bystanders to genocide," as Samantha Power put it in her powerful 2002 book, *A Problem from Hell*, wasn't a comfortable role.[2] The general sense was that the international community—led by the U.N. Security Council—

should have done more, or at least should have done *something*. Political leaders, the media, and advocacy groups all asked: Can it possibly be the case that it's acceptable, legally or morally, for the world to stand by idly while mass atrocities are committed? In particular, can the rest of us stand by when mass atrocities are committed against a population by its *own* government, or when a government seems unwilling or unable to protect its people from those who prey upon them?

## You Will Tell the World

Over the years, I've seen enough misery for these to feel like urgent moral questions, rather than academic or legal questions. When I read about the Lord's Resistance Army today, I still feel the same sick sense of helplessness I felt during that first trip to Northern Uganda in 1997. I remember the silent woman holding up her dying baby, and the little boy—another escaped LRA victim—clad in a ragged sweatshirt declaring, "I'm a Toys R Us Kid." The Toys R Us logo had mostly worn away; from a distance, his shirt just seemed to offer a silent reproach: "I'm a kid."

I remember a meeting with several dozen parents of schoolgirls abducted by LRA rebels in Uganda's Lira district. My Human Rights Watch colleague Yodon Thonden and I were apparently the first Americans to have shown any interest in their plight, and the parents, who had formed a group dedicated to lobbying the Ugandan government to rescue their girls, greeted us with such hope and gratitude that I felt instantly shamed. The group's spokesman was a man named Ben, whose adolescent daughter was still in captivity. One of his arms hung uselessly at his side, withered and immobile. "From the rebels," a woman whispered in explanation.

Ben greeted us with quiet formality. "Welcome. Welcome." He cleared his throat, and spoke slowly. "We have suffered greatly. But now you are here." (A murmur of soft approval from the crowd.)

Yes, you are here. We thank you. We thank you greatly, for we know you will return to America, and you will tell the world about our war here in Northern Uganda. You will tell your president Bill Clinton. Yes. You will tell him about how we suffer so much from the rebels, here in Northern Uganda. About how the rebels burn our homes, and beat us, and kill us, and take our children away from us, and do so many, many very bad things to them. (More murmurs.)

And your President Bill Clinton, when he learns this from you—when he learns of all these very bad things these rebels are doing here—then, we know he will send help to us here in Northern Uganda. Yes. You will go back to America and you will tell him all these things, you will carry this message to him. And your president will help us bring our children *home*. (Quiet applause.)

Later that night, I sat with Sister Rachele Fassera, an Italian nun who taught at the girls boarding school from which the LRA had abducted so many girls, and listened to her story. It went something like this:

On the night of October 9, 1996, Sister Rachele was fast asleep when she heard the screaming. As a teacher at a Catholic girls boarding school in the Ugandan town of Aboke, she had eaten with "her girls," presided over their evening study period, and seen them safely off to bed. Now, hearing screams, she jumped up and ran to open her door. But the door had been blocked from the outside, and it took Sister Rachele and several other nuns more than an hour to escape. When they made it out, they raced to the dormitories, where some hysterical younger girls told them that the LRA rebels had come and taken away scores of girls in a mass abduction. The girls who remained were the fortunate ones: they had hidden in cupboards and under beds, avoiding the rebels' notice.

Sister Rachele's fellow nuns proposed radioing the nearest Ugandan army post to ask for instructions, but Sister Rachele would hear none of this: the army, she feared (probably rightly, given its record), would either do nothing or, worse, would send out a unit that would end up killing the hostages alongside the rebels.

"I will go get our girls myself," she told her incredulous colleagues.

And she did. Along with John, the school handyman, she set out into the bush.

The trail wasn't hard to follow. Like modern-day Hansels and Gretels, the girls had left a trail of discarded items: scraps of paper, candy wrappers, the contents of their pockets. She and John tramped through the bush, and finally, around dawn, they caught up with the rebel party.

Sister Rachele walked right up to the rebel commander, a young man in his twenties, and demanded that he release her girls immediately.

The commander was used to terrified, cringing villagers. Sister Rachele was a tiny, birdlike little woman in her fifties with thick glasses and hair pulled severely back, and she seemed completely unafraid. Who was this nun?

Flummoxed, he said, "Sister, I cannot let these girls go. I must bring these girls back with me."

But Sister Rachele wouldn't take no for an answer. Ignoring the dozens of armed rebels, she told the commander he should be ashamed of himself. A big strong man, kidnapping young girls who only wanted to go to school and get an education so they could make their country better!

The rebel commander could have killed her, but instead, he proposed a compromise.

"Sister, I will pick the prettiest, strongest girls and take them with me. You may take the others back."

Sister Rachele refused the deal, insisting that she had to bring all the girls back with her.

By now the commander was growing irritated. "Sister, you can take back with you one hundred girls, but I will take the others with me. If you do not want to leave with a hundred girls, I will kill you, and take them all with me."

It wasn't much of a choice. The commander walked through the terrified ranks of schoolgirls, picking those he wanted to take back with him and pulling them aside. Then, shrugging magnanimously, he pointed at the hundred girls he had rejected: "Sister, you go now, and take these girls back to their school."

When Sister Rachele told me about her trek into the bush to retrieve her kidnapped charges, she was animated, reenacting the scene with Italian flair. But when she started to describe the moment she began to lead the hundred freed girls away from the rebels, something in her voice shifted. She still gesticulated dramatically, but all the energy was gone.

"Ah! So I kissed each of my girls who were going with the rebels, and they were crying."

Her voice cracked. "The commander was saying, 'Sister, you must leave us now!' and my girls, they were saying, 'Sister, don't leave me!' 'Sister, what about my asthma?' 'Sister, please stay with us, I am frightened!' 'Sister, my father will not survive this!' 'Sister, please, please take me with you!' "

By the end of her story, Sister Rachele was sobbing. She looked up at me. "I dream each night of those girls, their voices begging me not to leave them. But I left them. I do not see how God can ever forgive me for this."

I'm not religious. I'm the child and grandchild and great-grandchild of atheists: my ancestors turned their backs on Catholicism, Judaism, and Protestantism. If they had been Hindus or Muslims I'm sure they would have managed to reject those faiths too. So I was probably the worst person in the world to comfort a weeping nun.

I patted her shoulder awkwardly.

"Sister," I said, "God knows no one could have done more than you did."

. . .

A few days after that, I visited St. Mary's Hospital in Gulu, Uganda, where I met a doctor named Matthew Lukwena.

Matthew Lukwena spent virtually all his professional life at St. Mary's Hospital. He grew up poor in the neighboring district of Kitgum, went to school, and studied hard. Against all the odds, he made it to medical school at Makerere University in Kampala. Then he returned to Gulu, a few miles from his boyhood home. In 1989, when LRA rebels tried to kidnap some nuns from the hospital, Matthew insisted they take him away instead. They did. They walked him through the bush for days, but eventually—inexplicably—they let him go.

Most people with his credentials and skills would have abandoned Gulu after that, but Matthew stayed on. He struggled to provide medical care to a population suffering from both poverty and war, and he turned St. Mary's Hospital into a safe haven for the "night commuters": rural villagers who left their homes each evening to spend the night in the relative safety of Gulu, where LRA raids were less frequent. Each night, thousands of people would trudge quietly into the walled courtyard at St. Mary's, hauling sleeping mats and food. Each night, Matthew would make the rounds of the courtyard, offering water and basic medical care. As he walked through the camp of the night commuters, people would reach out their arms to touch him, as if his mere presence could keep them safe.

When I visited St. Mary's in 1997, Matthew walked me around the overcrowded hospital, pointing out the patients sleeping on the floor and in the hallways, the nearly empty medicine stockrooms, the bodies waiting in the morgue. Finally, he offered me a chair in his bleak cinder block office—nothing in it but a desk, and a bookshelf, and a few folding chairs. He sat down, rested his elbows on his desk, and then slumped with his head in his hands.

"The problem," he said tiredly, "is that we don't see an end to the problem. When you have a problem and you think it's coming to an end, then you say, let's persevere. But I really don't see how this is going to end. I foresee unlimited suffering." His eyes were wet.

I told you: everyone cried. Whether you were a doctor in Gulu or U.S. secretary of state Madeline Albright, who visited Northern Uganda later that year, it seemed impossible to think about the LRA and not cry.

"The last two years have been the worst in ten years. We cannot do anything, we cannot go outside in the community, we cannot do our work. It has to stop, it must stop . . ." His voice trailed off. When he continued, he was almost angry. "When you are in the medical field, you are trained always to look for solutions. But I cannot see one here. There is no point to my work. I can do nothing."

I listened and scribbled in my notebook, embarrassed by so much raw emotion in a stranger. It was late afternoon, and outside in the courtyard the night commuters were lighting their cooking fires, preparing for darkness. Matthew kept talking, in a low monotone: I think he had almost forgotten my presence. He did not even know how to keep his own children safe, he said; he had to shuttle them from relative to relative to protect them from rebel abduction. There was no truly safe place in Northern Uganda.

He wrung his hands, massaged his temples, fidgeted miserably with his pen. From time to time he blinked the tears from his eyes and looked up at me blankly.

Finally, I asked him what seemed like the obvious question to ask an educated professional living in Gulu in 1997: "Have you ever thought of leaving?"

He looked startled. "Leave? Where would I go?"

The Lord's Resistance Army made life so miserable in Gulu that when Ebola broke out there a few years after my first visit, many locals counted it as a lucky break. True, Ebola took the lives of thirty-six people—but the Ebola outbreak also brought the outside world to Gulu, in the form of an influx of unusually well-behaved Ugandan government troops, generous international aid organizations, journalists, and cable news crews. The foreigners handed out food and medicine, and spent money like water: they paid for local translators, drivers, expeditors, and aides. For a few weeks in the fall of 2000, Gulu made CNN nearly every day. During those same few weeks, there were no LRA attacks on Gulu.

For a short time—until the mobile medical units were packed up, the cable TV crews went home, and the rebels returned—farmers could harvest crops, people could walk around at night, and children could sleep in their homes rather than in schools and hospital compounds. Death by hemorrhagic fever was a risk, to be sure—but it was hardly worse than the risk of being hacked to pieces by machetes or clubbed to death with heavy sticks.

When Ebola came to Gulu in 2000, it was Matthew Lukwena who first identified the disease and reported it to national and then international authorities. Twelve of his nurses died helping Ebola patients, and others quit for fear of contracting the disease, but Matthew Lukwena stayed and continued to tend his patients. The outbreak was slowly brought under control, thanks in large part to his efforts.

In late November, he fell ill himself. On December 5, he died, the Gulu Ebola outbreak's last victim.[3]

## Inconsolable Sorrow

Everywhere I traveled, I met people like Matthew, Ben, and Sister Rachele. In Kosovo, I met a woman judge whose husband and sons had been gunned down in the street in front of her. In Indonesia, I met a man who had been tortured almost to death by an army unit notorious for such behavior. In Gaza, I met families whose homes had been mortared by Israeli forces, sometimes with their children still inside. In Sierra Leone I met dead-eyed children whose arms had been hacked off by Foday Sankoh's Revolutionary United Front. It was the same all over, in so many places, and everywhere I felt the same emotions: fear, and shame.

Fear, because wars and repression are terrifying things. You couldn't spend long hours each day listening to tales of grief, pain, and brutality and not find yourself lying awake in the night, wondering if that was gunfire you were hearing in the distance, and if it was getting closer, or if the creaking floorboards outside heralded the approach of something terrible.

No, nothing very dramatic ever happened to me: getting held up by armed bandits in Fallujah was as bad as it got. In the occasional moments of true danger, I found myself much calmer than in moments of quiet safety. When I was "invited" by a drunken and menacing group of Ugandan soldiers to ride with them to their barracks in their truck and interview some just captured LRA child soldiers, I was so distracted by my inability to find a working pen that I temporarily forgot that no one on earth knew where I was or where I was going. Reunited later that night with my more experienced Human Rights Watch colleague, I got a thorough scolding. Did I have *any* idea how stupid and irresponsible it was to go off like that without even letting anyone know I was going? No? Well, *never*, ever do something so juvenile and stupid again!

Similarly, when Israeli soldiers started firing into a crowd of civilians as I waited at a Ramallah border crossing, I found myself so full of foolhardy, righteous American outrage ("They're shooting! There are *children* here! They can't *do* that!") that my Palestinian escort had to grab my arm to keep me from racing toward the young soldiers and giving them a piece of my mind. And in Sierra Leone, flying in a rattling old Russian-made helicopter leased by the U.S. embassy, with a notorious war criminal panting sweatily on my right (Sam "Mosquito" Bockarie), an open door on my left, and treetops rushing by just a few feet beneath us, I somehow managed to fall asleep.

It was only at night, tucked comfortably into bed, that I felt my heart gallop with adrenaline-fueled panic.

The other recurring emotion was shame: shame at my privileged life; shame at my inability to cure sick babies, rescue terrified prisoners, or end brutal conflicts; shame at feeling, even when things got scary, the anticipatory pleasure of getting back home and telling friends and family about my adventures. Most of all, I felt shame at the knowledge that I *would* go home to safety, and virtually no one back in the prosperous, rich United States would likely lose a single moment of sleep wondering if we should do something to help those countless suffering people, so many worlds away.

A few years after returning from my first trip to Uganda, I was speaking on the phone with Angelina Atyam, the mother of one of the abducted Aboke schoolgirls. She had happy news: her own teen daughter had escaped from the LRA rebels, though she had been raped and given birth to a baby while in captivity. Still, she was alive, the baby was healthy, and she was back with her mother.

I digested that, then asked after Ben, the dignified man with the injured arm who had been so confident that once the world knew of their troubles, help would arrive. Had his daughter escaped or been rescued?

"Ah, no," said Angelina. "She is still with the rebels, maybe, or maybe she is dead. No one can say. No one knows."

And Ben himself, I asked? How was Ben?

"Ah," said Angelina. "Ben. He is dead."

I wasn't sure I wanted to hear the answer, but I asked anyway. "What did he die of?"

Through the crackling telephone line, Angelina's husky, lilting Ugandan voice made each syllable separate and distinct.

"Inconsolable sorrow."

## Responsibility to Protect

I was far from the only one mired in shame. By the late 1990s, the massacres in Rwanda and the Balkans had left the international community in full self-flagellation mode, pledging (again) that "never again" would atrocities be permitted to go on unhindered by international action—never again would the world stand by and do nothing in the face of genocide, ethnic cleansing, or other mass atrocities. Never mind principles of sovereignty—if necessary, the instruments of war would be used to restore peace. Just wars would save the unjustly threatened, and international courts, such as the criminal tribunals for Yugoslavia and Rwanda and the International Criminal Court, would prosecute the military and political leaders responsible for genocide.[4]

But even in the post–Cold War world, and even when faced with the most egregious of circumstances, the Security Council could not necessarily be relied upon to authorize military interventions for humanitarian purposes. The looming threat of vetoes had helped preclude meaningful Security Council action on Rwanda, and the same was true during the Kosovo crisis of 1998–1999. In Kosovo, though, when ethnic cleansing of Kosovar Albanians by the Serbian government seemed imminent, NATO states—led by the United States—decided not to wait for Security Council authorization: they went ahead and started bombing Serbian targets.

Interestingly, neither NATO nor the United States attempted to put forward a formal legal justification for the military intervention in Kosovo. They offered policy and humanitarian justifications for the use of force, but in the United States, the State Department Legal Adviser's Office made a deliberate decision to refrain from proffering a legal justification.[5] In part, U.S. and NATO lawyers feared that other states would not accept any legal justification they might put forward for a military intervention launched without Security Council approval—and in part, they were afraid that other states *would* accept their logic.

That is, they didn't want to put forward a legal theory that would be roundly repudiated by numerous other states: that would be embarrassing and would retard the development of any new norm permitting humanitarian intervention—but they were equally uneasy about the longer-term implications of *creating* a new norm permitting humanitarian interventions.

The problem with humanitarian emergencies is that they may lie in the eye of the beholder. Take away the requirement that military force must be authorized by the Security Council and you have a norm that can easily be abused. If the United States and other states could decide for themselves that a military intervention in Kosovo was justified, over Russian and Chinese objections, what was there to prevent China from asserting that humanitarian considerations required it to send Chinese troops into Indonesia or Taiwan? What could prevent Russia from claiming that humanitarian concerns required it to use force inside Georgia or Ukraine?

As more recent events have demonstrated, these concerns were well-founded. In 1999, the United States and other NATO powers weren't willing to just look the other way while another ethnic genocide began to unfold, but they were equally leery of opening the door to unilateral state decisions about the use of force. In the end, the NATO powers decided that discretion might well be the better part of valor, and opted to intervene without offering a legal basis for the intervention. NATO's justification for the Kosovo air campaign was fundamentally extralegal in nature: it rested, in effect, on a claim of moral necessity.[6]

But illegal or not, it saved thousands of lives, and history has judged it kindly. Even the Security Council eventually offered it tacit post hoc validation through a series of Security Council resolutions authorizing NATO forces to provide security in post-intervention U.N.-administered Kosovo.[7] Still, the legal and moral dilemma posed by mass atrocities remained acute. In a 1999 speech, then U.N. secretary-general Kofi Annan spelled out the conflict:

> To those for whom the greatest threat to the future of international order is the use of force in the absence of a Security Council mandate, one might ask . . . If, in those dark days . . . leading up to the [Rwandan] genocide, a coalition of States had been prepared to act . . . but did not receive prompt Council authorization, should such a coalition have stood aside and allowed the horror to unfold?
>
> To those for whom the Kosovo action heralded a new era when States . . . can take military action outside the established mechanisms for enforcing international law, one might ask: Is there not a danger of such interventions undermining the imperfect, yet resilient, security system created after the Second World War, and of setting dangerous precedents for future interventions without a clear criterion to decide who might invoke these precedents, and in what circumstances?[8]

By the beginning of the twenty-first century, the 1990s debates over humanitarian intervention had morphed into discussion of the Responsibility to Protect (R2P), a doctrine initially developed by the International Commission on Intervention and State Sovereignty (ICISS).[9] ICISS consisted of noted scholars, diplomats, and former high-level officials convened by the Canadian government, and in November of 2001, ICISS published a report called "The Responsibility to Protect."

In its report, ICISS did something novel and in many ways extraordinarily appealing: it sought to circumvent the tension between the moral pull of human rights and the moral pull of sovereignty by simply redefining the terms of the discussion.

In particular, ICISS sought to redefine sovereignty itself, arguing that sovereignty is not something that states possess simply by virtue of being states, but rather a matter of responsibilities as much as rights—and the most fundamental responsibility of a sovereign state is the protection of its own population. The right to be free of external intervention—long considered a fundamental attribute of Westphalian sovereignty—was, to ICISS, *contingent* upon a state's ongoing ability to protect its own population. A state that cannot (or will not) protect its population loses, to that same extent, the sovereign privilege of nonintervention.

ICISS offered a starkly different understanding of sovereignty than that taken for granted prior to World War II:

> State sovereignty implies responsibility. . . . Where a population is suffering serious harm, as a result of internal war, insurgency, repression or state failure, and the state in question is unwilling or unable to halt or avert it, the principle of non-intervention yields to the international responsibility to protect.[10]

ICISS was careful to note that military force should be a last resort, and that any military interventions *should* be authorized by the United Nations Security Council. But the Commission was unwilling to view Security Council authorization as an absolute requirement:

> If the Security Council rejects a proposal [to intervene to protect a population] or fails to deal with it in a reasonable time, alternative options . . . [include] action within area of jurisdiction by regional or sub-regional organizations under Chapter VIII of the Charter, subject to their seeking subsequent authorization.

Further, if the Security Council "fails to discharge its responsibility to protect in conscience-shocking situations crying out for action," warned ICISS, "concerned states may not rule out other means to meet the gravity and urgency of that situation."[11]

Logically, this made perfect sense: if the legitimacy and sovereign privileges of a particular state depend upon that state's willingness and ability to protect the human beings living within its borders, and if other states and the international community have an obligation to protect those same human beings, then surely any state that failed to act on that responsibility would similarly waive its own claims to legitimacy or to the full legal privileges of sovereignty. By extension, the same was true of organizations made up of states, such as the Security Council.

Either protection of human beings comes before legal and political fictions, or it doesn't: you can't have it both ways.

Within a decade, both the United States and the United Nations had offered the Responsibility to Protect doctrine at least a lukewarm embrace in speeches and General Assembly resolutions. And in March of 2011, the Security Council authorized the use of force to protect civilians both in Libya (where NATO took the lead) and in Côte d'Ivoire (where U.N. peacekeepers assisted by French troops used force to restore civil order following post-election violence). In both cases, the Security Council expressly invoked the Responsibility to Protect.[12]

This was the high-water point for the Responsibility to Protect norm. After Libya and Côte d'Ivoire, there was a brief period in which various commentators declared that the Responsibility to Protect had finally "grown up," achieving, or certainly getting within spitting distance of, the status of a norm of customary international law.[13] That period lasted only a few months, however, for the Libya intervention soon began to appear—at least to critics—more like a regime change intervention aimed at ousting Muammar Gaddafi than a civilian protection intervention.

Perhaps this was inevitable: it's not clear how an intervention intended to protect civilians from predation by their own government could avoid morphing into a regime change intervention in the face of continued government attacks on civilians. Regardless, the NATO shift toward a straightforward attack on Gaddafi's government forces triggered anxiety and anger in many states, including, most notably, Russia, China, and South Africa. From their perspective, the United States had tricked the Security Council into authorizing force for a limited, humanitarian purpose—and had then quickly moved to depose a sitting government.[14]

Even if the United States and other NATO powers had not initially intended the intervention to expand, the conflict illustrated that using force for civilian protection purposes could easily end up having unintended consequences.

After Libya, the pendulum again swung away from norms favoring humanitarian intervention and the responsibility to protect and toward an insistence on sovereign nonintervention—or, at the very least, a wariness of interventionist arguments. This has been reflected in the ongoing U.N. debate about Syria, where, despite more than 200,000 deaths, the Security Council has been unwilling even to use the phrase "responsibility to protect" in connection with the conflict.

In the United States, President Obama seems to have taken this to heart, as evidenced by his own conflicted response to the Syrian crisis. He's made it clear he has little appetite for a unilateral humanitarian intervention intended to protect civilians; he appears as concerned about slippery slopes as any U.S. critic.[15]

In August and September of 2013, however, Obama—trapped by his own rhetorical declaration that the use of chemical weapons in Syria would cross a U.S. "red line"—briefly declared his willingness to use military force for the limited purpose of ending Bashar al-Assad's regime's ability to use chemical weapons against his citizens. In the process, he articulated a legal argument justifying the potential unilateral use of force for the purpose of protecting civilians, even in the absence of Security Council authorization. The United Kingdom's prime minister did the same, asserting explicitly that a humanitarian intervention would be lawful under the circumstances.[16] In the United States, the United Kingdom, and France, key surrogates—such as former U.S. State Department legal advisor Harold Koh—also advanced legal arguments justifying a potential U.S. intervention in Syria.[17]

These arguments were far from universally accepted: the response both from domestic U.S. constituencies and even many close allies was sharply critical.[18] The British Parliament declined to authorize British participation in any use of force in Syria,[19] and in the United States, it seems quite likely that Congress would have done the same. Ultimately, this was not put to the test, as the United States opted against military action when Syria's government agreed to surrender its chemical weapons under international supervision.[20]

Despite the political backlash against U.S., U.K., and French arguments in favor of military intervention inside Syria, the 2013 debate marked an important turning point: it saw three permanent members of the Security Council explicitly embrace the view that humanitarian interventions inside other sovereign states can be lawful—even without Security Council authorization.

## Enter the "War on Terror"

The International Commission on Intervention and State Sovereignty had originally planned to issue its initial report on the Responsibility to Protect on September 12, 2001. The events of September 11 changed those plans, delaying the report's release by several months.

Like the Rwandan genocide and the atrocities in the former Yugoslavia, the terrorist attacks of September 2011 shook up traditional notions of sovereignty, self-defense, and armed conflict.

Prior to 9/11, most states had publicly accepted the general international law principle that force could not be used inside the territory of a sovereign state unless one of three things happened: the state at issue consented, the Security Council authorized the use of force under Chapter VII of the U.N. Charter, or the use of force was in self-defense following an "armed attack," as delineated in Article 51 of the U.N. Charter. NATO's Kosovo intervention could be seen as the exception that proves the rule—a onetime, "extralegal" intervention that shouldn't be used as a precedent.

U.N. Charter provisions on the use of force rest firmly on traditional understandings of sovereignty: as long as a state refrains in its external actions from threatening other states, the uninvited use of force inside its territory would be unlawful.[21] If a sovereign state chose to harbor terrorists, this would be its own business; unless those terrorists carried out attacks beyond the state's borders, no other state would have a legal basis to use force inside the harboring state.

But the 9/11 attacks made glaringly apparent the degree to which globalization and its drivers (changes in transportation, communication, and weapons technologies, for instance) had democratized the means of mass destruction, reduced the salience of international borders, and accelerated the speed with which money and matériel could travel. The attacks illustrated the growing difficulty in defining the realm of activities that was purely "internal" to a state, versus the realm of issues that can be regarded as purely "external."

For that matter, the events of 9/11 challenged standard definitions of terms such as "armed attack" and "armed force," long understood to refer to the use of traditional military force by foreign states. On 9/11, nineteen men—unaffiliated with any state or military force and armed only with box-cutters—hijacked civilian planes and brought about the deaths of thousands. It was hardly the kind of "armed attack" conceived of by the drafters of the U.N. Charter, who presumably imagined something more akin to Germany's 1939 invasion of Poland. But if the willful killing of thousands in an attack originating abroad *wasn't* an "armed attack," what was it?

Inevitably, the blurring of the lines between internal and external and between crime and war undermined the logic of sovereign non-intervention principles. The ethnic conflicts of the 1990s led the international community to define a state's predatory behavior toward its own people as a matter of global concern, and ICISS had articulated the "responsibility to protect" as triggered by a state's sustained failure to protect its *own* population. The events of 9/11 showed that a state's failure to control its "internal" affairs could lead to the "export" of harm to the populations of *other* states. Specifically, the Afghan state's inability or unwillingness to prevent its territory from being used by al Qaeda caused massive harm to populations living far beyond Afghanistan's borders (the thousands of Americans and others injured or killed in the 9/11 attacks).

Within the U.S. defense and national security communities, counterterrorism concerns after 9/11 sparked the rapid emergence of both policy and legal arguments for expanding the basis for using force within the territory of other states. There were several strands to these arguments.

First, the traditional self-defense-based justification for using force was expanded, most strikingly in the Bush administration's embrace of what it called "preemptive" self-defense, which was used to justify the war in Iraq. The logic underlying the Bush argument was straightforward (though the facts, inconveniently, were not): in the age of ballistic missiles and nuclear, chemical, and biological threats, states may only have a moment's notice before an imminent attack. Surely the framers of the U.N. Charter would not have required states to wait for such an armed attack to occur or be imminent, in the traditional sense, to lawfully use force in self-defense. Or, as President Bush put it, "Facing clear evidence of peril, we cannot wait for the final proof—the smoking gun—that could come in the form of a mushroom cloud."[22]

This extension of the principle of self-defense stretched traditional understandings of sovereignty—but the second strand of counterterrorism-based arguments justifying the use of force raised more fundamental challenges. The argument comes into sharpest focus when we consider drone strikes and other cross-border uses of force outside of hot battlefields. Since 2001, the United States has repeatedly used force inside the borders of sovereign states with which we are not at war, at times without the consent of the affected state. In October 2008, for instance, U.S. troops in Iraq crossed the Syrian border and attacked targets inside Syria.[23] The United States has also attacked targets inside Pakistan, Yemen, and Somalia. In some cases, the affected states have consented to the United States' use of force. In other cases, their consent is, at best, questionable.[24]

While the United States has been reluctant to offer much detail or legal justification for these actions, the underlying logic used appears structurally identical to that underlying the "responsibility to protect" concept: sovereignty implies responsibilities as well as rights; states must refrain from internal acts that threaten the citizens or basic security of other states, and must prevent nonstate entities from engaging in such acts inside their borders. If a state fails to fulfill this responsibility—by, for instance, harboring terrorists—other states are entitled to use force within its borders if doing so is necessary to protect themselves or uphold global security.[25]

As U.S. chief counterterrorism advisor John Brennan put it, "We reserve the right to take unilateral action if or when other governments are unwilling or unable to take the necessary actions themselves."[26]

## Two Sides of the Same Coin

The human rights and national security discourses appear to have developed parallel theories about the limits of sovereignty—though neither community is entirely comfortable with the logical implications taken for granted by the other community.[27]

One might even say that the "responsibility to protect" coin should logically be viewed as having two sides: On one side lies a state's duty to take action inside its own territory to protect its *own population* from violence and atrocities. On the other side lies a state's duty to take action inside its own territory to protect *other states' populations* from violence. A state that fails in either of these protective duties faces the prospect that other states will intervene in its internal affairs without its consent—and quite possibly without the Security Council's consent.[28]

There is a substantial irony here: human rights advocates and counterterrorism hawks make rather strange bedfellows. The "hard security" community, historically realist in its orientation, tends to be uncomfortable with the notion that states have a responsibility to protect the populations of other states from atrocities. The emerging Responsibility to Protect doctrine has largely been greeted in national security law quarters as irrelevant or pernicious, likely to draw the United States into diversionary foreign entanglements at the expense of protecting our core national security interests. Meanwhile, those in the human rights community tend to consider drone strikes and other uses of force outside of hot battlefields as little more than extraterritorial, extrajudicial executions—a flagrant violation of international human rights and rule of law principles.

Yet the logic of each sovereignty-limiting theory is virtually identical, and each theory reinforces and legitimizes the other. And Kofi Annan's 1999 warning still applies; it's all very well to argue that preventing ethnic cleansing and mass casualty terror attacks is everyone's responsibility (and, by extension, everyone's right), and that sovereignty should not shield an irresponsible state from outside intervention if that state can't or won't take appropriate action itself—and it's all very well to argue that states and other artificial entities, such as the

Security Council, can have no legitimacy if they fail to protect human beings from harm. But once you assert that every state can decide for itself that a military intervention inside another state's borders is justified, regardless of the Security Council, you're on a very slippery slope.

This is even more true in a world in which attacks can come from nonstate actors, and in which new technologies challenge old assumptions about imminence. If the United States can decide for itself that a single man inside a foreign state poses an imminent threat, and use that to justify deploying military force inside a foreign state, there's no reason for Russia, or China, or North Korea, or Iran not to do the same.

In theory, all these tensions could be resolved if we had more robust, responsive, and accountable forms of international governance. In the age of globalization, we need, more than ever, a strong global referee committed both to stability and to human dignity—a global referee that could make those difficult decisions about when and where to use force, so it wouldn't just be one state's views against another's. Only such a system could prevent the inevitable erosion of traditional norms of sovereignty from leading to a slide toward conflict and instability, at the expense of basic human rights.

# CHAPTER FIFTEEN

# Making the Military

## A Recent Innovation

States make and unmake war, and war makes and unmakes states. But although evidence of organized warfare can be found throughout humanity's earliest pictorial and written records, and human societies have long sought to tame and contain war through law, the existence of organized forms of warfare does not require the existence of a specialized institution called "the military."

Far from it: permanent, professionalized militaries are, like the state itself, a relatively recent human innovation. For much of human history, men—and sometimes women—assumed warrior identities on an as-needed basis. While elaborate rules and rituals often served to separate wars and warriors from ordinary, peacetime life, armies (and navies) were assembled for particular purposes—perhaps to go on a raid, or respond to an invasion—then disbanded until needed again. Until the third millennium BC, there is little evidence of professional, standing militaries, raised, funded, trained, and maintained by the state.

By 2700 BC, complex urban societies had developed in ancient Mesopotamia. Agriculture and the domestication of animals enabled the creation of surpluses, the amassing of wealth, and the development of what we would today call professions or "classes": merchants, craftsmen, farmers, bureaucrats, and soldiers. Sumerian cuneiform tablets from around the middle of the third millennium BC suggest the existence of at least a core group of six or seven hundred soldiers employed by the king, while the Stele of the Vultures, the world's oldest known historical document, portrays Sumerian infantry troops in helmets and body armor, fighting in elaborate phalanx formation. (The Stele of the Vultures memorializes King Eannatum's victory over the ruler and armies of Umma. "Their myriad corpses/I shall make stretch to the horizon," promises Eannatum, and the Stele indeed depicts Eannatum's forces marching past a pile of naked enemy corpses.)[1]

By midway through the second century BC, Egypt too had developed a highly professionalized military, maintained in part through conscription (each region being obligated to provide 10 percent of its young men to the pharaoh's army). Egypt was divided into military districts, and gifts of land were provided to families supplying officers; military schools and training centers were established. Ancient Persia, Greece, and Rome all had standing armies, and the science of warfare grew more elaborate in many societies. In some cases, mercenaries formed the core of state armies.[2]

Throughout the next two millennia, standing armies waxed and waned in many parts of the world. In Europe until the fifteenth century AD, armies were often hard to distinguish from roving groups of bandits, some of who might be hired temporarily by local lords. Armies were generally raised for particular campaigns, then demobilized when no longer required.

In 1181, for instance, King Henry II of England codified the obligation of his subjects to fight at his request. In the Assize of Arms, he specified the types of weapons with which each man must equip himself, according to his class (hauberks, helmets, shields, and lances for knights; quilted doublets, iron headpieces, and lances for burgesses and freemen). The Assize of Arms required every man to swear "he will possess these arms and will bear allegiance to the lord king, Henry . . . and that he will bear these arms in his service according to his order and in allegiance to the lord king and his realm."[3] But soldiering was still a part-time activity and a purely temporary identity: men fought when called upon to do so, but the rest of the time they returned to farming or trading or blacksmithing.

Only in 1445 did Charles VII of France create what is generally viewed as the first standing army of any European state. Britain's first peacetime standing army didn't come along for another two centuries, and it caused an immediate backlash: James II's 1685 creation of a standing army helped cement the distrust many powerful noblemen already felt for him. By 1688, James had been ousted in the Glorious Revolution, and was forced to flee to France. In 1689, the English Bill of Rights prohibited "the raising or keeping a standing army within the kingdom in time of peace, unless it be with consent of Parliament."[4]

The poet John Dryden summed up the prevailing hostility to standing armies in his 1697 poem "Cymon and Iphigenia": "Mouths without hands; maintained at vast expense, In peace a charge, in war a weak defence."[5]

The rebellious American colonists viewed standing armies with similar suspicion. In 1776, the Declaration of Independence denounced King George III for keeping "among us, in times of peace, Standing Armies" and "quartering large bodies of armed troops among us." The use of mercenaries and the impressment of American sailors was also seen as a sign of British tyranny: George III was condemned for "at this time transporting large Armies of foreign Mercenaries to compleat the works of death, desolation and tyranny," and "constrain[ing] our fellow Citizens taken Captive on the high Seas to bear Arms against their Country."[6] The American Constitution reflects the same mistrust of permanent military forces: it gives Congress the power to "raise and support Armies," but adds a caveat: "no Appropriation of Money to that Use shall be for a longer Term than two Years."[7]

Until well into the nineteenth century, the lines between bandits, mercenaries, mercantile entrepreneurs, lords, and soldiers remained quite indistinct, as did the lines between pirates, naval forces, and privateers operating pursuant to state letters of marque.

Consider the British East India Company, chartered in 1600 to trade in East and Southeast Asia and India.[8] Its first fleet was commanded by a former privateer, Sir James Lancaster, fresh from carrying out "a successful piratical attack . . . on the Portuguese settlement of Pernambuco."[9] Lancaster served not only as "general of the fleet" but as the Crown's accredited diplomatic representative to various Eastern rulers; according to Samuel Purchas's 1625 collection of documents relating to the voyage,

the queen provided Lancaster with "her friendly letters of commenda-
tion, written to divers princes of India, offering to enter into a league of
peace and amitie with them. . . . And because no great action can be well
carryed and accomplished without an absolute authoritie of justice, shee
granted to the generall of their fleet, Master James Lancaster, for his better command and government, a commission of martiall law."[10]

Although in its early years the East India Company employed only
a small number of guards for its ships, personnel, and warehouses, by
the middle of the eighteenth century, it was recruiting, training, and
maintaining substantial armies (manned mostly by natives) to expand
its dominion over India. In 1757, company forces under Robert Clive
defeated the Nawab of Bengal, who fought with assistance from French
troops. By 1778, the company employed more than 65,000 soldiers—far
more than the British Army.[11] From 1809 to 1861, it operated its own
military academy at Addiscombe.

The British East India Company was part profit-making corporate
enterprise, part government, and part military, and it acted in many
ways as the direct agent of the Crown. Throughout much of the first
half of the nineteenth century, it combined its own privately employed
forces with regular British Army units "lent" to the company by the
government. Only in 1858—after the Sepoy Mutiny triggered a general rebellion against company rule—did the Crown finally dissolve the
company, absorbing it formally into the British government.[12]

In the United States, concerns about tyranny kept the peacetime
military relatively small throughout most of the nineteenth and early
twentieth centuries. Only during the Civil War did the size of the American armed forces for the first time exceed one percent of the population. In both the Civil War and World War I, temporary conscription
brought participation in the armed forces up to about 3 percent of the
population; at virtually all other times before and after the Civil War
and World War I, the size of the military hovered at only about a quarter of one percent of the population.

During World War II, participation in the active duty military shot
up to about 12 percent of the overall population, before dropping to
just over 2 percent during the Korean War, just under 2 percent during

the Vietnam War, and about 0.5 percent prior to 9/11.[13] Today, participation in the active duty military still stands at about 0.5 percent of the total U.S. population; if we add in reservists and members of the National Guard, just over one percent of the population is a member of the armed services. Since the draft ended after the Vietnam War, this population has consisted entirely of volunteers.

In some sense, as these figures suggest, those who yearn for an earlier era in which more Americans had direct connections to the military harken after a time that never existed on more than a temporary basis. Today's relatively low military population is not aberrational: it was the larger, conscript-based militaries of World War I, World War II, Korea, and Vietnam that were anomalous.

Of course, just as the British East India Company's private armies often functioned as agents of the British Crown, the U.S. government supplements its military with what amounts to a substantial private force: contractors. According to a recent Congressional Research Center analysis, contractors accounted for more than 50 percent of the total U.S. Defense Department workforce in Afghanistan and Iraq.[14] Many other military and security contractors are employed by the Department of State and by other government agencies, including those in the intelligence community; while not under the authority of the Defense Department, many of these contractors function, in effect, as adjuncts to U.S. forces.

In modern U.S. military activities, it has once again become increasingly difficult to separate the roles of private and public actors. Consider the raid that killed Osama bin Laden. According to press reports, the raid was planned and carried out by a mix of civilian CIA and DoD employees, employees of private firms under contract to the intelligence community and the Defense Department,[15] and active duty military personnel. In practice, this too blurs the lines between military and civilians, intelligence and operations, public and private.

## What Makes a Soldier?

Military personnel are as confused by this as everyone else. A couple of years ago, I was speaking to an audience of majors and lieutenant col-

onels at the Army's School of Advanced Military Studies at Fort Leavenworth (SAMS). The school takes only those viewed as the Army's
best and brightest: creative officers likely to serve in important leadership positions throughout their careers. Most of the officers I spoke to
had recently returned from deployments in Iraq and Afghanistan, and
I asked them two questions: First, what did they see as the most significant security threats facing the United States in the coming decade or
two? Second, exactly what made a soldier a soldier?

The answers I got were interesting. I offered various options for
"most significant security threats," and asked for a show of hands.

—Al Qaeda? No hands went up.

—Islamic terrorism? One or two hands, but mostly I saw head
shakes.

North Korea and Iran generated no raised hands. Weapons of mass
destruction? A few hands went up.

—New conflicts and resource scarcity driven by climate change? A
lot of hands went up.

—Global economic collapse? Here too, lots of hands went up.

I moved on to what makes a soldier a soldier, asking for thoughts
from the assembled officers.

Some of the answers I got were tautological: "A soldier is someone
who serves in the Army." (And an army? "An army is a force made up of
soldiers.") Others were more functional: a soldier, I was told, is someone who is trained to fight in wars.

What, I asked, does it mean to "fight in wars"? The answers to this
one brought us around to the question of how to define war, and most
of the officers answered that the fighting done by soldiers is a) in the
service of the nation and b) involves the use of weapons that can injure
or kill human beings or physically destroy property.

Soldiers, they seemed to be telling me, are people who train to use
and actually use weapons to kill or injure enemies of their country.

Straightforward enough, until I asked each of them to tell me how
they had spent their most recent deployments. Most answered as I had
expected: they had supervised the building of wells, sewers, and bridges,
helped resolve community disputes, patrolled territory, worked with

local police, written press releases, analyzed intelligence data, engaged in cyber operations. A few of the unlucky ones had been in vehicles hit by IEDs. A far smaller number still had been in what most of us would consider combat, actively engaged with enemy forces.

In other words: most of them hadn't spent much time doing what they thought of as the essence of soldiering. They had trained to fight, but found, when deployed in America's two most recent ground wars, that most of the time there wasn't much call for fighting.

What, then, made them different from police officers, I asked, or from the armed employees of Blackwater and Triple Canopy who often worked alongside military personnel in conflict zones, and were also trained to fight, if necessary, on behalf of the United States? What made them different from the State Department's Foreign Service officers, or from local administrators or engineers?

This generated an uncomfortable silence. Soldiers conceive of themselves as profoundly different from civilians, even armed and well-trained civilians—but though soldiers maintain a strong sense of cultural identity, and inhabit a different legal order than civilians, the bright young officers at SAMS all understood my point. As the tasks we assign to the military expand, and as private contractors and intelligence community paramilitary operatives take on many of the tasks we used to assign to the military, it's gotten harder and harder to distinguish between the various players. What's more, if the military sees its job as protecting the nation from security threats, but the gravest security threats are things like climate change and financial collapse rather than war or even terrorism, it becomes increasingly difficult to define a uniquely "military" role and mission.

These days, the tautological answers are increasingly the only answers we can agree upon: soldiers are those who serve in the army, and the army is the institution in which soldiers serve. The military is the institution that plans, prepares for, and undertakes wars, and wars are whatever the military does.

# CHAPTER SIXTEEN

# An Age of Uncertainty

Stung by criticism of his foreign policy, in 2014 President Obama reminded an audience of Democratic donors that "the world has always been messy." His subtext was clear: it's easy and fun to throw stones, but *you* try fixing the world: you'll find out soon enough that many messes are stubbornly resistant to fixing, particularly by the United States.

He was surely right to remind us that today's tragic messes are hardly messier or more tragic than the past's tragic messes. Those who prefer their glasses half full can take comfort in reflecting that the recent Ebola pandemic had nothing on the Black Death, for instance, while the Syrian conflict pales beside the Thirty Years War. But with apologies to Tolstoy, each era of world messiness is messy in its own way.

Here's the nature of the current mess: the last century's technological revolutions have made our world more globally interconnected than ever. Power and access to power have become more democratized and diffuse in some ways, but more concentrated in other ways. For most individuals around the globe, day-to-day life is far less dangerous and brutal than in previous eras; for the species as a whole, however, the risk of future global catastrophe has increased. Meanwhile, the continuously accelerating rate of technological and social change makes it increasingly difficult to predict the geopolitical future.

Nothing is particularly original about these observations; they're repeated in some fashion in every major national strategic document produced over the last decade. They probably teach this stuff to kindergartners now. Indeed, we've heard it all so often that it's tempting to dismiss such claims as meaningless platitudes: *Been there; theorized that. Can we please get back to business as usual?*

Not if we want our children and grandchildren to live decent lives. If we care about the future at all, we need to do more than prattle on at cocktail parties about globalization, interconnectedness, complexity, danger, and uncertainty. We need to feel these seismic changes in our bones—and understand that this is the perilous context in which U.S. actions are further blurring the boundaries between war and peace, and further destabilizing the already shaky international order.

So bear with me, and let's try to breathe some life into the clichés.

Consider some facts. The world now contains more people living in more states than ever before, and we're all more interconnected. A hundred years ago, the world population was about 1.8 billion, there were roughly sixty sovereign states in the world, the automobile was still a rarity, and there were no commercial passenger flights and no transcontinental telephone service. Fifty years ago, the global population had climbed to more than three billion and there were 115 U.N. member states, but air travel was still for the wealthy and the personal computer still lay two decades in the future. Today, we've got seven billion people living in 192 U.N. member states and a handful of other territories. These seven billion people take 93,000 commercial flights a day from nine thousand airports, drive one billion cars, and carry seven billion mobile phones around with them.[1]

In numerous ways, life has gotten substantially better in this more crowded and interconnected era. Seventy years ago, global war killed scores of millions, but interstate conflict has declined sharply since then, and the creation of the United Nations ushered in a far more egalitarian and democratic form of international governance than existed in any previous era. Today, militarily powerful states are far less free than in the pre-U.N. era to use overt force to accomplish their aims, and the world now has numerous transnational courts and dispute-resolution bodies that collectively offer states a viable alternative to the use of force. The modern international order is no global utopia, but it's a substantial improvement over institutionalized racism, colonial domination, and world wars.

In the fifty years that followed World War II, medical and agricultural advances brought unprecedented health and prosperity to most parts of the globe. More recently, the communications revolution has enabled exciting new forms of nongovernmental cross-border alliances to emerge, empowering, for instance, global human rights and environmental movements. In just the last two decades, the near-universal penetration of mobile phones has had a powerful leveling effect: all over the globe, people at every age and income level can use these tiny but powerful computers to learn foreign languages, solve complex mathematical problems, create and share videos, watch the news, move money around, or communicate with far-flung friends.

We all know that this has had a dark side too. As access to knowledge has been democratized, so too has access to the tools of violence and destruction, and greater global interconnectedness enables disease, pollution, and conflict to spread quickly and easily beyond borders. A hundred years ago, no single individual or nonstate actor could do more than cause localized mayhem; today, we have to worry about massive bioengineered threats created by tiny terrorist cells and globally devastating cyberattacks devised by malevolent teen hackers.

Even as many forms of power have grown more democratized and diffuse, other forms of power have grown more concentrated. A very small number of states control and consume a disproportionate share of the world's resources, and a very small number of individuals control most of the world's wealth. (According to a 2014 Oxfam report, the eighty-five richest individuals on earth are worth more than the globe's 3.5 billion poorest people.)[2]

Indeed, from a species-survival perspective, the world has grown vastly more dangerous over the last century. Individual humans live longer than ever before, but a small number of states now possess the unprecedented ability to destroy large chunks of the human race and possibly the earth itself—all in a matter of days or even hours. Today, there are an estimated seventeen thousand nuclear warheads in the possession of some nine states—and though the near-term threat of interstate nuclear conflict has greatly diminished since the end of the Cold War, nuclear material is now less controlled and less controllable.

If you want to give yourself a good scare, do some bedtime reading on bioengineered threats or even the various possible lethal epidemics that might start without help from malign human actors and then spread around the world in weeks, thanks to modern travel technologies. Then there's climate change, which could flood coastal cities, cause drought and famine, and fuel civil conflict around the globe.

Amidst all these changes, our world has also grown far more uncertain. We possess more information than ever before and vastly greater processing power, but the accelerating pace of global change has far exceeded our collective ability to understand it, much less manage it. This makes it increasingly difficult to make predictions or calculate risks.

For most of human history, major technological and social transformations occurred over thousands of years. The Paleolithic period (or "Old Stone Age") is presumed to have lasted for a couple of million years, give or take; the Mesolithic and Neolithic eras got a five- to ten-thousand-year run; the Bronze Age and the Iron Age each took a few thousand years. In Europe, things sped up during the Renaissance and the Age of Exploration. Enter the Industrial Revolution, and the pace of change accelerates some more; today, in the age of Moore's Law, it's downright dizzying.

For the average European peasant, life in the year 300 AD wasn't all that different from life in 800 or 1300 or 1700: it revolved around hunting, fishing, or farming; the manufacture of goods was on a small scale; travel was by foot, horse, or ship. Most Americans living in 1900 would have had more daily experiences in common with Americans living in 1800—or 1700, for that matter—than with Americans living today.

We literally have no points of comparison for understanding the scale and scope of the risks faced by humanity today. Compared to the long, slow sweep of human history, the events of the last century have taken place in the blink of an eye. This should give us pause when we're tempted to conclude that today's trends are likely to continue. Rising life expectancy? That's great, but if climate change has consequences as nasty as some predict, a century of rising life expectancy could turn out to be a mere blip on the charts. A steep decline in interstate conflicts? Fantastic, but less than seventy years of human history isn't much to go on. No nuclear annihilation so far? Thank God—but what on earth would make you assume we've "solved" that problem, rather than just had a run of mostly unmerited good luck?

That's why one can't dismiss the risk of catastrophic events such as disastrous climate change or nuclear conflict as "high consequence, low probability." How do we compute the probability of catastrophic events of a type that has never happened? Does seventy years without nuclear annihilation tell us that there's a low probability of nuclear catastrophe— or just tell us that we haven't had a nuclear catastrophe *yet*?

Even when we have ample data going back over a long period of time, most of us aren't very good at evaluating risk. We tend to assume that the way things are is the way things are likely to remain. The mountain that has been there for thousands of years will probably be there for another hundred. But we forget that the same logic doesn't hold for everything. We say, "That tree in the backyard has survived snow and ice storms for a hundred years—it's not going to fall down tomorrow!" But when it comes to trees, having survived for a hundred years generally means there's now more, rather than less, chance of collapse tomorrow.

Lack of catastrophic change might signify a system in stable equilibrium, but sometimes—as with earthquakes—pressure may be building up over time, undetected. Often, the problem is that we just don't know enough: If you just planted a new tree in the backyard from a breed that's never before been planted outside the tropics, it's hard to know how it will fare in snow. If you're a scientist studying earthquakes, tornados, or tsunamis, it's one thing to understand the conditions under which they form, but we still have little ability to predict their precise time and locations sufficiently in advance to do any good. Is global stability more like a mountain, more like a tsunami, or more like a tree? And if it's a tree, is it the kind we're used to or a whole new kind of tree?

Most international security "experts" have about as much ability to predict the future as you or I would have to predict next year's weather by looking out the window today. The events of recent decades should undermine everyone's confidence in our collective ability to predict geopolitical change: most analysts assumed the Soviet Union was stable—until it collapsed. Analysts predicted that Egypt's Hosni

Mubarak would retain his firm grip on power—until he was ousted. How much of what we currently file under "Stable" should be recategorized under "Hasn't Collapsed Yet"?

We should try to feel the danger and uncertainty in your bones— not because it will build character, but because feeling afraid is the only thing likely to jolt us into action. Wouldn't it be better to try to actively manage the national and global risks we face, instead of muddling through with our eyes resolutely closed?

## The United States in the Mess

For Americans, the good news is that the United States remains an extraordinarily powerful nation. The United States has "the most powerful military in history," President Obama declared in a recent speech,[3] and measured by sheer destructive capacity, he is surely right. The U.S. military can get to more places, faster, with more lethal and effective weapons, than any military on the planet.

Even as its global influence and economic health have declined, the United States still has unprecedented power to destroy, as Saddam Hussein and Osama bin Laden both discovered to their detriment. We can kill; we can topple governments; we can demolish the conventional military capabilities of enemy states; we can wreak havoc on foreign states' economies.

The United States can also destroy or undermine international norms and institutions: despite our declining economic and political power, we still have disproportionate global influence. When our government embraces legal theories that accept the unilateral use of military force and destabilize principles of sovereignty—when we embrace the widespread use of covert targeted killings, or indefinite detention, or secret mass surveillance—we pave the way for other states to behave in similar ways. When we choose to bypass or ignore international institutions and rules we find inconvenient instead of working to create new and better ones, we further destabilize the already shaky international order.

Against this backdrop of uncertainty—some of it of our own making— we have to keep planning and adapting. We have to decide where to invest our tax dollars; when to use military force and when to avoid it; which legal norms to advance and which international institutions to support or reform; and how to structure our military and civilian institutions. Like it or not, the legal and policy decisions we make today will shape the world we must inhabit in the future. Yet as war blurs and expands, the fog of war expands as well, making it harder and harder to see the branches in the road ahead.

# PART IV

# Counting the Costs

# CHAPTER SEVENTEEN

# Car Bombs and Radioactive Sushi

For much of my childhood, my mother was a fellow at the Washington, D.C.-based Institute for Policy Studies. It's not surprising, then, that the 1976 murder of Orlando Letelier and Ronni Moffitt is seared into my memory.

Orlando Letelier was a hero to many Washington liberals. He had served as Chilean ambassador to the United States under left-wing president Salvador Allende, who then appointed Letelier his minister of defense. When the democratically elected Allende was overthrown in a violent 1973 coup staged by army General Augusto Pinochet, Letelier was imprisoned and tortured. Finally released by the military junta after intensive diplomatic pressure, Letelier fled Chile for the United States, where he became a fellow at the Institute for Policy Studies—and an outspoken critic of Pinochet's brutal dictatorship.

This was brave, but foolish: the Pinochet regime's reach was longer than Letelier could ever have imagined.

On the morning of September 21, 1976, Letelier was driving to work. With him were his young American assistant, twenty-five-year-old Ronni Moffitt, and her husband, Michael, who sat in the backseat.

As Letelier and the two young Americans drove through Washington's embassy district, a fierce explosion shook the car. Ronni and Michael Moffitt managed to crawl out of the burning vehicle, but Letelier's legs and much of his torso had been blown off. He died within minutes. Ronni Moffitt made it to the hospital, but died an hour later. Only Michael survived the explosion.[1]

Evidence gathered by the FBI quickly pointed to the Pinochet regime, and it later became clear that the brutal assassination had been engineered by Chile's intelligence service, on the orders of Pinochet himself.[2] Letelier's brazen murder—carried out on U.S. soil by a foreign regime—shocked the world, and was condemned by American law enforcement agencies and senior U.S. political officials, including President Gerald Ford. No one had any difficulty finding the right words to describe the incident: "I have just learned with shock and horror of the senseless and brutal assassination of your husband," presidential candidate Jimmy Carter telegrammed to Letelier's wife.[3]

The American left was galvanized by the murder. I was too young to fully understand the politics, but I remember the shock and the grief. A car bomb planted by a foreign government, in the streets of the nation's capital!

My mother took me to vigils and solidarity marches, and we chanted, in Spanish and English: "¡Chile sí, Junta no!" and "¡El pueblo unido jamás será vencido!" ("The people, united, will never be defeated!") At home, the songs of Víctor Jara, a Chilean musician tortured and murdered by the military junta, played endlessly on the record player in the living room, along with the haunting melodies of Holly Near, memorializing the many victims of the Pinochet regime:

> Hay una mujer desaparecida
> En Chile, en Chile, en Chile
>
> And the junta, and the junta knows. . . .
> And the junta knows where they are hiding her, she's dying
>
> . . . Hay un hombre, hay una niña
> Oh, los niños. . . .[4]

Of course, the Pinochet regime saw things rather differently. To Pinochet, the dead weren't murdered innocents. Chile was "at war" with left-wing "insurgents" and "terrorists," many connected to Salvador Allende's ousted government. Letelier's anti-Pinochet activities made him a direct threat to Chile's national security (as the term was understood by the ruling military junta). As such, he had to go.

Fast forward almost thirty years, to November 2006. In London, forty-four-year-old Russian dissident Alexander Litvinenko ate lunch at Itsu, a fashionable sushi restaurant, then drank a cup of tea at the Pine Bar in London's Millennium Hotel. A short time later, he fell ill. He was hospitalized, but became sicker and sicker as the days passed. Eventually, it became apparent that he was dying—slowly and agonizingly—of radiation sickness. Traces of deadly polonium-210 were later found in the sushi restaurant where he'd eaten lunch, in the Pine Bar, and in the apartment of a former KGB officer with whom he had met earlier in the day. The authorities ultimately concluded that Litvinenko, long a thorn in Russian president Vladimir Putin's side, had been assassinated on British territory by Russian government agents.[5]

As a matter of international law, there's no uncertainty about the killings of Orlando Letelier and Alexander Litvinenko: it was illegal for Chile and Russia to violate U.S. and U.K. sovereignty by using force inside their borders. And since neither Letelier nor Litvinenko was a combatant in an armed conflict with Chile or Russia, the killings were nothing more than murders.

The United States doesn't use car bombs or radioactive sushi to kill those we consider threats. Instead, we use drone strikes and special operations raids—and we tell ourselves that such strikes, which have by now killed an estimated four thousand people in several countries, don't violate international or domestic legal bans on murder or assassination. *We* only target "combatants" in our armed conflict with al Qaeda and its "associated forces"—and now, the so-called Islamic State—or those who pose "imminent threats" to the United States. But we don't make public the evidence supporting our assertions about the identity of those we target or the threat we say they pose, and we generally don't even acknowledge the strikes themselves.

We want to believe that we have nothing in common with Pinochet and Putin—but as the lines around war grow more indistinct, it becomes more and more difficult to draw principled distinctions between lawful and unlawful uses of force.

If we're truly in a war against al Qaeda and its "associated forces," and that war (and the law of war) extends to wherever our enemies go, and if we have correctly identified who should count as a combatant and what constitutes an imminent threat, well, then we're *nothing* like Pinochet or Putin. We're lawfully targeting enemy combatants in wartime—or, alternatively and additionally, we're engaging in lawful acts of international self-defense against imminent threats (always assuming, that is, that we either have the consent of the sovereign states in which we're using force, or we appropriately view those sovereign states as unwilling or unable to take appropriate action to address the threat).

That's a lot of "ifs," and in a world in which the boundaries of war have become impossible to define, we can't be sure we've got it right. If we're wrong—if we're using force without the consent of the sovereign states in which we're operating, or we've incorrectly concluded that a nonconsenting state is unwilling or unable to act against a threat, or if we've wrongly assessed as genuine and imminent a threat that's actually neither—then we may be breaking core international law rules on the use of force.

And: if we *can't* be said to be in a war with al Qaeda, or if that war can't be viewed as extending to its "associated forces," or if we're wrong about which groups should qualify as associated forces, or about which individuals can reasonably be viewed as members of such groups—or if we're wrong about what should count as "hostilities," or wrong about when and where the law of war applies—then U.S. targeted strikes are extrajudicial executions.

In international law, that's a polite way of saying "murders."

## High Stakes

A vast chasm lies between the law governing wartime and the law governing peacetime. In peacetime, the willful killing of human beings is a crime, excused only under certain narrowly defined circumstances, such as self-defense. Even law enforcement agents are forbidden to use lethal force except in defense of themselves or others: the police, for instance, can't decide to bomb an apartment building in which suspected criminals lie sleeping. If law enforcement agents knowingly kill innocent people as a by-product of using force against suspected criminals, we don't simply write off those deaths as "collateral damage." Furthermore, the intentional destruction of private property and severe restriction of individual liberties are generally impermissible.

In wartime, nearly everything changes. Many actions that are considered both immoral and illegal in peacetime are permissible—even praiseworthy—in wartime. Most notably, willful killing is permitted, as long as those targeted are enemy combatants or others participating directly in hostilities. Under the law of armed conflict, individuals can be targeted based on their *status*, rather than their activities. Thus, during a war, a combatant can lob a grenade into a building full of sleeping people, as long as he reasonably believes the sleeping people to be enemy soldiers. Even actions that a combatant *knows* will cause civilian deaths are lawful when consistent with the principles of necessity, humanity, proportionality, and distinction.[6]

Similarly, during wartime various lesser forms of coercion and intrusion are also permissible, even when the same acts would be unlawful in peacetime. In wartime, enemy combatants can be detained for the duration of the conflict, and even those determined to be civilians can be indefinitely detained for imperative reasons of security, at the discretion of the detaining power. In wartime, generally speaking, private communications can be lawfully restricted or intercepted, private property can be searched and destroyed, and so on.

If we're in a war, the continued indefinite detention of enemy combatants at Guantánamo is fine, and NSA wiretapping is perfectly reasonable. If we're not in a war, we're violating the provisions of a dozen international human rights law treaties by holding prisoners indefinitely without charge or trial, and violating a dozen other provisions through impermissible government infringements on privacy.

What if the 9/11 attacks were considered an armed attack sufficient to trigger a right to use force in self-defense, but not construed as the beginning of an armed conflict? Here, the rules lie somewhere in between those of the peacetime and wartime frameworks. Unlike the international law of armed conflict, the international law of self-defense permits states to use force only to *respond* to an armed attack or to prevent an *imminent* armed attack, and the use of force in self-defense must be both necessary and proportionate to achieving these ends. Status-based targeting is not permitted under self-defense rules: that is, an individual can be targeted only if his *current activities* pose an imminent threat. Furthermore, traditional interpretations of the international law of self-defense define the term "imminent" quite narrowly, restricting the use of force to situations in which force is necessary to address threats that are urgent and grave, rather than speculative, distant, or minor.[7]

As we know, after 9/11 the U.S. government opted for the legal frame that places fewest constraints on its use of coercion and lethal force. "Our war on terror begins with Al Qaeda, but it does not end there," President Bush told members of Congress on September 20, 2001.[8] His words proved more prophetic than perhaps even he could have realized, for once in war mode, there was no principled place to "end" the war, or draw any meaningful lines between war and nonwar.

A global "war on terror" was a war that could, by its nature, have no boundaries: no spatial limits, no limits on who could be targeted, captured, or killed, and no end. Start with the lack of geographic boundaries inherent in a war on "terror," or even an ostensibly more limited war on al Qaeda. If we are at war with "al Qaeda and its associates," these individuals, whoever they may be, are presumably targetable and detainable *wherever* they may be. Following this logic, the United States has used drone strikes and other forms of targeted killings to kill suspected terrorists in states ranging from Yemen and Libya to Syria and Somalia, and has detained suspected terrorists as far afield as Bosnia and Nigeria.

Limits on who can be targeted and detained are similarly elusive. Under the law of armed conflict, enemy combatants and civilians directly participating in hostilities are targetable and detainable, but who counts as a "combatant" in the war against al Qaeda and its associates? Is it reasonable to argue, as have some government lawyers, that the Islamic State is effectively the same as al Qaeda, despite the current hostility between the two groups, because ISIS was originally founded by al Qaeda members? And what are "hostilities" in this nontraditional conflict?

Further, the United States government has not offered any public explanation of which groups it considers to be "associated forces" of al Qaeda or the Taliban. The international law of war unquestionably permits parties to a conflict to target "co-belligerents" of the enemy. On a traditional battlefield, it would clearly be permissible for the United States to target individuals and groups that are literally fighting alongside the Taliban or al Qaeda. But identifying the enemy is far harder outside that traditional context, and executive branch officials have provided no clear criteria.

Take three examples. First, an easy one: say a group of Yemeni tribal leaders meets with al Qaeda representatives. In exchange for money and assistance fighting against local rivals, tribal leaders agree to work with al Qaeda by providing its fighters with arms, shelter, food, and a hundred young tribesmen who can serve as local guides, bodyguards, and soldiers, assisting with al Qaeda's Yemen-based military and terrorist activities as needed. Most people would agree that the tribal leaders—and the hundred young tribesmen—are now co-belligerents with al Qaeda under the international law of war, and could be detained and targeted by U.S. forces.

But here's a harder one. Say Boko Haram fighters in Nigeria decide to model their organizational structure and training programs on those of al Qaeda, and initiate limited communication with al Qaeda members. Boko Haram's exclusive focus is attacks against Nigerian Christians and Nigerian government interests inside Nigeria's borders, but Boko Haram leaders frequently express their view that they, like al Qaeda, are part of a global Islamic jihad. As a courtesy the two groups occasionally share information, but they do not coordinate their activities or act within the same geographic region. Can Boko Haram be said to be associated forces of Al Qaeda?

Or say a group of Pakistani tribal leaders plans a series of attacks against Pakistani military targets. Their activities have a purely local focus: they have no interest in global jihad, but simply want the Pakistani military out of their territory. To that end, they occasionally coordinate their efforts with those of the Pakistani Taliban, who also want to target the Pakistani military. These same Pakistani Taliban leaders also sometimes move across the Afghan border and help Afghan-based Taliban fighters in operations against the Afghan military. Are the Pakistani tribal leaders co-belligerents of the Afghan Taliban?

Add in more complexity, and it only gets more difficult. Is an Iraqi teenager who sends out social media messages on behalf of al Qaeda a "member" of al Qaeda? What about a Saudi financier who knowingly donates large amounts of money to an al Qaeda–linked charity? Is there a difference between being a "member" of al Qaeda and an al Qaeda "agent" or "operative"? Can either the Iraqi teen or the Saudi financier be considered, if not an al Qaeda member or agent or operative, a co-belligerent?

Terms such as "co-belligerent" and "combatant" add clarity only when we think of war in nineteenth-century terms. And if anything, it has only grown more difficult to define our "enemies" since 9/11. "Al Qaeda Central" has largely collapsed, but it has spawned numerous other networks and movements, loosely knit, nonhierarchical, geographically dispersed, and diverse in size, structure, methods, and aims. As former Defense Intelligence Agency director Lieutenant General Michael Flynn recently put it: "In 2004, there were 21 total Islamic terrorist groups spread out in 18 countries. Today, there are 41 Islamic terrorist groups spread out in 24 countries."[9] These groups range from ISIS, which controls substantial parts of Syria and Iraq and has more than forty affiliates around the world, to Nigeria's Boko Haram, Mali's al-Mourabitoun, Tunisia's Ansar Al Sharia, and numerous others.[10]

Given this, it is hardly surprising that recent U.S. drone strikes have reportedly killed numerous individuals whose activities and affiliations are literally unknown: although President Obama has frequently asserted that the United States only targets "specific senior operational leaders of al Qaida and associated forces" involved in the September 11, 2001, terror attacks who are plotting "imminent" violent attacks on Americans, classified CIA reports obtained by news outlets reportedly state that more than half of those killed by drone strikes in Pakistan in the year preceding September 2011 "were not senior al Qaida leaders but instead were 'assessed' as Afghan, Pakistani and unknown extremists." Similarly, "forty-three of 95 drone strikes reviewed for that period hit groups other than al Qaida, including the Haqqani network, several Pakistani Taliban factions and the unidentified individuals described only as 'foreign fighters' and 'other militants.'"[11]

There is also no apparent means of ending the war against al Qaeda and its associates. In a November 2012 speech, Defense Department general counsel Jeh Johnson raised this question: "Now that efforts by the U.S. military against al Qaeda are in their 12th year, we must also ask ourselves: how will this conflict end?"[12] That was several years ago, and the answer is even less clear today.

For the Obama administration, this question clearly causes substantial unease. "This war, like all wars, must end," President Obama told a National Defense University audience in May 2013. "That's what our democracy demands." He repeated the sentiment in 2015: "I do not believe America's interests are served by endless war."[13] But how do we end a nonterritorial armed conflict against an ill-defined, amorphous, protean enemy, with no leaders authorized to speak on its behalf, no set membership, and only the vaguest of goals?

## The Precedents We Set

I'm convinced that my former colleagues in the military, the Department of Defense, and the intelligence community are good people, acting in good faith. Despite my rule of law concerns, I trust them to act carefully and responsibly, doing their best to avoid mistakes and not abuse their power.

But there are a lot of other people in the world I don't trust at all—and when the United States asserts a unilateral right to use force in secret and with little accountability outside the executive branch, we are essentially handing every repressive and unscrupulous regime in the world a playbook for how to violate sovereignty and literally get away with murder.

Recall the 1976 murder of Orlando Letelier, and the murder of Alexander Litvinenko thirty years later. Imagine how the United States would respond if Russia—or China, or Iran, or North Korea—decided to engage in an expanded drone strike campaign against political critics living beyond their borders.

Say it was Vladimir Putin's Russia, and say Russian strikes in various European countries had by now killed hundreds of people, or even several thousand. U.S. authorities would protest, of course, and insist on the importance of free expression, due process, and human rights. But Putin would presumably respond by taking a page from America's playbook: he would refuse to confirm or deny any Russian strikes, while insisting that any Russian strikes that might or might not have occurred complied with all applicable laws, and that any targeted persons were terrorists posing an imminent threat to Russian national security. The United States would naturally ask to see some evidence of this—but once again, Putin could simply echo the United States: Sorry, that's classified.

And what could we say?

Let's not kid ourselves: the legal arguments that the United States is now making will come back and bite us in the future.

Putin himself has promised as much. In 2008, when the United States recognized Kosovo's unilateral declaration of independence from Serbia, Putin was furious; the U.N. had promised to respect Serbia's sovereign integrity. Putin argued that the U.S. decision to disregard what Russia saw as Serbia's right to sovereignty threatened to "blow apart the whole system of international relations." The United States, and other states opting to recognize Kosovar independence, should understand that their decision was "a two-sided stick," warned Putin, "and the second end will come back and hit them in the face."[14]

That particular two-sided stick has already been deployed by the Russians in the context of Ukraine and Crimea, where Putin greeted U.S. protestations about the importance of respecting Ukrainian sovereignty with little more than a cynical smirk.[15] In Syria too, Putin has highlighted inconsistencies in U.S. actions and legal arguments: if the United States can use military force inside Syria without the consent of the Syrian government, why should Russia be condemned for using force inside Ukraine?

The legal precedents we are setting risk undermining the fragil $\mid$ norms of sovereignty and human rights that help keep our world stable We should ask ourselves this: Do we want to live in a world in whic $\mid$ every state considers itself to have a legal right to kill people in othe states, secretly and with no public disclosure or due process, based o its own unilateral assertions of national security prerogatives?

# War Everywhere, Law Nowhere?

The "rule of law" is one of those terms people toss around freely, but often without much effort to explain just what they mean.[1] Here's the definition used by U.N. secretary-general Ban Ki-moon: the rule of law, he says, can be understood as:

> [A] principle of governance in which all persons, institutions and entities, public and private, including the State itself, are accountable to laws that are publicly promulgated, equally enforced and independently adjudicated, and which are consistent with international human rights norms and standards.
>
> It requires, as well, measures to ensure adherence to the principles of supremacy of law, equality before the law, accountability to the law, fairness in the application of the law, separation of powers, participation in decision-making, legal certainty, avoidance of arbitrariness and procedural and legal transparency.[2]

In the international sphere, the rule of law requires, at a bare minimum, the "avoidance of arbitrariness" and "procedural and legal transparency"; as legal scholar Simon Chesterman puts it, the law itself must be "accessible and clear."[3] This is essential for ensuring basic stability: If it is to have any value at all, international law must provide a reasonably clear basis for predicting state behavior and for holding states accountable when they break the law.[4]

Surprisingly enough, the international system generally works, despite the lack of a global Supreme Court, a global legislature, or a global

police force. The late Louis Henkin, one of America's most prominent international law experts, once observed, "almost all nations observe almost all principles of international law and almost all of their obligations almost all of the time."[5] States need each other, particularly given today's interconnected economies. Concerns about reputation, reciprocity, and retaliation give most states strong incentives to behave themselves, and when disagreements arise, most states are content to rely on diplomacy, arbitration, international and regional courts, and so on to settle disputes.

Not all states, of course. Occasionally, a state blatantly flouts international law. Iraq's 1990 invasion of Kuwait is one example; this led to the first Gulf War. Syria's use of chemical weapons is another example. But even the most egregious rule-breaking doesn't necessarily undermine the international rule of law any more than the continued existence of crime undermines the domestic rule of law. As long as serious rule-breaking is occasional rather than constant—and as long as *most* rule-breakers face consequences—the system itself can remain effective and intact. Ironically, uncertainty and ambiguity can undermine the rule of law far more than occasional blatant rule-breaking.[6]

The "rule of law" is most fundamentally concerned with constraining and ordering power and violence, and this concern led states to develop detailed legal rules governing the use of armed force.[7] But with no Supreme Court to deliver authoritative pronouncements on how to interpret the law, global peace and stability depends on the willingness of states to cooperate: to develop shared interpretations of legal rules and the concepts and terms on which the rules are premised.

Shared state interpretations of rules, terms, and concepts doesn't preclude some degree of vagueness and ambiguity in international law. Up to a point, legal vagueness and ambiguity can even be useful, giving states face-saving ways to avoid conflict by "looking the other way" when confronted with challenging but not manifestly illegal behavior.[8] But the introduction of excessive uncertainty wholly undermines the possibility of clarity, stability, predictability, and non-arbitrariness.

When key international law concepts vital to the regulation of violence lose any fixed meaning—when, for instance, an exceptionally powerful state begins to interpret international law in a substantially different way than most other states[9]—it becomes increasingly difficult to predict that state's behavior. And unpredictability can spread: one powerful outlier can pave the way for others, and as more states join the outlier, the foundations of the rule of law begin to crumble.[10]

U.S. counterterrorism practices—and the legal theories that under-pin them—are undermining the international rule of law in precisely this way. Critics of U.S. counterterrorism practices often assert that targeted killings, indefinite detention, and NSA eavesdropping are blatantly illegal, but would be more accurate to say that many U.S. counterterrorism practices simply defy straightforward legal categorization. In fact, the legal reasoning behind them constitutes a sustained challenge to the generally accepted meaning of core legal concepts, including "self-defense," "armed attack," "imminence," "necessity," "proportionality," "combatant," "civilian," "armed conflict," and "hostilities." The end result is increased uncertainty and unpredictability about both U.S. behavior and international legal rules—a dangerous state of affairs in a world that's already seeing rising tensions between great powers.

To understand how U.S. counterterrorism practices are increasing global uncertainty and unpredictability, return once again to the issue of U.S. drone strikes outside of traditional battlefields.

For political decision makers, unmanned aerial vehicles have obvious advantages: they're cheap and precise, and their use creates no short-term risk to American lives. As it happens, drone technologies improved dramatically just as the United States, struggling to respond to the threat of transnational terrorism after 9/11, began to perceive an increased need for low-cost, low-risk cross-border uses of force.[11]

Beginning in 2008, the United States began to make more frequent use of strikes from unmanned aerial vehicles. Most controversially, the United States has greatly increased its reliance on drone strikes outside of traditional, territorially bounded "hot battlegrounds." Yet almost everything about U.S. drone strikes is shrouded in secrecy. For the most part, the government does not comment on or acknowledge reported drone strikes that take place outside of hot battlefields, and does not release lists of those targeted or killed. Senior Obama administration officials have offered oblique accounts of the drone strike program, but these have been at an extremely high level of generality. As a result, it is impossible to describe current practices or internal procedures with any certainty, and also impossible to know exactly what legal constraints U.S. officials believe exist, and whether and how these have changed in the last few years.

From speeches delivered by senior officials and government court filings, we do know that the United States believes itself to be in an armed conflict, as defined by international law, with "al Qaeda and its associates." We know the United States therefore considers "al Qaeda operatives" to be targetable as "combatants," but we don't know precisely how it identifies or defines al Qaeda operatives, agents, or members, or how it defines the term "combatants" and applies it in the murky context of transnational terrorism. We also don't know precisely how the United States understands the term "civilian" in the context of terrorism, or the concept of "direct participation in hostilities." Finally, we don't know how the United States defines or identifies "associates" or "co-belligerents" of al Qaeda (although we know that the United States considers the Islamic State to be either a successor group to al Qaeda or an "associated force," despite the open enmity between the two organizations). Understanding U.S. legal arguments is made still more difficult by the fact that administration spokespersons often appear to oscillate between referencing the international law of armed conflict and referencing the law of self-defense when justifying drone strikes.[12]

When it comes to issues of sovereignty, U.S. officials have repeatedly stated that they only use force inside the borders of a sovereign state when that state either consents to the use of force or is "unwilling and unable" to take "appropriate action" to address the threat itself. We don't know, however, how the United States evaluates issues of consent in situations in which consent is ambiguous. In Pakistan, for instance, at least some elements of the executive branch gave tacit consent to U.S. drone strikes even as they publicly denied it, but the legislative branches and judicial branches have both denied consent. We also don't know what criteria the United States uses to determine whether a state is "unwilling or unable" to take appropriate action, or what action would be deemed "appropriate."

## Humpty Dumpty

That's a lot of unknowns. Nevertheless, if we piece together public statements by U.S. officials, court filings, leaked government documents, and the existing evidence about past strikes and their targets, the basic outlines of the United States' legal theory underlying targeted killings become visible. While much remains uncertain, it is clear that recent statements and practices by the United States represent a substantial challenge to international legal rules on the use of armed force.

The United Nations Charter prohibits the use of force by one state inside the borders of another sovereign state without that state's consent. The two big exceptions are Security Council authorization—cases in which the Security Council may respond to an act of aggression by taking action "by air, sea, or land forces as may be necessary to maintain or restore international peace and security"—and self-defense. The traditional understanding of the right to self-defense limits the unilateral use of force to situations in which a state is responding to a recent "armed attack" or to an "imminent" threat of future attack. But according to a leaked 2011 Justice Department memo—the most detailed legal justification that is publicly available—the United States is now taking a radically different approach to defining an "imminent threat."[13]

According to the Justice Department memo, the requirement that force only be used to prevent an "imminent" threat "does *not* require the United States to have clear evidence that a specific attack on U.S. persons and interests will take place in the immediate future."[14] This seems—and is—at odds with the traditional view—as well as with ordinary dictionary definitions of the word "imminent."

The Justice Department white paper goes on to assert that "certain members of al Qaeda are *continually* plotting attacks . . . and *would* engage in such attacks regularly [if] they were *able* to do so, [and] the U.S. government may not be aware of all . . . plots as they are developing and thus *cannot be confident that none is about to occur.*"[15] As a result, the white paper concludes that any person deemed to be an operational leader of al Qaeda or its "associated forces" inherently presents an imminent threat at all times—and as a result, the United States can lawfully target such persons at all times, even in the absence of specific knowledge relating to planned future attacks.

At the risk of belaboring the obvious, this understanding of imminence turns the traditional international law interpretation of the concept completely on its head. Instead of reading it to mean that states must have concrete knowledge or at least reasonable suspicion of an actual impending attack in the near future, the United States appears to construe *lack* of knowledge of a future attack as the *justification* for using force: that is, since the United States "may not be aware of all plots . . . and thus cannot be confident that none is about to occur," force is presumed *always* to be justified against the kinds of people considered likely to "engage in attacks . . . if they were able to do so."[16]

It's reminiscent of Humpty Dumpty's famous exchange with Alice in Lewis Carroll's *Through the Looking-Glass*:

"There's glory for you!" [said Humpty Dumpty].

"I don't know what you mean by 'glory,'" Alice said.

Humpty Dumpty smiled contemptuously. "Of course you don't—till I tell you. I meant 'there's a nice knock-down argument for you!'"

"But 'glory' doesn't mean 'a nice knock-down argument,'" Alice objected.

"When I use a word," Humpty Dumpty said, in rather a scornful tone, "it means just what I choose it to mean—neither more nor less."

"The question is," said Alice, "whether you can make words mean so many different things."

"The question is," said Humpty Dumpty, "which is to be master—that's all."[17]

From a rule of law perspective, the Justice Department white paper represents a radical assault on a once stable concept. If "imminent threat" can mean "lack of evidence of the absence of imminent threat," it is impossible to know, with any clarity, the circumstances under which the United States will in fact decide that the use of military force is lawful.

The rule of law conundrums don't end there. Under international law, the use of force in self-defense must also be consistent with the principles of necessity and proportionality.[18] The principle of necessity tracks the ancient "just war" requirement that force should be used only as a last resort, when measures short of force have proven ineffective, and the principle of proportionality relates to the amount and nature of the force used. But given the lack of transparency around U.S. drone strikes, it is impossible to say whether any given strike (or the totality of strikes) satisfies these legal and ethical principles.[19]

Are all U.S. drone strikes "necessary"? Could nonlethal means of combating terrorism—such as efforts to disrupt terrorist financing and communications—be sufficient to prevent future attacks? Might particular terror suspects be captured rather than killed? Do drone strikes inspire more terrorists than they kill? Also, to what degree does U.S. drone policy distinguish between terrorist threats of varying gravity? If drone strikes against a dozen targets prevented another attack on the scale of 9/11, few would dispute their appropriateness or legality—but we might judge differently a drone strike against someone unlikely to cause serious harm to the United States.

But if U.S. decision makers lack specific knowledge about the nature and timing of future attacks—which the Justice Department white paper acknowledges—judgments of necessity and proportionality become impossible. There's no way to determine if lethal force is "necessary" to prevent a possible future attack about which one knows nothing—and no way to decide how *much* force is proportionate to preventing a possible future attack of unknown magnitude?

Here again, the U.S. legal theory underlying targeted killing makes it impossible to apply key principles in a meaningful way. Both necessity and proportionality come to be evaluated in the context of hypothetical worst-case scenarios (in theory, any terror suspect *might* be about to unleash another catastrophic attack on the scale of 9/11). As a result, these "limitations" on the use of force establish no limits at all.

The problem goes still deeper. Should drone strikes be construed legally as a series of discrete uses of force, each of which must be independently evaluated for adherence to self-defense principles? Or do they constitute, in effect, an ongoing use of force made up of many individual strikes, which should be evaluated collectively?[20] If the latter, can the United States be said to be in an "armed conflict" with militants in Pakistan, suspected al Qaeda associates in Yemen, members of the Al Shabaab organization in Somalia, and assorted other unknown groups and individuals?

From a rule of law perspective, as we know, it is crucial that we be able to determine the existence or nonexistence of an armed conflict. In an armed conflict, it's lawful to target enemy combatants based simply on their status as enemy soldiers. If there is no armed conflict, such status-based targeting is unlawful, and force may be used only to ward off an imminent threat.

In a domestic context, disputes like this don't necessarily pose an ongoing challenge to the rule of law: although significant legal vagueness and ambiguity might persist for a time, the courts might eventually resolve the uncertainty by selecting one interpretation over the others, or new legislation might be passed to resolve the uncertainties.[21] In the international context, however, there is no referee able to make such vital calls. There is no judicial system and no legislature. States can enter into multilateral treaties, but there is no set procedure for creating such treaties—and in practice, treaties frequently take decades to be negotiated and further decades to enter into force.

Furthermore, the structure of the Security Council makes it near-impossible to imagine a Security Council–imposed resolution to any of these questions. Russia and China would likely block any U.S. effort to gain council authorization for drone strikes or to create some international force empowered to engage in such strikes. At the same time, the United States would use its veto to block any council criticism of its actions.

At the moment, the United States itself—as the globe's only military superpower—is judge, jury, and executioner all rolled into one. With zero transparency, it decides how to interpret the law to which it is subject; it decides what can be counted as evidence and how to evaluate that evidence; and, ultimately, it kills.

The concept of sovereignty itself has also been further destabilized by post-9/11 U.S. legal theories. In recent decades, globalization has reduced the salience of state borders even as the emergence of human rights law has chipped away at the state's legitimacy. Nevertheless, the concept of sovereignty—however frayed and problematic—has long served as a bulwark against unpredictable international conflict. Recent U.S. pronouncements suggest that this will not remain true for much longer.

It sounds superficially reasonable when U.S. officials assert that the United States will use force on the territory of other sovereign states only if that state either consents or is "unwilling or unable to suppress the threat posed by the individual being targeted." But the logic is in fact circular, since the United States is the self-appointed arbiter of whether a state is "unwilling or unable." Thus, if the United States— using its own malleable definition of "imminent"—decides that an individual in, say, Pakistan poses a threat to the United States and requires killing, sovereignty is a nonissue. Either Pakistan will consent to a U.S. strike inside its territory or it will not consent. And if Pakistan does not consent—on the grounds, perhaps, that it does not agree with the U.S. threat assessment—then Pakistan is, ipso facto, "unwilling or unable to suppress the threat posed by the individual being targeted."[22] It's a legal theory that more or less eviscerates traditional notions of sovereignty, and has the potential to significantly undermine the already shaky collective security regime created by the United Nations Charter.

## Remember the Duck-Rabbit

U.S. drone strikes present not an issue of lawbreaking, but of law's brokenness: sustained U.S. assaults on the meaning of core legal concepts have left international law on the use of armed force not merely vague or ambiguous but effectively indeterminate, eroding law's value as a predictor of state conduct and a means of holding states accountable.

But although the justifications for drone strikes proffered by the United States pose grave challenges to the international rule of law, it would be facile to condemn them out of hand. After all, though these strikes—or, more accurately, the legal theories that underlie them— challenge the international rule of law, they also represent an effort, on the part of the United States, to *respond* to gaps and failures in the international system.

The U.N. Security Council is paralyzed by anachronistic membership and voting rules, weakening arguments that the United States should wait for Security Council authorization before engaging in targeted strikes. Further, the United States is not wholly wrong to argue that traditional definitions of imminence are inadequate in the context of today's threats. And while it's easy to lambast circular U.S. arguments about sovereignty, here again, the United States is not necessarily wrong to argue that when many lives may be at stake, legal principles of sovereignty should not be an absolute bar to intervention.

However destabilizing U.S. counterterrorism legal theories are to the rule of law, they arose in response to real dilemmas—and it is not inconceivable that their very destabilizing qualities could ultimately help usher in a process of much needed legal change.

It wouldn't do to be Pollyannaish: the international order is a fragile one, and fragmentation, conflict, chaos, and collapse are just as likely. From a human rights perspective too, any changes to the international order sparked by the U.S. war on terrorism are as likely to be for the worse as for the better. But it would be just as much a mistake to dismiss U.S. counterterrorism policy as the selfish, destructive flailing of an arrogant, damaged superpower. It is that, but not only that.

Hegel famously defined tragedy as the conflict between two goods, each overly rigid in its claims.[23] That's not a bad way to conceptualize the legal debates triggered by the war on terrorism—but the end of this drama is not yet written.

## Democracy and Secret War

If I were a member of Congress right now, I would be hopping mad.

Since September 11, the United States has waged two very open wars in Afghanistan and Iraq, along with openly acknowledged airstrikes in Libya and Syria. But alongside these costly and visible wars, the United States has also been waging what amounts to a third, secret war, waged mainly by drone strikes and special operations raids.[24]

We don't know what this secret war has cost us in dollars, and we don't know its cost in human lives, either.[25] But we can say with confidence that in addition to undermining international legal rules, the whole idea of a secret war is deeply offensive to core principles of American democracy—in particular to any notion of constitutional checks and balances.

Our Constitution gives Congress vital powers relating to the use of military force: the power to declare war and the power to raise, support, and make rules regulating the armed forces and "captures on land and water."[26] Congress also has the constitutional power to call forth "the militia to execute the laws of the Union, suppress insurrections and repel invasions,"[27] as well as the power to "define and punish . . . offenses against the law of nations."[28]

Yet the secret war—which began under President Bush and accelerated under President Obama—has gotten us very far away from anything Congress contemplated in the 2001 Authorization for Use of Military Force (AUMF), passed just a few days after the September 11 attacks.[29]

For a document that has had such far-reaching consequences, the operative language of the 2001 AUMF is surprisingly short: it authorizes the president to "use all necessary and appropriate force against those nations, organizations, or persons he determines planned, authorized, committed, or aided the terrorist attacks that occurred on September 11, 2001, or harbored such organizations or persons, in order to prevent any future acts of international terrorism against the United States by such nations, organizations or persons."[30]

Look carefully at that language. It gives the executive branch authorization to use force, but note that it does not authorize the use of force against anyone, anywhere, anytime. Instead, it authorizes the use of force specifically and solely against those who "planned, authorized, committed, or aided" the September 11 attacks, or who harbored those who did. Furthermore, the AUMF authorizes force only for a specific *purpose*: to "prevent future acts" of terrorism against the United States by such organizations or states—not to prevent all future bad acts committed by anyone, anywhere.

In fact, even in those terrifying days right after September 11, when rescue personnel were still pulling corpses out of the wreckage of the Twin Towers and the west side of the Pentagon, Congress rejected a request from the Bush administration to pass a more expansive authorization to use military force. The administration initially asked that Congress authorize the use of force to "deter and preempt any future acts of terrorism or aggression."[31] But even in that moment of grief, anger, and fear, Congress rejected such an open-ended AUMF, understanding full well that when Congress cedes power to the executive branch, it rarely comes back.[32]

For much of the last dozen years, despite international controversies, the 2001 AUMF provided adequate domestic legal authority both for the conflict in Afghanistan and for initial U.S. drone strikes outside hot battlefields: most of the individuals targeted in early strikes were reportedly senior Taliban or al Qaeda operatives, putting them clearly in the category of targets contemplated by the AUMF. But this appears to have changed in the last few years, as the threat has metastasized.[33] As military action has decimated "Al Qaeda Central," U.S. drone strikes outside of hot battlefields have begun to target not only the remnants of "core" al Qaeda and Taliban, but also known or suspected members of other organizations.

For the moment, leave aside the question of whether the expanding range of groups targeted by the United States all pose a genuine threat (or the same degree of threat) to the United States. Maybe these groups and individuals all pose a threat to the United States, and maybe they don't—regardless, on its face, the 2001 AUMF just doesn't cover groups and individuals that were unconnected to the September 11 attacks.[34]

Obama administration lawyers have countered this argument by asserting that insofar as Congress intended the AUMF to be the functional equivalent of a declaration of war, the AUMF must be read to include the implied authority to target groups that are "associated forces" of al Qaeda or the Taliban.[35] However, it is far from clear that Congress actually did intend to authorize the use of force *outside* of traditional territorial battlefields against mere associates of those responsible for the September 11 attacks, particularly since many of those associated groups did not exist in 2001.[36]

In effect, the administration's assertion that the AUMF authorizes the use of force against al Qaeda's associated forces even outside of traditional battlefields appears to have become a backdoor way of expanding the AUMF far beyond Congress's intent. And to the extent that Congress accepts administration claims that force can be used against a broad category of persons and organizations determined (based on unknown criteria) to be al Qaeda "associates," this effectively turns the AUMF into exactly the kind of open-ended authorization to use force that Congress rejected back in 2001.

Call it AUMF mission creep. In recent years, the United States has targeted more and more people with no apparent connection to al Qaeda, no apparent connection to the September 11 attacks, and increasingly with no apparent connection to any imminent threat to the United States.

Take the Al Shabaab militants in Somalia targeted by drone strikes. I'm sure these were bad guys, and the world may be better off without them. Nonetheless, it's a huge stretch to shoehorn them into the 2001 AUMF. Even the Islamic State is, according to the U.S. government, covered by the AUMF: since the groups share a common ancestry despite their current enmity, government lawyers have argued that the 2001 AUMF can be construed to authorize the use of force against the Islamic State.

Saying that many recent U.S. drone strikes do not seem to fit well under the AUMF umbrella is not the same as saying that the president lacks any constitutional authority to use force in the absence of express congressional authorization. With or without an AUMF, the president unquestionably has the inherent constitutional power to use force against an imminent threat to the United States, no matter where and from whom it comes.[37] Nonetheless, that is a power that U.S. presidents have, generally speaking, used rarely and for the most part wisely.

The use of force without clear, ongoing congressional authorization should be the exception, not the norm. Ironically, President Obama seems to agree—at least some of the time. In 2013, he asserted that the 2001 AUMF is "flawed," and risks "keeping America on a perpetual wartime footing," and he declared his intention to eventually repeal it.

Despite this, he relied on it to justify the use of force against the Islamic State inside Syria.

I'm sure his intentions are good. But good intentions notwithstanding, we now have a state of affairs in which our government—the government of a democratic nation that was founded on the premise that all men are created equal, and endowed by their creator with certain unalienable rights, including the rights to life and liberty—is claiming for itself the power to kill any person, anywhere on earth, at any time, without express congressional approval, based on information that is secret and has been collected and evaluated according to secret criteria by anonymous individuals in a secret procedure.

Anyone who thinks this is consistent with American values should go back and reread the Declaration of Independence. The core notion of the rule of law is that *all* power must be constrained by law; even the state must be accountable to those it acts upon. If we truly believe in the unalienable rights championed in the Declaration of Independence— human rights, we would call them today—the lack of transparency and accountability characterizing America's secret war should chill us to the bone.

This is particularly true when we place the threat of terrorism into historical perspective. In the middle of the nineteenth century, the Civil War killed more than 600,000 Americans. Less than a century later, World War II killed more than 400,000 Americans. If you adjust for population size, these were horrific death tolls—and yet, even in the face of these existential threats, the United States didn't decide that we needed to give the executive branch wholesale authorization to use force against anyone, anywhere, anytime permanently, without geographic or temporal limitations.

Terrorism is a real threat, but keep it in perspective. We should be vigilant, particularly to ensure that terrorist groups don't gain access to weapons of mass destruction. But we should also keep in mind there has been no year except 2001 in which terrorism has killed more American citizens than lightning strikes. Do we really need to toss two-hundred-plus years of American values out the window?

## A Veritable Catch-22

Don't count on the American court system to hold the executive branch accountable. The secret war and the paradoxes it creates are enough to make even judges dizzy. Every now and then, honest judges come right out and say so.

In 2013, for instance, Judge Colleen McMahon of the Southern District of New York decided a case involving requests by the *New York Times* and the ACLU for government records relating to drone strikes against U.S. citizens[38] (such as Anwar al-Awlaki and his sixteen-year-old son, each killed in separate drone strikes in 2011). Judge McMahon began by acknowledging the legal complexities:

> There is and long has been robust debate about . . . whether antiterrorist operations in countries other than Afghanistan and adjacent territory in Pakistan can fairly or legally be classified as a war. . . . However, even if there were no such debate . . . some Americans question the power of the Executive to make a unilateral and unreviewable decision to kill an American citizen who is not actively engaged in armed combat operations against this country.
>
> As they gathered to draft a Constitution . . . the Founders—fresh from a war of independence from the rule of a King they styled a tyrant—were fearful of concentrating power. . . . That concern was described by James Madison in *Federalist No. 47* (1788): "The accumulation of all powers, legislative, executive, and judiciary, in the same hands, whether of one, a few, or many, and whether hereditary, self-appointed, or elective, may justly be pronounced the very definition of tyranny. . . ."
>
> Madison's statements echoed those of the great French philosopher Montesquieu, who wrote, in his seminal work *The Spirit of the Laws* (1748): "Were [the power of judging] joined to the executive power, the judge might behave with all the violence of an oppressor." . . . There are [thus] indeed legitimate reasons . . . to question the legality of killings unilaterally authorized by the Executive that take place otherwise than on a "hot" field of battle.

Judge McMahon made it clear that her substantive sympathies lay with those seeking greater transparency, noting that matters as important as the legal logic behind killing American citizens should not be kept secret from the citizenry itself. In the end, however, she ruled *against* the request for information made by the *New York Times* and the ACLU. Regardless of her views of the underlying issues, she acknowledged, the government's refusal to release the records appeared to be in accordance with the laws governing classified materials:

> I can only conclude that the Government . . . cannot be compelled by this court of law to explain in detail the reasons why its actions do not violate the Constitution and laws of the United States.
>
> The Alice-in-Wonderland nature of this pronouncement is not lost on me; but . . . I find myself stuck in a paradoxical situation . . . a veritable Catch-22. I can find no way around the thicket of laws and precedents that effectively allow the Executive Branch of our Government to *proclaim as perfectly lawful certain actions that seem on their face incompatible with our Constitution and laws, while keeping the reasons for their conclusion a secret.*[39]

## Trickle-Down War

The history of the Western nation-state is intimately entwined with the history of war.[40] The state makes war, both in the traditional sense of waging war and in the linguistic and legal senses—and when the state "makes" war in any of these ways, the shape of the state may itself begin to change.[41] World War II transformed Western states profoundly, ushering in the era of the regulatory welfare state. More recently, the "war on terror"—or, if you prefer, the armed conflict with al Qaeda and its associated forces—has begun to transform the state in new ways.

In the United States, it has led the state to invest in technologies to help it track and kill these enemies across the globe. This investment has driven a vast growth in the military/security corporate complex, as thousands of new firms have sprung up to help the government make war. These include private military and security companies such as the former Blackwater and Triple Canopy, as well as consulting firms that collect and analyze intelligence data, design cyber-defenses, create training materials for the military, or develop sophisticated nanobots. At the same time, the increased use of these new technological capabilities is changing the United States' relationship with other states, altering previously held ideas of sovereignty.

The war on terrorism is also altering the relationship between individuals and the state. After 9/11, human rights advocates and civil libertarians were quick to point out the ways in which laws and policies purportedly necessary to the war on terrorism have increased state power at the expense of transparency, accountability, and individual rights. After 9/11, the USA PATRIOT Act and similar legislation greatly enhanced the state's domestic search and seizure powers in national-security-related cases, for instance. Most of these post-9/11 state activities have been authorized by Congress and have been largely upheld—or at least tolerated—by the courts.[42]

But what is less well known is the way in which the war on terrorism is also transforming our courtrooms, police departments, and immigration services. Many of the U.S. practices and legal doctrines developed after 9/11 for war-making purposes are trickling down, subtly but perniciously, into ordinary law and law enforcement.[43]

### Domestic Policing

You can see it most obviously in domestic policing. The trend toward increased militarization of U.S. police predates 9/11, but accelerated after the attacks.[44] The first police SWAT teams, for instance, were created after the 1965 Watts riots in Los Angeles; initially, they were used primarily for emergencies such as hostage situations and domestic terror threats.[45] Over time, however, the number of SWAT teams expanded and such teams were increasingly used in routine policing— deployed to execute search and arrest warrants in drug-related cases, for instance. There were an estimated three thousand SWAT raids nationwide in 1980; by 2006, the number of annual SWAT raids had jumped to fifty thousand, and by 2012, there were as many as eighty thousand SWAT raids per year.[46]

The increased use of SWAT teams has been paralleled by a similar post-9/11 rise in police efforts to adopt other tactics developed by foreign militaries and intelligence services for counterterrorism purposes,[47] the proliferation of police academy programs modeled on military basic training,[48] the increased use of military-style battle dress uniforms for police on the streets,[49] and the growing use by police departments of weapons and other equipment developed for military purposes—from Humvees to surveillance drones.[50] Many of these weapons and equipment literally come direct from foreign war zones, through a Defense Department program that donates unneeded military equipment to police forces;[51] Homeland Security counterterrorism grants have also fueled the police acquisition of tools more commonly associated with war.[52]

Increasingly, war and policing have begun to converge both in terms of tactics and in terms of outward appearance. As legal scholar John Parry has noted, "War has changed in its functions, to become more like policing, [and] policing too has changed, to become more like war."[53] On the covert battlefields of the war on terrorism, outside of Iraq and Afghanistan, U.S. war making often superficially resembles policing in that it involves individuals and small teams rather than the large-scale armies associated with nineteenth- and twentieth-century warfare, and its victories and defeats are defined in terms of the activities of individuals and organizations, rather than in terms of terrain held or surrendered. As police departments increasingly use military tactics, weapons, equipment, and even apparel, domestic policing has come to look more and more like war.

### Secrecy in the Courtroom

In America's courtrooms, the effects of 9/11 are also apparent when judges confront the promiscuous use of the so-called state secrets privilege. The state secrets privilege is meant to prevent secrets damaging to national security interests from being released during a court case: if government officials fear that classified information might be revealed during litigation, they can ask the judge to block the release of that information—or even dismiss a lawsuit altogether. Technically, courts have the power to reject government claims of state secrets and release the information anyway, but judges are generally reluctant to do so, and tend to defer to executive branch requests.[54]

Examining docket records from the past thirty years and records from the "more than 1,300 case holdings since 1790 that refer to state secrets," Georgetown's Laura Donohue found that the state secrets privilege has increasingly been invoked by private litigants in cases relating to "breach of contract, patent disputes, trade secrets, fraud, and employment termination.... Wrongful death, personal injury, and negligence."[55]

On the surface, these are cases that have nothing at all to do with national security—but the expansive war on terrorism has led to increased interpenetration of the government and the private sector, with government agencies relying on private companies to provide a range of support services. Similarly, the government's desire to access information such as private Internet records has led to complex and generally secret new relationships among the military, the intelligence community, and private telecom and internet companies. As a result, more and more private actors are in possession of government "secrets," increasing the number of cases with no surface connection to national security in which private actors might nonetheless have to disclose classified information in the course of routine litigation.[56]

Donohue also noted the rise of a form of graymail, in which corporations that possess sensitive information as a result of government contracts seek to pressure the government to intervene in private litigation by suggesting that unless the government invokes the state secrets doctrine, they may be "forced" to reveal state secrets in order to defend themselves.[57] Such subtle threats create incentives for government intervention. Even when the government declines to intervene or when courts ultimately reject state secrets claims, efforts to invoke the state secrets doctrine can delay cases or force their removal to federal courts. In recent years, Donohue concluded, the state secrets doctrine has evolved into a "powerful litigation tool, wielded by both private and public actors. It has been used to undermine contractual obligations and to pervert tort law, creating a form of private indemnity for government contractors in a broad range of areas."[58]

In the context of criminal prosecutions, parallel dangers are raised by the Classified Information Procedures Act (CIPA). Under CIPA, the government can make an in camera ex parte submission to the court— that is, a secret submission made without the knowledge of the other party to the litigation—asking the court "to delete specified items of classified information from documents to be made available to the defendant."[59]

CIPA is not new, but in the post-9/11 context it has a newly worrisome impact. The government has been classifying documents at an unprecedented pace,[60] and an ever-growing number of private companies have become involved in the production and use of classified information.[61] As the sheer quantity and range of classified information increases and the number of private companies privy to classified information goes up, we can expect an increase in the number of ordinary criminal cases that touch upon classified national security information in a purely ancillary way. That means we can also expect an increase in the number of cases in which defendants may be deprived of the ability to use or even find out about information that might help their case.

"The impact of secret evidence upon the adversary system has yet to be acknowledged," argues law scholar Ellen Yaroshefsky, "in large measure because of the unstated belief that [CIPA is] confined to a narrow range of terrorism cases." But, she asserts, "secret evidence is seeping into the criminal justice system" as a result of overclassification, the growing number of individuals and companies involved in classified activities, and the tendency of prosecutors to overcharge ordinary crimes under antiterrorism statutes.[62]

## Immigration

Since 9/11, U.S. immigration law and policy have also become deeply bound up with counterterrorism efforts. The 9/11 attackers were all foreigners, and the apparent ease with which they entered the United States raised obvious questions about the adequacy of U.S. border control methods and screening programs. After 9/11, the Immigration and Naturalization Service was relocated into the newly created Department of Homeland Security and reorganized; most of its responsibilities shifted to DHS's new Immigration and Customs Enforcement division (ICE). The name change itself signaled a shift away from a "service" model to an "enforcement" model.[63]

There has been an enormous post-9/11 increase in funding for immigration programs with connections to homeland security;[64] in particular, as a 2011 Migration Policy Institute report documents, the post-9/11 era has given rise to unprecedented information collection and sharing between intelligence agencies, law enforcement agencies, and immigration agencies.[65]

The original purpose of this extensive data collection—including the collection of biometric data—was to identify those with connections to al Qaeda and prevent additional terrorist attacks. Numerous government organizations gather information—including fingerprints—from resident aliens and foreigners seeking entry into the United States at airports and land borders. At least in theory, the ability to cross-check such information with that gathered by intelligence and law enforcement agencies can enable officials to prevent potential terrorist plotters from gaining entry into the United States, and trace connections between foreign nationals already inside the United States and foreign terrorist organizations. But though only a tiny fraction of immigrants and foreign visitors have any link to terrorism, such extensive data collection and information sharing has become the norm for all immigrant groups and most foreign travelers to the United States.

This has costs: it has led to a huge post-9/11 increase in the number of annual immigrant detentions and deportations, as an information collection system designed to identify violent terrorists has been used to snag even those immigrants with only trivial criminal histories (a teen shoplifting incident, for instance, is more than enough to lead to deportation).[66] Information sharing between intelligence agencies and ICE has also led to increased scrutiny of immigrants from particular countries, ethnic groups, and religious backgrounds, leading to unequal enforcement of immigration laws.[67]

It is impossible to say whether these changes have reduced the risk of terrorism. What does seem clear, however, is that they have made individual immigrants and foreign nationals—particularly those from

Middle Eastern or Islamic backgrounds—far more vulnerable to various forms of surveillance, detention, and removal. As the threat of homegrown Islamic extremist terrorism increases, these immigrant and foreign-born communities are among those with which law enforcement officials most need friendly relations—but the increased threat of deportation has left many immigrants more fearful than ever of contact with local or federal authorities.

## Privacy and Surveillance

The war on terrorism has led the U.S. government to dramatically step up its efforts to collect and analyze an extraordinarily wide range of information, from cell phone metadata and Internet communications to biometric data (such as fingerprints, DNA, and retina scans). The government can now use facial recognition software, for instance, to track a person by sifting through countless images provided by social media or surveillance cameras.[68]

Technological leaps like these have made it possible to identify "enemies" through pattern analysis, even when there is no specific information linking them to hostile activities. This has led to an increase in so-called signature strikes: drone strikes against unidentified people presumed to be targetable enemies because of their communications patterns and travel patterns.[69]

The post-9/11 USA PATRIOT Act effectively eliminated the pre-9/11 firewall between foreign intelligence gathering and domestic law enforcement.[70] Today, law enforcement officials can access a wide range of sensitive information (including Internet records, telephone metadata, library records, and credit and banking information of U.S. citizens) as long as they can show "reasonable grounds to believe that the tangible things sought are *relevant* to an authorized investigation . . . to obtain foreign intelligence information not concerning a United States person or to protect against international terrorism or clandestine intelligence activities."[71] This has benefits, but it's also easy to imagine information gained in this manner—say, evidence of extramarital affairs or psychiatric treatment—being repurposed by law enforcement officials to put pressure on potential witnesses or informants in nonterrorism-related cases.[72]

Similarly, the sophisticated pattern recognition technologies originally developed for military and intelligence purposes can also easily be used by domestic law enforcement officials. Imagine, for instance, the police use of drone-based imaging technologies such as the military's Gorgon Stare, a platform that permits the visualization and videotaping of whole neighborhoods. Police will soon have the ability to use such technologies to track the movements and communications of thousands of people, searching for those whose travel patterns suggest links to gang activity.[73]

The trouble is, these powerful new technologies can also introduce powerful new errors, leading to faulty guilt-by-association assumptions. Say pattern recognition technologies determine that the same unidentified man is repeatedly driving to, from, and between the houses of known gang members, or telephone metadata indicate frequent calls between the man and the known gang members. The data might be assumed to indicate that the unidentified man is part of a criminal network—but in reality, he might simply be the pizza delivery guy.

Beyond this, widespread surveillance and government access to personal data can have obvious chilling effects on the exercise on constitutionally protected rights. Consider, for instance, the impact on journalists, who must rely heavily on information provided confidentially by sources.[74] "Some of our longtime trusted sources have become nervous and anxious about talking to us, even on stories that aren't about national security," Associated Press president Gary Pruitt commented in a 2013 speech. "And in some cases, government employees that we once checked in with regularly will no longer speak to us by phone, and some are reluctant to meet in person."

Trickle-down is inherently difficult to discern and measure,[75] and the problem is exacerbated by government secrecy. But it's past time to look at this phenomenon more comprehensively. Given the huge effects these changes could have on our country and our lives, can we afford not to?

# CHAPTER NINETEEN

# Institutional Costs

## Civil-Military Paradoxes

The blurring lines between war and peace also have costs for the U.S. military, and the relations between the military and civil society. Civil-military relations in modern America have come to be characterized more by paradox than by consistency:[1] ordinary Americans support the military more than ever, but know less about it than ever; meanwhile, elite Washington policymakers simultaneously overestimate the military's capabilities and mistrust the military leadership. We view our military as the strongest military in the history of the world, even as conventional military tools have less and less value. We no longer know what kind of military we need, or how to distinguish between civilian and military tasks and roles. And although today's military is better-educated and more professional than ever, its internal structures—from recruiting and training to personnel policies—still lag badly behind those in most civilian workplaces.

All this adds up to a recipe for tensions between civilian and military leaders, challenges to military morale, and, in the end, poor policy decisions.

• • •

Civilian-military gaps matter, but not in the ways we usually think. Lying beneath the more superficial civilian-military knowledge and opinion gaps reflected in public polls is a less obvious but more pernicious gap between elite civilian political leaders and elite military leaders: a gap of knowledge, and a gap of trust.

I'm speaking here not of elites as defined in public opinion polls, but of the tiny decision-making elite that runs the nation's capital: the few hundred people—certainly less than a thousand people—who occupy senior positions in the White House's West Wing, the Old Executive Office Building, the State Department's Seventh Floor, and the Pentagon's E-Ring. This elite group includes the service chiefs and their senior deputies, the president's top national security staff, the cabinet secretaries and their senior deputies. In Washington-speak, it's the principals and the deputies, together with a handful of influential advisors without line positions.

If there's any venue where civilians and military personnel work together side by side, day after day, it's in Washington's national security establishment. In theory, this constant interaction ought to breed respect and mutual understanding. In practice, it often produces the opposite: a mixture of suspicion and almost willful ignorance.

In Washington, many top civilian policymakers want the military to do anything and everything—but only when told to do so. They imagine that military power can be used to solve virtually any problem, and are baffled when military leaders take a more conservative approach. At the same time, they want military leaders to execute policy rather than making policy, making them suspicious of anything they view as military efforts to constrain or influence civilian policy decisions.

Too frequently, the favor is returned by military leaders, who mistrust civilians as "politicians" and are sometimes unwilling to accept their concerns as legitimate. Military leaders are often all too eager to stay in the narrowest of lanes, not understanding that this can be viewed as obstructionism by civilians searching for options and ideas. From the military perspective, civilian leaders constantly ask for the impossible, then get annoyed when the impossibilities are pointed out. Too many senior civilian officials know virtually nothing about the structure of military organizations, the chain of command, or the military planning process, while some senior military officers have forgotten that there's any other way to run an organization or think about problem solving.

Most fundamentally, civilian and military leaders often think of themselves and their roles in quite different ways, though the differences are generally unarticulated. Their experiences and training have led them to think differently about what it means to plan, to evaluate risk, and to define problems in the first place. As a result, they frequently talk past each other, using the same words to mean quite different things.

If any civilian-military gap matters, it is this one. Cultural or opinion gaps between the general public and the military community are media fodder, but there is little evidence that they cause actual harm. The mistrust and mutual ignorance that often characterize relations between high-level civilian and military decision makers is another story: here, misunderstandings and mistrust can lead to arbitrary decisions, and do genuine harm both to the military and to U.S. interests.

During my time serving in civilian jobs at the Pentagon and the State Department, I watched numerous interagency discussions devolve into exercises in mutual misunderstanding and frustration. Some of these discussions—such as Pentagon–White House squabbling over troop levels in Afghanistan and the split-the-baby outcome—made headlines. Others never came close to registering in the public consciousness, but rankled those involved.

## The Wrong Civilian

Take a small but typical example. In the spring of 2010, a minor crisis unfolded in Kyrgyzstan. Several hundred people were killed by police and ethnically aligned mobs, many more were wounded, and thousands of refugees (mostly from Kyrgyzstan's Uzbek minority population) fled their homes.

Within the White House, these events triggered fears of a possible ethnic cleansing campaign to come, or even genocide. At the time, I was still serving at the Pentagon, and one day I received a call from a member of the White House's National Security staff. With little preamble, he told me that Central Command needed to move a surveillance platform to a position from which it could monitor fast-breaking events in Kyrgyzstan.

This was a creative and interesting idea. Drones and other intelligence, surveillance, and reconnaissance assets have the potential to be powerful tools in human rights monitoring. The ability to watch troops or mobs or refugees move in real time, to see weapons being stockpiled or mass graves being filled, could potentially help the United States take timely and appropriate action to stop a genocide before it gets off the ground. Why not put drones to work for the cause of human rights?

But there was one big problem with my White House colleague's request: neither one of us had any authority to order Central Command to immediately shift a potentially vital asset from wherever it was currently being used to the skies over Kyrgyzstan.

I asked the obvious question: Had the president discussed this with the secretary of defense?

"We don't have time to spin up a whole bureaucratic process," he responded. "The president doesn't want another Rwanda. This is a top priority of his. I need you to just communicate this to CentCom and get this moving."

But the chain of command doesn't go from a White House staffer to an advisor to the under secretary of defense to U.S. Central Command—and the military doesn't put drones into foreign airspace without a great deal of planning, an enormous amount of legal advice, and the right senior officials signing off on the whole idea. Where would this drone come from? What was it doing now, and what tasks would it be unable to take on if it was shifted to Kyrgyzstan? Which personnel would control it, from what air base in what country? Whose airspace would it fly over? What budget would support the shift? What would the political consequences be if it fell or was shot down? Exactly where would it go? What precisely would it be looking for? Who would receive and analyze any imagery or other intelligence it gathered? How long would it stay? And so on.

My White House colleague was incredulous when I raised some of these concerns. "We're talking about, like, *one drone*. You're telling me you can't just call some colonel at CentCom and make this happen? Why the hell not? You guys"—by which he meant the Pentagon writ large—"are always stonewalling us on everything. I'm calling you from the *White House.* The president wants to prevent genocide in Kyrgyzstan. Whatever happened to civilian control of the military?"

He, I had to explain, was the wrong civilian.

It was a minor issue, but the exchange was far from unusual. My White House colleague—a smart, energetic, dedicated guy—went away upset, convinced that "the military" was refusing to take atrocity prevention issues seriously (an attitude that soured many later interagency discussions about Sudan, Libya, Syria, and more).

My military colleagues reacted to the request, when I relayed it, with equal irritation: How could a senior White House official fail to understand why the military could not, in fact, fight two major land wars, stop terrorists and pirates all over the world, foster economic development in Africa, stop human trafficking, *and* monitor and prevent atrocities in Kyrgyzstan using drones, all at the same time? They were appalled that a White House official seemed not to understand that sensitive, expensive military assets couldn't instantly be moved from a war zone to foreign airspace via a simple phone call from a midlevel staffer at the National Security Council to a Pentagon acquaintance. If the president wanted to make this happen, he could call the defense secretary and direct him to have CentCom undertake such a move (though he'd be unlikely to do so without plenty of discussion at lower levels first), but the chain of command can't be accessed midway down and more or less at random. My military colleagues were insulted by what looked, to them, like civilian arrogance and ignorance.

Some months later, similar misunderstandings plagued interagency planning on Sudan. With a referendum on South Sudanese independence in the offing, officials at the White House and the State Department were concerned about a resurgence of ethnic violence in the wake of a pro-independence vote. The Defense Department was asked—this time more formally, at the assistant secretary/deputy assistant secretary level—to produce plans for preventing or responding to mass atrocities, to "give the options" in the event of a rapidly deteriorating humanitarian situation.

Once again, the response from the Pentagon's military planners was to express polite frustration. What assumptions and constraints should guide planning? What kind of plans did the White House want? To respond to what kind of mass atrocities, against whom, and in what likely places? Respond for how long and through what means, and to what ultimate end? Peace in Sudan? Peace on earth? Would this mean fighting Sudanese government forces on northern Sudanese soil? Going to war with a foreign (and Muslim) state? If so, it was hard to imagine the president signing off on such a thing—the United States already had two ongoing wars—and it was a foolish waste of scarce planning resources to prepare for something that was never going to happen.

Or maybe the goals were narrower? Should the military be planning to evacuate displaced people? Where to? Should they just focus on protecting a humanitarian corridor? Where? For how long? Was the White House prepared to have boots on the ground, with the inevitable risk that events could easily spiral out of control if the troops were attacked? Did they want planning for targeted strikes designed to degrade the military capacity of the bad guys, whoever they might be? Did they even have a theory about who the bad guys would be?

The ensuing back-and-forth was tense, and occasionally broke out into open expressions of anger and mistrust. In a sense, it was a civilian-military version of the chicken-and-egg problem. White House staff wanted to be able to give the president a sense of his options: In the event of mass atrocities, what was it realistic for him to consider doing? How complicated, time-consuming, risky, expensive, and effective would it be to protect a humanitarian corridor, as opposed to engaging in limited military strikes to degrade the capacity of those committing atrocities?

Without help from military planners, White House staff couldn't properly advise the president. But without political and strategic direction from the White House on how much money they were willing to spend, how many troops they were willing to move, what tradeoffs they were willing to make in terms of other ongoing operations, and what would constitute success, military personnel couldn't properly advise their civilian counterparts.

Eventually, the issue got semi-resolved: the White House staff was forced to get more specific; the Pentagon was forced to let go of the elaborate planning process it preferred and cough up some back-of-the-envelope assessments. Fortunately for all, the feared genocide in Sudan didn't happen.

At the national level, however, the costs of the civilian-military gap are real, and high. Such mutual ignorance—and such systemic cultural differences in how to think about problems and solutions—leads frequently to misunderstanding, inefficient decision making, and, too often, bad policy.

There's an irony here: at the senior policymaking level, much of the civilian mistrust of the military derives from an exaggerated estimate of military capabilities. From the outside, the U.S. military appears able to do magic: get the combat elements of a full division deployed overseas in a single week, see in the dark, eavesdrop on global telecommunications, and fire missiles from invisible unmanned drones that strike only designated individual targets, leaving nearby structures undamaged.

Few outsiders understand just how much time, money, and effort lies behind these astonishing capabilities (indeed, today's military is so specialized and high-tech that even most military personnel understand only a small piece of the puzzle). As a result, civilian leaders often find it difficult to comprehend military claims that a particular task is too difficult, or will take longer than desired, or require more troops or other resources.

## Mission Failure

Take another example of high-level civilian-military misunderstandings: the 2009 debate about troop levels in Afghanistan. As a presidential candidate in 2008, Senator Obama had promised to "finish the job" in Afghanistan, and in early 2009 the newly inaugurated president got to work. He commissioned a sweeping interagency review of policy in Afghanistan, and announced that as an interim measure, he had authorized the deployment of an additional seventeen thousand troops to Afghanistan in response to a request from General David McKiernan, then the commander of the Afghan theater.

By the end of February 2009, the president had adopted the new strategic objectives recommended by his review team (led by diplomat Richard Holbrooke, former CIA official Brice Reidel, and the Pentagon's Michèle Flournoy, whom the president had appointed as under secretary of defense for policy).[2] Henceforth, the United States would seek to disrupt terrorist networks in Afghanistan and Pakistan, thus degrading al Qaeda and its associates' ability "to plan and launch international terrorist attacks." To that end, the U.S. would promote "a more capable, accountable and effective government in Afghanistan" and "develop increasingly self-reliant Afghan security forces" capable of operating with "reduced U.S. assistance."

These new strategic objectives proved easier to articulate than to achieve. By mid-May, General McKiernan had been ousted from his position—becoming the first of several Afghanistan theater commanders to discover just how elusive "finishing the job" would turn out to be.

McKiernan was succeeded by General Stanley McChrystal, who was in turn assigned the job of undertaking a sixty-day review of the situation in Afghanistan, with a view toward determining what course changes might be needed to achieve the president's new strategic objectives. McChrystal completed his review on schedule, but when word spread that he intended to propose a substantial troop increase—rumor put it as high as seventy to eighty thousand additional troops—Pentagon officials asked that he hold off on submitting his assessment for several weeks: even the rumor of such a large troop request had sent waves of dismay through the White House. In any case, it was late summer by then, and everyone from the president on down was taking a vacation.

Much behind-the-scenes skirmishing ensued, and in mid-September a preliminary copy of General McChrystal's assessment was leaked to the *Washington Post*. Although the leaked version of the report contained no numbers, the bottom line was clear: if the United States did not pour additional resources, including troops, into Afghanistan, McChrystal warned, the likely result would be "mission failure."[3]

Furious at the leak, which they blamed on the Pentagon, and unwilling to accept McChrystal's gloomy conclusions, senior White House staff engaged in strategic counter-leaks. In their version of the story,

McChrystal and the Pentagon were trying to "box in the president" by pushing tens of thousands more troops and "refusing" to consider other approaches.[4]

Eventually, a compromise was reached: thirty thousand more troops would be sent to Afghanistan. But the episode left scars. Senior White House officials suspected the military of exaggerating Afghanistan's problems and inflating their estimates of required troop numbers, viewing the military as having a vested interest in continuing a conflict the president had vowed to end. Civilian officials felt manipulated— and less than a year later, General McChrystal was out of a job, forced to resign after a *Rolling Stone* profile quoted his senior aides speaking mockingly of several senior civilian officials.

Of course, the military's take on the 2009 debate about Afghan troop levels was quite different—and it points to the real gulf between the military and its civilian leadership, a gulf that has more to do with differing perceptions of roles and missions than with the near-insubordination some White House officials suspected. As one former senior Pentagon official told me, "The [military's] general stance is 'We can do this, but we want you to acknowledge the mess, cost, and complexity.'"[5] To many in the military, General McChrystal fell victim in 2009 to a White House unwilling to acknowledge any of those things, and equally uninterested in understanding the military's methods, capabilities, or limits.

From the Pentagon's perspective, the White House's refusal to accept the costs of its own ambitious Afghan strategy was either naive or hypocritical. After all, the classic model of civil-military relations holds that it's civilian leaders who set overarching strategic and policy goals, while the job of military leaders is to determine how best to execute those goals. And the White House hadn't asked General McChrystal if he thought the president's strategy in Afghanistan was the right strategy or even a *good* strategy, or if he thought long-term U.S. interests might be better served by pursuing a radically scaled down counterterrorism mission, or even by withdrawing U.S. forces altogether. McChrystal was instead told to address a rather narrow question: What military resources were required for the existing strategy to succeed?

In response, McChrystal gave an equally narrow answer: to succeed in the mission as defined by the White House, many more troops would be required. If the president wanted a different answer, he needed to ask a different question.

Retired Lieutenant General Jim Dubik attributes miscommunications like those that characterized the 2009 debate about Afghanistan troop numbers to the differing models of civil-military relations assumed by military leaders and by the White House. There are several basic models of civil-military relations, he notes. "The first [is] traditional: civilians and military each occupy semiautonomous zones: civilians do policy; the military executes." In this model, the military leaves questions of strategy to the president, but the president leaves the means of carrying out his strategy to military commanders. The second model of civil-military relations is "a civilian control model. Civilians are the principals"—the bosses—and "the military are specialized employees. The military can advise, but they must do what the boss says in the way the boss wants, no more and no less."

Here's the problem, says Dubik: "Most people in the military still favor the traditional separate spheres model, while most people in the White House tend to think in terms of the employer-employee model. That's a recipe for unhappiness."

Of course, he notes, there's also a third model available: a "functional model, in which both sides realize that political leaders make final decisions, but neither has full expertise, so each side needs the other—they have shared responsibilities and need to work together collaboratively." You can't set strategy coherently if you don't understand the challenges of implementation, and it's impossible to implement an incoherent strategy.

For the functional model of civil-military relations to work, the military needs permission to engage in strategic discussions, and civilian leaders need some ability to understand and grapple with complex questions of how to make things work. Recently, however, such collaborative civilian-military relationships have proven as elusive as enduring success in Afghanistan.

During the 2013 debate about whether to intervene in Syria in response to the use of chemical weapons by the Assad regime, another recently retired senior general voiced his frustration with what he saw as lack of coherent strategic guidance from civilian leaders. "If war is the continuation of policy—an allusion to Clausewitz's famous maxim— "I'd like to know what that policy is—so I can avoid screwing it up, or wasting lives for no purpose. We need to know that force has a coherent purpose. Otherwise it's just killing for killing's sake."[6]

In part, he says, military recommendations go unheeded because senior White House staff have come to assume that a risk-averse Pentagon exaggerates every difficulty and inflates every request for troops or money. This assumption can turn every discussion into an antagonistic negotiation session.

"Sometimes you want to tell them, this isn't a political bargaining process," another retired senior military official says ruefully. "Where the military comes in high, they counter low, and we settle on an option that splits the difference. Needless to say, the right answer is not always in the middle."[7]

Over time, of course, the White House tendency to split the difference creates perverse incentives for military planners, and mutual mistrust becomes self-reinforcing. "If you believe the mission truly requires fifty thousand troops and $50 billion but you know that the White House is going to automatically cut every number in half, you'll come in asking for 100,000 troops and $100 billion," says a former White House official. "The military eventually starts playing the very game the White House has always suspected them of playing."

The stakes of this game are high, says Kathleen Hicks, a former senior Pentagon official. "The backdrop [today] is really tensions over budgets and money. Senior military officials worry that they're being asked to do all these [different] things, but who will fund it? Who's looking out for the military's institutional interests?" Meanwhile, "The White House suspects that the military is exaggerating the problems that will be caused by budget cuts, which just makes the military more frustrated."

## Dial 1-800-MILITARY

All the same, the White House can't do without the military. And for a president who entered office deeply committed to reversing the relentless post-9/11 militarization of U.S. foreign policy, this, in the end, may be what rankles most.

After 9/11, resources and authorities flowed to the Pentagon. The Bush administration "always wanted military guys between themselves and whatever the problem was," recalls a retired general who served in senior positions during that period,[8] and was more than willing to pour money into the Defense Department. As I noted earlier, it's a vicious circle: as the budgets and capacities of civilian agencies stagnate or decline, the military has stepped into the breach. But the more the military's role expands, the more civilian agencies such as the State Department find themselves sidelined—until finally, the military becomes virtually the only game in town.

And the White House knows it. However committed—in theory, at least—to expanding civilian capacity and "rebalancing" civilian and military roles, President Obama found himself turning again and again to the military in times of crisis, just like so many of his predecessors. "When the shit hits the fan," admits a former White House official, "the first place we turn is DoD."[9]

But this causes resentment among senior military leaders who feel alternately ignored and summoned to the rescue. "You have to have an ongoing relationship," says retired Lieutenant General Dave Barno. "You can't just dial 1-800-MILITARY when you need them."

## Welcome to Walmart

Many years ago, when I was in law school, I applied for a summer management consulting job at McKinsey & Company. During one of the interviews, I was asked to respond to a hypothetical business scenario: "Imagine you own a small general store. Business is good, but one day you learn that Walmart is about to open a store a block away from you. What do you do?"

"Roll over and die," I said immediately.

The interviewer's pursed lips suggested that this was the wrong answer, and no doubt a plucky mom-and-pop operation wouldn't go down without a fight: they'd look for a niche, appeal to neighborhood sentiment, maybe get boutiquey and artisanal and start serving hand-roasted organic chicory-soy lattes seasoned with Aztec spices. But we all know the odds would be against them: when Walmart shows up, the writing is on the wall.

With its boundaries and raison d'être increasingly uncertain, the relentlessly expanding U.S. military is becoming, says General Barno, more and more "like a Super Walmart with everything under one roof." Like Walmart, the military can marshal vast resources and exploit economies of scale in ways impossible for mom-and-pop operations. And like Walmart, the tempting one-stop-shopping convenience it offers has a devastating effect on smaller, more traditional enterprises—in this case, the State Department and other civilian foreign policy agencies.

It's fashionable to despise Walmart—for its cheap, tawdry goods, for the human pain we suspect lies at the heart of the enterprise, for its sheer vastness and mindless ubiquity. Most of the time, we prefer not to see it, and use zoning laws to exile its big box stores to the commercial hinterlands away from the center of town. But much as we resent Walmart, we can't, in the end, seem to live without it.

As the military struggles to define its role and mission, it evokes similarly contradictory emotions in its civilian masters. Civilian officials want a military that costs less but provides more, a military that stays deferentially out of strategy discussions but remains eternally available to ride to the rescue. "They hate the Pentagon," says a former DoD staffer,[10] "but boy do they love it when they're neck deep in crisis. They're racing for that Super Walmart every single bloody time."

Few senior officers *want* to preside over the remorseless Walmartization of the U.S. military: they fear that, in the end, overreliance on an expanding military risks destroying not only the civilian "competition" but the military itself. They worry that the military, under constant pressure to be all things to all people, could eventually find itself able to offer little of enduring value to anyone.

Ultimately, they fear, the military could come to resemble a Walmart after a Black Friday sale: stripped almost bare by a society both greedy for what it can provide and resentful of its dominance, with nothing left behind but some shoddy mass-produced items strewn haphazardly around the aisles.

## They Have More Money

F. Scott Fitzgerald, meticulous chronicler of American social class, famously confided to Ernest Hemingway that "the rich are different from the rest of us."

"Yes," was Hemingway's laconic reply. "They have more money."

These days, the same could be said of the American military. Is the military different from the rest of us? Yes—it has more money.

This is true in a multitude of ways. Start with the obvious: if we view military spending as synonymous with defense spending (which it's not, really, but pretend it is for now), boy, does it have more money. In 2011, the total defense budget—including both the base budget and supplemental budgets for "overseas contingency operations" (e.g., the wars in Afghanistan and Iraq) exceeded $768 billion. Defense spending has gone down since then, mainly because the Iraq and Afghanistan drawdowns caused a reduction in supplemental funding. The defense base budget also dipped for a few years, but has now begun to creep back up again—even in the age of sequestration and during a period in which nondefense discretionary spending has been cut for education, national parks, environmental protection, court operations, scientific research, and the like. In 2014, the Defense Department's base budget hovered a bit over $500 billion,[11] dwarfing most other government accounts; the poor little State Department, for instance, shared a measly $47 billion in base funding with the U.S. Agency for International Development and numerous other international programs.[12]

The United States spends more on defense than any other nation. In fact, it accounts for 41 percent of global defense spending: annually, we spend almost five times more on defense than China with its 1.3 billion people, and nine times more than Russia. We spend more on defense each year than the next fifteen biggest spenders *combined*.[13]

With its vast budget and complex accounting system, the Pentagon is an infamous money pit. Every couple of years, the inspector general or the Government Accountability Office discovers that large sums of DoD money have been spent on mysterious, never-accounted-for purposes. I have noted DoD's difficulty tracking humanitarian assistance projects, but the problem isn't unique to such efforts. DoD's a big place, and stuff gets lost: money, programs, people, organizations, weapons systems, the occasional small war.

It's not just from the perspective of national-level budgeting that the military has more money. According to the Congressional Budget Office, the average member of the military is paid better than 75 percent of civilian federal workers with comparable experience.[14] Members of the military and their families can also lay claim to many of America's most generous (though arguably unsustainable) public sector social programs.

As a military spouse, I'm delighted by the range of available benefits. Health care? Free. Groceries? Military commissaries save military families roughly 30 percent over shopping in civilian stores. Education benefits? Career personnel can expect the military to finance additional higher education, and the post-9/11 GI Bill provides up to thirty-six months of benefits to veterans, amounting, in effect, to full tuition and fees for four academic years, transferable to dependents. Housing? Free on base and subsidized off-base, with a higher housing allowance for personnel with dependents. Anyone who thinks there's no such thing as socialism in America has never spent time on a military base.

Pensions are equally generous. After twenty years of service, military personnel can retire and immediately begin to receive, at the ripe old age of forty or so, an annual pension equal to half their salary—for the rest of their lives. Veterans designated as disabled receive additional monthly payments, tax free.

It's a system ripe for reform. In some areas, costs have been spiraling out of control: health care already accounts for about 10 percent of the defense budget, and DoD spending on health care has grown twice as fast as health care spending in the civilian sector. In a goofy but illuminating exercise, an analyst at the Center for Strategic and Budgetary Assessments concluded that if the defense budget increases only in line with inflation each year while health care costs continue to increase at their current rate, virtually the entire defense budget would go to health care costs by 2039.[15]

Yet all this money doesn't always translate into higher-quality services, faster and better research and development, or rapid and efficient acquisitions processes. Too often, more money just translates into more pork. When I was a newly minted Pentagon employee, one of the things that astounded me most was how hard it was to get Congress to stop funding stupid stuff. This should not have surprised me, since funding stupid stuff is one of Congress's constitutional functions, but it surprised me nonetheless. I recall, for instance, former defense secretary Robert Gates's "heartburn letters" to congressional appropriators. Most of his complaints related not to proposed funding cuts, but to Congress's insistence on giving DoD money for programs the military did not want or need, such as extra VH-71 helicopters or C-17 Globemaster IIIs.[16]

## Borrowed Credibility

Our willingness to throw money at the military, heedless of the need or cost, reflects a deep anxiety about the changing world we live in, combined with a general sense that the military is one of the few remaining functional public institutions. This probably also helps account for another somewhat odd phenomenon: the increased tendency of advocacy groups, on both right and left, to try to associate themselves in some way with the military.

Politicians have always vied to demonstrate their love for all things military. For as long as there have been soldiers, there have been politicians eager to stand beside them and soak up a bit of reflected glory. What's more unusual is how eagerly the rest of us have lined up to imitate the candidates. From human rights activists to nutritionists, everyone now seems to look to the military for some borrowed credibility.

Take human rights. During the Bush administration, human rights organizations struggled to convince Americans to oppose "enhanced interrogation" (that's torture, when it's at home). In the years immediately following the 9/11 attacks, the American public appeared to have little sympathy for abstract arguments about the rights of suspected terrorists. Searching for a more effective way to change public opinion, Human Rights First assembled a group of retired generals and admirals willing to make the military case against torture. In a letter to President Bush, the group (which included the former commanding general of CENTCOM) asserted that the U.S. use of torture has "put American military personnel at greater risk [and] undermined U.S. intelligence gathering efforts."[17] The group of retired officers assembled by Human Rights First remains active today.

It's not just human rights advocates who have sought to enhance their credibility with the American public by associating themselves with the military. With conservatives taking aim at recent efforts to reduce the caloric content of school lunches and public attention waning, health care advocates have also brought in the big guns: in their case, a group of senior officers who can frame obesity not as a health problem, but as a military recruitment and readiness problem. In a report called *Too Fat to Fight*,[18] dozens of retired generals and flag officers proclaimed the obesity epidemic a threat to national security. According to the report, more than a quarter of young Americans are now too fat to qualify for military service. This, obviously, is bad news for military recruiters, and for the rest of us too—how can a flabby bunch of couch potatoes defend America as we face off against the Third World's lean, hungry masses?

*Too Fat to Fight* goes on to call for the kind of reforms the left generally loves and the right generally hates, such as greater attention to the relationship between poverty, hunger, and obesity; increased federal funding of school lunch programs for the poor; and more government money for "the development, testing and deployment of proven public-health interventions." A recent follow-up report (*Still Too Fat to Fight*),[19] funded by foundations such as the Robert Wood Johnson Foundation, called for the elimination of junk food in school vending machines—again in the name of military readiness.

The last decade has seen similar efforts to frame everything from climate change to low-quality public education as military issues.[20] And why not? Obesity and poor nutrition surely will hurt military recruitment and readiness, and the U.S. use of torture surely does endanger troops and produces unreliable information. Similarly, low-quality public education threatens military readiness[21]—illiterate and innumerate recruits are as bad as obese ones—and climate change will certainly cause migration and conflict over resources, creating new challenges for the military.[22]

It's more than that, though. In an era in which all military personnel have officially been labeled "heroes," former military personnel make fantastic spokespeople for causes that might otherwise languish. After all, polls suggest that Americans have lost faith in virtually every other profession and public institution, and defense budgets have been holding steady or rising even as other discretionary federal budgets drop.

Here's what it adds up to: if you want to get something funded in the United States today, you need to find a way to shoehorn it into the defense budget. (See: Vicious Circle; Walmart.) Congress seems increasingly disinclined to fund civilian diplomacy and development initiatives, much less education, environment, and antipoverty programs—but call something a military program, and presto, money falls from the heavens.

I'm exaggerating—but not by much. As larger and larger swaths of the federal budget fall victim to Jack the Ripper–style cuts, it's the military that increasingly provides the vital services once offered by other parts of the federal government.

Little wonder, then, that service members have become a must-have accessory for political candidates and issue advocates. Our cynical political culture devalues social welfare programs and snickers at communitarian impulses, and most of us trust neither our neighbors nor the public institutions that are meant to serve us. The distrust is not unmerited; the more we devalue public programs, the less we fund them—and the less they can offer us, the less we trust them, and so on. The military is all that's left: the last institution standing.

No question, there's an element of self-serving jingoism in the efforts of politicians and interest groups to snuggle up with the military—a desire to benefit from a little heroism by association, combined with a shameless appeal to the public's most bellicose and mindless "us versus them" instincts. But perhaps it's more than that. Perhaps we're simply desperate to be reassured that there is an "us" in the first place—that the United States is something more than simply 300 million people who don't much like or trust one another, and who definitely don't trust their government.

Perhaps we try to associate every issue and platform with the military not because we're self-serving cynics, but because we secretly yearn for a domain that's free of cynicism. The military has come to symbolize those lost American virtues of public-spiritedness, generosity, sacrifice, self-discipline, and service to something larger than the self. It also represents that most elusive of American dreams: a government institution that actually works.

. . .

Of course, it *doesn't* always work.

Here's another paradox: today's military is more professionalized and better educated than ever before—certainly far healthier than most other government institutions—but at the same time it's increasingly hamstrung by its own organizational rigidities. The military has been locked into a defensive crouch, semi-paralyzed by interservice rivalries, dysfunctional budget politics, and personnel and acquisition systems that seem diabolically designed to discourage creativity and innovation.

Virtually every military leader understands that as an institution, the military still lacks many of the core skills and attributes that are essential to addressing today's security challenges—but though military leaders universally proclaim the need for flexibility, adaptability, decentralization, and creativity in today's military personnel, our recruiting system has changed little in the last century. Similarly, military training and education remain focused primarily on skills that are relevant only in a diminishing number of situations. The acquisitions process is cumbersome and slow. Meanwhile, the personnel system makes it difficult to bring in new skills or allow servicemembers to specialize, and a zero-defect internal culture rewards conformity and punishes creativity. In all, as the Defense Science Board declared in a 2010 review, "DoD's processes are complex, time-consuming, and often do not align well with the timeframes dictated by today's operational environment."[23]

Take just a few examples, starting with recruiting. In some ways, much has changed. Seventy years ago, the United States had a segregated military, but today people of every race, color, and creed train and fight side by side. Twenty-five years ago, women were excluded from half the occupational specialties in the Army and 80 percent of Marine Corps jobs; today, women can serve in every military job. Just a few years ago, gay and lesbian service members risked discharge; today, they can serve openly.

But there's one thing that has changed hardly at all. Each year, the overwhelming majority of new military recruits are young and male. In that sense, the American military of 2016 still looks a great deal like the American military of the 1970s, the 1940s, the 1860s, or the 1770s. For that matter, it still looks a lot like virtually every group of warriors in virtually every society during virtually every period of human history.

For most of human history, having an army full of young men made sense for two reasons. First, young males are usually stronger, on average, than any other demographic group: they can run fast and carry heavy loads. Second, they're biologically "expendable": from a species-survival perspective, women of child-bearing age are the limiting factor in population growth. A society can lose a lot of young men without a devastating impact on overall population growth.

Today, these characteristics don't matter as much as they once did. Overall birthrates are much lower in modern societies than they were during earlier periods, but life expectancy is much longer. Early societies worried about sustaining their populations; today we worry less about ensuring population growth than about overburdening the planet's capacity.

Simple brawn also offers far less advantage in our high-tech age. In modern warfare, brutal hand-to-hand combat is no longer the norm, and warfare is no longer a matter of sending out wave after wave of troops to overwhelm the enemy through sheer mass. Increasingly, much modern warfare involves a mixture of high-tech skills and low-tech cultural knowledge rather than "fighting" in the traditional sense.

Being young, male, and strong offers no particular advantage to an Air Force remote drone pilot, an Army financial services technician, or a cyberwarrior assigned to the NSA. Even for service members in combat positions, the physical strength that young men are more likely to possess no longer offers as much of an advantage: even the most impressive musculature is no match for an IED.

It's not that the physical strength of soldiers has no further military relevance. Notwithstanding all our high-tech gadgets, military personnel—particularly in the infantry—often still find themselves doing things the old-fashioned way: hauling heavy equipment up a winding mountain trail, or slugging it out hand-to-hand during a raid. The infantry, along with specialized groups such as the Navy SEALs, will continue to view strength and endurance as essential to their mission. But for increasing numbers of military personnel, the marginal benefits of sheer physical strength and youth have plummeted relative to earlier eras—and this trend seems likely to continue.

Meanwhile, an increasing number of tasks we now assign to the military require quite different skills and attributes: technical experience, scientific know-how; foreign language and regional expertise; an anthropological cast of mind; media savvy; maturity and good judgment.

If military recruiting were better calibrated toward ensuring the mix of skills we need, we might make an effort to recruit far more women, more older personnel, more college graduates, and many more immigrants with unusual language skills. Not everyone will have the physical strength and endurance needed for certain combat jobs, but as noted earlier, 85 percent of military personnel serve in non-combat positions. Why not differentiate in recruiting, and focus on ensuring a better match between recruits and the positions in which we will need them?

We might also look for ways to make it easier for Americans to move back and forth between the military and civilian worlds. At the moment, it's virtually impossible to move laterally into and out of the military. CYBERCOM's commander can't bring on a dozen top experts from Google for five-year stints at ranks commensurate with their experience. That's because if a forty-five-year-old top technical expert at Google wanted to join the military, he'd need an age waiver and would have to start as a first lieutenant with a commensurate salary. This would make it impossible for him to hold positions of authority for years to come. Nor can CYBERCOM's commander send his ten brightest young officers off to work in Silicon Valley for a few years: by doing so, they would risk promotions within the military. As it is, many military officers fear that taking "broadening" assignments will work against them when it comes to promotion and command opportunities: despite rhetoric from senior military leaders about the value of gaining diverse experiences, it's often those who have followed the straight and narrow path who end up in top positions.[24]

The current all-or-nothing approach to military careers doesn't serve the nation well. It keeps talented people out of the military, and makes it risky or impossible for military personnel to branch out and still return without career penalties.

Granted, there are military positions that require substantive skills that can be gained only by many years in the military itself—civilian life, no matter how rich and varied, doesn't tend to give people the ability to operate tanks in close formation in a combat setting while coordinating air support. But there are many other military positions for which this is far less true, particularly ones where new skills are needed, be they technical or linguistic. You can't learn combined arms maneuvers in civilian life, but you *can* learn to be a computer programmer, a medic, an agricultural expert, or an Arabic interpreter. At the moment, the near-impossibility of lateral moves between the military and civilian worlds forces an overreliance on contractors. That's one way to bring in skills, but probably not the best way, and it carries with it risks of its own.

During World Wars I and II, the urgent need for officers led the military to grant temporary wartime commissions to lawyers, doctors, and others deemed to possess valuable skills; those with comparable civilian experience could enter the military at ranks commensurate with their civilian career levels. Today's military urgently needs to experiment with similar flexible programs, both to bring in outside talent and to permit talented military personnel to gain new skills in the civilian world, then return without career penalties.

At the same time, the zero-defect nature of military evaluations discourages risk taking and pushes out many talented officers.[25] Shifting from one occupational specialty to another is difficult, and transcending poor assessments in one area is next to impossible, even if ratings are exceptionally high in other areas.[26] I recall a three-star general with responsibility for cyber operations lamenting that his most talented aide was likely to be involuntarily separated from the Army because he had a mediocre record as an infantry officer. Despite his talents in the cyber domain, even his three-star mentor couldn't save the young officer's career.

Meanwhile, rigid bureaucratic rules also push out many of the military's best and brightest. Tim Kane, the author of *Bleeding Talent* and a vocal critic of the military personnel system, notes that "talented senior officers [are often] badly mismatched with . . . optimal jobs because the Pentagon continue[s] to use a command-and-control personnel system right out of a Soviet playbook, rather than trusting the voluntary nature of their volunteers. Surveys reveal that the main drivers of attrition [are] not high op-tempo [operational tempo: the pace of new tasks and deployments] but frustration with the personnel bureaucracy."[27] If you speak Korean and want to be stationed in Korea, you may find yourself posted involuntarily to Kuwait, while an Arabic speaker is sent off to Korea. Your kids may have one more year of high school and your spouse may need one more year to finish her nursing degree at the local university, but none of this matters to the military; you can still be shipped off posthaste to Germany, even though someone else might be better suited to your assignment in any case. You may be an expert in nuclear engineering, but that won't necessarily stop the military from plunking you down in a Pentagon job where you'll spend your days on counterinsurgency planning.

When rigid bureaucracy drives out many talented people, you're left mainly with people who aren't bothered by rigid bureaucracy—but they may not be the right people to lead the military through uncharted waters.

In a recent study, Stephen J. Gerras and Leonard Wong of the Army War College examined some of the reasons the military is often resistant to change and transformation.[28] They evaluated the degree to which some of the Army's most successful officers exhibited "openness," which "is manifested in a strong intellectual curiosity, creativity and a comfortable relationship with novelty and variety. . . . People with low scores on openness tend to have more conventional, traditional interests, preferring familiarity over novelty. They tend to be conservative and resistant to change. . . ." Meanwhile, "Leaders high in openness . . . solicit alternate points of view and are comfortable debating with those whose perspectives differ from their own. They are generally more receptive to change," making them more adept at navigating complex, rapidly changing, and uncertain environments.

Senior military personnel didn't score very highly on openness, Gerras and Wong found. "Personality data gathered at the US Army War College from lieutenant colonel and colonel students show that the most successful officers score lower in openness than the general US population. Upon reflection, this makes sense. People with lower openness scores would probably be more inclined to join the Army in the first place. . . . To make matters worse, though, those Army War College students selected for brigade command"—a traditional indicator of success for full colonels—"score even lower than the overall Army War College average. This raises an interesting paradox: the leaders recognized and selected by the Army to serve at strategic levels—where uncertainty and complexity are the greatest—tend to have lower levels of one of the attributes most related to success at [a] strategic level." It's the Peter Principle in action, Army style.

## The Strongest Military in the History of the World

Here's a final paradox—and one that lies at the heart of the high-level civilian-military tensions described in this book. The United States has what President Obama has called "the strongest military in the history of the world,"[29] but that same military seems increasingly incapable of addressing many of today's most pressing threats.

In many ways, the military is a victim of its own success: our conventional military dominance makes direct challenges nearly suicidal for other states, pushing adversaries toward asymmetric strategies designed to neutralize our strengths and play on our weaknesses.

Thus, we handily defeated Saddam Hussein's armies in 1991 and again in 2003—but were caught flat-footed by the rise of terrorism and insurgency inside Iraq and by the challenges of post-conflict stabilization and reconstruction. In Afghanistan, CIA and Special Forces advisors plus American airpower helped the Northern Alliance gain rapid victory over the Taliban—but top al Qaeda leaders slipped across the porous Pakistani border, the U.S. occupation helped the Taliban generate new recruits, and our troops were frequently confounded by an invisible enemy that left IEDs in roadways, then melted back into the civilian population.

Conventional U.S. military force, designed to combat the militaries of peer and near-peer states, has only limited value when it comes to many of the more distributed and complex challenges we currently face. Tanks and fighter jets can't stop disaffected teenagers in Birmingham or Paris or Detroit from being inspired by al Qaeda or ISIS; they can't stop ISIS from posting gruesome footage of beheaded hostages on YouTube, or halt the spread of Ebola, or prevent cyber espionage and attack.

Part of the problem is our own false assumptions. "I know not with what weapons World War III will be fought," Albert Einstein warned President Harry Truman, "but World War IV will be fought with sticks and stones."[30] Implied in Einstein's famous adage is an assumption that right up until the moment we knock ourselves back into the Stone Age, the technologies of warfare will evolve in one direction only: they will become ever more advanced, complex, sophisticated, and lethal.

Today, much rhetoric about future wars makes this assumption. We assume that military technological innovation is a one-way ratchet. High-tech measures taken by one side will be followed by high-tech countermeasures taken by the other, which will be met with still more advanced counter-countermeasures, and so on, ad infinitum—or at least until some Einsteinian nuclear catastrophe ends the cycle, crashing us back to the age of sticks and stones.

But Einstein's cautionary words overlook one detail: for all our technological sophistication, warfare has never truly moved past sticks and stones—and even today, their bone-breaking power remains surprisingly potent.

Certainly, history offers plentiful examples of escalating technological "measure, countermeasure, counter-countermeasure" cycles: As swords and spears grew more lethal, armor became heavier. As armor became heavier, horses were needed to increase speed and maneuverability, and the invention of the stirrup further increased the lethal effectiveness of mounted cavalry. The development of the longbow and crossbow enabled distance warfare and the decimation of mounted troops armed with swords and spears, but then guns and artillery displaced bows, automatic weapons displaced single-shot weapons, and so on through the atom bomb—for which Einstein's work so ambivalently paved the way.

Or consider electronic warfare. During World War II, for instance, Allied forces developed active sonar to locate submerged German U-boats, while ship-based high-frequency radio direction finders were produced to intercept radio transmissions sent by surfaced U-boats. Germany then equipped U-boats with radar detectors, which led the Allies to deploy newly developed centimetric radar, which German radar detectors could not detect. In the context of aerial warfare, the evolution of radar systems to detect incoming aircraft led to the use of chaff and the development of radar jammers, which in turn led to new counter-countermeasures intended to making jamming more difficult, such as frequency hopping and radiation homing.

Here's what we seem eager to forget: military technological evolution can go in both directions. In biological evolution, there's no teleology: the simple doesn't inevitably become more complex, and while life-forms change and evolve in response both to random mutation and environmental conditions, they don't inevitably "advance." In modern warfare, the same is true. High-tech measures aren't inevitably countered by more high-tech measures. Sometimes, the opposite is true: the most successful countermeasures are low-tech—and historically, this has been demonstrated just as often as has the opposite.

We know this, of course. We just don't like it. Consider, most recently, the U.S. experience in Afghanistan. The United States brought overwhelming technological superiority to the battlefield—and with it, we also brought new blind spots. The Taliban, a low-budget but by no means low-innovation adversary, quickly developed low-tech responses to our high-tech blind spots.

Unable to prevail in direct combat with U.S. troops, for instance, the Taliban turned to improvised explosive devices made of readily available materials and detonated by cell phones. We countered by developing costly vehicle-based cell phone jammers, designed to prevent the long-distance detonation of IEDs as our vehicles drove by them. These often had the unintended consequence of disrupting our own communications, and they also led the Taliban to shift to using IEDs with mechanical triggers. We responded by equipping our forces with ground-penetrating radar designed to detect the metallic signature of IED components. The Taliban countered by moving even further in the direction of sticks and stones, constructing pressure-plated IEDs out of foam rubber, plastic, and wood.

We've seen similar Taliban low-tech countermeasures in other areas. We have invested heavily in both encryption technologies and surveillance technologies designed to thwart adversaries' use of encryption, for instance, but since we took it for granted that potential adversaries would have made similar high-tech communications commitments, we allowed our ability to locate simple FM radios to degrade.

Most of the time, Taliban forces don't bother with encryption; they communicate openly over simple handheld walkie-talkies, using multiple mobile FM repeaters to retransmit these weak signals over longer distances. U.S. forces initially lacked the equipment to intercept these transmissions, and reportedly had to rely on purchasing cheap "commercially available radio scanners in the Kabul souk" to listen in.[31] The equipment needed to intercept Taliban radio communications became standard, but it has proven far more difficult for us to locate the enemy themselves; we can locate the repeater towers, but not a Taliban soldier on his handheld radio.

Al Qaeda too is a learning organization. Threatened by U.S. drones, al Qaeda supporters are reportedly turning to low-tech countermeasures, encouraging militants to use mud and grass mats to hide vehicles from overhead surveillance.[32] This tactic won't be successful for long, but it's a good bet that AQ and its offshoots will find new low-tech means to thwart U.S. drones in the coming years.

A misplaced confidence in our technological superiority dangerously increases our vulnerability to low-tech countermeasures. In the 1970s, we convinced ourselves that there would be no more Vietnams, and turned our backs on whatever wisdom we had gained during that brutal, protracted conflict (wisdom about the nature of asymmetric and guerrilla warfare, the strength of nationalism, and the perils of occupation). Then, in Iraq and Afghanistan, we painfully relearned many of Vietnam's grim lessons—just in time for the wars to wind down and the public to lose interest.

Now many leaders in both the military and civilian world seem determined to repeat our post-Vietnam head-in-the-sand routine. We won't have any more Iraqs or Afghanistans, we tell ourselves—we won't invade or occupy states or territories with vast ground forces, and we won't be engaged in messy counterinsurgency or stability operations, so we don't need to remember our mistakes—we can just move on! The lessons of Afghanistan will have no applicability to future wars, for these future wars, if any, will be high-tech conflicts with sophisticated state or state-backed adversaries.

Maybe so, maybe not. Even if most future wars will be with sophisticated, high-tech states, it's a big mistake to imagine that sticks and stones will play no role in future conflicts. After all, it took the Taliban remarkably little time to realize that high-tech U.S. capabilities could frequently be thwarted by lower-tech countermeasures. ISIS has been quick to exploit U.S. overreliance on high-tech precision weapons as well, and our related refusal to consider "boots on the ground."

Near-peer states such as China and Russia have also taken notice. The Russians have already begun to reshape their strategic assumptions around these changes. In a 2013 article in a Russian military journal, for instance, Valery Gerasimov, Russia's deputy defense minister and chief of the General Staff of the Armed Forces, wrote of the need for his country's military to adapt to this new world: "In the 21st century we have seen a tendency toward blurring the lines between the states of war and peace. Wars are no longer declared and, having begun, proceed according to an unfamiliar template." Gerasimov went on:

> The very "rules of war" have changed. The role of nonmilitary means of achieving political and strategic goals has grown, and, in many cases, they have exceeded the power of force of weapons in their effectiveness. . . . From this proceed logical questions: What is modern war? What should the army be prepared for? . . .
>
> These days . . . frontal engagements of large formations of forces at the strategic and operational level are gradually becoming a thing of the past. Long-distance, contactless actions against the enemy are becoming the main means of achieving combat and operational goals. . . .
>
> [Warfare was once] handled exclusively by the armed forces. But conditions have changed.[33]

In Ukraine, Russia has already shown an impressive ability to mix the conventional and the unconventional, the high-tech and the low-tech. Russia has relied mainly on proxy forces in Ukraine, arming and advising separatist paramilitary groups. Many of the deaths in Ukraine were due to low-tech tools deployed by separatist groups: arms and simple IEDS. Russia used high-tech jammers to block communications between Ukrainian military units, but also deployed one of the oldest tricks in the book, placing sensitive Russian equipment next to schools and hospitals to make it politically impossible for Ukrainian forces to target them. Russian cyberattacks paralyzed Ukrainian government computers, while crudely doctored photos helped spread anti-Ukraine misinformation.[34]

* * *

The U.S. military's most thoughtful leaders are taking note as well, and have a keen understanding of the gaps between our current capabilities and the evolving and complex threats we face. The Army's Special Operations Command recently produced a white paper urging greater emphasis on "political warfare," for instance, which the paper defined as "a persistent and purposeful synergy of diplomatic, economic, informational, and military efforts in unified campaigns where military contributions support the attainment of broader strategic end states."

The logic behind this is much like that behind emerging Chinese and Russian military strategies:

> Rather than a binary opposition between "war" and "peace," the conduct of international relations is characterized by continuously evolving combinations of collaboration, conciliation, confrontation, and conflict. As such, during times of interstate "peace," the U.S. government must still confront adversaries aggressively and conclusively through all means of national power. When those adversaries practice a form of Hybrid Warfare employing political, military, economic, and criminal tools below the threshold of conventional warfare, the U.S. must overmatch adversary efforts.

Sounds simple on paper: if our adversaries seamlessly blend diplomacy, economic power, media and information campaigns, and so on, making full, though often covert, use both of traditional state and military tools and of the private sector, the United States will need to learn to do the same. But it's relatively simple for authoritarian regimes to coordinate "all means of national power": authoritarian and totalitarian regimes don't need to bother with domestic legal restrictions, and private citizens can be coerced into doing the state's bidding. It's not so easy for a democracy—at least, not for a democracy that hopes to stay that way.

# PART V

# Managing War's Paradoxes

On the morning of September 11, 2001, I was driving to work from my home in rural Free Union, Virginia. I was six months pregnant with my first child, and in my first semester teaching at the University of Virginia's School of Law. I didn't want to be late for my criminal law class. As I drove through the rolling foothills of the Blue Ridge, I turned on the radio. It was a few minutes before nine.

The voices on the radio were talking about the World Trade Center and a crash and a fire. I frowned. Why was the World Trade Center on the news? I wondered if they were doing some sort of retrospective on the 1993 truck bomb attack, which had killed six people, and I almost changed the station: I wasn't interested in a nearly ten-year-old story.

But then there was something about a plane flying into a tower, and I realized that this was breaking news. An accident, maybe? A few minutes later, one of the voices said something about a second plane, hitting the other tower. By now the news anchors were beginning to sound flustered. Could it be a terrorist attack, they wondered? Or just a coincidence?

I snorted. Two planes hitting the Twin Towers within twenty minutes? A coincidence didn't seem likely.

Arriving at work, I found several colleagues standing around. No one seemed to know what to do. One woman was sobbing: her daughter was in New York and she couldn't reach her; all the phone lines were tied up. Someone hugged her awkwardly, and we all stood around some more. Suddenly someone shouted, from inside an office, "The tower is collapsing!" We all raced in to stare dumbstruck at his computer, but the screen only showed streets full of thick smoke. A few minutes later, the university canceled classes, and I went home.

We had only moved to Virginia the previous month, and we hadn't yet purchased a television. This seemed as good a time as any to acquire one, so my then husband and I drove to Best Buy. But walking into the store, it was clear right away that no one would be doing any buying or selling today: the employees were all clustered toward the rear of the store, where they stood gaping at dozens of display televisions, all tuned to various news channels.

I hadn't watched television in months, and suddenly there were TV screens everywhere I looked. Tiny six-inch kitchen counter TVs stood beside vast six-foot home theater flat-screens and medium-sized living room sets. Vividly colored images were everywhere: in front of us, on the side walls. One enormous television even seemed to be suspended from the ceiling. The sound was off, but as we joined the stunned group of Best Buy staff, we could see that every single television was showing some version of the same scenes, all in the same eerie silence: planes smashing into glass and metal, and flames pouring out from gashes in the towers. Smoke and fire, then, unbearably, human bodies, jumping and twisting and falling soundlessly through the air. Finally, the towers collapsing in slow motion, one after the other, endlessly, silently replayed.

After a few moments I turned away, sick. Everything will be different now, I thought. The child I'm carrying will be born into a different world.

· · ·

But it doesn't have to be a world in which everything is war.

In the years since 9/11, we've slid further and further toward such a grim future. We have allowed the rules and habits of wartime to pervade ordinary life, blinding us to the ways in which we're becoming both less principled and less secure.

The horrors of 9/11 can't be wished away, any more than we can wish away the brutality of ISIS, the looming specter of catastrophic climate change, or the coming era of bioengineered threats and autonomous weapons. Reality will always be crueler and less orderly than the neat rules and categories we humans try to create, but this is no reason to abandon our efforts to tame and constrain the human capacity for violence, or give up on our efforts to ensure that power is exercised fairly and accountably.

History tells us that rules and rituals can lose their force over time, or be turned to different ends—but history also tells us that we need to keep trying. War's paradoxes can never be fully resolved, but with creativity and determination they can, perhaps, be managed more justly and sensibly.

Lawmaking is an imaginative enterprise: legislators, diplomats, and policymakers look at the existing world, project onto it an image of a better, tidier future, and then try to develop contingency plans for dealing with various forms of future untidiness. Thus, the mid-twentieth-century diplomats who negotiated the U.N. Charter, the Geneva Conventions, and the core human rights treaties took the raw materials at hand, drawn from older legal documents and customs, and coupled these with their own searing sense of what had gone wrong in the world war just ended. By laying out new rules for a world more orderly than the one they had inherited, they hoped to encourage life to imitate law—and for a time, it almost worked.

Inevitably, the post–World War II legal and institutional framework was slightly out of date from the moment it was created. The law speaks of civilians and combatants, of states and "organized armed forces under responsible command," of "international peace and security" and "domestic affairs," but there have always been actors and actions that didn't fit into these neat boxes. In the decades immediately following World War II, the world saw plenty of partisans and guerrillas, for instance, along with terrorist groups ranging from the Irish Republican Army to violent Basque separatists. Proxy conflicts in Africa, Asia, and Latin America put pressure on international rules relating to sovereignty and the use of force, as did the covert action and espionage of the Cold War era. For decades, the number of things that "didn't fit" stayed well clear of the tipping point. It was only after 9/11 that the categories and rules of the post–World War II world became fundamentally incoherent.

Look further back in time, and there have been many other moments in which the post–World War II categories so familiar to most of us could not have been easily applied. The British East India Company was, for the better part of two hundred years, part profit-making private company, part government, and part army, and it wasn't unique: throughout history, all these categories have frequently been murky, along with the lines between pirate and naval officer, bandit leader and feudal lord, mercenary and patriot, citizen and soldier.

And these categories are culture-specific. As our brief foray into history and anthropology demonstrated, virtually all human societies have sought to draw clear lines between war and peace, warriors and nonwarriors, but they have drawn these lines in quite different places at different times, used different rituals in an attempt to keep them clear, and found, repeatedly, that every line they drew eventually had to be redrawn.

Perhaps the problem we face today is not that categories which have long been clear have suddenly become hazy; perhaps the problem is that we briefly convinced ourselves of the permanence and clarity of lines drawn in the sand. Perhaps the anomaly we should study is not the recent emergence of line-blurring threats such as transnational terrorism or cyberattacks, but that strange and halcyon period between World War II and the 9/11 attacks, in which we in the West thought we had finally figured it all out: we thought we understood the world around us, and could lock into place the international order best suited to maintaining peace and stability and enabling humans to thrive. We built a global system based on the assumption that the state is the ultimate and best form of human social organization, and convinced ourselves that war could be locked in a box and made subject to unchanging rules.

But though the current blurriness may be less historically anomalous than we often assume, one important thing *has* changed in the years since the British East India Company controlled an entire subcontinent: we live today in the age of human rights. Human rights may not be universally respected, but the idea of human rights is now almost universally accepted, with its promises of dignity, fairness, and justice.

Two or three hundred years ago, very few individuals had high expectations of their states or rulers. Few people dared to imagine that opportunity should be equal, or that hereditary governing privilege was wrong, or that governments should be accountable to their people, or that power should only be exercised in accordance with fair rules. Virtually no one imagined, except in their most utopian dreams, that the nations and peoples of the world should all be expected—even, perhaps, required!—to work together for good: to feed the hungry, help the victims of natural disasters, or collaborate to stop repression, slaughter, and war.

After the carnage of World War II, the dream of human rights spread rapidly around the globe, along with dreams of democracy and rule of law. And over the course of little more than a century, human expectations have changed radically—not for everyone on earth, but for many people, all around the globe.

As a result, the weakened constraints on state power that stem from the blurring—or reblurring—of lines between war and peace trouble us today as they might not have troubled our great-grandparents. Today, our expectations are different, and higher. We no longer accept predation by the powerful as inevitable; instead, we view it as something that should be eliminated. We no longer consider government secrecy entirely acceptable; today, most of us believe that governments have an obligation to be transparent and accountable, with only narrow exceptions. We no longer consider sudden violent death at the hands of government authorities something that can be expected to happen with some degree of frequency: we view it as shocking.

All this could change once more. The globalization of the human rights discourse has never been entirely consistent, and it may not endure. But if we believe that a world in which governments respect basic rights and the rule of law is a better world than one in which they don't, we should be troubled by the recent blurring and expansion of war. If the rules we have created for wartime stay the same, but war continues to expand, we will eventually find ourselves living permanently under wartime rules, with their reduced constraints on lethal force and reduced expectations about accountability.

Back in 1999, Chinese army colonels Qiao and Wang warned that when the boundaries between war and nonwar, military and nonmilitary have eroded, both law and morality will begin to lose their force. If the boundaries between war and nonwar are socially constructed, that doesn't make them any less vital.

If we can't figure out whether or not there's a war—or where the war is located, or who's a combatant in that war and who's a civilian—we have no way of deciding whether, where, or to whom the law of war applies. And if we can't figure out what legal rules apply, we lose any principled basis for making the most vital decisions a democracy can make: What is the appropriate sphere for the military? When can a government have "secret laws," and when must government decisions and actions be submitted to public scrutiny? Which communications and activities can be monitored, and which should be free of government eavesdropping? What matters can the courts decide, and what matters should be beyond the scope of judicial review? Who can be imprisoned, for how long, and with what degree, if any, of due process? When can lethal force be used inside the borders of a sovereign country? Who is a duck, and who is a rabbit?

Ultimately: Who lives, and who dies?

. . .

It may be tempting to shrug all this off as unduly melodramatic: Yes, the world is changing, and our laws and institutions may now be badly out of sync with the realities of the world in which we live, but why treat this as an urgent problem requiring our collective attention? Throughout history, we humans have always managed, eventually, to adapt our laws and institutions in response to changing technologies and changing conditions. Somehow, we've always managed to muddle through.

This shouldn't be a source of much comfort. True, the human species has always muddled through, but the muddling through has generally been a slow, brutal, and agonizing process.

Think of the major inflection points in the modern international order: the Peace of Westphalia, or the post–World War II creation of the U.N. Charter system. Despite the teleological fervor of some history and international law books, the bursts of creativity and change symbolized by the emergence of the post-Westphalian nation-state or the U.N. system were not the happy culmination of decades or centuries of peaceful evolution.[1] On the contrary, these dramatic changes in the international system arose out of cataclysm.

The religious wars that wracked Europe before the Peace of Westphalia left nearly a third of the population dead in much of Central Europe.[2] World Wars I and II were nearly as devastating, leaving tens of millions dead and many of Europe's great cities in ruins.[3] Out of the ashes, we developed new categories, new rules, and new institutions, ones that worked better—for a time, at least. But the process wasn't much fun for the humans who had to live through it. It was even less fun for the humans who didn't live through it.

Perhaps we'll muddle through once more, and our laws and institutions will evolve in constructive ways without need of any anxious efforts to steer them—but perhaps they won't. Perhaps today's international system will gradually and peacefully morph into a more stable, equitable, and effective system of global governance without any conscious collective effort on our part—but perhaps it won't. Perhaps instead we'll get an increasingly repressive and Orwellian state, and an increasingly vicious and unstable international order. Perhaps the current system will collapse as catastrophically as the pre–World War II international order.

Change is inevitable, but not inevitably for the better; even when the ultimate outcome is good, the process of change may be neither pleasant nor gentle. It will take both a concerted effort and a whole lot of luck for us to stagger and stumble our way toward a stronger, more stable, and more human-rights-friendly system of law and institutions. If we don't bother to make an effort, and we run out of luck, we could find ourselves, all too quickly, back in an era of domestic repression and bloody global conflict.

## What Is to Be Done?

Since the 9/11 attacks, the blurring of the boundaries between war and peace has enabled successive presidential administrations to embrace indefinite detention, massive secret surveillance programs, covert cross-border targeted killings, the use of military force outside the U.N.

Charter framework, and a host of other troubling practices. We've also seen the steady militarization of U.S. foreign policy as our military has been assigned many of the tasks once given to civilian institutions, and the steady trickling down of war-related doctrines and practices into ordinary law, law enforcement, and domestic politics.

So what is to be done?

The easiest option is to bury our heads deeply in the sand and pretend nothing has changed. We can pretend that wars are temporary, bounded, and exceptional affairs, that the current "war" on terror is fundamentally no different from World War I or World War II, and that "peace" is the norm, to which we will shortly and inevitably return. Most Americans are selecting this first option, because to do otherwise requires us to face too many frightening realities.

A second option is to try to jam war back into its old box. We can denounce U.S. government practices and legal interpretations that undermine human rights and the rule of law, and insist that the root of the problem is a simple category mistake: the United States has labeled as "war" too many things that should correctly be labeled "crime" or "social problems," and labeled as "military" too many tasks that should properly be labeled "civilian." If the root of our current problems is a category mistake, the way to remedy these problems is to urge politicians, policymakers, military leaders, and judges to recognize that counterterrorism should not truly be conceived of as war, any more than the "war on drugs" or the "war on poverty" led us to apply the law of armed conflict to those efforts. Similarly, this argument would suggest that we should stop viewing cyber threats, economic threats, and a dozen other threats through the lens of war, and return to our pre-9/11 understanding of the world.

This is the approach that has been taken by many in the human rights and civil rights communities since 9/11. But a decade and a half after those planes crashed into the Twin Towers, this approach is a waste of time and energy—and an exercise in self-deception. We can argue all we want about category errors and the importance of ridding ourselves of the "war paradigm," but events march inexorably on. The war on terrorism continues to open new fronts, from Syria and Libya to Mali and Nigeria, and it's hard to see this changing under any future administration, Democratic or Republican. It's difficult to imagine *any* politician, judge, or elected leader declaring the war on terrorism "over," or labeling it a fifteen-year mistake.

Regardless, trying to jam war back into its old box rests on a faulty assumption about the world we live in. Messy forms of conflict have always been part of human reality, and most likely always will be. Until we accept this, the post-9/11 erosion of human rights is likely to continue.

Paradoxical as it may seem, the best route to upholding human rights and the rule of law lies in accepting that some degree of global violence, conflict, and coercion is likely to remain the norm, not the exception. The best route to upholding human rights and the rule of law lies in recognizing that war and peace are not binary opposites, but lie along a continuum.

This is our third and best option: we can accept the world as it is, but change the categories we use to make sense of it, and develop new rules and institutions to manage the paradoxes of perpetual war.

· · ·

We humans created the categories, rules, and institutions under which we live, and if they are no longer doing the work we want them to do, we should change them.

We call ourselves *Homo sapiens*, but we might more accurately describe ourselves as *Homo categoricus*.[4] It is in our nature to create categories: plants/animals; wet/dry; good/evil; ducks/rabbits; raw/cooked; us/them . . . war/peace. As psychologist Jerome Bruner wrote in a famous 1957 essay, "Whatever is perceived is placed in and achieves its 'meaning' from a class of precepts with which it is grouped."[5] To Bruner, it doesn't necessarily matter whether the categories we create correspond to something "real" and external to our minds—to the world of noumena, in Kant's formulation, rather than the world of phenomena. To categorize is to assign meaning, and to be human is to be a seeker of meaning.

We see a drawing of what could be either a duck or a rabbit, and in the absence of other cues, we don't know how to make sense of it. We see an adult slap a child's cheek: until we identify the "correct" category for the act we have seen, we don't know how to react. Was it child abuse? Parental discipline? Part of a game? An accident? An effort to squash a mosquito before it could bite? End a dangerous fit of hysterics? We need context to determine the "right" category. If we also see the same adult drunkenly insult or beat the same child, we'll categorize the slap as "child abuse"; if we see the adult laugh and slap at a buzzing mosquito on his own arm, we'll categorize the slap quite differently.

Legal categories also assign meaning. In particular, law is one of the most important mechanisms human societies have developed to give moral meaning to aggression, violence, suffering, and death.[6] Every human society experiences some degree of conflict and suffering, and a central question for every society is how to make sense of the kinds of violence and suffering that occur. In societies without law in the modern sense, myths, customs, and rituals reinforce the categorizations that give moral meaning to violence. Stories, songs, and symbols may tell us, for instance, that killing a relative is bad, but killing an "enemy" from another group is good, or that death in battle is blessed, while death through illness is shameful, or that illness is sent by God to test a person's mettle, or is caused by witchcraft and must be avenged, or that a brave person turns the other cheek. There are as many ways to organize and make sense of violence and suffering as there have been human societies in the world.

In modern states, legal process is itself a form of ritual. Law, to use anthropologist Paul Bohannan's phrase, is a set of "double-institutionalized" norms: it consists of norms that first solidify into customs, then are given additional power through their incorporation into the formal mechanisms of the law (police, courts, trials, prisons).[7] Formal law is most effective when its rituals are widely acknowledged as meaningful and appropriate, and when the norms and customs it embodies are widely shared by its subjects. But whether or not law's subjects regard it as legitimate, law always represents an effort—at least on the part of those who create and interpret it—to organize and give moral and social meaning to violence and suffering.

Law doesn't necessarily operate to *reduce* violence and suffering, but it labels and categorizes it. Law labels violence as socially beneficial or socially detrimental, deliberate or accidental, preventable or inevitable. Through law, we plant moral flags; through law, we tell people how we want them to behave, and where we want our society to go.

One person kills another: the law tells us how to regard this killing. It gives us categories for attaching moral meaning to the killing: if we label it "accidental" or "self-defense," it is excusable; if it was a "wartime" killing of an "enemy," it was heroic; if it was none of those things, it will be condemned and punished as "murder." Modern U.S. law defines most state-sponsored violence as good or appropriate violence, while defining most private violence as bad. Thus, the pain and suffering caused by imprisonment or the death penalty are deemed acceptable, while the murderer's acts fill most of us with horror and are punished by the law.

Recall the story of Drazen Erdemovic, and the International Criminal Tribunal's struggle to decide his fate. Erdemovic killed scores of innocent civilians at Srebrenica, but he did so under duress: his commander told him that if he didn't follow orders, he could stand in line with the doomed civilians, "and we will kill you too." Yet the tribunal insisted on punishing Erdemovic as a criminal—not because the judges doubted his story or thought they would have acted differently themselves, or because they thought his continued resistance might have saved lives, but because they believed that legal rules should reflect what *ought* to be, not merely what is.

"The law," they insisted, "should not be the product or slave of logic or intellectual hair-splitting, but must serve broader normative purposes in light of its social, political and economic role. . . . There is no avoiding the essential relationship between law and politics." The law should serve as a warning and a guide, reminding us that the contours of darkness are as indistinct as the contours of war, and the future will be the one we choose.

## War Is Interested in You

"I do not believe America's interests are served by endless war, or by remaining on a perpetual war footing," President Obama said on February

11, 2015. That this statement came as the president asked Congress to authorize military force against yet another enemy—the Islamic State this time—was an irony lost on few observers.

No modern politician will praise war. American political culture regards war as an occasional but regrettable necessity, at best, and more often as a tragic and avoidable failure. Either way, we persist in viewing war as the exception, and peace as the norm. As President Obama put it in a different speech, "Our systematic effort to dismantle terrorist organizations must continue. But this war, like all wars, must end. That's what history advises."[8]

But history advises no such thing. As we have seen, some degree of war has been the norm for much of human history, and pure "peace" has been the exception, though we Americans have been largely blind to this reality: foreign attacks on U.S. soil have been few and far between, and for most of our history, our wars have been fought by a small and highly professionalized military, making them largely invisible to the bulk of the population.

The American Civil War—one of the few to visit its harms on the nation as a whole—occasioned the first U.S. government effort to codify the laws of armed conflict. "Modern times are distinguished from earlier ages by the existence, at one and the same time, of many nations and great governments related to one another in close intercourse," declared the Lieber Code; "Peace is their normal condition; war is the exception. The ultimate object of all modern war is a renewed state of peace."[9]

This was an optimistic perspective in 1863, coming, as it did, in the middle of a century kicked off in Europe by the Napoleonic Wars, which lasted for over a decade and killed more than three million people, and during a bloody civil war that killed some 2 percent of the U.S. population. The nineteenth century was wracked by conflict, from uprisings in Serbia and Greece to the Crimean War and the Wars of Italian Unification.

The preceding centuries were marred by even more widespread conflict, punctuated less by periods of peace than by periods of smaller-scale conflicts. Look back further, and the same is true. As historian

Michael Howard puts it in *The Invention of Peace*, "Archaeological, anthropological, as well as all surviving documentary evidence indicates that war, armed conflict between organized political groups, has been the universal norm in human history."[10]

The century that followed the Lieber Code's historical misremembering was no better: two world wars wiped out tens of millions, to say nothing of the numerous non-Western conflicts that engulfed parts of Africa, Asia, and Latin America. The United States too was in a state of near-constant conflict throughout the twentieth century, with two world wars supplemented by Korea, Vietnam, and more than a dozen "small wars" (not to speak of the numerous Central American, Asian, and African Cold War proxy wars fomented or intervened in by the United States).

There's little reason to expect something different from the twenty-first century. In the century's first fifteen years, the United States has already fought two large-scale ground wars, one in Iraq and one in Afghanistan, and used airpower and special operations forces to kill perceived enemies in a dozen other places, from Pakistan, Yemen, and Libya to Somalia, the Philippines, and Syria. As I write, there are U.S. military personnel stationed in almost every country in the world. Violence and conflict are escalating in both the Middle East and Central Asia, and the United States is getting pulled back into conflicts we thought were over.

The stunning rise of the Islamic State is yet another reminder that turning the page on war is easier said than done. (As Leon Trotsky's grim quip puts it, "You may not be interested in war, but war is interested in you.") The notion that states can monopolize violence seems increasingly quaint: the technologies of destruction are cheap and widely available, and acts of brutality can easily be broadcast on YouTube and Twitter. New methods of warfare continue to emerge, from fully autonomous "robot" weapons and DNA-linked bioweapons to a range of nonlethal mechanisms of coercion and control. Meanwhile, potential causes of global conflict are plentiful. Tensions between the United States and Russia are higher today than at any period since the end of the Cold War, and tensions with China are increasing. Cyberattacks are rising, and climate change is creating new spheres of competition over water and other resources.

Warfare will keep changing, but it's unlikely to disappear. We are, as the military puts it, in an era of persistent conflict.[11] It won't end soon.

. . .

"War appears to be as old as mankind, but peace is a modern invention," wrote Sir Henry Maine in 1888.[12] This isn't a fashionable sentiment, and for most of us, accepting that "wartime" is unlikely to end goes against the grain.

We resist seeing war and peace as points along a continuum: we long for them to be starkly differentiated. Like the Mekeo of Papua New Guinea, we recognize on some level that war is toxic; if allowed to leach into ordinary life, if may destroy all that we value.

It is because so much is at stake that we humans have dedicated so much energy, over the millennia, to policing the lines between war and peace. In wartime, we permit violence and coercion that we deem immoral and illegal in peacetime—and we permit these wartime deviations from the usual peacetime rules because, despite war's historical frequency, we persist in viewing it as an exceptional state of affairs.

There are many things we are willing to tolerate on an exceptional basis, but not if they become the norm. Thus, indefinite detention "for the duration of the conflict" is one thing if a conflict is likely to last for two years, or five, or even ten. It's another thing altogether when a conflict can confidently be expected to last a lifetime. The suspension of civil liberties is one thing during an emergency of short duration, and another thing over the long term. The killing of human beings without due process or any mechanisms for accountability is one thing in the trenches of World War I, and another thing when the killings can take place anywhere on earth, at any time, against an ill-defined, nonuniformed, and changing foe.

When war is relatively bounded—when it is something that happens in a defined place and time, and involves a clearly defined group of actors—we can tolerate its relatively unconstrained violence. But the nature of modern security threats resists our efforts at categorization.

In a war against a geographically diffuse terrorist network, the spatial boundaries of conflict are necessarily arbitrary. A war against constantly morphing organizations that often lack centralized leadership structures cannot "end" with a peace treaty. A war against a constantly changing set of actors who move from place to place and from organization to organization can have no clearly defined "enemy."

Some may be inclined to dismiss the increasing haziness of the boundaries between war and peace as merely a product of disingenuous U.S. government rhetoric, but they are wrong to do so. No question, there has been plenty of disingenuous rhetoric—but the changes in the geopolitical landscape are real, significant, and most likely irreversible: revolutionary technological changes have reduced the salience of state borders and physical territory, and increased the lethality and disruptive capabilities of nonstate actors and even individuals. The changes that have blurred the lines between war and peace are real, not just figments of militaristic American imaginations.

But the fact that they are real doesn't lessen the degree to which these changes are undermining hard-won global gains in human rights and the rule of law. Most of the institutions and laws designed to protect rights and prevent the arbitrary or abusive exercise of state power rest on the assumption that we can readily distinguish between war and peace. When there is no longer any consistent or principled way to do so, many of our existing legal frameworks become little more useful to us than the lines Navajo warriors once drew in the sand.

• • •

It's time to stop relying on lines drawn in the sand: the wind and waves are washing them away.

We can deny that any of this is happening, or we can try to shoehorn war back into its box, insisting on an end to the "war" on terror, a wholesale rejection of the war paradigm, and a return to the law enforcement framework that we associate with times of peace. But our best option is to focus instead on developing norms and institutions that support human rights and the rule of law, but are not premised on the existence of sharp lines between war and peace. If we recognize war not as a rare state of exception but as a constant companion to human affairs, and thus something that requires permanent management, rather than episodic denial, we can, perhaps, develop rules and institutions for the space that lies between total war and total peace.

As legal historian Mary Dudziak puts it in her book *War•Time*,

> Military conflict has been ongoing for decades, yet public policy rests on the false assumption that it is an aberration. This enables a culture of irresponsibility, as "wartime" serves as an argument and an excuse for national-security-related ruptures of the usual legal order. If we abandon the idea that war is confined in time we can see more clearly that our law and politics are not suspended by an exception to the regular order of things. . . . Wartime has become the only time we have, and therefore it is a time when American politics must function. . . . A cultural framing of wartimes as discrete and temporary occasions, destined to give way to a state of normality, undermines democratic vigilance.[13]

It's time to accept that "war" and "peace" are not binary opposites, but rather the outer limits of a continuum. Indeed, add in cyber, individualized weapons, and various nonlethal forms of coercion and control and a two-dimensional continuum may not be enough: we may need to conceptualize warfare in three dimensions, or even more.

For now, though, let's stick with the world we inhabit today, in which we already find ourselves, more often than not, operating in the murky territory between what we traditionally conceptualize as "war" and what we traditionally conceptualize as "peace." In the last few years, more and more thinkers have tried to find a way to label and describe this murky terrain. The Army's Special Operations Command calls it "the missing middle," while Nora Bensahel of the Center for a New American Security and retired Lieutenant General David Barno call it "a 'gray zone' between traditional notions of war and peace." They write:

> Gray zone conflicts are not formal wars, and little resemble traditional, "conventional" conflicts between states. . . . They involve

some aggression or use of force, but in many ways their defining characteristic is ambiguity—about the ultimate objectives, the participants, whether international treaties and norms have been violated, and the role that military forces should play in response.

Gray zone conflicts abound in today's world. . . . Each of these confrontations is characterized by "hybrid" threats that may combine subversion, destabilizing social media influence, disruptive cyber attacks, and anonymous "little green men" instead of recognizable armed forces making overt violations of international borders.[14]

Nadia Schadlow, a former Defense Policy Board member now at the Smith Richardson Foundation, offers a different formulation, arguing that the United States must learn to operate in "the space between war and peace." This space "is not an empty one," she argues, "but a landscape churning with political, economic, and security competitions that require constant attention"—and the United States needs "an active operational approach to managing that space between peace and war."[15]

## The Space Between

What would it mean, in practice, to manage this churning, changing "space between"—to develop laws, politics, and institutions premised on the assumption that we will forever remain unable to draw sharp boundaries between war and peace, and that we will frequently find ourselves in the space between?

This will be the work of many minds and many years. But the task is surely not impossible if we remind ourselves that we human beings can make and unmake categories and rules. And it is surely not inconsistent with the core principles enshrined both in America's founding documents and in human rights law: that life and liberty are unalienable rights, that no person should be arbitrarily deprived of these rights, and that no one—no individual, no organization, no government, and no state—should be permitted to exercise power without being held accountable for mistakes or abuses.

If we take these principles seriously, we might, for instance, develop better mechanisms to prevent arbitrariness, mistake, and abuse in targeted killings. At the moment, debates about targeted strikes (whether conducted via drones, manned aircraft, or special operations forces) fall prey to meaningless war/peace dichotomies: some insist that no person should be executed by the state without the full range of due process protections provided by criminal law, while others insist that fighting wars effectively requires that we accept a high risk of mistake, since judicial oversight of the "battlefield" would be absurd and unduly burdensome.

But there is surely an alternative: better laws and institutions. Threats in "the space between" often bring with them an urgency rarely encountered in a traditional law enforcement context, and sometimes a related need for at least temporary secrecy. At the same time, laws and institutions designed for an age when ongoing decentralized threats are the norm rather than the exception should be more rigorous in oversight, with greater transparency and more effective accountability mechanisms than would be required in a hot conflict between states on a temporally and territorially bounded battlefield.

In hot wars, we all understand the absurdity of requiring judicial approval prior to battlefield killings. You couldn't have military lawyers opining on targeting decisions during the invasion of Normandy, much less judges; Allied soldiers were much too busy just trying to stay alive. In any case, we could reasonably assume that virtually everyone present on the beaches of Normandy was a combatant.

Meanwhile, in law enforcement settings, we all understand the dangers of failing to require judicial oversight of police searches, arrests, and uses of force. Ordinary crime is mostly individual and episodic, and the harm it does to society and the innocent is relatively contained. In these circumstances, it's reasonable to expect a higher degree of due process and after-the-fact judicial scrutiny.

U.S. targeted killings lie in the space between. They involve the use of military force against individuals who hope to inflict harm far exceeding that associated with ordinary crime, and they often take place in geographic areas in which ordinary law enforcement activities are impossible: the area is physically inaccessible, or too violent and disorderly for the slow work of policing to succeed.

At the same time, U.S. targeted strikes aren't spur-of-the-moment actions against targets of opportunity: those we kill have often been on "kill lists" for weeks, months, and even years. The precise moment of a strike may be opportunistic, but officials have had plenty of time to consider evidence and make decisions about status and threat.

The logic underlying the law of armed conflict's permissive rules on status-based killing doesn't apply here. In the space between, unlike the beaches of Normandy, there's plenty of time for careful process—including some judicial or quasi-judicial process—before an individual goes on a list of those who can be killed. There's also plenty of time afterward to review strikes, determine if any mistakes were made, compensate victims for damages, and review or change procedures to prevent similar mistakes in the future. So why not develop categories, rules, institutions, and processes that take this into account?

Already, several scholars and policy experts—myself included—have outlined a number of ways to bring greater transparency and accountability to U.S. targeted strikes, ranging from independent commissions with the power to review targeting policies and past strikes to judicial bodies that might issue "strike warrants" or order damages for inappropriate strikes.[16] None of the current proposals completely fixes the problem, but there are many straightforward and feasible ways to improve on the current situation—if Congress and the White House choose to do so.

Much the same could be said of detention, surveillance, and secrecy in the space between. In this murky middle space, we need to reevaluate all our assumptions, neither mechanically seeking to apply the laws of war nor mechanically applying law enforcement and peacetime rules. We should focus not on trying to jam activities in the space between into the old categories—war/peace, foreign/domestic, and so on—but on ensuring that this space, like every space, remains a zone subject to the rule of law.

Ultimately, the concept of "the space between" probably won't offer enough precision; we may need to identify multiple different points along the continuum between war and peace, and develop different rules and accountability mechanisms for each. But to do this, we will need to abandon our obsession with forcing everything into outmoded categories and instead keep our focus on protecting human dignity, preventing the arbitrary exercise of power, increasing predictability, and ensuring accountability.

We will need to do this on at least three different levels: the level of the individual, the level of the state, and the level of the international system. With regard to individuals, our goal should be the development of categories, rules, and institutions that balance the right of each individual to life, liberty, and fair process with the need to protect others. With regard to the nation, we need categories, rules, and institutions that enable meaningful democratic control of government decisions that affect liberty and lives.

With regard to the international system, we need categories, rules, and institutions that prevent powerful states from committing abuses with impunity behind the cloak of state sovereignty, but that also prevent the instability that would result from expanding a unilateral right to use force. Bluntly: the United States will need to accept some further loss of sovereignty in exchange for more just and effective mechanisms for solving collective global problems. No state can combat disease, climate change, or international terrorist organizations on its own—but any state can play a destructive and destabilizing role on its own.

If we don't want to keep setting precedents that will come back to haunt us, we will need to learn how to share power, authority, and resources with other states—on issues from targeted killings and surveillance policy to refugee flows and the emerging technologies likely to shape future warfare. Doing this will go beyond tinkering with Security Council voting and membership rules: we will need to thoroughly overhaul existing international governance structures, and pour both money and diplomatic energy into persuading other powerful states to join us.

None of this will be easy or uncontroversial, and technologies will continue to evolve, continually creating new challenges. But none of this should be impossible. On the level of individuals, we already have decent models for protecting individuals from the arbitrary exercise of state power, while also protecting society from the harm that can be inflicted by malevolent individuals. On the level of the nation, we can look to existing democratic accountability and oversight regimes for ways to bring "the space between" under the rule of law.

Even on the global level, where rule of law and governance traditions are weakest, we don't need to start entirely from scratch. Strong and effective international institutions already oversee and adjudicate many significant economic interactions, for instance, and even the globe's most powerful states have willingly consented to allowing institutions such as the World Trade Organization to limit and constrain their economic activities. We can look to some of these institutions for ideas that may also be useful in governing state activities in the space between war and peace.

•  •  •

And what about the military? What about the human institutions that make up our foreign policy and national security establishments: the State Department, the United States Agency for International Development, the Defense Department, the intelligence community, and so on?

They too will need to be reimagined and reformed to operate effectively and responsibly in the space between—and here again, we will need to abandon our fixation on the artificial lines we have drawn, and focus instead on how to organize our government to do what we need and want it to do.

At the moment, U.S. civilian-military tensions remain high. As the military continues to expand its activities into traditionally civilian spheres, we keep going in circles with the usual sterile debates: Are we witnessing the militarization of U.S. foreign policy? Shouldn't the military stick to what it's good at—drilling, training to shoot, conducting military exercises, and, if needed, actually fighting—and leave development, governance, information activities, humanitarian aid, and so on to civilian experts?

In response to such concerns, military officials usually offer a somewhat halfhearted defense. They concede that in an ideal world, such activities would be undertaken by a reinvigorated civilian sector, but note that civilian agencies currently lack the needed resources and capacity, creating a temporary need for the military to fill the gaps between what national security requires and what the civilian sector can provide.

This is an unsatisfying state of affairs for all concerned. Advocates of civilian power watch in dismay as the military takes on more and more jobs that, in their view, ought to be done by civilian agencies—and proceeds, much of the time, to do them badly. Since the military has only recently come to see these activities as part of its mission, its doctrine, training, and skills inevitably lag behind.

For many military personnel, the current situation is equally frustrating. If civilian agencies lack the resources and capacity to undertake critical missions on an appropriate scale, the military is more or less forced to step in, taking on unfamiliar jobs and subject to little but criticism from their civilian agency counterparts.

Both military and civilian leaders frequently assert that the key to resolving this uncomfortable situation is to reinvigorate the government's civilian agencies, restoring them—at a minimum—to their Cold War funding levels. But the hope—or, I should say, pretense—that one of these days civilian agencies will be funded at a level adequate to take over these activities from the military is becoming a dangerous delusion. There's virtually no chance that Congress and the executive branch will summon up the resources or the political will to reinvigorate the government's civilian sector—and in any case, as we know, the lines between "civilian" and "military" tasks are arbitrary to begin with.

Just as it's a mistake to imagine that we can shove war back into a neat box, it's a mistake to imagine that we will someday be able to simply return our government agencies to their traditional roles and missions. Such a fantasy lands us in the worst of all possible worlds, one in which the military continues to expand into traditionally "civilian" missions, but does so in an ad hoc and often ambivalent manner rather than a planned and thoughtful way. After all, to do otherwise would require a politically unpalatable acknowledgment that the degradation of the civilian sector is likely irreversible.

We need to think about military and civilian roles in a very different way.

Try two thought experiments. First, imagine what the civilian sector would look like if the military could reinvent it, freed from all constraints. If we take at their word the many defense officials who insist that the military is only engaged in development, reconstruction, rule of law, information campaigns, and so forth because the civilian sector currently lacks capacity and resources, what capacities and resources would civilian agencies need to "return" to their traditional role? If we want the civilian sector to expand so it can respond rapidly, flexibly, and effectively to prevent conflicts and promote stability and reconstruction, how big would the international affairs budget need to be? How many more people, with what skills, would civilian agencies need? And is it remotely realistic to imagine that this will happen anytime in the next few decades, given current political and fiscal realities?

If the answer to that last question is "no"—and I am afraid it is—move on to the second thought experiment. Imagine what the U.S. military would need to do—imagine the required skills, resources, personnel, and organizational changes—if we were to accept that waiting for a reinvigorated civilian sector is like waiting for Godot. How might the Defense Department need to change, in the coming decades, to prevent and respond with agility not only to conventional military threats, but to the complex and often inchoate threats that may stem from cyberattacks, refugee flows driven by climate change, ethnic conflict, economic collapse, or terrorist efforts to develop biological weapons?

To develop the needed capabilities, the military would have to start looking a whole lot more like a civilian agency itself. Within a single large but agile organization, traditional "military" skills would have to be fully integrated with traditional "civilian" skills, including expertise in development, education, public health, governance, communications, and languages and cultures. Today, threats don't come neatly packaged as "civilian" versus "military" threats—and to operate effectively in the space between, we'll need to knock down the walls we've created between our civilian agencies and the military.

Here too, knocking down walls will be difficult, but not impossible.

Imagine if we stopped calling the military "the military," and instead recognized that "national security" depends on many different things, from the strength and quality of our schools, roads, and hospitals to the creativity we can bring to solving global problems like climate change.

Sometimes, our national security interests—and global stability—will require us to use coercive and destructive technologies. Rwanda, Bosnia, Syria, and Iraq aren't onetime glitches in a peaceful world order, but recurring themes, and sometimes the United States and other capable global actors will need to use force to respond. But despite the inherent risks, the lines we draw between those who carry guns and those who carry stethoscopes and hammers will need to become more porous.

War, for all its horrors, has long been one of the best and only means of harnessing collective human talent and energy to serve the group as a whole, and the military has long been the institution we use to bring talent together. If the military is becoming everything, why not use this as an opportunity to engage *everyone*—to include millions more Americans in the project of making the nation stronger, and the world a little less cruel?

Imagine a revamped public sector premised on the idea of universal service—an America in which every young man and woman spends a year or two engaged in work that fosters national and global security. Some might choose to carry the traditional weapons of a soldier; some might teach or build roads; some might write computer code to protect vulnerable systems; some might work on international development or public health projects.

Expensive, at least in the near term? Yes, though a universal service program would also be a massive investment in a safer, stronger future—an investment that would ultimately pay off a hundred times over. Ambitious? Yes.

But in this as in so much else, we're held back not by the laws of physics—or even the laws of politics—but only by our limited imaginations.

Every grand undertaking seems impossible until it happens. Three hundred years ago, American independence must have seemed impossible. Two hundred years ago, ending slavery seemed impossible. A hundred years ago, the establishment of Social Security and Medicare was a pipe dream. Reimagining the military and combining it with a broad program of universal national service would be complicated and, in the short run, expensive—but in the long run, how else can we harness the creativity, energy, and talent we will need, in this uncertain and dangerous world?

Most of us cringe reflexively at the idea of a vastly expanded "military," one that takes on an ever broader range of traditionally civilian activities as our civilian agencies, defunded and demoralized, shrink gradually into irrelevance. But aside from intellectual laziness and sheer habit, nothing solid stands behind our instinct that this would be a dangerous state of affairs. As we know, the terms "military" and "civilian" weren't handed down by a divine power; they are human constructs, and the assumption that there are (and must be) sharp lines between the two is of relatively recent vintage.

When critics lament the militarization of foreign policy, they often point to the diminution of civilian control over the military, worrying that any expansion of responsibilities, resources, and power in the same organization that controls so many lethal weapons is inherently dangerous. But our concept of civilian control of the military needs updating. Most who invoke it apply it mechanistically: "Nonuniformed people must trump uniformed people in political decision making." To say this, however, is to make a fetish of increasingly meaningless symbols.

We would do better to ask why we have a concept of civilian control of the military in the first place. Ultimately, we care about what we call civilian control of the military not because we happen to dislike uniforms, but because we want to ensure the responsible use of force in the public interest; we want to prevent arbitrariness, ensure accountability, and safeguard human rights and the rule of law.

In a world in which the maintenance of power depends solely upon brute force, civilian control of those who possess (and know how to use) the tools of brute force matters: it's the only way to keep the palace guard from deciding that the throne is more comfortable than the barracks, and acting accordingly. But today, power is maintained through far more subtle and varied means. Brute force still matters, but so does technical know-how. As warfare becomes both more personalized and less dependent on indiscriminate lethality, control over money, networks, and information is becoming as crucial as control over tanks and grenades.

Given this, our current civilian control paradigm is surely neither the only way nor the best way to achieve the goals of preventing arbitrariness or abuses of power. On the contrary: if anything, it is the political establishment's current reluctance to acknowledge the blurry lines between war and peace, civilian and military that presents the greatest threat to the core values that underlie the notion of civilian control.

Recall the civilian-military tensions and misunderstandings of 2009, or the more recent executive branch legal gymnastics around the 2001 Authorization for Use of Military Force. If this is the best our current models of civilian control of the military can get us, it's time to toss them aside. The best route to preventing the misuse of the tools of coercion remains what it has always been: robust laws, processes, and institutions designed to ensure that all forms of power are exercised accountably, combined with an engaged and informed citizenry and a military that is integrated with society as a whole.

## The Game of Law versus the Game of Life

To a lawyer, nothing beats a good game of law.

It stands to reason: law is the game lawyers are trained to play. In law school, the pedagogic emphasis is on "learning to think like a lawyer," and law students quickly come to understand that law and justice are two quite different things: the law is about rules and precedents, and the careful parsing of words and phrases. Often, the law is precisely what the International Criminal Tribunal's Appeals Chamber said it *shouldn't* be: "the product or slave of logic or intellectual hair-splitting."

"Justice" is a far messier and more dangerous concept: mention justice, and emotions quickly start running high. This gives lawyers even more incentive to stick to law.

When lawyers talk about war, they like to talk about "armed conflict," the legal distinctions between international and noninternational armed conflicts, and the legislative definition of "traditional military activities." Lawyers like to talk about "collateral damage" and "proportionality" and "incidental harm," and debate the quantum of activity that constitutes "direct participation in hostilities." To buttress their arguments, lawyers cite other lawyers and legal scholars and judges. They argue by syllogism and analogy, citing past cases and commentaries to prove that the concept of co-belligerency can be mapped onto the newer notion of "associated forces," or that the newly articulated "unwilling or unable" doctrine merely restates older rules about neutrality.

It's probably not a coincidence that President Obama is a former University of Chicago law lecturer, or that it was lawyers and legal academics like UC Berkeley's John Yoo who came up with justifications for CIA black sites and "enhanced interrogation" during the Bush administration. More than half of U.S. senators hold law degrees, along with more than a third of the House of Representatives. The secretary of state and the secretary of homeland security are lawyers too.

Somehow, lawyers have come to dominate Washington debates about war, and that's a shame. Legal categories should reflect a society's deepest moral beliefs. But ask a lawyer if something's a good idea, and odds are he'll tell you instead whether he thinks it's legally permissible. If we live today in a world in which everything has become war and the military has become everything, it is partly because far too many top decision makers have spent the last fifteen years playing the game of law, instead of the game of life.

For lawyers, the game of law is safe and rule-bound: he who hews to the law can do no wrong. Whatever is not prohibited is permitted, we reason: if indefinite detention and mass surveillance aren't clearly illegal, they must be legal. If U.S. targeted killings are not manifestly unlawful, they must be lawful, and if they're lawful, they needn't keep us up at night, dreaming of dead and broken bodies.

•　•　•

When you leave the game of law for the game of life, you're thrown back into the messy world of policy and morality. Suddenly you have to argue about right and wrong, good and evil, fear and hope, cruelty and compassion. Few lawyers are good at that sort of conversation, but it's a conversation we need to have.

As technologies and geopolitics have changed, the legal categories and institutions we once thought we could rely upon to protect our rights and our lives have become more and more arbitrary, with potentially fearsome consequences for American democracy, for individual rights and the rule of law, and for the fragile international order that for decades has stood between us and global chaos.

As we have seen, there is nothing natural or inevitable about the legal and cultural categories with which we are currently operating, or the rules associated with those categories. No divine power proclaimed that war should be defined in a particular manner, or that certain tasks and no others should be the proper province of those wearing uniforms. *We* came up with the concepts, definitions, laws, and institutions that have come to be so freighted with significance—and we can change them.

In particular, there is nothing eternal about the legal constructs inherited by post-9/11 America. The modern law of war is hardly sacred. It should be viewed as no more than what it is: a somewhat arbitrary set of legal constructs and categories created mainly by the post–World War II West to reflect the realities, assumptions, and aspirations of that time. Like Melanesian or Liberian or Native American war rituals, the modern law of war represents only a particular society's efforts to label, order, and constrain violence at a particular moment in time.

Law never does this more than imperfectly, but law and institutions can—and should—be reimagined when the imperfections grow too glaring.

We don't have to accept a world in which the globe is a battlefield in a boundary-less war that can never end, and law has lost any ability to guide or constrain us. If the secrecy and lack of accountability of U.S. targeted killings bothers us, or we worry that mass surveillance will enable government abuses, we can mandate new checks and balances that transcend the traditional war/peace and foreign/domestic categories. If we don't want future technologies to encourage the reckless use of force or coercion, we can search for new rules and institutions to manage them. If we don't want our military to become too hidebound to adapt to new challenges, we can change the way we recruit, train, and treat those who serve, and change the way we define the military's role. If we worry that the tensions between human rights, national self-defense, and sovereignty are pushing us toward global instability, we can create new rules and institutions for global decision making.

We tend to forget this. Instead, we defer to the lawyers: we ask, Does the law define such and such kinds of contested relationships as "armed conflict"? Does the law permit State A to use force inside the borders of State B in such and such circumstances? Does the law permit us to locate an ordinary young man thousands of miles away, and guiltlessly transform him, with the push of a button, into a mass of pulverized flesh and bone?

We should be asking a far more urgent question: What kind of world do we want to live in—and how do we get from here to there?

· · ·

It's never too late to be brave. Think of those flawed but visionary men who signed the Declaration of Independence, pledging their lives, their fortunes, and their "sacred honor" to a revolutionary dream of "unalienable rights." Think of Francis Lieber and Henri Dunant, who longed to make the battlefield less cruel, or young Drazen Erdemovic, torn apart by guilt and shame, but still determined to tell the world of the slaughter "burning at [his] conscience."

Think of Sister Rachele, who rescued so many girls from the Lord's Resistance Army, or Matthew Lukwena, who stayed when he could have left. Or think of those exhausted diplomats at the United Nations' conference in 1945, struggling to look beyond the smoldering battle-fields of Europe and Japan—beyond the crematoria of the Nazi con-centration camps, the devastated ruins of Tokyo and Dresden, and the sixty million dead—and draw up the plans, instead, for a world in which aggressive war would be illegal and every state would respect "the dig-nity and worth of the human person."[17]

None of them achieved everything they hoped for. Drazen Er-demovic couldn't bring back the innocents he killed. Sister Rachele couldn't save all her girls; Matthew Lukwena couldn't save himself. And the planners of the United Nations never came close to achieving their most ambitious goals.

Still.

Without their courage—without their stubborn insistence on imagining a better future—think how much we'd have lost. The American democracy created by the Declaration of Independence was far from perfect, but it was better than tyranny and the divine right of kings; the Lieber Code and the Geneva Conventions didn't eliminate suffering on the battlefield, but they made many wars less indiscriminately vicious. Erdemovic, Sister Rachele, and Lukwena couldn't rescue everyone, but they brought a little bit of humanity to the earth's dark places. And though the United Nations didn't end war, it helped rein in conflict for decades. If the dream of human rights embedded in the U.N. Charter has never been fully realized, it has inspired millions of activists to demand justice and freedom, all around the world. We try and we try and we try, and sometimes things get better.

Today, as the boundaries around war grow indistinct and war's toxins begin to bleed into ordinary life, it's time to try again.

# Acknowledgments

I started working on this book a decade ago, though I didn't realize it at the time. In hindsight, I can see shadowy precursors to the themes and arguments in this book in dozens of my past articles, and I'm deeply grateful to the many people who helped me refine my thinking or offered other forms of support over the years.

My agent, Kris Dahl at ICM, waited patiently for two decades while I dithered over whether or not to write another book. John Davis, former Warden of All Souls College at Oxford and my anthropology tutor, taught me that the four horsemen of the apocalypse never truly appear out of nowhere. Lois Whitman at Human Rights Watch sent me to Uganda, and never pretended to grow accustomed to terrible things. Aryeh Neier at the Open Society Foundations gave me time and space to work when I needed it, and commissioned me to write a short 2004 memo that turned into a law review article and eventually became the seed for the book. Harold Koh at Yale Law School taught me the value of both toughness and charm; Jane Stromseth of Georgetown Law encouraged me to go into teaching, and Paul Stephan of the University of Virginia School of Law let me talk him into going on a trip to Iraq. Michael Kinsley gave me a column at the *Los Angeles Times* for no good reason, and Nick Goldberg and Cherry Gee kindly put up with me. Michèle Flournoy hired me at the Pentagon and let me loose to explore.

Dean Bill Treanor at Georgetown Law told me he didn't care if I wrote more law review articles, but he thought I should write a book. Andrés Martinez, Steve Coll, and Anne-Marie Slaughter gave me several years of generous fellowship funding at New America and brought me into a community of smart, supportive journalists and thinkers. Daniel Rothenberg at Arizona State University helped make sure the fellowship support would continue. Susan Glasser hired me to write for *Foreign Policy* and gave me the freedom to write about anything that interested me; many of the arguments in this book first appeared in my *Foreign Policy* columns. At *Foreign Policy*, Peter Scoblic and Ben Pauker made me smarter, and David Rothkopf, *Foreign Policy*'s CEO, refused to reduce my pay when I told him I needed to write fewer columns and focus on this book. Without such generous support from *Foreign Policy*, New America, Arizona State University, and Georgetown Law, this book would never have seen the light of day. Finally, Priscilla Painton and her fantastic team at Simon & Schuster offered enthusiasm and wise editorial advice.

There's no way to properly thank the dozens of others who have, variously, taught me the ropes, shared their knowledge, read my work, argued with me and inspired me. In no particular order, they include Laura Dickinson, Tom Perriello, Charlie Brown, Peter Singer, Doug Ollivant, Kath Hicks, Damon Stevens, Austin Branch, Kori Schake, Mike Williams, Steve Rickard, Lisa Magarrell, Julie Smith, Wendy Patten, George Soros, Sue Gough, Pete Verga, Stan McChrystal, David Luban, Paul Eaton, David Koplow, Marty Lederman, Jeh Johnson, Jonathan Morgenstein, David Cole, Bob Wieler, Wayne Porter, Puck Mykleby, Laura Donohue, Michael Mullen, Janine Davidson, Phil Carter, Bill Lietzau, Bruce Ackerman, Jack Balkin, Tim Noah, Yochai Benkler, David Petraeus, Shawn Brimley, Jim Mattis, Chris Stone, Brigid Schulte, Liza Mundy, Konstantin Kakaes, Tom Nachbar, Dave Martin, Liz Magill, Jennifer Mnookin, Janet McIntosh, Mary Dudziak, Greg Corn, Bobby Chesney, Charlie Dunlap, Laurie Blank, Greg O'Neil, Steve Vladeck, Heather Hurlburt, Dan Feldman, Kori Schake, Price Floyd, Doug Wilson, Tom Ricks, John Abizaid, Kristen Lord, John Bellinger, Phil Mudd, Lincoln Bloomfield, Rachel Stohl, Jim Dubik, Oona Hathaway, David Barno, and Jeff Smith. There are many more people whose names should also be on this list. Please forgive my memory lapse: You know who you are.

I've also been lucky enough to have many brilliant students and research assistants over the years. Particular thanks are owed to Kevin

Hillery, Kim Hsu, Ido Kilovaty, Richard Kraus, Keinan Meginnis, and Sam Moss. I'm also deeply grateful to Betsy Kuhn at Georgetown, who read a draft, helped with end notes, and generally served as the world's best-natured and most overqualified faculty assistant.

Several people read early drafts of this manuscript and gave me generous and thoughtful comments. I'm grateful to my mother, Barbara Ehrenreich; my father, John Ehrenreich; my stepmother, Sharon McQuaide; and my godmother, Deirdre English, for serving as my first test audience. Michèle Flournoy, David Petraeus, Kath Hicks, and Julie Smith also read and commented on drafts and sometimes tried to save me from myself. The mistakes that remain are all mine.

Most of all, I'm grateful to my family. My husband, Joe, read everything I wrote, encouraged me, argued with me, shared his insights and stories, and took care of the kids whenever I needed to disappear for a few days to write. My daughters, Anna and Clara, were patient and loving throughout this book's long germination. Thank you, my sweet girls.

# Notes

## Part I: Tremors

1. See Anthony H. Cordesman, "Trends in Iraqi Violence, Casualties and Impact of War: 2003–2015," Center for Strategic and International Studies, September 4, 2015, csis.org/files/publication/150904_Cordesman_Iraqi_violence_casualties _war.pdf; Neta Crawford, "Civilian Death and Injury in the Iraq War, 2003–2013," Costs of War Project, Watson Institute, Brown University, March 2013, accessed January 24, 2016, http://watson.brown.edu/costsofwar/files/cow/imce/papers /2013/Civilian%20Death%20and%20Injury%20in%20the%20Iraq%20War,%20 2003-2013.pdf; Neta Crawford, "War-Related Death, Injury, and Displacement in Afghanistan and Pakistan, 2001–2014," Costs of War Project, Watson Institute, Brown University, May 22, 2015, http://watson.brown.edu/costsofwar/files/cow /imce/papers/2015/War%20Related%20Casualties%20Afghanistan%20and %20Pakistan%202001-2014%20FIN.pdf.

2. Stephan Grundy, "Shapeshifting and Berserkergang," *Disputatio* 3, ed. Carol Poster and Richard Utz (Evanston, IL: Northwestern University Press, 1998), 104.

3. Mark S. Mosko and Frederick H. Damon, *On the Order of Chaos: Social Anthropology and the Science of Chaos* (New York: Berghahn Books, 2005), 182.

4. D. W. Murray, "Transposing Symbolic Forms: Actor Awareness of Language Structures in Navajo Ritual," *Anthropological Linguistics* 31, no. 3/4 (Fall/Winter 1989): 195–208.

5. Qiao Liang and Wang Xiangsui, *Unrestricted Warfare*, Parts 1 and 2 (Beijing: PLA Literature and Arts Publishing House, 1999), available at www.cryptome.org/cuw .htm.

6. Alan Taylor, "World War II: Pearl Harbor," *The Atlantic*, July 31, 2011, www.the atlantic.com/photo/2011/07/world-war-ii-pearl-harbor/100117/.

7. Carl von Clausewitz, *On War*, Michael Howard and Peter Paret, trans. (Princeton, NJ: Princeton University Press, 1989), 75.

8. "Bush, in Florida, Pressures Congress on Education," *Inside Politics*, CNN, September 10, 2001, http://edition.cnn.com/2001/ALLPOLITICS/09/10/bush .education/.

9. White House, *An International Strategy for Cyberspace* (2011), www.whitehouse .gov/sites/default/files/rss_viewer/international_strategy_for_cyberspace.pdf.

10. Harold H. Koh, "International Law in Cyberspace," remarks at Fort Meade, September 18, 2012, Department of State, www.state.gov/s/l/releases/remarks/197924 .htm.

11. James Fallows, "The Tragedy of the American Military," *The Atlantic*, January/ February 2015, www.theatlantic.com/features/archive/2014/12/the-tragedy-of -the-american-military/383516/.

12. Sabrina Tavernise, "As Fewer Americans Serve, Growing Gap Is Found Between Civilians and Military," *New York Times*, November 24, 2011, www.nytimes .com/2011/11/25/us/civilian-military-gap-grows-as-fewer-americans-serve. html?_r=0.

13. While Americans over 60 account for less than 20 percent of the general population, roughly half the U.S. veteran population is over 60. Department of Veterans Affairs, *Living Veterans by Age Group/Gender, 2010–2040*, www.va.gov/vetdata /docs/demographics/new_vetpop_model/1l_vetpop2014.xlsx.

14. See generally Jim Golby, Lindsay Cohn, and Peter D. Feaver, "Thanks for Your Service: Civilian and Veteran Attitudes After Fifteen Years of War," in James Mattis and Kori Schake, eds., *Warriors and Citizens: American Views of Our Military* (Palo Alto, CA: Hoover Institution Press, 2016).

15. See Rosa Brooks, "A Military Isolated from Society?," in Schake and Mattis, *Warriors and Citzens.* See also Department of Defense, "Active Duty Military Strength by Service," https://www.dmdc.osd.mil/appj/dwp/dwp_reports.jsp.

16. See Golby, Cohn, and Feaver, "Thanks for Your Service."

17. CNN, "Joint Chief to Graduates: I Fear They Do Not Know Us," May 21, 2011, www .cnn.com/2011/US/05/21/new.york.mullen.military/.

18. Department of Defense, accessed February 26, 2016, www.dmdc.osd.mil/dcas /pages/casualties.xhtml.

19. "America's $1 Trillion National Security Budget," Straus Military Reform Project, Center for Defense Information, Project on Government Oversight, March 13, 2014, www.pogo.org/our-work/straus-military-reform-project/defense-budget /2014/americas-one-trillion-national-security-budget.html.

20. Congressional Budget Office, "Analysis of Federal Civilian and Military Compensation," January 20, 2011, www.cbo.gov/sites/default/files/cbofiles/ftpdocs/120xx /doc12042/01-20-compensation.pdf.

21. Gallup, "American Confidence in 16 Institutions, 2015," www.gallup.com/poll /183593/confidence-institutions-below-historical-norms.aspx.

22. William Shakespeare, *Henry V*, Act III, Scene 1, shakespeare.mit.edu/henryv /henryv.3.1.html.

23. Clausewitz, *On War*, 87.

24. Rosa Ehrenreich, "Support the Troops: Resist," *Harvard Crimson*, Jan. 18, 1991, www.thecrimson.com/article/1991/1/18/support-the-troops-resist-pbtbhe-bush/.

25. See Dana Priest, "CIA Holds Terror Suspects in Secret Prisons," *Washington Post*, November 2, 2005; see also BBC News, "Bush Admits to Secret Prisons," September 7, 2006, http://news.bbc.co.uk/2/hi/americas/5321606.stm.

26. Rosa Ehrenreich Brooks, "War Everywhere: Rights, National Security Law, and the Law of Armed Conflict in the Age of Terror," 153 *University at Pennsylvania Law Review* 675 (2004).

## Part II: The New American Way of War

### Chapter 1: Pirates!

1. "Mother of Somali Pirate on Trial Says He Was Brainwashed," Associated Press via Fox News, April 21, 2009, www.foxnews.com/story/2009/04/21/mother-somali -pirate-on-trial-says-was-brainwashe-1841212140/.

2. Larry Neumeister and Colleen Long, "Pirate Comes to NY, World Away from Home in Africa," Associated Press via ABC30, April 22, 2009, http://abc30.com /archive/6770075/.

3. Peter Eichstaedt, *Pirate State: Inside Somalia's Terrorism at Sea* (Chicago: Chicago Review Press, 2010), 23.

4. Prepared Statement of Theresa Whelan, Deputy Assistant of Defense for African Affairs, "Piracy on the High Seas: Protecting Our Ships, Crews and Passengers," Senate Hearing 111-427, May 5, 2009, www.gpo.gov/fdsys/pkg/CHRG-111shrg51472 /html/CHRG-111shrg51472.htm.

5. Government Accountability Office, *Maritime Security: Ongoing Counterpiracy Efforts Would Benefit from Agency Assessments* (Washington, DC, June 2014), 19, www.gao.gov/assets/670/664268.pdf.

6. Weston Jones, "Obangame Express 2014 Concludes," Navy News Service, April 23, 2014, www.navy.mil/submit/display.asp?story_id=80539.

7. Kris Arvind, "New Radar System Improves Nigerian Maritime Capability," U.S. Africa Command Newsroom, March 15, 2011, www.africom.mil/newsroom/article /8075/new-radar-system-improves-nigerian-maritime-capabi; Amanda McCarty, "Djibouti's Head General Says Partnership with U.S. Provides Stability," U.S. Africa Command Newsroom, December 29, 2010, www.africom.mil/newsroom/article /7923/djiboutis-head-general-says-partnership-with-us-pr.

8. Government Accountability Office, *Maritime Security*, 19.

9. Rick Gladstone, "Global Piracy Hits Lowest Level Since 2007, Report Says," *New York Times*, January 14, 2015, www.nytimes.com/2014/01/16/world/africa/global-piracy-hits-lowest-level-since-2007-report-says.html.

10. "Counter-Piracy at Sea Will Likely Fail," *The Maritime Executive*, November 11, 2014, www.maritime-executive.com/article/CounterPiracy-at-Sea-Will-Likely-Fail-2014-11-11; Alan Cowell, "West African Piracy Exceeds Somali Attacks, Report Says," *New York Times*, June 18, 2013, www.nytimes.com/2013/06/19/world/africa/west-african-piracy-exceeds-somali-attacks-report-says.html.

11. Brandon Prins, "The Continuing Threat of Maritime Piracy in Sub-Saharan Africa," Scholars Strategy Network, July 2014, www.scholarsstrategynetwork.org/sites/default/files/ssn_key_findings_prins_on_the_continuing_threat_of_piracy_in_sub-saharan_africa.pdf.

12. Government Accountability Office, *Maritime Security*, 2.

13. Robert F. Turner, "President Thomas Jefferson and the Barbary Pirates," *Newport Papers* 35 (Naval War College, 2010): 160.

14. Francis D. Cogliano, *Emperor of Liberty: Thomas Jefferson's Foreign Policy* (New Haven: Yale University Press, 2014), 44.

15. Turner, "President Thomas Jefferson and the Barbary Pirates," 160.

16. Gerard W. Gawalt, "America and the Barbary Pirates: An International Battle Against an Unconventional Foe," Library of Congress: American Memory, http://memory.loc.gov/ammem/collections/jefferson_papers/mtjprece.html.

17. Elizabeth Huff; rev. by Priscilla and Richard Roberts, "The First Barbary War," Monticello, 2011, www.monticello.org/site/research-and-collections/first-barbary-war#footnote10_trdpc84.

18. Sarah Schoenberger, "Piracy in the South China Sea: Petty Theft in Indonesia, Kidnapped Ships in Malaysia," *Asia-Pacific, Global Analysis*, Center for International Maritime Security, September 6, 2014, http://cimsec.org/piracy-south-china-sea-petty-theft-indonesia-kidnapped-ships-malaysia/12899.

## Chapter 2: Wanna Go to Gitmo?

1. Agreement Between the United States and Cuba for the Lease of Lands for Coaling and Naval Stations, February 23, 1903, http://avalon.law.yale.edu/20th_century/dip_cuba002.asp.

2. Agreement Between United States and Cuba, Article 3. See also Paul Kramer, "A Useful Corner of the World: Guantánamo," July 20, 2013, *New Yorker*, www.newyorker.com/news/news-desk/a-useful-corner-of-the-world-guantnamo.

3. Patrick Gavigan, "Migration Emergencies and Human Rights in Haiti," Conference on Regional Responses to Forced Migration in Central America and the Caribbean, 1997, www.oas.org/Juridico/english/gavigane.html.

4. Harold H. Koh, "The Haitian Refugee Litigation: A Case Study in Transnational Public Law Litigation," 18 *Maryland Journal of International Law* 1 (1994), 5, 12.

5. See Harold H. Koh, Department of State, "The Obama Administration and International Law," paper presented at the annual meeting of the American Society of International Law, March 25, 2010. See also Harold Koh, Department of State, "Remarks to Oxford Union: How to End the Forever War?," May 17, 2013, www.state.gov/s/l/releases/remarks/139119.htm.

6. Katharine Q. Seelye, "A Nation Challenged: The Prisoners; First 'Unlawful Combatants' Seized in Afghanistan Arrive at U.S. Base in Cuba," *New York Times*, January 12, 2002, www.nytimes.com/2002/01/12/world/nation-challenged-prisoners-first-unlawful-combatants-seized-afghanistan-arrive.html.

7. Katharine Q. Seelye, "A Nation Challenged: Captives; Detainees Are Not P.O.W.'s, Cheney and Rumsfeld Declare," *New York Times*, January 28, 2002, www.nytimes.com/2002/01/28/world/a-nation-challenged-captives-detainees-are-not-pow-s-cheney-and-rumsfeld-declare.html.

8. Alberto Gonzales, U.S. Attorney General, Memorandum for the President, January 25, 2002, www.hereinreality.com/alberto_gonzales_torture_memo.html#.VKrfF4rF9H0.

9. Donald Rumsfeld, Secretary of Defense, "Memorandum for Chairman of the Joint Chiefs of Staff," January 19, 2002, http://lawofwar.org/Rumsfeld%20Torture%20memo_0001.jpg.

10. Seelye, "A Nation Challenged: Captives; Detainees."

11. Department of Justice, Office of the Inspector General, *A Review of the FBI's Involvement in and Observations of Detainee Interrogations in Guantánamo Bay, Afghanistan, and Iraq* (Washington, DC, May 2008), www.justice.gov/oig/special/s0805/final.pdf.

12. Josh White, "Abu Ghraib Tactics Were First Used at Guantánamo," *Washington Post*, July 14, 2005, www.washingtonpost.com/wp-dyn/content/article/2005/07/13/AR2005071302380.html.

13. Department of Justice, *A Review of the FBI's Involvement*.

14. James Risen, "The Struggle for Iraq: Treatment of Prisoners; G.I.'s Are Accused of Abusing Iraqi Captives," *New York Times*, April 29, 2004, www.nytimes.com/2004/04/29/world/struggle-for-iraq-treatment-prisoners-gi-s-are-accused-abusing-iraqi-captives.html.

15. Neil A. Lewis, "Bush Didn't Order Any Breach of Torture Laws," *International New York Times*, June 9, 2004, www.nytimes.com/2004/06/09/politics/09TORT.html; Jay Bybee, Memorandum for Albert Gonzales, Counsel to the President, Re: Standards of Conduct for Interrogation, Aug. 1, 2002, http://fl1.findlaw.com/news/.findlaw.com/nytimes/docs/doj/bybee80102mem.pdf.

16. *Rasul v. Bush*, 124 S. Ct. 2686 (2004).

17. "European Court Award for Rendition Victim Khaled al-Masri," BBC, December 13, 2012, www.bbc.com/news/world-europe-20712615.

18. Mark Denbeaux, Joshua Denbeaux, et al., *Report on Guantánamo Detainees*, Seton Hall University School of Law, February 8, 2006, http://law.shu.edu/publications /guantanamoReports/guantanamo_report_final_2_08_06.pdf.

19. Ibid.

20. *Hamdan v. Rumsfeld*, 548 U.S. 557 (2006).

21. The War Crimes Act of 1996, 18 U.S.C. 2441 (2000).

22. Melissa McNamara, "Bush Says He Wants to Close Guantánamo," CBS/AP, March 8, 2006, www.cbsnews.com/news/bush-says-he-wants-to-close-guantanamo/.

23. Andrei Scheinkman, Margot Williams, et al., "The Guantánamo Docket: Timeline," *New York Times*, http://projects.nytimes.com/guantanamo/timeline.

24. "White House Wants to Close Guantánamo Bay Prison 'As Soon as Possible,'" Associated Press via Fox News, June 22, 2007, www.foxnews.com/story/2007/06/22 /white-house-wants-to-close-guantanamo-bay-prison-as-soon-as-possible/.

25. "Cheney: Gitmo Holds 'Worst of the Worst,'" Associated Press via NBC News, June 1, 2009, www.nbcnews.com/id/31052241/ns/world_news-terrorism/t/cheney-gitmo -holds-worst-worst/.

26. "Facts and Figures: Military Commissions v. Federal Courts," Human Rights Watch, www.hrw.org/features/guantanamo-facts-figures; "Guantánamo by the Numbers," American Civil Liberties Union, https://www.aclu.org/national-security /guantanamo-numbers; "Guantanamo by the Numbers," Human Rights First, www .humanrightsfirst.org/sites/default/files/gtmo-by-the-numbers.pdf.

27. President Barack Obama, "Executive Order: Review and Disposition of Individuals Detained at the Guantánamo Bay Naval Base and Closure of Detention Facilities," White House, January 22, 2009, www.whitehouse.gov/the_press_office/Closure _Of_Guantanamo_Detention_Facilities.

28. Rosa Brooks, "Obama's Bold First Week," *Los Angeles Times*, January 29, 2009, http://articles.latimes.com/2009/jan/29/opinion/oe-brooks29.

29. Sheryl Gay Stolberg, "Obama Is Said to Consider Preventive Detention Plan," *New York Times*, May 20, 2009, www.nytimes.com/2009/05/21/us/politics/21obama.html.

30. President Barack Obama, "Remarks on National Security," White House: Office of the Press Secretary, May 21, 2009, www.whitehouse.gov/the-press-office /remarks-president-national-security-5-21-09.

31. Jo Becker and Scott Shane, "Secret 'Kill List' Proves a Test of Obama's Principles and Will," *New York Times*, May 29, 2009, www.nytimes.com/2012/05/29/world /obamas-leadership-in-war-on-al-qaeda.html.

32. Rep. Jan Schakowsky, "My Trip to Guantánamo: It Must Be Closed," *World Post*, July 26, 2009, www.huffingtonpost.com/rep-jan-schakowsky/a-beautiful-ocean -view-my_b_220968.html.

NOTES

## Chapter 3: Lawyers with Guns

1. See Rosa Ehrenreich Brooks, "The New Imperialism," 101 *Michigan Law Review*, 2275–2340 (2003); Rosa Brooks, "By Force of Will—Can the Rule of Law in Iraq Come from the Barrel of a Gun?," *Legal Affairs*, November/December 2003, 24–25.

2. Rosa Brooks, Jane E. Stromseth, and David Wippman, *Can Might Make Rights? Building the Rule of Law After Military Interventions* (Cambridge, UK: Cambridge University Press, 2006).

3. Department of Defense, Office of the Assistant Secretary of Defense for Readiness and Force Management, *Defense Manpower Requirements Report: Fiscal Year 2015* (Washington, DC: Department of Defense, June 2014), http://prhome.defense.gov /Portals/52/Documents/RFM/TFPRQ/docs/F15%20DMRR.pdf.

4. Defense Institute of International Legal Studies, website, www.diils.org/node /1455541/news?page=1.

5. Armed Services Committee, U.S. Senate, "Advance Policy Questions for Harry B. Harris, U.S. Navy," Dec. 2, 2014, www.armed-services.senate.gov/imo/media/doc /Harris_12-02-14.pdf.

6. Judge Advocate General's Legal Center and School, U.S. Army Center for Law and Military Operations, *Rule of Law Handbook: A Practitioner's Guide for Judge Advocates*, ed. Lt. Col. Mike Cole (Charlottesville, VA, 2010), www.loc.gov/rr/frd /Military_Law/pdf/rule-of-law_2011.pdf.

7. Neetzan Zimmerman, "Sen. Lindsey Graham: Not Enough 'Angry White Guys' to Sustain GOP," Gawker, August 30, 2012, http://gawker.com/5939404/sen-lindsey -graham-not-enough-angry-white-guys-to-sustain-gop.

## Chapter 4: The Full Spectrum

1. Department of Defense, *Military Support for Stability, Security, Transition and Reconstruction Operations*, DoD Directive 3000.5, Washington, DC, November 28, 2005, https://www.fas.org/irp/doddir/dod/d3000_05.pdf.

2. Joint Chiefs of Staff, *Doctrine for Joint Operations*, Joint Publication (JP) 3-0, August 11, 2011, www.dtic.mil/doctrine/new_pubs/jp3_0.pdf.

3. Bradley Graham, "Pentagon Officials Worry Aid Missions Will Sap Military Strength," *Washington Post*, July 29, 1994, A29.

4. Samuel P. Huntington, "New Contingencies, Old Roles," *Joint Force Quarterly* (Autumn 1993): 43.

5. Presidential Debate in Winston-Salem, October 11, 2000, American Presidency Project: Presidential Debates, University of California, Santa Barbara, www.presidency .ucsb.edu/ws/?pid=29419.

6. David Kirkpatrick, *The Facebook Effect: The Inside Story of the Company That Is Connecting the World* (New York: Simon & Schuster, 2010), 296.

7. Department of Defense, Office of the Assistant Secretary of Defense, "U.S. Security Strategies for Sub-Saharan Africa" (August 1, 1995), www.defense.gov/speeches /speech.aspx?speechid=943.

8. George W. Bush, "The National Security Strategy of the United States," March 2006, http://georgewbush-whitehouse.archives.gov/nsc/nss/2006/.

9. Sara Wood, American Forces Press Service, "Africa Command Will Consolidate U.S. Efforts on Continent," February 6, 2007, http://archive.defense.gov/news /NewsArticle.aspx?ID=2946.

10. See Rosa Brooks, "The Pivot to Africa," *Foreign Policy*, August 16, 2012, http:// foreignpolicy.com/2012/08/16/the-pivot-to-africa/.

11. Donna Miles, "New Malaria Task Force," June 14, 2012, www.defense.gov/news /newsarticle.aspx?id=116721.

12. Magharebia News website, accessed September 10, 2014, http://magharebia.com /cocoon/awi/xhtml1/en_GB/document/awi/footer/about/about.

13. U.S. Africa Command, "Maritime Safety and Security Seminar one piece of AFRICOM effort," AFRICOM Blog, March 29, 2012, http://africom.wordpress .com/2012/03/29/maritime-safety-security-africom/.

14. U.S. Africa Command, "2013 AFRICOM Posture Statement," www.africom.mil /Doc/10432.

15. U.S. Africa Command, "TRANSCRIPT: General Ham Briefs Pentagon Press on Operation Odyssey Dawn," March 21, 2011, www.africom.mil/newsroom/article /8105/transcript-general-ham-briefs-pentagon-press-on-op.

16. Thomas A. Schweich, "The Pentagon Is Muscling in Everywhere. It's Time to Stop the Mission Creep," *Washington Post*, December 21, 2008, www.washingtonpost .com/wp-dyn/content/story/2008/12/19/ST2008121902949.html.

17. Statement of John H. Pendleton, Director, Defense Capabilities and Management, "Interagency Collaboration Practices and Challenges at DoD's Southern and Africa Commands," Testimony Before the Subcommittee on National Security and Foreign Affairs, Committee on Oversight and Government Reform, House of Representatives, July 28, 2010, www.gao.gov/assets/130/125154.pdf.

18. Mark Mazzetti and Borzou Daragahi, "U.S. Military Covertly Pays to Run Stories in Iraqi Press," *Los Angeles Times*, November 30, 2005, http://articles.latimes.com /2005/nov/30/world/fg-infowar30.

19. James Dao and Eric Schmitt, "Pentagon Readies Efforts to Sway Sentiment Abroad," *New York Times*, February 19, 2002, www.nytimes.com/2002/02/19/international /19PENT.html.

20. "The Office of Strategic Influence Is Gone, but Are Its Programs in Place?," FAIR

(Fairness and Accuracy in Reporting), November 27, 2002, http://fair.org/press-release/the-office-of-strategic-influence-is-gone-but-are-its-programs-in-place/.

21. M. E. Roberts, *Villages of the Moon: Psychological Operations in Southern Afghanistan* (Baltimore: PublishAmerica, 2005); ARSTRAT IO Newsletter, Joint Training Integration Group for Information Operations (JTIG-IO), Information Operations (IO) Training Portal; Arturo Munoz, "U.S. Military Information Operations in Afghanistan: Effectiveness of Psychological Operations, 2001–2010," RAND Corporation, 2012, www.rand.org/content/dam/rand/pubs/monographs/2012/RAND_MG1060.pdf.

22. John A. Nagl, *Knife Fights: A Memoir of Modern War in Theory and Practice* (New York: Penguin, 2014).

23. Ibid., 18. Portions of this section draw on a review of Nagl's book originally published in *The Washington Post*. See Rosa Brooks, "Book Review: Knife Fights: A Memoir of Modern War in Theory and Practice," *Washington Post*, November 28, 2014, https://www.washingtonpost.com/opinions/book-review-knife-fights-a-memoir-of-modern-war-in-theory-and-practice-by-john-a-nagl/2014/11/28/87412bbe-4d97-11e4-aa5e-7153e466a02d_story.html.

24. Eliot Cohen, Lt. Col. Conrad Crane, et al., "Principles, Imperatives, and Paradoxes of Counterinsurgency," *Military Review* 86, no. 2 (Fort Leavenworth, KS: Combined Arms Center, March/April 2006), www.au.af.mil/au/awc/awcgate/milreview/cohen.pdf.

25. Ibid.

26. Ibid.

27. Thomas E. Ricks, "Gen. Petraeus Warns Against Using Torture," *Washington Post*, May 11, 2007, www.washingtonpost.com/wp-dyn/content/article/2007/05/10/AR2007051001963.html.

28. NATO, International Security Assistance Force, *Tactical Directive*, Kabul, Afghanistan, July 6, 2009, www.nato.int/isaf/docu/official_texts/Tactical_Directive_090706.pdf.

29. Nagl, *Knife Fights*, 85.

30. Government Accountability Office, "Humanitarian and Development Assistance: Project Evaluations and Better Information Sharing Needed to Manage the Military's Efforts" (GAO-12-359) (Washington, DC, 2012), www.gao.gov/assets/590/588334.pdf.

31. Government Accountability Office, "Defense: Stabilization, Reconstruction, and Humanitarian Assistance Efforts," *Opportunities to Reduce Duplication, Overlap and Fragmentation, Achieve Savings, and Enhance Revenue* (GAO-12-342SP) (Washington, DC, 2012), www.gao.gov/modules/ereport/handler.php?1=1&path

=/ereport/GAO-12-342SP/data_center/Defense/6._Stabilization,_Reconstruc
tion,_and_Humanitarian_Assistance_Efforts.

32. See Cynthia Brassard-Boudreau and Don Hubert, "Shrinking Humanitarian Space? Trends and Prospects on Security and Access," blog post, website of *The Journal of Humanitarian Assistance*, https://sites.tufts.edu/jha/archives/863.

33. See "The Aid Worker Security Database—About the Project," accessed January 22, 2016, https://aidworkersecurity.org/.

34. James Pfiffner, "US Blunders in Iraq: De-Baathification and Disbanding the Army," *Intelligence and National Security* 25, no. 1 (February 2010): 76–85.

35. Anthony H. Cordesman, "Iraq's Sunni Insurgency: Looking Beyond Al Qa'ida," Center for Strategic and International Studies, 2006, www.comw.org/warreport /fulltext/070716cordesman.pdf.

36. Sabrina Tavernise and Andrew W. Lehren, "A Grim Portrait of Civilian Deaths in Iraq," *New York Times*, October 22, 2010, www.nytimes.com/2010/10/23/world /middleeast/23casualties.html?_r=0.

37. "Afghanistan Index," Brookings Institution, accessed January 22, 2016, www.brook ings.edu/about/programs/foreign-policy/afghanistan-index.

38. Howard LaFranchi, "In Afghanistan War, US Civilian Surge Peaks as Pentagon Be-gins Pullback," *Christian Science Monitor*, June 23, 2011.

39. Quoted in Rajiv Chandrasekaran, *Little America: The War Within the War for Af-ghanistan* (New York: Alfred A. Knopf, 2012), 308.

40. Sajjan Gohel, "Afghanistan: Green-on-Blue Attacks Show There's No Easy Way Out," CNN, September 18, 2012.

41. "US Building Projects in Afghanistan 'A Waste,'" Al Jazeera English, July 30, 2012, www.aljazeera.com/news/asia/2012/07/2012730181354495196.html.

42. "Warlord, Inc.: Extortion and Corruption Along the U.S. Supply Chain in Af-ghanistan," Report of the Majority Staff, Subcommittee on National Security and Foreign Affairs Committee on Oversight and Government Reform, U.S. House of Representatives, June 2010, doi:10.1037/e629812012-001.

43. Donald P. Wright, *A Different Kind of War: The United States Army in Operation Enduring Freedom (OEF), October 2001–September 2005*, 245 (Fort Leavenworth, KS: Combat Studies Institute Press, U.S. Army Combined Arms Center, 2010).

44. Interview notes on file with author.

45. Ibid.

46. Secretary of Defense Robert M. Gates, "Landon Lecture," University of Kansas, No-vember 26, 2007, https://www.k-state.edu/media/newsreleases/landonlect/gates text1107.html.

47. Department of State and the Broadcasting Board of Governors, Office of the In-spector General, "Report of Inspection: The Bureau of African Affairs," Report Number ISP-I-09-63, August 2009.

48. Interview notes on file with author.

49. *Cost of National Security Counter*, National Priorities Project, www.nationalpri orities.org/cost-of/; Ernesto Londoño, "Study: Iraq, Afghan Wars Costs to Top $4 trillion," *Washington Post*, March 28, 2013, www.washingtonpost.com/world /national-security/study-iraq-afghan-war-costs-to-top-4-trillion/2013/03/28 /b82a5dce-97ed-11e2-814b-063623d80a60_story.html.

## Chapter 5: The Secret War

1. "CIA 'Killed al-Qaeda Suspects' in Yemen," BBC News, World Edition, November 5, 2002, http://news.bbc.co.uk/2/hi/2402479.stm; "U.S. Kills al-Qaeda Suspects in Yemen," Associated Press in *USA Today*, November 5, 2002, http://usatoday30 .usatoday.com/news/world/2002-11-04-yemen-explosion_x.htm.

2. Associated Press, "US Kills al-Qaeda Suspects in Yemen."

3. I have written extensively elsewhere about drone warfare and U.S. targeted strikes. This section draws in part on material originally prepared as congressional testimony, which I later adapted to form a book chapter for a volume edited by Peter Bergen and Daniel Rothenberg. Some of the language from my congressional testimony also found its way into the Stimson Commission's report on U.S. drone policy, for which I served as primary author. See Rosa Brooks, "Drone Wars: The Constitutional and Counterterrorism Implications of Targeted Killing," Hearing Before the Subcommittee on the Constitution, Civil Rights and Human Rights of the Subcommittee on the Judiciary, 113th Cong., April 23, 2013; Rosa Brooks, "Drones and Cognitive Dissonance," in Peter L. Bergen and Daniel Rothenberg, eds., *Drone Wars: Transforming Conflict, Law, and Policy* (New York: Cambridge University Press, 2015), 230–52; John P. Abizaid, Rosa Brooks, and Rachel Stohl, "Recommendations and Report of the Task Force on US Drone Policy," Stimson Center, May 12, 2014, www.stimson .org/spotlight/recommendations-and-report-of-the-stimson-task-force-on -us-drone-policy/.

4. Mark Mazzetti, "A Secret Deal on Drones, Sealed in Blood," *New York Times*, April 6, 2013, www.nytimes.com/2013/04/07/world/asia/origins-of-cias-not-so-secret -drone-war-in-pakistan.html?pagewanted=all.

5. David Rohde and Mohammed Khan, "Ex-Fighter for Taliban Dies in Strike in Pakistan," *New York Times*, June 19, 2004, www.nytimes.com/2004/06/19/international /asia/19STAN.html; Mazzetti, "A Secret Deal on Drones, Sealed in Blood."

6. These numbers are drawn from the New America Foundation's data sets. See New America, "Drone Wars Pakistan: Analysis," http://securitydata.newamerica.net /drones/pakistan/analysis.

7. New America, "Drone Wars Yemen: Analysis," http://securitydata.newamerica

.net/drones/yemen/analysis. See also "Get the Data: Drone Wars," Bureau of Investigative Journalism, www.thebureauinvestigates.com/category/projects/drones/drones-graphs/.

8. Mazzetti, "A Secret Deal on Drones, Sealed in Blood."

9. President Barack Obama, *Remarks by the President at the "Change of Office" Chairman of the Joint Chiefs of Staff Ceremony*, at Fort Myer, VA, September 30, 2011, Office of the Press Secretary, www.whitehouse.gov/the-press-office/2011/09/30/remarks-president-change-office-chairman-joint-chiefs-staff-ceremony.

10. Greg Miller, "Brennan Speech Is First Obama Acknowledgment of Use of Armed Drones," *Washington Post*, April 30, 2012, www.washingtonpost.com/world/national-security/brennan-speech-is-first-obama-acknowledgement-of-use-of-armed-drones/2012/04/30/gIQAq7B4rT_story.html.

11. President Barack Obama, *Remarks by the President at the National Defense University*, Fort McNair, Washington, DC, May 23, 2013, Office of the Press Secretary, www.whitehouse.gov/the-press-office/2013/05/23/remarks-president-national-defense-university.

12. See "The Drone Papers," *The Intercept*, October 15, 2015, https://theintercept.com/drone-papers/.

13. Eric Roth, *With a Bended Bow: Archery in Medieval and Renaissance Europe* (Stroud: Spellmount, 2012), Part I, Section 7.

14. See J. F. C. Fuller, *Armament and History: The Influence of Armament of History from the Dawn of Classical Warfare to the End of the Second World War* (New York: Da Capo, 1998), 91–92.

15. Philip Alston and Hina Shamsi, "A Killer Above the Law?," *Guardian*, February 8, 2010, www.guardian.co.uk/commentisfree/2010/feb/08/afghanistan-drones-defence-killing.

16. Daniel Klaidman, "Daniel Klaidman on the Mind of a Drone Strike Operator," *Daily Beast*, June 8, 2012, www.thedailybeast.com/articles/2012/06/08/daniel-klaidman-on-the-mind-of-a-drone-strike-operator.html.

17. Rachel Martin, "Report: High Level of 'Burnout' in US Drone Pilots," NPR, December 18, 2011, www.npr.org/2011/12/19/143926857/report-high-levels-of-burnout-in-u-s-drone-pilots.

18. "Attack of the Drones," *Economist*, September 03, 2009, accessed January 22, 2016, www.economist.com/node/14299496; Dan Parsons, "Air Force F-35s, Drones May Square Off in Budget Battle," *National Defense Magazine*, February 2012, www.nationaldefensemagazine.org/archive/2012/February/Pages/AirForceF-35s, DronesMaySquareOffinBudgetBattle.aspx; Deloitte, "Public Sector, Disrupted: How Disruptive Innovation Can Help Government Achieve More for Less," accessed January 22, 2016; "AeroWeb | AGM-114 Hellfire Missile," *AeroWeb*, accessed January 22, 2016, www.bga-aeroweb.com/Defense/AGM-114-Hellfire

-Missile-System.html; "Air Force's Newest Fighter Jet, F-22 Raptor Makes Combat Debut," PBS, accessed January 22, 2016, www.pbs.org/newshour/rundown/air -forces-newest-fighter-jet-f-22-raptor-makes-combat-debut/.

19. "White House Report on U.S. Actions in Libya," *New York Times*, June 15, 2011, accessed January 22, 2016, www.nytimes.com/interactive/2011/06/16/us/politics /20110616_POWERS_DOC.html?ref=politics.

20. Scott Shane, "The Moral Case for Drones," *New York Times*, July 14, 2012, accessed January 22, 2016, www.nytimes.com/2012/07/15/sunday-review/the-moral-case -for-drones.html.

21. Greg Miller, "Increased U.S. Drone Strikes in Pakistan Killing Few High-Value Militants," *Washington Post*, February 21, 2011, www.washingtonpost.com/wp -dyn/content/article/2011/02/20/AR2011022002975.html; Peter Bergen, "Drone Is Obama's Weapon of Choice," CNN, September 19, 2012, www.cnn.com/2012/09 /05/opinion/bergen-obama-drone/.

22. See "The Drone Papers," *The Intercept*. See also "U.S. Drones Can Now Kill Joe Schmoe Militants in Yemen," Wired.com, April 26, 2012, www.wired.com/danger room/2012/04/joe-schmoe-drones/.

23. See Abizaid, Brooks, and Stohl, "Recommendations and Report of the Task Force on US Drone Policy"; "Deadly Drone Strike on Muslims in the Southern Philippines," Brookings Institution, March 5, 2012, www.brookings.edu/research/opinions /2012/03/05-drones-philippines-ahmed.

24. Lt. Robert George McFarlane, CEF Soldier Detail, Canadian Great War Project, accessed June 1, 2015, www.canadiangreatwarproject.com/searches/soldierDetail .asp?ID=36; Lt. Robert George McFarlane, Victim Detail, Lijssenthoek Military Cemetery, accessed June 1, 2015, www.lijssenthoek.be/en/address/2621/-robert -george-macfarlane.html; Cpl. Charles Lawrence Amas, 54th Battalion Details, accessed June 1, 2015, www.54thbattalioncef.ca.

25. Not all targeted killings involve drone strikes—some may involve bombs dropped from manned aircraft, or missiles fired from an aircraft carrier, or a boots-on-the-ground raid—just as not all drone strikes are targeted killings. Drones can be used to provide close air support to ground troops, for instance.

26. Mark Mazzetti, *The Way of the Knife: The CIA, a Secret Army, and a War at the Ends of the Earth* (New York: Penguin, 2013), 301.

27. Matthew Power, "Confessions of a Drone Warrior," *GQ*, October 23, 2013, www.gq .com/news-politics/big-issues/201311/drone-uav-pilot-assassination?printable=true.

28. Becker and Shane, "Secret 'Kill List' Proves a Test of Obama's Principles and Will."

29. See "The Bay of Pigs," John F. Kennedy Presidential Library and Museum, accessed January 22, 2016, www.jfklibrary.org/JFK/JFK-in-History/The-Bay-of-Pigs.aspx. See also Duncan Campbell, "638 Ways to Kill Castro," *Guardian*, August 2, 2006, www.guardian.co.uk/world/2006/aug/03/cuba.duncancampbell2.

30. See Elizabeth Bazen, "Report for Congress: Assassination Ban and E.O. 12333: A Brief Summary," Congressional Research Service, January 4, 2002.

31. Marshall Curtis Erwin, "Report for Congress: Sensitive Covert Action Notifications: Oversight Options for Congress," Congressional Research Service, April 10, 2013.

32. See A. John Radsan, "The Unresolved Equation of Espionage and International Law," 28 *Michigan Journal of International Law* 595 (2006).

33. The 9/11 Commission, *Final Report of the National Commission on Terrorist Attacks Upon the United States* (Washington, DC: Government Printing Office, 2011).

34. Central Intelligence Agency, "Devotion to Duty: Responding to the Terrorist Attacks of September 11," December 8, 2010, https://www.cia.gov/library/publica tions/resources/devotion-to-duty/15601-pub-FINAL-web.pdf.

35. Greg Miller and Julia Tate, "CIA Shifts Focus to Killing Targets," *Washington Post*, September 1, 2011, www.washingtonpost.com/world/national-security/cia-shifts -focus-to-killing-targets/2011/08/30/gIQA7MZGvJ_story.html.

36. Becker and Shane, "Secret 'Kill List' Proves a Test of Obama's Principles and Will"; Eric Schmitt, "U.S. to Step Up Drone Strikes Inside Yemen," *New York Times*, April 25, 2012, www.nytimes.com/2012/04/26/world/middleeast/us-to-step-up-drone -strikes-inside-yemen.html.

37. See "White House Rejects Requests for 'Targeted Killing' Papers," Fox News, June 21, 2012, www.foxnews.com/politics/2012/06/21/white-house-rejects-requests -for-targeted-killing-papers/. See also Brief for Appellee at 43, *ACLU v. CIA*, No. 11-5320 (D.C. Cir. May 21, 2012).

38. Letter from Dolores M. Nelson, CIA Information and Privacy Coordinator, to Jonathan Manes, ACLU, March 9, 2010, https://www.aclu.org/files/assets/20100309 _Drone_FOIA_CIA_Glomar_Response.pdf.

39. Andrew Rosenthal, "Secrets and Lies." *New York Times*, March 29, 2012, http:// takingnote.blogs.nytimes.com/2012/03/29/secrets-and-lies/.

40. Julian E. Barnes, "Panetta Makes Cracks About Not-So-Secret CIA Drone Program," *Wall Street Journal*, Oct. 7, 2011, at http://blogs.wsj.com/washwire/2011/10 /07/panetta-makes-cracks-about-not-so-secret-cia-drone-program.

41. Scott Horton, "Blair Addresses the CIA, Drones and Pakistan," *Harper's Magazine*, December 1, 2011, www.harpers.org/archive/2011/12/hbc-90008329.

42. Andrew Feichert, "Special Operations Forces (SOF) Technical Analysis and Evaluation," Congressional Research Service, November 19, 2015.

43. Eric Schmitt, Mark Mazzetti, and Thom Shanker, "Admiral Seeks Freer Hand in Deployment of Elite Forces," *New York Times*, February 12, 2012, www.nytimes.com/2012 /02/13/us/admiral-pushes-for-freer-hand-in-special-forces.html?pagewanted=all.

44. Marshall Curtis Erwin, "Covert Action: Legislative Background and Possible Policy Questions," Congressional Research Service, April 10, 2013, www.fas.org/sgp/crs /intel/RL33715.pdf.

45. Abizaid, Brooks, and Stohl, "Recommendations and Report of the Task Force on US Drone Policy."

46. Moshe Schwartz and Joyprada Swain, "Department of Defense Contractors in Afghanistan and Iraq: Background and Analysis," Congressional Research Service, May 13, 2011, https://www.fas.org/sgp/crs/natsec/R40764.pdf.

47. Rosa Brooks, "Deniable, Disposable Casualties," *Los Angeles Times*, June 1, 2007, http://articles.latimes.com/2007/jun/01/opinion/oe-brooks1.

48. Rosa Brooks, "Why Obama's Assurance of 'No Boots on the Ground' Isn't So Reassuring," *Washington Post*, September 26, 2014, www.washingtonpost.com /opinions/why-obamas-assurance-of-no-boots-on-the-ground-isnt-so-reassuring /2014/09/26/c56d859e-44bf-11e4-9a15-137aa0153527_story.html.

49. Dana Priest and William Arkin, "A Hidden World, Growing Beyond Control," *Washington Post*, July 19, 2010, http://projects.washingtonpost.com/top-secret -america/articles/a-hidden-world-growing-beyond-control/.

50. "How Many People Have Security Clearances?," ClearanceJobs, September 25, 2011, http://news.clearancejobs.com/2011/09/26/how-many-people-have-security -clearances/.

51. National Archives and Records Administration, "Report to the President," 2011, www.archives.gov/isoo/reports/2011-annual-report.pdf.

52. Elizabeth Gotein and David M. Shapiro, *Reducing Overclassification Through Accountability* (New York: Brennan Center for Justice, 2011).

53. 9/11 Commission Report.

54. "Report to the President: Transforming the Security Classification System," Public Interest Declassification Board (PIDB), 2012, www.archives.gov/declassification /pidb/recommendations/transforming-classification.pdf.

55. "Weekly Situation Report on International Terrorism," Central Intelligence Agency, December 17, 1974, www.gwu.edu/~nsarchiv/NSAEBB/NSAEBB90/dubious-01a .pdf.

56. Executive Order 12958, "Classified National Security Information," 60 *Federal Register* 19825, April 20, 1995, www.fas.org/sgp/clinton/eo12958.html.

57. Gotein and Shapiro, *Reducing Overclassification Through Accountability*; PIDB, "Transforming the Security Classification System."

58. Eric Lipton, "Don't Look, Don't Read: Government Warns Its Workers Away from WikiLeaks Documents," *New York Times*, December 4, 2010, www.nytimes.com /2010/12/05/world/05restrict.html.

## Chapter 6: Future Warfare

1. See "US Military Cybersecurity by the Numbers," Nextgov, March 19, 2015, www.nextgov.com/cybersecurity/2015/03/us-military-cybersecurity-numbers

/107637/; Federal News Radio, "DHS Defends FY 2016 Cyber Budget Before Senate Subcommittee," April 15, 2015, http://federalnewsradio.com/budget/2015/04 /dhs-defends-fy-2016-cyber-budget-before-senate-subcommittee/.

2. Charles J. Dunlap, Jr., "The Hyper-Personalization of War: Cyber, Big Data and the Changing Face of Conflict," *Georgetown Journal of International Affairs* 15 (2014): 111.

3. Gabriella Blum, "The Individualization of War: From War to Policing in the Regulation of Armed Conflicts," *Law and War*, ed. Austin Sarat et al. (Redwood City, CA: Stanford University Press, 2013).

4. Daniel Ventre, ed., *Cyberwar and Information Warfare* (Hoboken, NJ: John Wiley & Sons, 2012).

5. "'ISIL Website' Names and Urges Killing of 100 US Troops," Al Jazeera, March 22, 2015, www.aljazeera.com/news/2015/03/website-names-urges-killing-100 -troops-150321214110673.html.

6. Andrew Hessel, Marc Goodman, and Steven Kotler, "Hacking the President's DNA," *The Atlantic*, November 2012, www.theatlantic.com/magazine/archive /2012/11/hacking-the-presidents-dna/309147/.

7. "Call to Action," Campaign to Stop Killer Robots, accessed January 23, 2016, www .stopkillerrobots.org/call-to-action/.

8. "Seize the Opportunity for Action," Campaign to Stop Killer Robots, accessed January 23, 2016, www.stopkillerrobots.org/2013/11/seize-the-opportunity-for -action/; www.stopkillerrobots.org/.

9. John Markoff, "Planes Without Pilots," *New York Times*, April 6, 2015, www.nytimes .com/2015/04/07/science/planes-without-pilots.html; Rachel Nuwer, "Computers Can Tell if You're Really in Pain—Even Better than People Can," *Smithsonian*, April 30, 2014, www.smithsonianmag.com/smart-news/computers-are-better-people -differentiating-between-real-and-faked-expressions-pain-180951263/?no-ist; Rachel Fobar, "Meet the Machine That Could Replace Anesthesiologists," *Popular Science*, May 12, 2015, www.popsci.com/meet-machine-could-replace-anesthesi ologists.

10. "Shaking the Foundations: The Human Rights Implications of Killer Robots," *Human Rights Watch*, 2104, www.hrw.org/sites/default/files/reports/arms0514 _ForUpload_0.pdf.

11. "Offense Analysis: United States, 2010–2014," Federal Bureau of Investigation, August 17, 2015, https://www.fbi.gov/about-us/cjis/ucr/crime-in-the-u.s/2014 /crime-in-the-u.s.-2014/tables/table-7; "Decrease in 2014 Violent Crimes, Property Crimes," FBI, September 28, 2015, https://www.fbi.gov/news/stories/2015 /september/latest-crime-stats-released/latest-crime-stats-released.

12. Stanley Milgram, "Behavioral Study of Obedience," *The Journal of Abnormal and Social Psychology* 67, no. 4 (1963): 371. See also Thomas Blass, ed., *Obedience to*

*Authority: Current Perspectives on the Milgram Paradigm* (Hove, UK: Psychology Press, 1999).

13. Department of Defense, "Active Denial Technology Fact Sheet," Non-Lethal Weapons Program (April 10, 2015), http://jnlwp.defense.gov/PressRoom/FactSheets /ArticleView/tabid/4782/Article/577989/active-denial-technology-fact-sheet.aspx.

14. Maj. Darrin Haas, "Flash-Bang Mortars: Nonlethal Stun Grenades in Development Could Enable Troops to Counter Insurgent Attacks Without Risking Civilian Casualties," *In the News*, Department of Defense, Non-Lethal Weapons Program, May 5, 2015, http://jnlwp.defense.gov/PressRoom/InTheNews/tabid/4777/Article /587950/flash-bang-mortars-nonlethal-stun-grenades-in-development-could -enable-troops-t.aspx.

15. Department of Defense, "Ocular Interruption," Non-Lethal Weapons Program, http://jnlwp.defense.gov/DevelopingNonLethalWeapons/OcularInterruption .aspx; Department of Defense, "Radio Frequency Vehicle Stopper," Non-Lethal Weapons Program, http://jnlwp.defense.gov/FutureNonLethalWeapons/Radio FrequencyVehicleStopper.aspx.

## Chapter 7: What's an Army For?

1. Gen. Ray Odierno, "Regionally Aligned Forces: A New Model for Building Partnerships," *Army Live: The Official Blog of the U.S. Army*, March 22, 2012, http:// armylive.dodlive.mil/index.php/2012/03/aligned-forces/.

2. Interview notes on file with author.

3. Farnaz Fassihi, "Two Novice Gumshoes Charted the Capture of Saddam Hussein," *Wall Street Journal*, December 18, 2003, http://online.wsj.com/news/articles /SB107170894237083800.

4. Lance Bacon, "New World-Wide Deployments: Who's Going Where," *Army Times*, June 3, 2013, www.armytimes.com/article/20130603/NEWS/306030006/New -world-wide-deployments-Who-s-going-where.

5. Sgt. Daniel Stoutamire, "Classes Prepare Soldiers for AFRICOM," *Fort Riley News*, May 14, 2013, www.riley.army.mil/News/ArticleDisplay/tabid/98/Article/471811 /classes-prepare-soldiers-for-africom.aspx.

6. "3-2 Stryker and Japanese Unit Conclude Their First Decisive Action Rotation," *High Desert Warrior: Aerotech News*, February 7, 2014, www.aerotechnews.com /ntcfortirwin/2014/02/07/3-2-stryker-brigade-combat-team-7th-id-and-japanese -unit-conclude-their-first-decisive-action-rotation/.

7. Maj. Will Cox, "Georgia's Army National Guard Building Security in the Americas," Defense Video and Imagery Distribution System, January 24, 2014, www.dvidshub .net/news/119615/georgias-army-national-guard-building-security-americas# .Ux9Ie_RdW1I.

8. Eric Schmitt, "U.S. Army Hones Antiterror Strategy for Africa, in Kansas," *New York Times*, October 18, 2013, www.nytimes.com/2013/10/19/world/africa/us -prepares-to-train-african-forces-to-fight-terror.html?_r=0.

9. Nick Turse, "Why Is the US Military Averaging More Than a Mission a Day in Africa?," *The Nation*, March 27, 2014, www.thenation.com/article/why-us-military -averaging-more-mission-day-africa/.

10. Jason Ditz, "Into Africa: US to Send Troops to 35 Nations Next Year," blog post on Antiwar.com, December 24, 2012, http://news.antiwar.com/2012/12/24/into -africa-us-to-send-troops-to-35-nations-next-year/.

11. Interview notes on file with author.

12. Gary Sheftick, "ARCENT Says Future Hinges on Regional Alignments," U.S. Army Website, October 28, 2013, www.army.mil/article/114027/ARCENT_says_future _hinges_on_regional_alignments/.

13. Schmitt, "U.S. Army Hones Antiterror Strategy for Africa, in Kansas."

14. Mindy Anderson, "USARAF Training Provides Africans Insight into the Greater Need," U.S. Army Africa Public Affairs, United States Africa Command, February 6, 2014, www.africom.mil/Newsroom/Article/11801/usaraf-training-provides -africans-insight-into-the-greater-need.

15. Interview notes on file with author.

16. Ibid.

17. Prepared Statement of Gen. Ray Odierno, Chief of Staff of the Army, to House Appropriations Subcommittee on Defense, House of Representatives, May 8, 2013, www.army.mil/article/103164/May_8__2013____CSA_testimony_to_House _Appropriations_Subcommittee_on_Defense/.

18. "The Army Vision: Strategic Advantage in a Complex World," U.S. Army, 2015, accessed January 23, 2016, http://usacac.army.mil/sites/default/files/publications /TheArmyVision.pdf.

## Chapter 8: What We've Made It

1. Ernesto Londoño, "Study: Iraq, Afghan War Costs to Top $4 Trillion," *Washington Post*, March 28, 2013, https://www.washingtonpost.com/world/national-security /study-iraq-afghan-war-costs-to-top-4-trillion/2013/03/28/b82a5dce-97ed-11e2 -814b-063623d80a60_story.html.

2. Clausewitz, *On War*, 75.

3. "Military Careers," U.S. Bureau of Labor Statistics 2015, accessed January 23, 2016, www.bls.gov/ooh/military/military-careers.htm.

4. Dave Baiocchi, *Measuring Army Deployments to Iraq and Afghanistan*, RAND Corporation, 2013, www.rand.org/content/dam/rand/pubs/research_reports/RR 100/RR145/RAND_RR145.pdf.

5. Nese F. DeBruyne and Anne Leland, *American War and Military Operations Casualties: Lists and Statistics* (CRS Report No. RL32492) (Washington, DC: Congressional Research Service, January 2, 2015), www.fas.org/sgp/crs/natsec/RL32492 .pdf.

6. See Greg Jaffe, "U.S. Model for a Future War Fans Tensions with China and Inside Pentagon," *Washington Post*, August 1, 2012, www.washingtonpost.com/world /national-security/us-model-for-a-future-war-fans-tensions-with-china-and -inside-pentagon/2012/08/01/gJQAC6F8PX_print.html. Just as the services jostle for preeminence, so too do the combatant commands. The shift in the balance power from the services to the combatant commands—particularly the geographic combatant commands—is another interesting story of the last few decades. Contrary to popular assumptions, "the Army" and "the Navy" don't make operational decisions about where, when, and how to fight: these days, it's the geographic combatant commands such as Central Command and Pacific Command that control such decisions, with the services unhappily reduced to mere providers of people, equipment, and money.

7. Department of Defense, *2013 Demographics: Profile of the Military Community*, accessed January 22, 2016, www.militaryonesource.mil/12038/MOS/Reports/2013 -Demographics-Report.pdf.

8. "Military Recruitment 2010," National Priorities Project, 2011, accessed January 23, 2016, http://nationalpriorities.org/analysis/2011/military-recruitment-2010/; Sherea Watkins and James Sherk, "Who Serves in the U.S. Military? The Demographics of Enlisted Troops and Officers," Heritage Foundation, August 21, 2008, www.heritage.org/research/reports/2008/08/who-serves-in-the-us-military-the -demographics-of-enlisted-troops-and-officers.

9. Richard Pérez-Peña, "U.S. Bachelor Degree Rate Passes Milestone," *New York Times*, February 23, 2012, www.nytimes.com/2012/02/24/education/census-finds -bachelors-degrees-at-record-level.html?_r=0.

10. "Profile of Veterans: 2011," *National Center for Veterans Analysis and Statistics*, March 2013, www.va.gov/vetdata/docs/SpecialReports/Minority_Veterans_2011 .pdf; Rosa Brooks, "Uncle Sam Wants Who?," *Foreign Policy*, July 31, 2013, http:// foreignpolicy.com/2013/07/31/uncle-sam-wants-who/.

11. Jason K. Dempsey, *Our Army: Soldiers, Politics, and American Civil-Military Relations* (Princeton, NJ: Princeton University Press, 2009), 93.

12. Heritage Foundation, "Military Enlisted Recruit to Population Ratios, By Region," accessed January 22, 2016, www.heritage.org/static/reportimages/E8F05D 884C7E78E45A200DC953ED3854.gif.

13. Tim Kane, "The Demographics of Military Enlistment After 9/11," November 2005, www.heritage.org/research/reports/2005/11/the-demographics-of-military -enlistment-after-9-11.

14. In 2010, the 10 most densely populated states produced 1.8 recruits per thousand 18–24 year olds, while the 10 least densely populated states produced 2.4 recruits per thousand. My analysis is drawn from recruit numbers provided by the National Priorities Project, "Military Recruitment 2010."

15. Department of Defense, *2013 Demographics*.

16. National Priorities Project, "Military Recruitment 2010."

## Part III: How We Got Here

### Chapter 9: Putting War into a Box

1. Evidence of organized warfare goes back at least 10,000 years. In the 1960s, archaeologists working in Northern Sudan found cemeteries full of 13,000-year-old bodies showing evidence of violent death; some had stone arrowheads and spear tips embedded in their bones. In Australia, 10,000-year-old rock art depicts scenes of combat between groups. As Harvard archaeologist Steven LeBlanc and Kathleen Register conclude in *Constant Battles: The Myth of the Peaceful, Noble Savage*, "*everyone* had warfare in *all* time periods" (New York: St. Martin's Press, 2003), 8. See also Raymond C. Kelly, "The Evolution of Lethal Intergroup Violence," *Proceedings of the National Academy of Sciences U.S.A.* 102, no. 43 (October 25, 2005): 15294–98, www.ncbi.nlm.nih.gov/pmc/articles/PMC1266108/; F. Wendorf, "Site 117: A Nubian Final Paleolithic Graveyard Near Jebel Sahaba, Sudan," in F. Wendorf, ed., *The Prehistory of Nubia* (Dallas, TX: Southern Methodist University, 1968), 954–87; Paul Tacon and Christopher Chippindale, "Australia's Ancient Warriors: Changing Depictions of Fighting in the Rock Art of Arnhern Land," *Cambridge Archaeological Journal* 4, no. 2 (1994): 211–48.

2. Toby A. H. Wilkinson, "What a King Is This: Narmer and the Concept of the Ruler," *The Journal of Egyptian Archaeology* (2000): 23–32.

3. Andrew George, trans., *The Epic of Gilgamesh* (London: Penguin, 1999), 197–98.

4. *Jacobellis v. Ohio*, 378 U.S. 184 (Potter Stewart concurrence) (June 22, 1964).

5. "War," *Stanford Encyclopedia of Philosophy*, http://plato.stanford.edu/entries/war/.

6. Clausewitz, *On War*, 87.

7. Sir Michael Howard and John F. Guilmartin, "Two Historians in Technology and War," U.S. Army Strategic Studies Institute, July 1994, accessed January 24, 2016, www.au.af.mil/au/awc/awcgate/ssi/2hist.pdf.

8. Andreas Paulus and Mindia Vashakmadze, "Asymmetrical War and the Notion of Armed Conflict—A Tentative Conceptualization," *International Review of the Red Cross* 91, no. 873 (March 2009): 97, https://www.icrc.org/eng/assets/files/other/irrc-873-paulus-vashakmadze.pdf. In a 1993 essay, H. P. Gasser suggests that "any

use of armed force by one State against the territory of another, triggers the applicability of the Geneva Conventions between the two States. . . . It is . . . of no concern whether or not the party attacked resists." Modern German military regulations add that "an international armed conflict exists if one party uses force of arms against another party. . . . The use of military force by individual persons or groups of persons will not suffice." See "How Is the Term 'Armed Conflict' Defined in International Humanitarian Law?," International Committee of the Red Cross (ICRC) Opinion Paper, March 2008, accessed January 24, 2016, https://www.icrc .org/eng/assets/files/other/opinion-paper-armed-conflict.pdf. Meanwhile, Swedish scholars at Uppsala University propose adding a quantitative component, defining armed conflict as "a contested incompatibility which concerns government and/or territory where the use of armed force between two parties, of which at least one is the government of a state, results in at least 25 battle-related deaths." See "Definition of Armed Conflict," Department of Peace and Conflict Research, Uppsala Conflict Data Program, Uppsala University, accessed January 30, 2016, www.pcr.uu.se/research/ucdp/definitions/definition_of_armed_conflict/.

9. International Criminal Tribunal for the Prosecution for the former Yugoslavia (ICTY), *The Prosecutor v. Dusko Tadic*, Judgment, IT-94-1-T, 7 May 1997, para. 561–68, emphasis added. Meanwhile, the International Committee of the Red Cross suggests that "in order to distinguish an armed conflict . . . from less serious forms of violence, such as internal disturbances and tensions, riots or acts of banditry. . . . First, the hostilities must reach a minimum level of intensity. This may be the case, for example, when the hostilities are of a collective character or when the government is obliged to use military force against the insurgents, instead of mere police forces. Second, non-governmental groups involved in the conflict must be considered as 'parties to the conflict,' meaning that they possess organized armed forces. This means, for example, that these forces have to be under a certain command structure and have the capacity to sustain military operations." See ICRC, "How Is the Term 'Armed Conflict' Defined in International Humanitarian Law?"

10. John C. Ewers, "Blackfoot Raiding for Horses and Scalps," in *Law and Warfare: Studies in the Anthropology of Conflict*, ed. Paul Bohannan (Garden City, NY: Natural History Press, 1967), 32–44.

11. See David J. Wishart, *Encyclopedia of the Great Plains Indians* (Lincoln: University of Nebraska Press, 2007), 48; Colin Calloway, *The Shawnees and the War for America* (New York: Penguin, 2007), 16; Nancy Bonvillain, *The Teton Sioux* (New York: Chelsea House, 2004), 35; Stan Hoig, *The Cherokees and Their Chiefs: In the Wake of Empire* (Fayetteville: University of Arkansas Press, 1998), 13; Mark S. Mosko and Frederick H. Damon, *On the Order of Chaos: Social Anthropology and the Science of Chaos* (New York: Berghahn Books, 2005), 184–85.

12. George W. Harley, "Masks as Agents of Social Control in Northeast Liberia," *Papers of the Peabody Museum of American Archaeology and Ethnology* 32 (Cambridge, MA: Harvard University Press,1950).

13. Keith Otterbein, "The Evolution of Zulu Warfare," in Bohannan, ed., *Law and Warfare*.

14. Rafael Karsten, *The Civilization of the South American Indians* (New York: Routledge, 2010), 39.

15. Simon Harrison, *The Mask of War: Violence, Ritual, and the Self in Melanesia* (Manchester: Manchester University Press, 1993), 113, 121.

16. Harrison, *The Mask of War*, 95

17. Damon and Mosko, *On the Order of Chaos*, 182.

18. King James, Numbers 31:19, accessed January 24, 2016, http://biblehub.com/numbers/31-19.htm.

19. Bernard J. Verkamp, *The Moral Treatment of Returning Warriors in Early Medieval and Modern Times* (Scranton, PA: University of Scranton Press, 1993), 11.

20. See Shannon French, *The Code of the Warrior: Exploring Warrior Values Past and Present* (Lanham, MD: Rowman & Littlefield, 2003).

21. Steven Silver and John P. Wilson, "Native American Healing and Purification Rituals for War Stress," in John P. Wilson, Zev Harel, and Boaz Kahana, eds., *Human Adaptation to Extreme Stress: From the Holocaust to Vietnam* (New York: Plenum Press, 1988), 337.

22. Paulo Granjo, "Back Home: Post-War Cleansing Rituals in Mozambique," in B. Nicolini, ed., *Magical Practices, Witchcraft, and Warfare in the African Continent (XIX–XX Century)* (Lampeter, UK: Edwin Mellen Press, 2006), www.ics.ul.pt/rdonweb-docs/cleansing%20rituals%20Livro.pdf.

23. See, e.g., Peter Uvin and Charles Mironko, "Western and Local Approaches to Justice in Rwanda," vol. 9, *Global Governance*, p. 219 (2003).

24. All quotes are from Rosa Ehrenreich and Yoden Thonden, "The Scars of Death: Children Abducted by the Lord's Resistance Army in Uganda," Human Rights Watch, 1997, www.hrw.org/legacy/reports97/uganda/.

25. For a fuller account of the origins, rituals, and actions of the LRA, see ibid. See also Rosa Ehrenreich, "The Stories We Must Tell: Ugandan Children and the Atrocities of the Lord's Resistance Army," *Africa Today* 45 (1998): 79–102.

26. United States Military Academy, "Bugle Notes: Learn This!," accessed January 23, 2016, www.west-point.org/academy/malo-wa/inspirations/buglenotes.html.

## Chapter 10: Taming War

1. F. Max Müller and Georg Bühler, *The Laws of Manu: With Extracts from the Seven Commentaries* (Kessinger Publishing, 2004), www.sacred-texts.com/hin/manu/manu07.html.

2. Sheng Hongsheng, "The Evolution of Law of War," *Chinese Journal of International Politics* 1, no. 2 (2006): 267–301.

3. Adriaan Lanni, "The Laws of War in Ancient Greece," *Law and History Review* 26, no. 3 (2008): 469–89.

4. Marcus Tullius Cicero, *De Officiis*, trans. Walter Miller (Project Guttenberg, 2014), accessed January 24, 2016, www.gutenberg.org/files/47001/47001-h/47001-h.html.

5. St. Augustine, *City of God*, trans. Marcus Dods (Catholic Way Publishing, 2015), Book 1, 21.

6. Roy Jackson, *What Is Islamic Philosophy?* (New York: Routledge, 2014), 347. See also Majid Khadduri, *War and Peace in the Law of Islam* (Clark, NJ: The Lawbook Exchange, 2006).

7. See Theodor Meron, "Medieval and Renaissance Ordinances of War: Codifying Discipline and Humanity," in *War Crimes Law Comes of Age* (Oxford, UK: Oxford University Press, 1999), 1.

8. Shakespeare, *Henry V*, Act III, Scene 6.

9. Meron, "Medieval and Renaissance Ordinances of War," 5.

10. Marcus Tullius Cicero, *Pro Milone* (Torino, Italy: Paravia, 1969), 17.

11. Thomas Sergeant Perry, ed., *The Life and Letters of Francis Lieber* (Boston: James R. Osgood & Company, 1882), 12.

12. Ibid., 404.

13. Ibid., 316–17.

14. John Fabian Witt, *Lincoln's Code: The Laws of War in American History* (New York: Free Press, 2012), 187.

15. Quoted in ibid., 187.

16. Rick Beard, "The Lieber Codes," Opinionator Blog, *New York Times*, April 24, 2013, http://opinionator.blogs.nytimes.com/2013/04/24/the-lieber-codes/.

17. Instructions for the Government of the Armies of the United States in the Field (Lieber Code), General Order No. 100 (Department of War, April 24, 1863), www.yale.edu/lawweb/avalon/lieber.htm.

18. Henri Dunant, A *Memory of Solferino* (Geneva, Switzerland: International Committee of the Red Cross, 1959), 16, https://www.icrc.org/eng/assets/files/publications/icrc-002-0361.pdf.

19. Ibid., 19.

20. Ibid., 44.

21. Ibid., 127.

22. Convention Between the United States and Other Powers Respecting the Laws and Customs of War on Land, Oct. 18, 1907, 36 Stat. 2277; Regulations Respecting the Laws and Customs of War on Land, October 18, 1907, 36 Stat. 2295.

23. Treaty Between the United States and Other Powers Providing for the Renunciation of War as an Instrument of National Policy (Kellogg-Briand Pact), August 27, 1928, art. I, 46 Stat. 2343, 2345.

24. Portions of this section are drawn from Rosa Brooks, "Civilians and Armed Conflict," originally published in Jared Genser and Bruno Stagno Ugarte, eds., *The United Nations Security Council in the Age of Human Rights* (New York: Cambridge University Press, 2014), 35–67.

25. See Tony Long, "March 9, 1945: Burning the Heart Out of the Enemy," *Wired*, March 9, 2011, www.wired.com/thisdayintech/2011/03/0309incendiary-bombs-kill -100000-tokyo/.

26. Charter of the United Nations (1945), http://treaties.un.org/doc/Publication/CTC /uncharter.pdf.

27. See, e.g., Joshua Goldstein, *Winning the War on War: The Decline of Armed Conflict Worldwide* (New York: Dutton, 2012). But how much violence has declined, and whether this trend will be lasting, is disputed. See "The Forum: The Decline of War," *International Studies Review* 15, no. 3 (September 2013): 396–419.

28. While enforcement of human rights law remains wildly inconsistent, the post–World War II sea change should not be underestimated. In the years following the war, human rights were elaborated and codified into binding treaties: in 1948, the U.N. General Assembly passed the Universal Declaration of Human Rights, and the next decades saw the drafting and entry into force of treaties protecting civil and political rights, along with treaties prohibiting genocide, torture, and racial discrimination. Some of these treaties contained mechanisms through which individuals who felt that their rights had been violated could complain to international bodies, and most treaties obligated states to pass domestic laws to enable people to go to court over violations of their internationally guaranteed rights. Over time, new regional and international bodies—including courts—sprang up to resolve and adjudicate claims of human rights violations.

29. In 1977, an international conference led to two Additional Protocols to the Geneva Conventions, both of which have been widely ratified. Human rights treaties have also added constraints on wartime behavior: for instance, the Genocide Convention, which entered into force in 1951, declares that genocide—defined as "acts committed with intent to destroy, in whole or in part, a national, ethnical, racial or religious group"—is a crime under international law "whether committed in time of peace or in time of war." The Convention Against Torture, which entered into force in 1987, similarly states that "No exceptional circumstances whatsoever, whether a state of war or a threat of war, internal political instability or any other public emergency, may be invoked as a justification of torture." See Protocol Additional to the Geneva Conventions of 12 August 1949, and Relating to the Protection of Victims of International Armed Conflicts, June 8, 1977, 1125 U.N.T.S. 4;

Protocol Additional to the Geneva Conventions of 12 August 1949, and Relating to the Protection of Victims of Non-International Armed Conflicts, June 8, 1977, 1125 U.N.T.S. 609; Genocide Convention; Convention Against Torture and Other Cruel, Inhuman or Degrading Treatment or Punishment (1984). More recently, the international criminal tribunals for Yugoslavia and the recently created International Criminal Court have begun to develop an increasingly elaborate jurisprudence on war crimes, genocide, and crimes against humanity.

30. Richard P. DiMeglio, "Training Army Judge Advocates to Advise Commanders as Operational Law Attorneys" (2013), accessed January 24, 2016, www.loc.gov/rr/frd/Military_Law/pdf/Training-Army-JA.pdf.

31. Field Manual 1-04, *Legal Support to the Operational Army* (2013), accessed January 24, 2016, http://armypubs.army.mil/doctrine/DR_pubs/dr_a/pdf/fm1_04.pdf.

32. Janine Davidson, *Lifting the Fog of Peace: How Americans Learned to Fight Modern War* (Ann Arbor: University of Michigan Press, 2011); U.S. Army Center of Military History, "Rebuilding the Army: Vietnam to Desert Storm," in *American Military History*, Vol. 2, 372–73, accessed January 24, 2016, www.history.army.mil/books/amh-v2/pdf/chapter12.pdf.

33. See "Judge Advocate and Other Military Service Careers for Lawyers," Chapman University School of Law, www.chapman.edu/law/_files/students/military-careers.pdf.

34. Testimony of Geoffrey Corn, "The Law of Armed Conflict, the Use of Military Force, and the 2001 Authorization for Use of Military Force," Hearing Before the Committee on Armed Services, United States Senate, 113th Cong, 1st Sess., May 16, 2013, www.armed-services.senate.gov/imo/media/doc/lawofarmedconflict_useofmilitaryforce_2001aumf_hearing_051613.pdf.

35. Michael M. Phillips, "Civilians in Crosshairs Slow Troops," *Wall Street Journal*, February 21, 2010, www.wsj.com/articles/SB10001424052748704751304575079741450028512.

36. "Obama's Rules of Engagement: Calling Lawyers for Permission to Kill Terrorists," *HotAir*, February 23, 2010, http://hotair.com/archives/2010/02/23/obamas-rules-of-engagement-calling-lawyers-for-permission-to-kill-terrorists/.

37. Alberto Gonzales, "Memorandum for the President, Subject: Decision to Re Application of the Geneva Convention on Prisoners of War to the Conflict with Al Qaeda and the Taliban," January 25, 2002, http://nsarchive.gwu.edu/NSAEBB/NSAEBB127/02.01.25.pdf.

38. See generally Brooks, "War Everywhere." This argument also draws on Rosa Brooks, "The Politics of the Geneva Conventions: Avoiding Formalist Traps," 46 *Virginia Journal of International Law*, 197–207 (2005).

39. Rosa Brooks, "Bush's Jane Fonda-esque Mistake," *Los Angeles Times*, July 30, 2005, http://articles.latimes.com/2005/jul/30/opinion/oe-brooks30.

## Chapter 11: An Optimistic Enterprise

1. This section is adapted from an article I originally published in the *Virginia Journal of International Law*. See Rosa Brooks, "Law in the Heart of Darkness: Atrocity and Duress," 43 *Virginia Journal of International Law*, 861–88 (2003).

2. See Judgment, *Prosecutor v. Erdemovic*, Case No. IT-96-22-A (I.C.T.Y., Appeals Chamber, Oct. 7, 1997). This and all other ICTY documents relating to the Erdemovic case, including trial chamber transcripts, are available at www.icty.org/case/erdemovic/4.

3. See Elizabeth Neuffer, "War Crimes Probe Pains Srebrenica Genocide; Charges Stir Range of Emotions in Bosnian City," *Boston Globe*, April 2, 1996; "Serbia Delivers Witnesses to Bosnia War Crimes Tribunal," *Los Angeles Times*, March 31, 1996.

4. Joint Separate Opinion of Judge MacDonald and Judge Vohrah, *Prosecutor v. Erdemovic*, 1997.

5. Separate and Dissenting Opinion of Judge Cassese, *Prosecutor v. Erdemovic*, 1997.

6. Separate and Dissenting Opinion of Judge Stephen, *Prosecutor v. Erdemovic*, Appeals Chamber, 1997.

7. The Srebrenica massacre eventually had substantial political fallout in the Netherlands. See "Dutch Government Quits over Srebrenica," BBC, April 16, 2002, http://news.bbc.co.uk/2/hi/europe/1933144.stm; "Dutch State Liable for 300 Srebrenica Massacre Deaths," Associated Press via *Guardian*, July 16, 2014, www.theguardian.com/world/2014/jul/16/dutch-liable-srebrenica-massacre-deaths.

## Chapter 12: Making War

1. Charles Tilly, "Reflections on the History of European State Making," in Charles Tilly, ed., *The Formation of National States in Western Europe* (Princeton, NJ: Princeton University Press, 1975), 42.

2. See Rosa Brooks, "The Trickle-Down War," 32 *Yale Law & Policy Review*, 583–602 (2014).

3. Tilly, "Reflections on the History of European State Making." See also Charles Tilly, *Coercion, Capital, and European States, AD 900–1992* (Oxford, UK: Blackwell, 1990).

4. See, e.g., John A. Hall and G. John Ikenberry, *The State* (Minneapolis: University of Minnesota Press, 1989), 40–41; Anthony Giddens, *The Nation State and Violence* (Berkeley: University of California Press, 1985), 112; Jan Glete, *War and the State in Early Modern Europe* (London: Routledge, 2002), 216; Timothy Besley and Torsten Persson, "The Origins of State Capacity: Property Rights, Taxation, and Politics," *American Economic Review* 99, no. 4 (September 2009), 1218–1244.

5. Paul Waldman, "The 13-Year War," *The American Prospect*, January 18, 2013, http://prospect.org/article/13-year-war.

6. "Chart: US Troop Levels in Iraq," CNN, October 21, 2011, www.cnn.com/2011/10

/21/world/meast/chart-us-troops-iraq/index.html. Overall, some 2.5 million U.S. military personnel had deployed to Iraq or Afganistan by 2013. See Chris Adama, "Millions Went to War in Iraq, Afghanistan, Leaving Many with Lifelong Scars," McClatchy News, March 14, 2013, www.mcclatchydc.com/2013/03/14/185880 /millions-went-to-war-in-iraq-afghanistan.html.

7. A version of this section previously appeared in the *Stanford Law & Policy Review*. See Rosa Brooks, "Duck-Rabbits and Drones: Legal Indeterminacy in the War on Terror," 25 *Stan. L. & Pol'y Rev*. 301–15 (2014).

8. Antonio Cassese, "Terrorism Is Also Disrupting Some Crucial Legal Categories of International Law," 12 *European Journal of International Law* 993, 993 (2001).

9. Michael James, "Senate Republicans Block James Cole, Key Obama Nominee at Justice Dept.," ABC News, May 9, 2011, http://abcnews.go.com/blogs/politics/2011 /05/senate-republicans-block-james-cole-key-obama-nominee-at-justice-dept.

10. James M. Cole, "A Prosecutor Must Protect Rights of All," *Legal Times*, September 9, 2002, www.law.com/jsp/article.jsp?id=900005532110.

11. Amnesty International, "Yemen: The Rule of Law Sidelined in the Name of Security," September 23, 2003, www.amnesty.org/en/library/asset/MDE31/006/2003 /en/1201e721-d6a7-11dd-ab95-a13b602c0642/mde310062003en.pdf. More than a decade later, variants of this view continue to have strong adherents, particularly within the European legal community and within the human rights community. As a recent European Council on Foreign Relations report by Anthony Dworkin notes, most European legal scholars and courts "[reject] the notion of a de-territorialised global armed conflict between the U.S. and al-Qaeda," and believe that although a "confrontation between a state and a non-state group" can in theory rise to the level of an armed conflict, it can only do so if "the non-state group meets a threshold for organization [when] . . . there are intense hostilities between the two parties . . . [and] fighting [is] concentrated within a specific zone (or zones) of hostilities. . . . The default European assumption would be that the threat of terrorism should be confronted within a law enforcement framework." Anthony Dworkin, "Drones and Targeted Killing: Defining a European Position," European Council on Foreign Relations, 2013, accessed January 24, 2016, http:// ecfr.eu/page/-/ECFR84_DRONES_BRIEF.pdf.

12. "Bush's Remarks to the Nation on the Terrorist Attacks," *New York Times*, September 12, 2001, www.nytimes.com/2001/09/12/us/a-day-of-terror-bush-s-remarks -to-the-nation-on-the-terrorist-attacks.html.

13. George W. Bush, "News Conference," *Washington Post*, September 13, 2001, www .washingtonpost.com/wp-srv/nation/transcripts/bushtext2_091301.html.

14. John C. Yoo and James C. Ho, "The Status of Terrorists," 44 *Virginia Journal of International Law* 207, 211 (2003). State Department Legal Advisor William H. Taft agreed: "The law of armed conflict provides the most appropriate legal framework

for regulating the use of force in the war on terrorism." See William H. Taft IV, "The Law of Armed Conflict After 9/11: Some Salient Features," 28 Yale J. Int'l L. 319, 320 (2003).

15. Ari Shapiro, "Obama Team Stops Saying 'Global War on Terror' but Doesn't Stop Waging It," NPR, March 11, 2013, www.npr.org/sections/itsallpolitics/2013/03 /11/174034634/obama-team-stops-saying-global-war-on-terror-but-doesnt-stop -waging-it.

16. John O. Brennan, "Remarks: Strengthening Our Security by Adhering to Our Values and Laws," White House, September 16, 2011, www.whitehouse.gov/the -press-office/2011/09/16/remarks-john-o-brennan-strengthening-our-security -adhering-our-values-an.

17. Barack Obama, "Remarks at National Defense University," May 23, 2013. "Crime" and "war" were not the only ways to conceptualize the 9/11 attacks. The events of 9/11 might also have been understood as an "armed attack" of sufficient gravity to trigger an international law right to use armed force for the limited purpose of self-defense, but without triggering a full-scale "armed conflict" between the United States and the perpetrators of the attacks. Understood thusly, the U.S. response to 9/11 would be shaped and constrained not by the laws of war, which permit status-based targeting, but by the somewhat different *jus ad bellum* rules relating to the use of force in self-defense, presumably in conjunction with international human rights law. See generally Laurie R. Blanc, "Targeted Strikes: The Consequences of Blurring the Armed Conflict and Self-Defense Justifications," 38 *William Mitchell Law Review* 1655 (2012).

18. I made an early version of this argument in a 2004 article. See Brooks, "War Everywhere."

19. Ludwig Wittgenstein, *Philosophical Investigations*, trans. G. E. M. Anscombe, 4th ed. (Hoboken, NJ: Wiley-Blackwell, 2009), 22.

20. Ibid., 205.

## Chapter 13: Making the State

1. The concept of "the state" is complex and controversial in and of itself, and scholars have long sought to distinguish between varieties of states and varieties of sovereignty. For the classic legal definition of statehood, see the Montevideo Convention, Article 1: "The state as a person of international law should possess the following qualifications: (a) a permanent population; (b) a defined territory; (c) government; and (d) capacity to enter into relations with the other states." Convention on Rights and Duties of States, Dec. 26, 1933, Art. 1, 49 Stat. 3097, 3100, 165 L.N.T.S. 19, 25. For classic functional definitions of statehood, see Max Weber, *Essays in Sociology*, pp. 77, 78 (H. H. Gerth and C. Wright Mills, eds. and trans.,

1958) ("[the] state is a human community that (successfully) claims the monopoly of the legitimate use of physical force within a given territory"). See also Ernest Gellner, *Nations and Nationalism* 3 (1983); and see generally Norbert Elias, *The Civilizing Process*, Edmund Jephcott, trans. (London: Blackwell Publishing, 2001); Robert Cooper, *The Breaking of Nations: Order and Chaos in the Twenty-First Century* (New York: Grove Press, 2004); Alexander Wendt, "Why a World State Is Inevitable," 9, *European Journal of International Relations* 491 (2003).

2. This section is adapted from an essay originally published in the *University of Chicago Law Review*. See Rosa Brooks, "Failed States, or the State as Failure?," 72 *University of Chicago Law Review* 1159–96 (2005).

3. See Michael J. Mazarr, "The Rise and Fall of the Failed-State Paradigm." *Foreign Affairs* 93, no. 1 (2014).

4. See, e.g., Jonathan Di John, "The Concept, Causes and Consequences of Failed States: A Critical Review of the Literature and Agenda for Research with Specific Reference to Sub-Saharan Africa," *European Journal of Development Research* 22, no. 1 (2010): 10–30; Robert I. Rotberg, "The New Nature of Nation-State Failure," *Washington Quarterly* 25 (Summer 2002): 85–96.

5. Global Security, "Islamic State of Iraq and the Levant/Al-Qaeda in Iraq (AQI): ISIS/ Caliphate—Funding and Strength," accessed January 23, 2016, www.globalsecurity .org/military/world/para/isil-2.htm.

6. Sam Ro, "Apple Has More Cash on Hand than All These Different Countries," *Business Insider*, April 7, 2014, www.businessinsider.com/global-cash-reserves-companies -nations-2014-4; James Kirkup, "Sony vs North Korea: Some Companies Are Bigger than Countries. So What?," *The Telegraph*, December 18, 2014, www.tele graph.co.uk/news/worldnews/asia/northkorea/11300895/Sony-vs-North-Korea -some-companies-are-bigger-than-countries.-So-what.html.

7. See, e.g., Peter Andreas and Angelica Duran-Martinez. "The International Politics of Drugs and Illicit Trade in the Americas," Watson Institute for International Studies Research Paper 2013-05 (2013); Liana Eustacia Reyes, and Shlomi Dinar, "The Convergence of Terrorism and Transnational Crime in Central Asia," *Studies in Conflict & Terrorism* 38, no. 5 (2015): 380–93; Michael Miklaucic, Jacqueline Brewer, and James G. Stavridis, *Convergence: Illicit Networks and National Security in the Age of Globalization* (Washington, DC: National Defense University Press, 2013).

8. See, e.g., Steven D. Krasner, "The Hole in the Whole: Sovereignty, Shared Sovereignty, and International Law," 25 *Michigan Journal of International Law* 1075, 1077 (2004).

9. A vast and influential body of literature has documented this. See, e.g., William McNeill, *A History of Human Community, Prehistory to Present* (Boston: Pearson, 1996); E. J. Hobsbawm, *Nations and Nationalism Since 1780*, 2nd ed. (Cambridge, UK: Cambridge University Press, 2012); Hans Kohn, *The Idea of Nationalism: A*

*Study in Its Origins and Background* (New York: Macmillan, 1944); Alexander Wendt, *Social Theory of International Politics* (Cambridge, UK: Cambridge University Press, 1999).

10. Henry Samuel, "Vendée French Call for Revolution Massacre to Be Termed 'Genocide,'" *The Telegraph*, December 26, 2008, www.telegraph.co.uk/news/world news/europe/france/3964724/Vende-French-call-for-revolution-massacre-to -be-termed-genocide.html.

11. Jonathan Fenby, *France on the Brink: A Great Civilization in the New Century* (New York: Arcade, 2014), Ch. 9.

12. See, e.g, Benedict Anderson, *Imagined Communities: Reflections on the Origin and Spread of Nationalism* (London: Verso, 1983), 4, 6 ("Nationality, or, as one might prefer to put it in view of the world's multiple significations, nation-ness, as well as nationalism, are cultural artifacts of a particular kind," and, quoting Gellner: "Nationalism is not the awakening of nations to self-consciousness: it invents nations where they do not exist"). See also Paul Kahn, *The Question of Sovereignty*, 40 *Stanford Journal of International Law* 259, 268–69 (2004); Eugene Weber, *Peasants into Frenchmen* (Redwood City, CA: Stanford University Press, 1976); Thomas Hylland Eriksen, *Ethnicity and Nationalism: Anthropological Perspectives* (London: Pluto Press, 2002); Leonard M. Thompson, *The Political Mythology of Apartheid* (New Haven, CT: Yale University Press, 1985).

13. See Rosa Brooks, "Making a State by Iron and Blood," *Foreign Policy*, August 19, 2015, http://foreignpolicy.com/2015/08/19/making-a-state-by-iron-and-blood-isis -iraq-syria/.

14. See Charles Tilly, "War-Making and State-Making as Organized Crime," in Peter B. Evans, Dietrich Rueschemeyer, and Theda Skocpol, eds., *Bringing the State Back In* (Cambridge, UK: Cambridge University Press, 1999), 169.

15. See generally Anthony Giddens, *The Nation-State and Violence*, Vol. 2 (Berkeley: University of California Press, 1985); Robert H. Holden, *Armies Without Nations: Public Violence and State Formation in Central America, 1821–1960* (Oxford, UK: Oxford University Press, 2004); Kahn, "The Question of Sovereignty."

16. See Gellner, *Nations and Nationalism*, 125.

## Chapter 14: Un-Making Sovereignty

1. Francis M. Deng, *The Global Challenge of Internal Displacement*, 5 *Washington University Journal of Law & Policy* 141, 154 (2001).

2. Samantha Power, *A Problem from Hell: America and the Age of Genocide* (New York: Basic Books, 2002).

3. For a fine account of Matthew Lukwena's work during the Ebola epidemic, see Blaine Harden, "Dr. Matthew's Passion," *New York Times*, February 18, 2001.

4. See generally Rosa Brooks, "Remarks, Humanitarian Intervention: Evolving Norms, Fragmenting Consensus," 29 *Maryland Journal of International Law*, 161–83 (2014). See also Brooks, "Civilians and Armed Conflict."

5. See Adam Roberts, "NATO's 'Humanitarian War' over Kosovo," 41 *Survival*, 102–120 (1999).

6. The Kosovo air campaign was arguably illegal under international law, since intervening states could offer neither plausible self-defense arguments nor Security Council authorization. See, e.g., Thomas Franck, *Recourse to Force: State Action Against Threats and Armed Attacks* (New York: Cambridge University Press, 2002), 174–91. See also Bruno Simma, "NATO, the UN and the Use of Force: Legal Aspects," *European Journal of International Law* 10, no. 10 (1999): 1, 22.

7. See, e.g., U.N. Security Council Resolution 1244 (1999).

8. Kofi A. Annan, "Two Concepts of Sovereignty," *Economist*, September 18, 1999, www.un.org/news/ossg/sg/stories/kaecon.html.

9. International Commission on Intervention & State Sovereignty, *The Responsibility to Protect* (Ottawa: International Development Research Centre, December 2001), http://responsibilitytoprotect.org/ICISS%20Report.pdf.

10. Ibid., XI.

11. Ibid., XIII.

12. See U.N. Security Council Resolutions 1973 and 1975.

13. See, e.g., Gareth Evans, "Responding to Mass Atrocity Crimes: The Responsibility to Protect (R2P) After Libya and Syria," Public Lecture at the Central European School of Public Policy, October 24, 2012.

14. Louis Charbonneau, "Russia U.N. Veto on Syria Aimed at Crushing West's Crusade," Reuters, February 8, 2012, www.reuters.com/article/2012/02/08/us-un-russia-idUSTRE8170BK20120208.

15. Frederik Pleitgen and Tom Cohen, "'War-Weary' Obama Says Syria Chemical Attack Requires Response," CNN, August 30, 2013, www.cnn.com/2013/08/30/world/europe/syria-civil-war/.

16. "Syria Crisis: David Cameron Makes Case for Military Action," BBC News, August 29, 2013, www.bbc.co.uk/news/uk-politics-23883427.

17. See, e.g., Harold Koh, "Strike on Syria for Chemical Weapons—Not Illegal," *Yale-Global Online*, October 3, 2013, http://yaleglobal.yale.edu/content/strike-syria-chemical-weapons-%25E2%2580%2593-not-illegal.

18. See Colum Lynch, "U.N. Chief Ban Ki-moon Warns G-20 Leaders Against Possible Military Action in Syria," *Washington Post*, September 6, 2013; Krishnadev Calamur, "Where U.S. Allies Stand on a Strike Against Syria," NPR, August 30, 2013, www.npr.org/blogs/parallels/2013/08/30/217189600/where-u-s-allies-stand-on-a-strike-against-syria.

19. Nicholas Watt and Nick Hopkins, "Cameron Forced to Rule Out British Attack

on Syria After MPs Reject Motion," *Guardian*, August 29, 2013, www.theguardian
.com/world/2013/aug/29/cameron-british-attack-syria-mps.

20. See Mark Landler and Jonathan Weisman, "Obama Delays Syria Strike to Focus on
a Russia Plan," *New York Times*, September 11, 2003.

21. See, e.g., "Case Concerning Military and Paramilitary Activities in and Against
Nicaragua" (*Nicaragua v. United States*) ICJ Reports (1986) 14, 25 ILM 1023.

22. "Bush: Don't Wait for Mushroom Cloud," CNN, October 8, 2002, http://edition
.cnn.com/2002/ALLPOLITICS/10/07/bush.transcript/.

23. The cross-border raid reportedly killed several people, including an Iraqi suspected
of being an al Qaeda operative. See, e.g, Nicholas Blandford, "What's Behind the
US Military Raid on Syria?," *Time*, October 27, 2008, www.time.com/time/world
/article/0,8599,1854169,00.html.

24. One difficulty is raised by the fact that the affected state may agree in private to
allow U.S. strikes but object in public. This, and the secrecy surrounding most of
these strikes, makes it difficult to fully evaluate the degree to which consent has
been obtained.

25. See, e.g., U.N. Security Council Resolution 1373, which notes that state must prevent and suppress, in their territories through all lawful means, the financing and
preparation of any acts of terrorism. SC Res. 1373 (2001).

26. John O. Brennan, "Strengthening Our Security by Adhering to Our Values and
Laws," Remarks by John Brennan, Harvard Law School, Cambridge, MA, September 16, 2011, www.whitehouse.gov/the-press-office/2011/09/16/remarks-john
-o-brennan-strengthening-our-security-adhering-our-values-an. Note the circu-
larity: the United States views the use of force as permissible when a state consents,
and also views the use of force as permissible when a state does *not* consent, since
the United States is sole judge of "unwilling or unable."

27. This section draws on arguments I originally made in Rosa Brooks, "Be Careful
What You Wish For: Changing Doctrines, Changing Technologies, and the Lower
Cost of War," *American Society of International Law Proceedings* 106 (2012); Rosa
Brooks, "Strange Bedfellows: The Convergence of Sovereignty-Limiting Doctrines
in Counterterrorist and Human Rights Discourse," *Georgetown Journal of Interna-
tional Affairs* 13, no. 2 (2012); Rosa Brooks, "Lessons for International Law from the
Arab Spring," 28 *American University International Law Review*, 107–12 (2013).

28. From a strictly legal perspective, the security case is arguably stronger than the humanitarian case, since it is bound up with the right to self-defense, which predates
and is reflected in the U.N. Charter.

## Chapter 15: Making the Military

1. See Richard Gabriel and Karen Metz, "A Short History of War: The Armies of Sumer and Akkad, 3500–2200 B.C." (Montgomery, AL: U.S. Air Force Air War College, 1992), accessed January 23, 2016, www.au.af.mil/au/awc/awcgate/gabrmetz /gabr0004.htm; Richard A. Gabriel, *Man and Wound in the Ancient World: A History of Military Medicine from Sumer to the Fall of Constantinople* (Washington, DC: Potomac Books, 2012); The Louvre, "Work: The Stele of Vultures," accessed January 23, 2016, www.louvre.fr/en/oeuvre-notices/stele-vultures.

2. Gabriel and Metz, "A Short History of War." See also Sarah Percy, "Mercenaries," in the *Oxford Bibliography of Military History*, accessed July 24, 2013, www.oxford bibliographies.com/view/document/obo-9780199791279/obo-9780199791279 -0105.xml.

3. David Charles Douglas and George William Greenaway, *English Historical Documents, 1042–1189* (London: Eyre Methuen, 1981), 448.

4. English Bill of Rights, 1689: "An Act Declaring the Rights and Liberties of the Subject and Settling the Succession of the Crown," accessed January 22, 2016, http:// avalon.law.yale.edu/17th_century/england.asp.

5. John Dryden, "Cymon and Iphigenia," in John Hammond and David Hopkins, eds., *The Poems of John Dryden: Volume Five: 1697–1700* (New York: Routledge, 2014), 582.

6. "The Declaration of Independence," accessed January 22, 2016, www.archives.gov /exhibits/charters/declaration_transcript.html.

7. "The Constitution of the United States," accessed January 22, 2016, www.archives .gov/exhibits/charters/constitution_transcript.html.

8. "Charter Granted by Queen Elizabeth to the East India Company, 31 December 1600," accessed January 22, 2016, www.sdstate.edu/projectsouthasia/loader.cfm ?csModule=security/getfile&PageID=857407.

9. James Lancaster, C. R Markha, and John Knight, *The Voyages of Sir James Lancaster, Kt., to the East Indies, with Abstracts of Journals of Voyages to the East Indies, During the Seventeenth Century, Preserved in the India Office: And the Voyage of John Knight (1606) to Seek the North-West Passage* (London: Hakluyt Society, 1877), accessed January 24, 2016, http://archive.org/stream/voyagesofsirjame 00markrich/voyagesofsirjame00markrich_djvu.txt.

10. Samuel Purchas, *Hakluytus Posthumus, Or, Purchas His Pilgrimes: Contayning a History of the World in Sea Voyages and Lande Travells by Englishmen and Others.* (Glasgow: J. MacLehose & Sons, 1905), accessed January 24, 2016, http://archive .org/stream/hakluytusposthum02purcuoft/hakluytusposthum02purcuoft_djvu .txt.

11. Gerald Bryant, "Officers of the East India Company's Army in the Days of Clive

and Hastings," *The Journal of Imperial and Commonwealth History* 6, no. 3 (1978): 203–27.

12. "Government of India Act, 1858," in Cyril Henry Philips and Harischandra Lal Singh, *The Evolution of India and Pakistan, 1858 to 1947: Select Documents*, Vol. 4 (London: Oxford University Press, 1962).

13. David Segal and Mady Wechsler Segal, "America's Military Population," Population Reference Bureau, 2004, accessed January 23, 2016. doi:10.13111/2066-8201.

14. Schwartz and Swain, "Department of Defense Contractors in Afghanistan and Iraq."

15. See Kerry Patton, "Hold Your Applause: It Wasn't the CIA Alone Who Found Osama Bin Laden," *Business Insider*, January 21, 2014, www.businessinsider.com /cia-osama-bin-laden-seals-intelligence-2014-1.

## Chapter 16: An Age of Uncertainty

1. See generally Rosa Brooks, "Embrace the Chaos: Strategy in an Age of Uncertainty," *Foreign Policy*, November 14, 2014, foreignpolicy.com/2014/11/14/embrace-the -chaos/.

2. OXFAM, "Working for the Few: Political Capture and Economic Inequality," 2014, accessed January 23, 2016, www.oxfam.org/sites/www.oxfam.org/files/bp-working -for-few-political-capture-economic-inequality-200114-summ-en.pdf.

3. Barack Obama, "Remarks by the President to the American Legion National Convention," White House, August 26, 2014, www.whitehouse.gov/the-press-office /2014/08/26/remarks-president-american-legion-national-convention.

## Part IV: Counting the Costs

## Chapter 17: Car Bombs and Radioactive Sushi

1. See generally Pamela Constable and Arturo Valenzuela, *A Nation of Enemies: Chile Under Pinochet* (New York: W. W. Norton, 1991).

2. John Dinges, "A Bombshell on Pinochet's Guilt, Delivered Too Late, " *Newsweek*, October 14, 2015, www.newsweek.com/2015/10/30/bombshell-pinochets -guilt-delivered-too-late-383121.html.

3. Quoted in Vanessa Walker, "At the End of Influence: The Letelier Assassination, Human Rights, and Rethinking Intervention in US-Latin American Relations," *Journal of Contemporary History* 46, no. 1 (2011): 109–35.

4. Holly Near, "Hay Una Mujer Desaparecida." Full lyrics available on www.hollynear .com.

5. "Litvinenko Case: UK Inquiry Says Putin Probably Approved Ex-Spy's Killing," CNN, January 21, 2016, www.cnn.com/2016/01/21/europe/litvinenko-inquest-report/.

6. The principle of necessity requires parties to a conflict to limit their actions to those that are indispensable for securing the complete submission of the enemy as soon as possible (and that are otherwise permitted by international law). The principle of humanity forbids parties to a conflict to inflict gratuitous violence or employ methods calculated to cause unnecessary suffering. The principle of proportionality requires parties to ensure that the anticipated loss of life or property incidental to an attack is not excessive in relation to the concrete and direct military advantage expected to be gained. Finally, the principle of discrimination or distinction requires that parties to a conflict direct their actions only against combatants and military objectives, and take appropriate steps to distinguish between combatants and noncombatants. See generally William Johnson and David Lee, eds., *Operational Law Handbook* (Charlottesville, VA: U.S. Army Judge Advocate General's Legal Center and School, 2014), www.loc.gov/rr/frd/Military_Law/pdf /operational-law-handbook_2014.pdf; International Committee of the Red Cross, "Customary International Humanitarian Law, Rule 1," accessed January 24, 2016, www.icrc.org/customary-ihl/eng/docs/v2_rul_rule1; International Committee of the Red Cross, "Customary International Humanitarian Law, Rule 14," accessed January 24, 2016, www.icrc.org/customary-ihl/eng/docs/v1_cha_chapter4_rule14.

7. The traditional rule, as articulated in 1842 by Secretary of State Daniel Webster during a dispute with Great Britain over an attack on the U.S. ship *Caroline*, is that a state may use preemptive force only where the "necessity of that self-defense is instant, overwhelming, and leaving no choice of means, and no moment for deliberation." See Martin A. Rogoff and Edward Collins, Jr., "The Caroline Incident and the Development of International Law," 16 *Brooklyn Journal of International Law* 493 (1990). See also "Armed Activities on the Territory of the Congo (Dem. Rep. Congo v. Uganda)," 2005 I.C.J. 116 (Dec. 19); U.N. Secretary-General Kofi Annan, "In Larger Freedom: Report of the Secretary-General," paras. 124–25, U.N. Doc. A /59/2005/Add.3, May 26, 2005.

8. President George W. Bush, "Address Before a Joint Session of the Congress on the United States Response to the Terrorist Attacks of September 11, 2001," 2 Pub. Papers 1140, 1141 (September 20, 2001).

9. James Kitfield, "Flynn's Last Interview: Iconoclast Departs DIA with a Warning," *Breaking Defense*, August 7, 2014, http://breakingdefense.com/2014/08/flynns -last-interview-intel-iconoclast-departs-dia-with-a-warning/.

10. See Karen Yourish, Derek Watkins, and Tom Giratikanon, "Recent Attacks Demonstrate Islamic State's Ability to Both Inspire and Coordinate Terror," January 14, 2016, www.nytimes.com/interactive/2015/06/17/world/middleeast/map -isis-attacks-around-the-world.html; Tim Lister, "Map of ISIS," CNN, December 31, 2015, www.cnn.com/2015/12/17/world/mapping-isis-attacks-analysis/. See also United Kingdom Home Office, "Proscribed Terrorist Organizations," October

30, 2015, www.gov.uk/government/uploads/system/uploads/attachment_data/file /472956/Proscription-update-20151030.pdf; Department of State, *Country Reports on Terrorism 2014* (Washington, DC, June 2015), www.state.gov/documents /organization/239631.pdf.

11. Johnathan Landay, "Obama's Drone War Kills 'Others,' Not Just Al Qaida Leaders," McClatchy DC, April 9, 2013, www.mcclatchydc.com/2013/04/09/188062 /obamas-drone-war-kills-others.html#.UkiL5xZGvy9#storylink=cpy. See also "The Drone Papers," *The Intercept*.

12. Jeh Charles Johnson, "Remarks: The Conflict Against Al Qaeda and Its Affiliates: How Will It End?," November 30, 2012, Department of State, www.state.gov/docu ments/organization/211954.pdf.

13. "Obama Proposes War Authorization Against Islamic State," *PBS NewsHour*, February 11, 2015, www.pbs.org/newshour/rundown/obama-proposes-war-authori zation-islamic-state/.

14. "Putin Calls Kosovo Independence 'Terrible Precedent,'" *Sydney Morning Herald*, February 23, 2008, www.smh.com.au/news/world/putin-calls-kosovo-indepen dence-terrible-precedent/2008/02/23/1203467431503.html.

15. Vladimir Putin, "Address to Joint Session of Russian Parliament," March 18, 2014, in Julia Percha, "Transcript: Putin Says Russia Will Protect the Rights of Russians Abroad," *Washington Post*, March 18, 2014, www.washingtonpost.com/world /transcript-putin-says-russia-will-protect-the-rights-of-russians-abroad/2014/03 /18/432a1e60-ae99-11e3-a49e-76adc9210f19_story.html.

### Chapter 18: War Everywhere, Law Nowhere?

1. This section is adapted from an article I originally published in the *Journal of Ethics and International Affairs*. See Rosa Brooks, "Drones and the International Rule of Law," 28 *Journal of Ethics and International Affairs.*, 83–103 (2014). See also Stromseth, Wippman, and Brooks, *Can Might Make Rights?*; and see generally Stephane Beaulac, "The Rule of Law in International Law Today," in *Relocating the Rule of Law*, eds. Gianluigi Palombella and Neil Walker (Portland, OR: Hart, 2009), 201; Simon Chesterman, "International Rule of Law?," *American Journal of Comparative Law* 56 (2008): 359.

2. United Nations Secretary General, "Report of the Secretary-General on the Rule of Law and Transitional Justice in Conflict and Post-Conflict Societies," S/2004/616, August 23, 2004, www.un.org/en/ga/search/view_doc.asp?symbol=S/2004/616.

3. Chesterman, "International Rule of Law?," 342. This is a familiar concept in the U.S. legal system: consider the *ex post facto* clause of Article I, Section 9, of the Constitution, or the court-made "void-for-vagueness" doctrine.

4. In a November 2012 resolution (adopted without a vote), the General Assembly declared, "We recognize that the rule of law applies to all States equally, and to international organizations, including the United Nations and its principal organs, and that respect for and promotion of the rule of law and justice should guide all of their activities and accord predictability and legitimacy to their actions. [But] we also recognize that all persons, institutions and entities, public and private, including the State itself, are accountable to just, fair and equitable laws and are entitled without any discrimination to equal protection of the law. . . . We rededicate ourselves to support all efforts to uphold the sovereign equality of all States." "Declaration of the High-Level Meeting of the General Assembly on the Rule of Law at the National and International Levels," U.N. Doc. A/RES/67/1, paras. 2 and 3 (November 3, 2012).

5. Louis Henkin, *How Nations Behave*, 2nd ed. (New York: Columbia University Press, 1979), 47 (emphasis omitted).

6. See Jacob Cogan, who argues that in the absence of highly developed international law enforcement mechanisms, "operational noncompliance" is a good thing. Jacob Katz Cogan, "Noncompliance and the International Rule of Law," *Yale Journal of International Law* 31 (2006): 209.

7. See, e.g, "Case Concerning Military and Paramilitary Activities in and against Nicaragua" (*Nicaragua v. United States*), separate opinion of President Singh, at para. 153 ICJ Reports (1986) 14 (noting that international law on the use of force is "the very cornerstone of the human effort to promote peace in a world torn by strife").

8. Vagueness and ambiguity can also sometimes offer an efficient way for consensus-based changes in the law: amending the language of international treaties might be cumbersome or impossible, for instance, but some degree of vagueness and ambiguity in treaty language can permit shared interpretations to be modified over time, thus providing the community of states with a relatively simple "backdoor" means of changing the effect of a treaty.

9. When one or more powerful states challenge the generally accepted meaning of core legal concepts, other states face a choice. They can accept the "new" interpretations, in which case (if a sufficient number of states will go along with it) international law will quietly change. Alternatively, they can take the opposite tack, directly confronting those states seeking to reinterpret the law and demanding fidelity to previously shared interpretations. This route is risky: if it succeeds, legal stability is restored, but if it fails, legal disputes can escalate into open conflict between states. Finally, states dismayed by new interpretations of once fixed legal concepts can take a middle ground, quietly questioning new interpretations of the law while reaffirming their own interpretations. This route reduces the likelihood of conflict between states, but by enabling disparate legal interpretations to coexist

without any obvious means of reconciling them, it can also prolong or increase legal uncertainty.

10. Since international law remains, in its current incarnation, a product of state consensus, this process doesn't inevitably doom the rule of law—ultimately, if enough states shift their positions, it may end up creating robust new norms and new law. The rule of law is most threatened when an old consensus breaks down and a new consensus has yet to emerge.

11. See Larry Greenemeier, "The Drone Wars: 9/11 Inspired Advances in Robotic Combat," *Scientific American*, available at *Live Science*, September 3, 2011, www.livescience.com/15908-drone-wars-september-11-anniversary.html.

12. See statement of Attorney General Eric Holder: "Because the United States is in an armed conflict, we are authorized to take action against enemy belligerents under international law. The Constitution empowers the President to protect the nation from any imminent threat of violent attack. And international law recognizes the inherent right of national self-defense. None of this is changed by the fact that we are not in a conventional war." Eric Holder, "Attorney General Eric Holder Speaks at Northwestern University School of Law," Department of Justice, March 5, 2012, www.justice.gov/iso/opa/ag/speeches/2012/ag-speech-1203051.html. See also Harold Hongju Koh, "The Obama Administration and International Law," speech at the Annual Meeting of the American Society of International Law, Washington, DC, March 25, 2010, www.state.gov/s/l/releases/remarks/139119.html ("As a matter of international law, the United States is in an armed conflict with al-Qaeda, as well as the Taliban and associated forces, in response to the horrific 9/11 attacks, and may use force consistent with its inherent right to self-defense under international law"). And see also John O. Brennan, "Strengthening Our Security by Adhering to Our Values and Laws," White House, September 16, 2011, www.whitehouse.gov/the-press-office/2011/09/16/remarks-john-o-brennan-strengthening-our-security-adhering-our-values-an.

13. See "Department of Justice White Paper: Lawfulness of a Lethal Operation Directed Against a US Citizen Who Is a Senior Operational Leader of Al-Qa'ida or an Associated Force," Department of Justice (released February 4, 2013), http://msnbcmedia.msn.com/i/msnbc/sections/news/020413_DOJ_White_Paper.pdf.

14. Ibid., 7 (emphasis added).

15. Ibid., 8 (emphasis added).

16. Ibid.

17. Lewis Carroll, *Through the Looking-Glass* (Project Gutenberg, 1991), www.gutenberg.org/files/12/12-h/12-h.htm.

18. See Nicaragua Case, para. 176 ("There is a specific rule whereby self-defence would warrant only measures which are proportional to the armed attack and necessary to respond to it, a rule well established in customary international law"). See also

Judith Gardam, *Necessity, Proportionality and the Use of Force by States* (New York: Cambridge University Press, 2011).

19. President Obama has stated that "America does not take strikes when we have the ability to capture individual terrorists; our preference is always to detain, interrogate, and prosecute," Barack Obama, "Obama's Speech on Drone Policy," but no one outside the U.S. executive branch has any real ability to determine whether the strikes are necessary.

20. This conundrum has led some commentators to propose a new *jus ad vim*, a set of rules concerning uses of force that fall short of armed conflict. See Daniel Brunstetter and Megan Braun, "From *Jus ad Bellum* to *Jus ad Vim*: Recalibrating Our Understanding of the Moral Use of Force," *Ethics and International Affairs* 27, no. 1 (Spring 2013).

21. New uncertainties would eventually arise—perhaps even new uncertainties created by judicial language—but these too can be clarified or corrected via subsequent judicial decisions, or via new legislation made in response to judicial decisions.

22. A Pakistani court has rejected this argument and held that U.S. drone strikes within Pakistan's borders violate international law. See Jonathan Horowitz and Christopher Rogers, "Case Watch: A Court in Pakistan Addresses U.S. Drone Attacks," *Open Society Foundations*, May 28, 2013, www.opensocietyfoundations.org/voices /case-watch-court-pakistan-addresses-us-drone-attacks. The court's decision is available at www.peshawarhighcourt.gov.pk/images/wp%201551-p%2020212.pdf.

23. See G. W. F. Hegel, *Hegel on Tragedy*, eds. Anne Paolucci and Henry Paolucci (Westport, CT: Greenwood, 1978).

24. This section draws on remarks I gave at the 2014 Federalist Society Annual Student Symposium at the University of Florida in Gainesville, Florida, later adapted and published as Brooks, *Cross-Border Targeted Killings*. Note: I use "U.S. drone strikes" as a shorthand way to refer to the expansive U.S. campaign of lethal, cross-border counterterrorist strikes outside of traditional, territorially defined battlefields. To be clear, however, the issue is not "drones" or "drone strikes"; drones are simply another way of delivering ordnance from a distance. The availability of armed unmanned aerial vehicles has enabled an expanded U.S. campaign of cross-border targeted killings, but my concern is with the expanded use of such targeted killings, rather than the specific platforms used to carry them out.

25. Noah Schachtman, "Not Even the White House Knows the Drones' Body Count," *Wired*, September 29, 2012, www.wired.com/2012/09/drone-body-count/.

26. U.S. Constitution art. I, § 8, cl. 11–12, 14.

27. Ibid., cl. 15.

28. Ibid., cl. 10.

29. This discussion of the AUMF draws on congressional testimony I gave in 2013. See "Prepared Statement of Rosa Brooks: Oversight: The Law of Armed Conflict,

the Use of Military Force, and the 2001 Authorization for Use of Military Force," Hearing Before the Senate Committee on Armed Services, 113th Cong. (2013).

30. Pub. L. No. 107-40, § 2(a), 115 Stat. 224, 224 (codified at 50 U.S.C. § 1541 note).

31. See 147 Congressional Record S9950-51 (daily ed. October 1, 2001) (statement of Sen. Byrd) (providing the text of the administration's initial proposal).

32. See, e.g., Susan Milligan, "Congress Gives Bush Power to Hunt Terrorists," *Boston Globe*, September 15, 2001, www.boston.com/news/packages/underattack/globe _stories/0915/Congress_gives_Bush_power_to_hunt_terroristsP.shtml.

33. Landay, "Obama's Drone War Kills 'Others,' Not Just al Qaida Leaders."

34. See Pub. L. No. 107-40, § 2(a), 115 Stat. 224, 224 (codified at 50 U.S.C. § 1541 note); Jennifer Daskal and Stephen I. Vladeck, "After the AUMF," 5 *Harvard National Security Journal* 115, 115–16 (2014).

35. Rosa Brooks, "Mission Creep in the War on Terror," *Foreign Policy*, March 14, 2013, www.foreignpolicy.com/articles/2013/03/14/mission_creep_in_the_war_on _terror.

36. See Oona Hathaway, "The Power to Detain: Detention of Terrorism Suspects After 9/11," 38 *Yale Journal of International Law* 123, 130–31 (2013).

37. David Abramowitz, "The President, the Congress, and Use of Force: Legal and Political Considerations in Authorizing Use of Force Against International Terrorism," 43 *Harvard International Law Journal* 71, 78 (2002).

38. *New York Times Co. v. U.S. Dep't of Justice*, 915 F. Supp. 2d 508, 521 (S.D.N.Y. 2013) aff'd in part, rev'd in part, 752 F.3d 123 (2d Cir. 2014)

39. Ibid., United States District Court, S.D. New York. January 3, 2013, 915 F. Supp. 2d 508 (emphasis added).

40. Tilly, "Reflections on the History of European State Making."

41. This section is derived from an article I originally published in the *Yale Law & Policy Review*. See Brooks, "The Trickle-Down War."

42. The Supreme Court did impose some limits on early Bush administration detention-related policies and efforts to remove detainees from the jurisdiction of U.S. courts. See, e.g., *Hamdi v. Rumsfeld*, 542 U.S. 507 (2004); *Rasul v. Bush*, 542 U.S. 466 (2004); *Hamdan v. Rumsfeld*, 548 U.S. 557 (2006); *Boumediene v. Bush*, 553 U.S. 723 (2008). Similarly, Congress sought to rein in the U.S. use of interrogation techniques amounting to torture. For the most part, however, Congress and the courts have acquiesced in the executive branch's post-9/11 policies; even with regard to claims of torture, federal courts have found numerous reasons to prevent lawsuits seeking damages for torture from going forward. Indeed, as Stephen Vladeck has noted, "not a single damages judgment has been awarded in any of the dozens of lawsuits arising out of post–September 11 U.S. counterterrorism policies alleging violations of plaintiff's individual rights." Stephen I. Vladeck, "The New National Security Canon," 61 *American University International Law Review*, 1295, 1296 (2012).

43. I'm not the first commentator to note the potentially distorting effect of national security practices and doctrines on seemingly unrelated areas of law and law enforcement. In September 2002, the Lawyers' Committee for Human Rights (now renamed Human Rights First) published a report called "A Year of Loss: Reclaiming Civil Liberties Since September 11." This report looked at the impact of post-9/11 law and policy on such areas as general government transparency, the right to privacy, the treatment of immigrants, refugees and minorities, and the criminal justice system. See "A Year of Loss: Reclaiming Civil Liberties Since September 11," Human Rights First, accessed December 12, 2015, https://www.humanrightsfirst.org/wp-content/uploads/pdf/loss_report.pdf.

44. Abigail R. Hall and Christopher J. Coyne, "The Militarization of U.S. Domestic Policing," *The Independent Review* (Spring 2013): 485. See generally Radley Balko, *Rise of the Warrior Cop: The Militarization of America's Police Forces* (New York: PublicAffairs, 2013).

45. Balko, *Rise of the Warrior Cop*, 53.

46. See generally Tim Gurrister, "Why More SWAT-Style Raids? A 'Militarized' World," *Standard-Examiner*, August 10, 2013, www.standard.net/stories/2013/03/23/why-more-swat-style-raids-militarized-world; Sarah Stillman, "SWAT-Team Nation," *New Yorker*, August 8, 2013, www.newyorker.com/online/blogs/comment/2013/08/swat-team-nation.html.

47. Consider stop-and-frisk programs. See, e.g., Patrice O'Shaughnessy, "NYPD Gathering Intel, on Lookout for Terrorists Around the World," *New York Daily News*, July 6, 2008, www.nydailynews.com/news/world/nypd-gathering-intel-lookout-terrorists-world-article-1.351616; William Finnegan, "The Terrorism Beat: How Is the N.Y.P.D. Defending the City?," *New Yorker*, July 25, 2005, www.newyorker.com/archive/2005/07/25/050725fa_fnact2; Anya Sostek, "Taking Action: New York's State of Mind," Manhattan Institute for Policy Research (October 2004), www.manhattan-institute.org/html/_govmag-out_of_the_twin_towers.htm; David Reeder; "NYPD's Elite E-Men: Ready to Counter Attack Terror," *Tactical-Life* (July 2009), www.tactical-life.com/magazines/tactical-weapons/nypds-elite-e-men/.

48. Karl W. Bickel, "Recruit Training: Are We Preparing Officers for a Community Oriented Department?," *Community Policing Dispatch*, June 2013, http://cops.usdoj.gov/html/dispatch/06-2013/preparing_officers_for_a_community_oriented_department.asp.

49. Karl W. Bickel, "BDUs and Community Policing?," *Community Policing Dispatch*, November 2012, http://cops.usdoj.gov/html/dispatch/11-2012/bdus-community-policing.asp.

50. John Hanrahan, "Local Police Forces Are Now Little Armies. Why?," *Nieman Watchdog*, October 6, 2011, www.niemanwatchdog.org/index.cfm?fuseaction=ask_this.view&askthisid=529; "Defense Department Gives Local Police Equip-

ment Designed for a War Zone," FoxNews.com, November 27, 2013, www.fox news.com/us/2013/11/27/defense-department-gives-local-police-equipment -designed-for-warzone/; Michael Shank and Elizabeth Beavers, "The Militarization of U.S. Police Forces," Reuters, October 22, 2013, www.reuters.com/article /2013/10/22/us-opinion-shank-idUSBRE99L12420131022.

51. Michael Shank and Elizabeth Beavers, "America's Police Are Looking More and More Like the Military," *Guardian*, October 7, 2013, www.theguardian.com/com mentisfree/2013/oct/07/militarization-local-police-america.

52. Andrew Becker and G. W. Schulz, "Local Cops Ready for War with Homeland Security-Funded Military Weapons," *Daily Beast* (December 21, 2011), www.the dailybeast.com/articles/2011/12/20/local-cops-ready-for-war-with-homeland -security-funded-military-weapons.html.

53. John T. Parry, "Terrorism and the New Criminal Process," 15 *William & Mary Bill of Rights Journal*, 765, 768 (2007).

54. See generally Todd Garvey and Edward C. Liu, "The State Secrets Privilege: Preventing the Disclosure of Sensitive National Security Information During Civil Litigation," Congressional Research Service, August 16, 2011, https://www.fas.org /sgp/crs/secrecy/R41741.pdf. See also Erin E. Bohannon, "Breaking the Silence: A Challenge to Executive Use of the State Secrets Privilege to Dismiss Claims of CIA Torture in Mohamed v. Jeppesen Dataplan, Inc.," 65 *University of Miami Law Review* 621 (2010); D.A. Jeremy Telman, "Intolerable Abuses: Rendition for Torture and the State Secrets Privilege," 63 *Alabama Law Review* 429 (2012); Geoffrey R. Stone, "Secrecy and Self-Governance," 56 *New York Law School Law Review* 81 (2012); "100 Days: End the Abuse of the State Secrets Privilege," Center for Constitutional Rights, accessed April 10, 2014, https://ccrjustice.org/learn-more/faqs/100-days%3A-end -abuse-state-secrets-privilege.

55. Laura Donohue, "The Shadow of State Secrets," 159 *University of Pennsylvania Law Review* 77 (2010), 87–88.

56. Thus, an employment discrimination case against a private contractor might require disclosure of the existence and nature of a classified program operated in support of the government. See generally Anjetta McQueen, "Security Blanket: The State Secrets Privilege Threat to Public Employment Rights," 22 *Labor Law Journal*, 329, 335 (2007).

57. Donohue, "The Shadow of State Secrets," 88.

58. Ibid., 91.

59. See Title 18, U.S.C. App III § 4.

60. See, e.g, Joshua L. Dratel, "Section 4 of the Classified Information Procedures Act: The Growing Threat to the Adversary Process," 53 *Wayne Law Review*, 1041 (2007). See also Ellen Yaroshefsky, "Secret Evidence Is Slowly Eroding the Adversary System: CIPA and FISA in the Courts," 34 *Hofstra Law Review*, 1063 (2006). And see

also Anna Maria Martignetti, "The Classified Information Procedures Act (CIPA) and Suspected Terrorists in Federal Civilian Courts: Subject to the Most Exacting Demands of Justice?" (Spring 2010) (unpublished LLM thesis, Lund University), accessed January 24, 2016, http://lup.lub.lu.se/luur/download?func=download File&recordOId=1670606&fileOId=1670607.

61. See Dana Priest and William M. Arkin, *Top Secret America: The Rise of the New American Security State* (New York: Little Brown and Company, 2011).

62. Yaroshefsky, "Secret Evidence Is Slowly Eroding the Adversary System," 1080.

63. Michelle Mittelstadt, Burke Speaker, Doris Meissner, and Muzaffar Chishti, "Through the Prism of National Security: Major Immigration Policy and Program Changes in the Decade Since 9/11," Migration Policy Institute, August 2011, www .migrationpolicy.org/pubs/FS23_Post-9-11policy.pdf.

64. Ibid. CBP's budget more than doubled since FY2002, and the staff increased 43%, including a 104.6% increase in Border Patrol personnel. The ICE budget also more than doubled and increased 39.7% in manpower.

65. Ibid. US-VISIT collects fingerprints and photographs for all noncitizens entering the country and stores them in the IDENT database, which is interoperable with the FBI's Integrated Automated Fingerprint Identification System. The Student and Exchange Visitor Information System (SEVIS), authorized by the 1996 reforms, permits the tracking of international students. Other databases abound.

66. See Paige Scheckla, "Personal Security for Citizens and Non-Citizens in Post-9/11 US Immigration Policy," University of Chicago International Human Rights Clinic, November 19, 2013, https://ihrclinic.uchicago.edu/blog/personal-security -citizens-and-non-citizens-post-911-us-immigration-policy-paige-scheckla-1l. See also Samantha Hauptman, *The Criminalization of Immigration: The Post 9/11 Moral Panic*, (El Paso, TX: LFB Scholarly Pub Llc, 2013).

67. Deepa Iyer and Jayesh M. Rathod, "9/11 and the Transformation of U.S. Immigration Law and Policy," *Human Rights Magazine* 38 (Winter 2011), www.american bar.org/publications/human_rights_magazine_home/human_rights_vol38_2011 /human_rights_winter2011/9-11_transformation_of_us_immigration_law_policy .html.

68. See generally Laura K. Donohue, "Technological Leap, Statutory Gap, and Constitutional Abyss: Remote Biometric Identification Comes of Age," 97 *Minnesota Law Review*, 407 (2012).

69. See, e.g., David S. Cloud, "CIA Drones Have Broader List of Targets," *Los Angeles Times*, May 5, 2010, http://articles.latimes.com/2010/may/05/world/la-fg -drone-targets-20100506. See also Cora Currier and Justin Elliott, "The Drone War Doctrine We Still Know Nothing About," *ProPublica*, February 26, 2013, www.pro publica.org/article/drone-war-doctrine-we-know-nothing-about.

70. USA PATRIOT Act, Pub. L. No. 107-56, § 218, 115 Stat. 272 (codified at 50 U.S.C.

§1804 *et seq.*). Previously, foreign intelligence gathering had to be a "primary" purpose. See generally Susan Landau, "National Security on the Line," 4 *Journal on Telecommunications & High Technology Law*, 409 (2006); Daniel J. Solove, "Reconstructing Electronic Surveillance Law," 72 *George Washington Law Review*, 1264 (2004).

71. USA PATRIOT Act, §215, codified as amended at 50 U.S.C. § 1861 (emphasis added). The court conducts an *in camera* review, and issues *ex parte* approval orders. See also 18 U.S.C. § 2709(b); Right to Financial Privacy Act (RFPA), 12 U.S.C. § 3414(a)(5)(A); Fair Credit Reporting Act (FCRA), 15 U.S.C. §§ 1681u(b), 1681v(a); National Security Act, 50 U.S.C. § 436(a)(3). The National Security Agency's program to collect telephone metadata on U.S. citizens was approved under Section 215 of the PATRIOT Act. See Privacy and Civil Liberties Oversight Board, "Report on the Telephone Records Program Conducted Under Section 215 of the USA PATRIOT Act and on the Operations of the Foreign Intelligence Surveillance Court," January 23, 2014, www.pclob.gov/SiteAssets/Pages/default/PCLOB-Report-on-the-Telephone-Records-Program.pdf.

72. Timothy B. Lee, "Here's How Phone Metadata Can Reveal Your Affairs, Abortions, and Other Secrets," *Washington Post*, August 27, 2013, www.washingtonpost.com/blogs/the-switch/wp/2013/08/27/heres-how-phone-metadata-can-reveal-your-affairs-abortions-and-other-secrets.

73. Imagine, for instance, the use of pattern recognition technologies to identify, investigate, and potentially entrap users of prohibited drugs. See generally Marc Jonathan Blitz, "Video Surveillance and the Constitution of Public Space: Fitting the Fourth Amendment to a World That Tracks Image and Identity," 82 *Texas Law Review* 1349, 1351–52 (2004).

74. See Emily Bell et al., "Comment to Review Group on Intelligence and Communications Technologies Regarding the Effects of Mass Surveillance on the Practice of Journalism," October 4, 2013, http://towcenter.org/wp-content/uploads/2013/10/Letter-Effect-of-mass-surveillance-on-journalism.pdf.

75. Perhaps 9/11 merely accelerated pre-existing trends; perhaps it had no causal impact at all. Perhaps some or all of the trends hinted at above would have emerged with or without 9/11 and the war making that followed. As Steven Vladeck notes, "the Rehnquist and Roberts courts have systematically made it more difficult for civil plaintiffs to obtain damages in cases arising out of governmental misconduct." Steven Vladeck, "The New National Security Canon," 1297. See also Laura Donohue, "The Limits of National Security," 48 *American Criminal Law Review*, 1573 (2011) (charting the timelines of national-security-discourse-driven laws and suggesting that 9/11 likely just accelerated the expansion of state power vis-à-vis individuals); Jack M. Balkin, "The Constitution in the National Surveillance State," 93 *Minnesota Law Review*, 1 (2008) (arguing that increased government surveillance

is driven by accelerating developments in information technology, and that the war on terror is not its sole or most important cause). And see also John T. Parry, "Terrorism and the New Criminal Process," 15 *William & Mary Bill of Rights Journal*, 765, 834–35 (2007) (noting that while 9/11 "accelerated the development of a new criminal process," the post-9/11 changes also "reflect trends in ordinary criminal procedure.").

## Chapter 19: Institutional Costs

1. This section draws on several articles I originally published in *Foreign Policy*; a draft book chapter that will appear in James Mattis and Kori Schake, eds., *Warriors and Citizens* (Palo Alto, CA: Hoover Institution Press, 2016); and an article originally published in *Politico Magazine*: "Obama vs. the Generals," *Politico Magazine*, November 8, 2013, www.politico.com/magazine/story/2013/11/obama-vs-the-generals-099379.

2. *White Paper of the Interagency Policy Group's Report on U.S. Policy Towards Afghanistan and Pakistan*, White House, 2009, accessed January 23, 2016, www.whitehouse.gov/assets/documents/Afghanistan-Pakistan_White_Paper.pdf.

3. Bob Woodward, "McChrystal: More Forces or 'Mission Failure,'" *Washington Post*, September 21, 2009, www.washingtonpost.com/wp-dyn/content/article/2009/09/20/AR2009092002920.html.

4. Peter Baker, "How Obama Came to Plan for 'Surge' in Afghanistan," *New York Times*, December 5, 2009, www.nytimes.com/2009/12/06/world/asia/06reconstruct.html?pagewanted=all.

5. Interview notes on file with author.

6. Ibid.

7. Ibid.

8. Ibid.

9. Ibid.

10. Ibid.

11. Pat Towell and Amy Belasco, "Defense: FY2014 Authorization and Appropriations," Congressional Research Service, January 8, 2014, https://www.fas.org/sgp/crs/natsec/R43323.pdf.

12. Office of Management and the Budget, "Department of State and Other International Programs," 2014, accessed January 23, 2016, https://www.whitehouse.gov/sites/default/files/omb/budget/fy2014/assets/state.pdf.

13. "The 15 Countries with the Highest Military Expenditure in 2011 (table)," Stockholm International Peace Research Institute (SIPRI), 2011, accessed January 23, 2016, www.sipri.org/research/armaments/milex/resultoutput/milex_15/the-15-countries-with-the-highest-military-expenditure-in-2011-table/view.

14. Congressional Budget Office, "Analysis of Federal Civilian and Military Compensation."

15. See "A Real Domestic Threat: How Health-Care Spending Strains the U.S. Military," Center for Strategic and Budgetary Assessments, March 12, 2012, www .csbaonline.org/2012/03/12/a-real-domestic-threat-how-health-care-spending -strains-the-u-s-military/; Ezra Klein, "Defense Has a Health Care Spending Problem," *Washington Post*, January 6, 2012, www.washingtonpost.com/blogs /ezra-klein/post/defense-has-a-health-care-spending-problem/2012/01/06 /gIQAWI4PfP_blog.html.

16. Megan Scully, "Appropriator Expects Defense Bill to Pay for 10 More C-17s." *Government Executive*, October 22, 2009, www.govexec.com/defense/2009/10/appro priator-expects-defense-bill-to-pay-for-10-more-c-17s/30178/

17. "Letter to Bush from Military Leaders, January 18, 2006," Human Rights First, accessed January 22, 2016, www.humanrightsfirst.org/wp-content/uploads/pdf /06118-etn-ltr-bush-from-military.pdf.

18. "Too Fat to Fight," Mission: Readiness, 2010, accessed January 22, 2016, http://cdn .missionreadiness.org/MR_Too_Fat_to_Fight-1.pdf.

19. "Still Too Fat to Fight," Mission: Readiness, 2012, accessed January 22, 2016, www .rwjf.org/content/dam/farm/reports/reports/2012/rwjf401381.

20. "Senior Military Leaders Announce Support for Climate Bill," *ThinkProgress*, April 29, 2010, http://thinkprogress.org/climate/2010/04/29/205887/senior-military -leaders-announce-support-for-climate-bill/?mobile=nc.

21. "Ready, Willing, and Unable to Serve: 75 Percent of Young Adults Cannot Join the Military," Mission: Readiness, 2009, accessed January 23, 2016, www.missionread iness.org/2009/ready_willing/.

22. John Broder, "Climate Change Seen as Threat to U.S. Security," *New York Times*, August 8, 2009, www.nytimes.com/2009/08/09/science/earth/09climate.html?page wanted=all&_r=0.

23. Defense Science Board, "Enhancing Adapatability of US Military Forces," Summer 2010, accessed January 22, 2016, www.nationaldefensemagazine.org/blog/Docu ments/EnhancingAdaptabilityOfUSMilitaryForces.pdf.

24. Leonard Wong, "Fashion Tips for the Field Grade," U.S. Army, *Strategic Studies Institute Newsletter*, October 2006, www.strategicstudiesinstitute.army.mil/pubs /display.cfm?pubID=731.

25. Amy Schafer, "What Stands in the Way of the Pentagon Keeping Its Best and Brightest?," *Defense One*, July 14, 2014, www.defenseone.com/ideas/2014/07/what -stands-way-pentagon-keeping-its-best-and-brightest/88630/?oref=d-channel river.

26. Tim Kane, "An Army of None," *Foreign Policy*, January 10, 2013, http://foreign policy.com/2013/01/10/an-army-of-none/.

27. Ibid.

28. Stephen Gerras and Leonard Wong, "Changing Minds in the Army," Strategic Studies Institute, October 2013, www.strategicstudiesinstitute.army.mil/pdffiles /PUB1179.pdf.

29. "Carter 'Will Help Keep Our Military Strong,' President Says," DoD News, Defense Media Activity, February 12, 2015, www.defense.gov/news/newsarticle.aspx?id= 128174.

30. Quoted in M. Alex Johnson, "The Culture of Einstein," MSNBC.com, April 18, 2005, www.nbcnews.com/id/7406337/.

31. Matthew M. Aid, "The Troubled Inheritance: The National Security Agency and the Obama Administration," in Loch K. Johnson, ed., *The Oxford Handbook of National Security Intelligence* (Oxford, UK: Oxford University Press, 2010).

32. John Keller, "The Continuing Drone War of Low-tech vs. High-tech—Military and Aerospace Electronics," *Atom*, February 26, 2013, www.militaryaerospace.com /blogs/aerospace-defense-blog/2013/02/the-continuing-drone-war-of-low-tech -vs-high-tech.html; Rukmini Callimachi, "Al-Qaida Tipsheet on Avoiding Drones Found in Mali," Yahoo! News, February 22, 2013, http://news.yahoo.com/al-qaida -tipsheet-avoiding-drones-found-mali-173015912.html.

33. Mark Galeotti, "The 'Gerasimov Doctrine' and Russian Non-Linear War," Blog: *In Moscow's Shadows*, July 6, 2014, https://inmoscowsshadows.wordpress.com/2014 /07/06/the-gerasimov-doctrine-and-russian-non-linear-war/.

34. Reuben Johnson, "Russia's Hybrid War in Ukraine 'Is Working,'" *IHS Jane's 360*, February 26, 2015, www.janes.com/article/49469/update-russia-s-hybrid-war-in -ukraine-is-working; Kevin McCaney, "Russia's Hybrid Warfare Tactics Gain Upper Hand in Ukraine," *Defense Systems*, March 24, 2015, http://defensesystems .com/articles/2015/03/24/russia-hybrid-warfare-ukraine-nato.aspx.

## Part V: Managing War's Paradoxes

1. See Derek Croxton, "The Peace of Westphalia of 1648 and the Origins of Sovereignty," *International History Review* 21(1999): 569, 582.

2. Thomas H. Greer and Gavin Lewis, *A Brief History of the Western World* (Belmont, CA: Wadsworth, 2005), 398.

3. "WWI Casualty and Death Tables," PBS, accessed February 8, 2014, www.pbs.org /greatwar/resources/casdeath_pop.html.

4. See Mahzarin Banaji and Anthony Greenwald, *Blind Spot: Hidden Biases of Good People* (New York: Delacorte, 2013).

5. Jerome S. Bruner, "On Perceptual Readiness," *Psychological Review* 64 (1957): 123–52.

6. See generally Brooks, "The New Imperialism."

7. Paul Bohannon, "The Differing Realms of Law," in Paul Bohannan, ed., *Law and Warfare*, 43.

8. Peter Baker, "Pivoting from a War Footing, Obama Acts to Curtail Drones," *New York Times*, May 23, 2013.

9. Lieber Code, art. 29.

10. Michael Howard, *The Invention of Peace: Reflections on War and International Order* (New Haven, CT: Yale University Press, 2001), 1.

11. Michael R. Gordon, "After Hard-Won Lessons, Army Doctrine Revised," *New York Times*, February 7, 2008, www.nytimes.com/2008/02/08/washington/08strategy .html?pagewanted=all.

12. Sir Henry Maine, *International Law* (London: John Murray, 1888), 8, http://avalon .law.yale.edu/19th_century/int01.asp.

13. Mary Dudziak, *War Time: An Idea, Its History, Its Consequences* (Oxford, UK: Oxford University Press, 2012), 8.

14. David Barno and Nora Bensahel, "Fighting and Winning in the 'Gray Zone,'" *War on the Rocks*, May 19, 2015, http://warontherocks.com/2015/05/fighting-and -winning-in-the-gray-zone/?singlepage=1.

15. Nadia Schadlow, "Peace and War: The Space Between," *War on the Rocks*, August 18, 2014, http://warontherocks.com/2014/08/peace-and-war-the-space-be tween/. See also Daniel Brunstetter and Megan Braun, "From *Jus ad Bellum* to *Jus ad Vim*: Recalibrating Our Understanding of the Moral Use of Force," *Ethics and International Affairs* 27, no. 1 (Spring 2013).

16. See, e.g., Rosa Brooks, "Ten Ways to Fix the Drone War," *Foreign Policy*, April 11, 2013, http://foreignpolicy.com/2013/04/11/10-ways-to-fix-the-drone-war/. See also Abizaid, Brooks, and Stohl, "Recommendations and Report of the Task Force on US Drone Policy"; Steven Vladeck, "Judicial Review, but Not Secretive Drone Courts," *New York Times*, April 24, 2015, www.nytimes.com/roomfordebate /2015/04/24/should-a-court-approve-all-drone-strikes/judicial-review-but-not -secretive-drone-courts; Brunstetter and Braun, "*Jus ad Vim*"; Micah Zenko, "Reforming US Drone Strike Policies," No. 65, Council on Foreign Relations, 2013, www.cfr.org/wars-and-warfare/reforming-us-drone-strike-policies/p29736.

17. U.N. Charter, Preamble.

# Index

# About the Author

Rosa Brooks is the daughter of left-wing antiwar activists and the wife of a U.S. Army Special Forces officer. Her varied career has included work for international human rights NGOs and a recent stint as a high-level Pentagon official. From 2009 to 2011, Brooks served as counselor to Under Secretary of Defense for Policy Michèle Flournoy, one of the Pentagon's highest-ranking civilians. In 2011, Brooks was awarded the Secretary of Defense Medal for Outstanding Public Service. Over the years, her work has brought her to dozens of countries around the globe, from Afghanistan, Iraq, China, and Indonesia to the Balkans and sub-Saharan Africa.

Brooks is currently a tenured law professor at Georgetown University Law Center and a senior fellow at New America. She is an expert on international law, constitutional law, human rights, and national security law, and has authored dozens of scholarly articles on these subjects, along with a book, *Can Might Make Rights?: Building the Rule of Law After Military Interventions* (co-authored with Jane Stromseth and David Wippman, Cambridge University Press, 2006). She regularly speaks before public audiences on matters relating to the changing nature of warfare, including recent testimony before both the Senate Armed Services Committee and the Senate Judiciary Committee, and both scholars and journalists frequently cite her comments on these issues.

Brooks has combined her government and academic work with a successful career in journalism. From 2005 to 2009, she wrote a popular weekly opinion column for the *Los Angeles Times*, and she currently writes a weekly column on war, politics, and the military for *Foreign Policy* magazine; her column routinely hits the top of ForeignPolicy.com's "most popular" list. (ForeignPolicy.com attracts four million online readers each month.) Brooks's articles and essays have appeared in dozens of other publications as well, and she is a frequent radio and television guest, with appearances on the *Charlie Rose* show (PBS and Bloomberg TV), *The Rachel Maddow Show* (MSNBC), *Meet the Press*, the *Today* show, and *Erin Burnett OutFront* (CNN). Brooks lives in Alexandria, Virginia, with her husband, Joe, her children, Anna and Clara, and her dog, Scout.